GREAT HATRED

RONAN McGREEVY

GREAT HATRED

The Assassination of
Field Marshal
Sir Henry Wilson MP

faber

First published in the UK in 2022
by Faber & Faber Limited
Bloomsbury House
74–77 Great Russell Street
London WC1B 3DA
First published in the USA in 2022

Typeset by Ian Bahrami
Printed and bound by CPI Group (UK) Ltd, Croydon, CRO 4YY

The author and publishers are grateful to United Agents Ltd for permission
to publish lines from W. B. Yeats's poem 'Remorse for Intemperate Speech',
from *The Winding Stair and Other Poems*, 1933

A CIP record for this book
is available from the British Library

ISBN 978–0–571–37280–5

For my parents, Chris (RIP) and Eamonn

Contents

List of Illustrations   ix

Timeline   xiii

1   Assassination: 'Here, in the middle of our own metropolis, he has been murdered'   1

2   Henry Wilson – The Early Years: 'I am an Irishman'   39

3   Wilson – The Post-war Years: 'Never daunted, never dismayed'   76

4   Henry Wilson and Ulster: 'The Orange Terror'   101

5   Reginald Dunne: 'The blood that's in them'   131

6   Joseph O'Sullivan: An Old Fenian Family   164

7   Planning: 'The Wilson job is on'   190

8   Aftermath: 'The assassination has horrified the whole civilised world'   218

9   Rescue: Kidnapping the Prince of Wales   247

10   Execution: 'The felon's cap is the noblest crown an Irish head can wear'   272

11   The Irish Civil War: 'The madness from within'   294

12   Repatriation: 'The Irish Government's attitude is strictly illogical'   333

13   Conclusion: Ireland's Sarajevo   366

Glossary of Terms   399

Acknowledgements   405

Notes   407

Select Bibliography   429

Index   435

List of Illustrations

1 Liverpool Street Station, 22 June 1922: Wilson at the unveiling of the war memorial to the men from the Great Eastern Railway who had died in the First World War (*Illustrated London News*, 1 July 1922)

2 Field Marshal Sir Henry Wilson (Library of Congress)

3 Dunne and O'Sullivan either side of the front door at Eaton Place (*Illustrated London News*, 1 July 1922)

4 The scene of the murder and the escape route of the assassins (*The Times*)

5 Crowds gathered outside 36 Eaton Place at the corner with Belgrave Place (*Assassination* by Rex Taylor, 1961)

6 Michael Collins in 1922 (Hulton Archive/Getty Images)

7 Currygrane House, County Longford (Ronan McGreevy)

8 General Wilson and Marshal Foch, the *Illustrated News*, 1 July 1922

9 Terence MacSwiney on his deathbed, *Le Petit Journal*, 19 September 1920 (Gallica/Bibliothèque National de France)

10 Wilson declined to attend the state opening of the Northern Ireland parliament on 22 June 1921 as he was a serving soldier (Artist William Connor/Northern Ireland Assembly)

11 The Belfast IRA kept a handwritten list of those who had been killed in the Belfast pogroms between 1920 and 1922 (Irish Military Archives/Brigade Activity Reports)

12 Snapshot of Reggie with three friends at St Mary's College,

Hammersmith, 1920. All were in the IRA (National Library of Ireland)

13 John and Mary Ann O'Sullivan with their eleven surviving children, c.1902–3 (Michael Boulton)

14 Joe in his First World War uniform (Professor Paul Raffield)

15 Cathal Brugha arriving by bicycle at a Dáil Éireann meeting in Dublin University, 1 December 1921 (Hulton Archive/ Getty Images)

16 The death of the third man, Denis Kelleher, merited an article in the *Cork Examiner* of 14 November 1971 (Irish Newspaper Archives)

17 *Punch* of 28 June 1922 illustrates that many in the British press regarded the Irish as an incorrigibly violent race more interested in the gun than democratic politics

18 Wilson's assassination made the front page of the *New York Times* on 23 July 1922

19 Wilson's funeral was one of the biggest that London had ever seen (*Illustrated London News*, 1 July 1922)

20 Lady Wilson is escorted down the steps of St Paul's by Marshal Foch (*Illustrated London News*, 1 July 1922)

21 The wedding of Lord Louis Mountbatten and Miss Edwina Ashley at St Margaret's, Westminster, 18 July 1922 (*Illustrated London News*, 22 July 1922)

22 Regatta Week, Cowes, in the 1920s (Topical Press Agency/ Getty Images)

23 Extract from Reggie's last letter to his mother (National Library of Ireland)

24 Relatives and supporters praying outside Wandsworth Prison before the execution of Dunne and O'Sullivan (Bettman/ Getty Images)

25 Free State forces shell the Four Courts, where anti-Treaty

rebels had been based for more than two months, July 1922 (South Dublin County Libraries)

26 On 30 June the destruction of the Public Records Office, where the munitions were stored, sent a huge cloud of smoke over Dublin city (Photo12/Universal Images Group via Getty Images)

27 Currygrane outhouses, the only buildings still standing on the Wilson estate (Ronan McGreevy)

28 Harry Boland, Michael Collins and Éamon de Valera, 1 January 1920 (Independent News and Media/Getty Images)

29 The repatriation of the remains of Dunne and O'Sullivan was widely covered in the *Irish Press* of 7 July 1967 (Irish Newspaper Archives)

30 Reggie and Joe's final resting place in the republican plot of Deansgrange Cemetery, Dublin (Ronan McGreevy)

MAPS

1 Ireland

2 Dublin, 1922

3 Irish Civil War

PLATE SECTION

1 The portrait of Field Marshal Sir Henry Wilson by his childhood friend Sir William Orpen was painted in 1919 (National Portrait Gallery, London)

2 The memorial at Liverpool Street Station to the men from the Great Eastern Railway Company who died in the First World War was unveiled by Field Marshal Sir Henry Wilson MP on 22 June 1922 (Ronan McGreevy)

3 The Northern Ireland parliament was opened by King

George V on 22 June 1921, a year to the day before Wilson was assassinated (Northern Ireland Assembly)

4 The St Ignatius College cricket first XI from 1914–15 includes Reginald Dunne (Irish National Archives)

5 Joseph O'Sullivan's last will and testament was acquired by the National Museum of Ireland at auction in 2014, along with that of Dunne (National Museum of Ireland)

6 Wilson's assassination made the front cover of the leading Paris weekly *Le Petit Journal* in the week after his assassination (Private Collection Stefano Bianchetti/Bridgeman Images)

7 Wilson's funeral was one of the largest London has seen, outside of members of the royal family (*The Sphere*, 1 July 1922)

8 This memorial in County Kerry recalls the Ballyseedy massacre of March 1923 (Ronan McGreevy)

9 Michael Collins's death on 22 August 1922 ensured he would forever be known as Ireland's great lost leader (Sir John Lavery, *Michael Collins (Love of Ireland)*, 1922. Collection and image © Hugh Lane Gallery (Reg. 744). Lady Lavery Memorial Bequest through Sir John Lavery, 1935)

10 Currygrane Lake provided water for Currygrane House, the home of the Wilson family (Ronan McGreevy)

11 This small pet cemetery contains the remains of three dogs that lived on the Wilson estate (Ronan McGreevy)

12 The inscription on the tomb of Reginald Dunne and Joseph O'Sullivan states in Gaelic (Irish) that they gave their lives for Ireland in England. Also remembered on the headstone is Michael McInerney (Ronan McGreevy)

13 The memorial to Henry Wilson at Liverpool Street Station was erected a year after his death and is located underneath the one to the men from the Great Eastern Railway Company (Ronan McGreevy)

Timeline

1606–1630: King James I orders the plantation of Ulster following the defeat of northern Gaelic chieftains and the Flight of the Earls in 1603. The king grants land in six counties west of the Bann – Derry, Donegal, Fermanagh, Tyrone, Cavan and Armagh – to English and Scottish settlers.

1641: Ulster explodes into open warfare between English and Scottish settlers and the native Irish.

1690: William of Orange defeats the exiled King James II at the Battle of the Boyne. The battle is decisive in consolidating Protestant domination in Ireland. Around this time the Wilson family arrive in Ireland.

1782–1800: Short-lived Irish parliament, which ends following the 1798 rebellion against British rule. The parliament is abolished in 1800 under the Act of Union. Henceforth, Irish MPs will sit only in Westminster. For the whole of the nineteenth century, Irish nationalists campaign for an end to the Act of Union.

1864: Henry Wilson is born in Currygrane, County Longford.

1867: The Fenians stage a short-lived rebellion.

1870: Isaac Butt forms the Home Rule Association, which campaigns for self-government for Ireland within the United Kingdom.

1874: The Irish Parliamentary Party is created to elect MPs to the Westminster parliament, with the goal of achieving home rule for Ireland. The party dominates Irish electoral politics until 1918.

1886: The first Home Rule Bill is introduced into the House of
Commons by British prime minister William Gladstone but
is defeated. Sectarian riots hit Belfast and dozens are killed.
Unionist opposition coalesces to oppose home rule with the
phrase 'Ulster will fight and Ulster will be right'.

1893: A second Home Rule Bill is passed in the House of
Commons but defeated in the House of Lords.

April 1912: The Irish Parliamentary Party again holds the balance
of power in Westminster. A third Home Rule Bill is passed in
the House of Commons. This time the power of the House of
Lords to defeat it is curbed. It is due to become law in 1914.

January 1913: The Ulster Volunteer Force (UVF) is formed to
defend any attempt to impose the Home Rule Bill on Ulster.

November 1913: The Irish Volunteers is formed as a
counterweight to the UVF.

March 1914: The Curragh Incident occurs. More than fifty
British army officers based in Ireland indicate that they will
resign their commissions rather than move against Ulster. The
proposed mutiny convinces many Irish nationalists that the
British cannot be trusted to implement home rule. Wilson is
involved behind the scenes.

April 1914: The UVF smuggle twenty thousand German rifles
with three million rounds of ammunition into the port of
Larne.

July 1914: The Buckingham Palace conference takes
place between nationalist and unionist leaders over the
implementation of home rule, but no agreement is reached.

4 August 1914: The First World War breaks out and Wilson's
plan to deploy the British Expeditionary Force (BEF) on the
left of the French army comes to fruition. The Germans are
stopped at the Battle of the Marne in early September.

September 1914: The Home Rule Act becomes law but is suspended for the duration of the war.

April 1916: The Easter Rising occurs in Dublin. Rebels who take up arms against the British reject home rule, which would have given Ireland self-government within the United Kingdom. Instead they want an independent Irish republic. The British execute sixteen leaders of the Rising.

February 1918: Wilson takes over as Chief of the Imperial General Staff from Field Marshal Sir William Robertson.

March 1918: Legislation to introduce conscription into Ireland is passed after the German Spring Offensive begins. Plans to assassinate the British cabinet are put in place but dropped when conscription is not implemented.

January 1919: Sinn Féin, which wins a landslide victory in Ireland in the 1918 British general election, convenes the first Dáil. On the same day the Irish War of Independence begins with the Soloheadbeg ambush.

September 1919: Unionist leader Sir James Craig says he will not oppose a parliament for Ulster provided it consists of six counties with a Unionist majority rather than the nine counties of the historic province.

October 1920: The Lord Mayor of Cork Terence MacSwiney dies on hunger strike in Brixton Prison. Michael Collins orders the assassination of members of the British cabinet in retaliation.

December 1920: The Government of Ireland Act 1920 becomes law. It creates two home rule parliaments and divides Ireland on a twenty-six/six-county basis. The act is rejected by Sinn Féin, which demands full independence, but Ulster unionists accept it.

22 June 1921: King George V opens the Northern Ireland parliament and makes a conciliatory speech, saying: 'I appeal

to all Irishmen to pause, to stretch out the hand of forbearance and conciliation, to forgive and to forget, and to join in making for the land which they love a new era of peace, contentment, and goodwill.'

11 July 1921: A truce is called between crown forces and republicans to allow for talks about the future of Ireland.

6 December 1921: The Anglo-Irish Treaty is signed, setting up the Irish Free State. Nationalists believe partition will be a temporary issue as Clause 12 of the Treaty provides for a Border Commission. Many nationalists are confident that the commission will make Northern Ireland so small as to render it unviable. Wilson regards the Treaty as a surrender to the 'murder gang'.

7 January 1922: The Treaty is ratified narrowly by the Dáil by sixty-four votes to fifty-seven. On 16 January Dublin Castle, the administrative centre of British rule in Ireland, is handed over to the Provisional Government. Michael Collins and Sir James Craig agree a pact to end the violence in the North, but it quickly breaks down.

February 1922: Field Marshal Sir Henry Wilson retires as Chief of the Imperial General Staff on 19 February and is elected unopposed as MP for North Down two days later.

March 1922: Sir James Craig announces that Wilson is to be the military advisor to the Northern government. Wilson writes to Craig telling him that Ireland is in a 'welter of chaos and murder difficult to believe, impossible to describe'. He also says that Britain needs to re-establish order in the South of Ireland. The worst atrocity of the Belfast pogroms occurs on 24 March, when six members of the McMahon family are murdered in their homes. A second Craig–Collins pact is signed but it again breaks down.

14 April 1922: Anti-Treaty IRA militants, led by Rory
O'Connor, occupy the Four Courts and several other
buildings in central Dublin in defiance of the Provisional
Government.

16 June 1922: The Irish constitution is published on the
morning of the general election. The constitution retains the
oath of allegiance to the British monarch. The twenty-six
counties go to the polls for the first time as an independent
country, with pro- and anti-Treaty Sinn Féin candidates on the
ballot, along with Labour, independents and other parties who
are largely pro-Treaty.

16–20 June 1922: The result of the general election shows an
almost four to one split to candidates in favour of or neutral to
the Treaty. The Provisional Government see it as a mandate to
govern.

21 June 1922: Reginald Dunne and Joseph O'Sullivan, two
ex-British servicemen, meet in Mooney's pub in Holborn,
London. They discover in the evening newspaper that Wilson
is to unveil a memorial at Liverpool Street Station. They
travel to the station to reconnoitre the spot, but decide an
attempted assassination there is impossible.

22 June 1922: 12.50 p.m.–1.50 p.m. Wilson unveils a monument
at Liverpool Street Station.
2.30 p.m.: Wilson is shot dead on the doorstep of his Eaton
Place home by Dunne and O'Sullivan. They are immediately
arrested and taken to Gerald Road police station.
6.30 p.m.: British prime minister David Lloyd George sends a
letter post-haste to Michael Collins, warning him to clear the
anti-Treaty rebels out of the Four Courts: 'The ambiguous
position of the Irish Republican Army can no longer be
ignored by the British army.'[1]

26 June 1922: An anti-Treaty raiding party seize fifteen cars imported in defiance of the Belfast Boycott from Ferguson's garage in Lower Baggot Street. Anti-Treaty officer Leo Henderson is arrested by government troops. In retaliation, an anti-Treaty unit kidnaps Lieutenant General Jeremiah Joseph (J. J.) 'Ginger' O'Connell. Winston Churchill makes it clear in the House of Commons that he expects the Provisional Government to take action against the anti-Treaty rebels. Otherwise, 'We shall regard the Treaty as having been formally violated.'

27 June 1922: Collins gives a final ultimatum to the Four Courts garrison to surrender before they are attacked. The Provisional Government tell the people of Ireland that they intend to take action against the anti-Treaty side: 'Outrages such as these against the nation and the government must cease at once and cease forever.'

28 June 1922: The National Army shells the Four Courts and the Irish Civil War begins.

30 June 1922: The Four Courts garrison surrenders. The Public Records Office, containing centuries' worth of priceless documents, is destroyed in a massive explosion.

18 July 1922: Dunne and O'Sullivan are sentenced to be hanged.

10 August 1922: They are hanged at Wandsworth Prison.

12 August 1922: Their testimony justifying their actions, which was disallowed at their trial, is published in the *Irish Independent*. Arthur Griffith, founder of Sinn Féin, dies of natural causes at the age of fifty-one.

16 August 1922: Currygrane House, Wilson's childhood home, is burned to the ground.

22 August 1922: Michael Collins is killed in an ambush at Béal na mBláth.

May 1923: The Irish Civil War ends with Frank Aiken calling
on anti-Treaty forces to dump arms. No peace treaty is ever
signed.

July 1967: The bodies of Dunne and O'Sullivan are removed
from the grounds of Wandsworth Prison and reburied in
Deansgrange Cemetery, south Dublin.

Out of Ireland have we come.
Great hatred, little room,
Maimed us at the start.
I carry from my mother's womb
A fanatic heart.

From 'Remorse for Intemperate Speech',
W. B. Yeats, 1933

1

Assassination: 'Here, in the middle of our own metropolis, he has been murdered'

Liverpool Street Station was once the biggest railway station in the biggest city in the world.[1] In the 1920s its proximity to the City of London, to the engines of commerce and law in Shoreditch, Bank and Holborn and to the heart of the British Empire brought 220,000 commuters and 1,250 trains under its glass-covered roof every weekday.[2] First came the workmen in their hardwearing fustian, followed by the clerks in their homburgs and straw boaters, and finally the professionals in their bowler hats who arrived late and stayed late. After the morning rush hour came the shoppers, the ladies and gentlemen who lunched, and then the theatre-goers.

Departing from the station were the daily excursion trains, which had been suspended for the duration of the First World War but were restored in 1920 and which took working-class families from the East End of London to the seaside resorts of Clacton-on-Sea, Southend, Lowestoft and Yarmouth. The station, like the city it served, was ceaseless.

On 22 June 1922 the bustle stopped for an allocated hour to remember the men from the Great Eastern Railway (GER) Company who had died in the Great War. At 12.50 p.m. the doors of the station were locked to all but the invited guests gathered in the booking hall under the high arches of the station roof. Outside, the flags on the roof of the station were at half-mast. It was midsummer, but an unseasonably cool and showery day.

For those gathered inside, the focal point of their sorrow was a marble memorial, seven metres high and eight wide, with laurel-twisted, fluted columns bearing the names in black lettering on a white background of 1,220 men from the company who had died in the First World War. At the centre of the memorial was the GER crest representing the areas of the east of England served by the company – Essex, Maldon, Ipswich, Norwich, Huntingdonshire, Hertfordshire and Northamptonshire. The inscription in red lettering read: 'To the Glory of God and in grateful memory of the Great Eastern Railway Company staff who, in response to the call of their King and Country, sacrificed their lives during the Great War'.

This memorial was situated beside one unveiled in 1917 to Captain Charles Fryatt, a GER employee, who had been executed by the Germans the previous year . In March 1915, while in command of the SS *Wrexham* in the North Sea, he had attempted to ram a German U-boat that was about to torpedo his vessel. A year later he was captured while in command of the SS *Brussels*. The German authorities deemed that he had acted as a civilian and was therefore not entitled to the protections afforded to a prisoner of war. In 1919 his body had been repatriated with much solemnity via Liverpool Street Station, as, in that same year, were the remains of Edith Cavell, the nurse executed by the Germans in 1915 for her part in smuggling British servicemen out of occupied France and Belgium.[3,4]

Less than four years had passed since the end of the war. From the United Kingdom 886,000 men had died; from the entire British Empire the dead numbered 1.1 million. Britain was one of the victors, but victory was relative. Every country had lost. No family, community or company was untouched.[5]

London, once considered inviolable, had been attacked from the air, and the station had been hit twice. On 8 September 1915 bombs dropped by German Zeppelins fell on the tracks without loss of life. On 13 June 1917 a raid by German Gotha planes on the East End of London dropped bombs on platforms 8 and 9, killing thirteen commuters. It was witnessed by the war poet Siegfried Sassoon, who was home on leave from the front. Sassoon recalled that 'an invisible enemy sent destruction spinning down from a fine weather sky'. The raid was more terrifying for having happened in daylight and for the huge loss of life. The 162 civilians who were killed in the East End that day presaged the even greater terrors of the Blitz a generation later.[6]

The memorial service began with the boys of St Stephen's Choir from London, assisted by members of the station staff, singing the hymn 'Let Saints on Earth in Concert Sing'. The Bishop of Norwich, Dr Bertram Pollock, stepped forward to offer prayers for the dead and for peace. He was followed by Lord Claud Hamilton, the successful railway entrepreneur and GER chairman, in his last public appearance in the role. The memorial was 'beautiful and dignified', he stated. It would stand in perpetuity in the middle of Liverpool Street Station in full view of commuters to honour the men who had left the safety of their railway employment to serve in the war. They had died that others might live.

He then introduced his good friend and the principal guest, Field Marshal Sir Henry Wilson, to unveil the memorial. Wilson was fifty-eight, an Ulster Unionist MP and a former career soldier. His four-year term as the Chief of the Imperial General Staff (CIGS), the British government's most senior military advisor, had ended in February 1922. Within days he was elected unopposed as the Ulster Unionist MP for North Down in Northern Ireland.[7]

Although no longer an active soldier, Wilson was received like one. He was greeted at the entrance to the station and a guard of

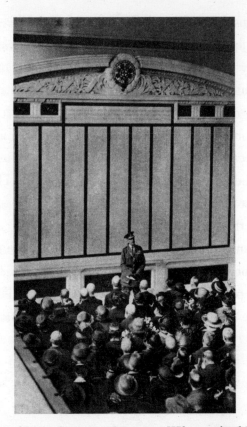

1 Liverpool Street Station, 22 June 1922: Wilson makes his speech
at the unveiling of the war memorial to the men from the Great
Eastern Railway who had died in the First World War

honour was formed on Platform 9 by ex-servicemen now back in
civilian life as railway employees. Wilson was in good spirits as he
passed along the ranks, making small talk and commending those
who had won medals for gallantry in the war. At 6ft 4in he had lost
the ungainliness that made him something of a figure of fun when
he was a young subaltern cavalry officer, his knees jutting upwards
from the stirrups as he rode horses too small for his extended gait.
Wilson made the most of his physical presence. He was peculiar-
looking, with a receding hairline, a greying moustache, a lined face

and, most conspicuously, a scar on the right side of his eyeball socket which made his face droop. His right eye would often water and he frequently gave the impression of crying. Given his propensity for occasional emotional outbursts, it was never clear whether he was weeping or not. He was described by one female contemporary, Mary Garstin, as 'the tall ugly Irishman whose torturous spirit seemed reflected in his twisted face'.[8] He was fond of telling the story that when he was based in Belfast in 1891, a letter addressed to the 'ugliest man in the army' found an accurate recipient in him. Wilson had the confidence to laugh off the sobriquet and mentioned it often at public gatherings where he was invited to speak.

Wilson's personality filled every room he entered as much as his physical presence did. Friends spoke of his 'wild Irish ways' and his sense of fun, accentuated by a loud laugh and a forthright

2 Field Marshal Sir Henry Wilson

manner. He could be admirably focused but also flippant in the
gravest of circumstances, and this made people wary of him. He
often called people by their nicknames, even august personages
such as the French prime minister Georges Clemenceau, whom
everybody called 'Tiger' behind his back, but Wilson did not hesitate to address him as such to his face.[9]

His physical and intellectual energies were inexhaustible. He
had an engaging delivery that he had perfected at the British
army's Staff College, Camberley, as an instructor in the early years
of the twentieth century. Students recalled his clarity of thought
and delivery, attributes which he deployed at the highest levels of
decision-making in the First World War. Sir George Barrow, a
contemporary of Wilson at Staff College, regarded him as:

> the most original, imaginative and humorous man I have ever
> known. He riveted the attention and made the dullest subjects
> bright. He brought something new, something nobody else
> had thought of into the discussions of lectures and problems,
> and his summings-up at conferences and on Staff tours were
> models of well-balanced judgements.[10]

Wilson was dressed in his field marshal's uniform. The highest
rank in the British army had not been given for his command in
the field – he had spent just nine months as a general in the war –
but for his services as an advisor. Wilson was one of the four men
who won the war, according to many of his contemporaries. He,
along with the Supreme Allied Commander Marshal Ferdinand
Foch of France, the British prime minister David Lloyd George
and Clemenceau, were seen by many as the principal architects
of the Allied victory that brought Germany to sign a humiliating
armistice in November 1918 and the Treaty of Versailles seven
months later, in June 1919.

Wilson's decisive interventions bookended the conflict. His far-sighted planning had ensured that the British Expeditionary Force (BEF) could deploy on the left flank of the French army in the first full month of the war in August 1914. Throughout the war he had advocated greater co-operation between the Allies. He assumed the role of CIGS in February 1918 and was one of the instigators of the joint Allied command under his good friend Foch. The Allied all-arms strategy, exploiting advantages of materiel and manpower, along with the entry of the Americans, brought the war to a swifter end in November 1918 than most had anticipated.

The early post-war years were beset with unrest throughout the Empire. The UK was tasked with demobilising the biggest army in its history and sending millions of veterans back to civilian life. There were old problems for Britain from her pre-war colonies – Ireland, Egypt and India – all restive and demanding more freedoms. There were new ones, too, in the Middle East mandates given to Britain after the war. The Empire had never been so big nor so overstretched. In Britain there were strikes in the coal mines and in the docks and unrest on the streets. Fears of socialism and Bolshevism, both real and imagined, stalked the country.

Wilson vacated the role of CIGS in good standing with the public but not the coalition government of Lloyd George, from whom he had become increasingly estranged. Wilson could not abide the nationalist turn his native land, Ireland, had taken towards independence. He was not just a unionist, but a Southern unionist from the Midlands county of Longford, an overwhelmingly nationalist county that had played a disproportionate part in the Irish War of Independence between 1919 and 1921. Wilson was self-consciously an Irishman, who considered himself also to be British and saw no contradiction between the two identities. He was Anglo-Irish, an imperialist, and his country was the British Empire.

In December 1921 the British had negotiated the Anglo-Irish Treaty with the leaders of Sinn Féin, setting up the Irish Free State. Wilson saw the Treaty as a betrayal of the values of law and order and a surrender to the 'murder gang', as he was wont to call his fellow Irishmen in Sinn Féin and the Irish Republican Army (IRA), with whom the British had negotiated. He did not believe the Irish had the ability to govern themselves. Outside Ulster few people in Ireland agreed with him.

* * *

Before he began to speak, a woman carrying a large wreath burst into tears and sobbed so abjectly that many thought she was going to faint. Wilson approached and steadied her. No longer constrained by the forced reticence of the professional soldier, Wilson could now speak his mind.[11]

He had given valedictory talks during the preceding weeks in Belfast and Manchester, where, in the course of honouring the war dead, he had made caustic comments about the Lloyd George government and its Irish policy. At Liverpool Street Station his remarks were, unusually for him, brief and emotional, and contained no reference to Ireland.

It is always a proud duty for one soldier to speak of others. All over our country there are these memorials to those who carried out their duty in the Great War. We soldiers count as our gains our losses. These names that we love to honour are those who died in a great cause. On this table are placed the

8

names of 1,200 or 1,400 of your comrades who, doing what they thought was right, paid the penalty.

He finished with the ever-quotable Rudyard Kipling, who had lost his son John in the war, killed at the Battle of Loos in September 1915 while serving with the Irish Guards.

> The tumult and the shouting dies;
> The Captains and the Kings depart;
> Still stands Thine ancient sacrifice,
> A humble and a contrite heart;
> Lord God of Hosts, be with us yet,
> Lest we forget – lest we forget![12]

Those present at the unveiling knew too well the human cost of the war. The service was punctuated by the soft sobbing of mothers and widows. The grief of the war was still viscerally present, and Britain had inherited a bitter peace. After the dedication by the Bishop of Norwich, all present sang 'Oh God, Our Help in Ages Past'. 'The Last Post' was sounded by the Grenadier Guards, followed by 'Reveille' and 'God Save the King'. The ceremony over, Wilson repaired to the office of Admiral Sir Reginald Hall, known as Blinker Hall, the Director of Naval Intelligence, who was responsible in 1916 for intercepting the *Aud*, the German vessel that was due to land weaponry for those planning the Easter Rising, and in 1917 for intercepting the Zimmerman telegram, which brought the United States into the war.

'Well, old sailor,' said Wilson. 'Well, old soldier,' came the response. Wilson told Hall he could not dally as he had an appointment in the House of Commons at 3.30 p.m. and had to go home to change.[13]

Wilson left the station and took a District Line underground train west in the company of Lieutenant Colonel Harold Charley, the officer commanding the Royal Ulster Rifles, established after the creation of Northern Ireland the previous year. Wilson was the regiment's honorary colonel.

Wilson and Charley travelled in the first-class carriage reserved for army officers and alighted at Charing Cross Station. From there, Wilson said goodbye to Charley and hailed a cab to go home. He first stopped off at the Travellers Club in Pall Mall to read the news off the ticker-tape machine and pick up his mail. He then travelled on to his home at 36 Eaton Place, which he had acquired in 1910. The handsome three-storey house was bigger than the needs of the childless Wilsons and was rented out frequently to pay their bills. It was also their well-loved home.[14]

* * *

At around 1 p.m. Joe O'Sullivan left his office in the Ministry of Labour in Whitehall, where he worked as a clerk, and walked to the clock at Vauxhall Bridge Road for 1.30 p.m. He told a colleague to sign him in if he did not come back in the afternoon. O'Sullivan was of average height, slightly built and with a diffident manner.[15] He wore standard office attire: a black jacket, trousers and a brown trilby hat. He had served with the 3rd (City of London) Battalion, London Regiment, in the war, losing a leg in August 1917 during the Battle of Passchendaele, the muddy apocalypse that 'tipped the survivors into the slough of despond', as the military historian John Keegan described it.[16]

O'Sullivan was needed to positively identify Wilson, who had often called into the offices of the Ministry of Labour on CIGS business, and O'Sullivan knew his address.[17] Waiting for

O'Sullivan was Reginald 'Reggie' Dunne. Dunne was 6ft tall, well built running to stout, with brown hair. He walked with a slight limp as a result of an exploding shell that had damaged his knee-cap in the First World War. He wore a fawn sports coat and a trilby hat, heavy clothing for the time of year.

O'Sullivan was twenty-five and Dunne twenty-four, but Dunne was the more forceful of the two, a leader of men and the officer commanding the IRA in London. Dunne and O'Sullivan had been engaged in acts of destruction, execution and gun smuggling in the name of Ireland, a country that neither man, unlike Wilson, had been born in. Dunne served with the 1st Battalion of the Irish Guards, a regiment that reflected his background and his height – recruits were usually at least 5ft 9in and therefore well nourished. These two war veterans often wore the large sterling silver lapel badge, known as the 'wound badge', in public, but not today. Nobody noticed them. Why would they? There were millions of men like them in Britain, visibly and physically broken by the war, scuttling about the streets attracting pity but not much attention.

O'Sullivan carried a long-barrelled Webley .450, a standard-issue British army service revolver, with six extra rounds; Dunne the short version of the same weapon. Dunne waited anxiously for a third man, an able-bodied volunteer, to help in their dangerous enterprise. He had left a coded telephone message at this man's place of work, but time was passing and he had not turned up. Dunne looked at O'Sullivan and momentarily regretted his decision to call on him, given his obvious disability, but then he recalled how O'Sullivan had previously been involved in dangerous missions and had not lacked for courage or resolve. He knew O'Sullivan would not waver despite the risks to both of them.

They walked from Victoria Station to Wilson's home, arriving soon after 2 p.m. Eaton Place in Belgravia is a stately terrace of stucco-fronted buildings with white porticoes built in the 1820s, a prime address and favoured by those who wanted to be physically close to the centre of government in London.

The road outside Wilson's home was under repair and workmen busied about. A battery of horse-drawn artillery came down the road. O'Sullivan and Dunne's already frayed nerves were set further on edge. Dunne gestured to O'Sullivan that they would have to call off the attack if the battery was Wilson's escort. It departed, however, as quickly as it arrived. The minutes passed slowly. Several pedestrians walked past, but none thought anything of the two men loitering around.

Presently, Wilson's cab drew up. Wilson paid the taxi driver and got out. He walked around the roadworks and towards the steps of his house, which lay at the corner of Eaton Place and Belgrave Place. O'Sullivan brazenly crossed the road in a straight line and raised his weapon. At a distance of just three metres he fired two

THE WILSON MURDER: THE SCENE OF THE CRIME; AND THE PRISONERS.

3 Dunne and O'Sullivan either side of the front door at Eaton Place. A bullet can be seen in the door

shots at Wilson, hitting him both times. Wilson staggered up the doorsteps. Dunne intercepted him and fired several more shots at close range from the hip. Wilson cried out in pain as bullets penetrated his lungs, his left armpit and shoulder joint.[18]

A story would circulate later that Wilson, a warrior to the last, had drawn his sword from his scabbard and raised it in a final act of defiance, but he never got that far, according to a workman (known as witness No. 1) who saw the shooting: 'He tried to recover himself before he fell and made a movement with his right hand to his left side. He was wearing a sword on his left side. After that he collapsed completely.'[19]

As he reached for his sword, O'Sullivan finished him off with another shot. Wilson was almost at his own front door. Had it been open he might have stumbled inside and shut it behind him. A bullet lodged in the door, and the former field marshal's blood on the steps was later covered up with sand.[20]

The sound of the shots on a still midsummer's afternoon brought residents from their homes. Wilson's butler emerged almost immediately from the front door and called for help. Lady Wilson was in the drawing room when she heard the shots and, rushing to the window, saw her husband lying prostrate on the steps. She ran out with a cup of water, but he was already too far gone. 'He is dying, he is dying. Isn't there someone who can help? Cannot someone bring a doctor?' she cried out.[21] The couple's butler and a neighbour helped carry the dying field marshal inside. Lady Wilson was heard to exclaim, 'Well, they have done their cruel work at last, but you have died like a soldier. God will be merciful to you.' By the time Dr John Evans, the surgeon attached to the Gerald Road police station, was summoned, Wilson was dead.

Two doors away a member of the household of Lord Channing rushed out and, spotting the assassins, shouted 'Murder!' and

'Stop thief!' O'Sullivan and Dunne walked briskly away from the scene down Eaton Place, but they did not start to run until they heard a policeman's whistle. A workman dropped his shovel and ran after the two men. As they hurried away, O'Sullivan dragging his wooden leg behind him, Dunne noticed his friend's discomfort and concluded it was only a matter of time before they were caught. The two men turned left into Eaton Terrace, the pursuing crowd swelling at every moment.[22]

Police Constable Walter Marsh, who had been patrolling nearby Eaton Square, joined the chase. Marsh caught up with Dunne and wrestled him to the ground, but as he did so, O'Sullivan shot him in the chest. The bullet lodged in his back, yet he survived. Dunne and O'Sullivan stopped a Victoria cab, a horse-drawn covered carriage with two passenger seats, and ordered the driver, John William Puxley, to drive to Marble Arch. 'Even at the time I was amused at the energy with which the prim, liveried, old driver whipped up the horses, very much conscious that two guns were pointed at his back,' Dunne recalled. The pair did not get far before a mob stopped the cab, and they continued on foot.[23]

Detective Constable Cecil Sayer heard the shots that badly injured Marsh, and he too chased after Dunne and O'Sullivan. He crossed the King's Road (now renamed Eaton Square) and followed them from South Eaton Place. Sayer bravely flung his truncheon at O'Sullivan, hitting him on the head. Dunne turned around and shot Sayer in the ankle, and the constable fell to the ground. Dunne and O'Sullivan paused for a moment to reload their weapons. They passed the home of the American ambassador, Colonel George Harvey, who had as his guest the US Chief Justice and former president William Howard Taft. Both men heard shots and thought they were being targeted.

An American eyewitness noticed between fifty and sixty civilians in pursuit, along with half a dozen unarmed policemen. More shots brought more constables onto the street. Two emerged from the Gerald Road police station and started pursuing the fugitives.[24]

Dunne and O'Sullivan were flagging now and out of breath, O'Sullivan exhausted and struggling with his wooden leg, Dunne aching from his war wound and walking backwards, pointing his gun to keep the crowds at bay while also trying to reload. They fired a few more shots at constables Walter Bush and James Alexander Duff but missed.

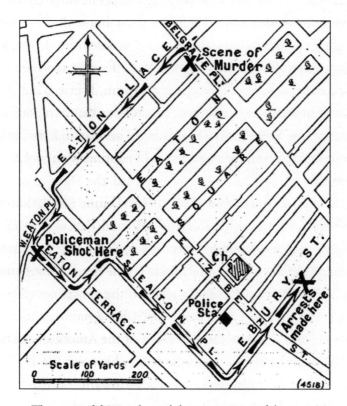

4 The scene of the murder and the escape route of the assassins

An eyewitness who joined in the pursuit remembered Dunne and O'Sullivan as the 'ruffian type and I thought they had been guilty of robbery and violence'.[25] Bush caught up with Dunne as he was trying to reload and with one expertly aimed flourish of the truncheon felled the big man as he ran down Ebury Street. Duff flung his truncheon at O'Sullivan, and for the second time O'Sullivan experienced the sharp thud of heavy wood on the back of his head. He squeezed the trigger of his revolver, but he was out of ammunition. The truncheon was followed by an empty milk bottle flung by a passer-by, which hit O'Sullivan in the face. A melee followed, with the public joining in, and a shot was fired by either Dunne or O'Sullivan. 'You are a dirty blackguard,' one passer-by shouted at Dunne. 'I was only firing blank shots at the last,' Dunne responded. PC Ernest Upcott from Gerald Road police station estimated that a crowd of about 130 people descended on the pair as they were caught.

The chase was over. 'Have mercy,' one of the men was reported by a passer-by to have shouted, to which came the retort, 'A lot of mercy you have shown.' The police then turned from pursuers to rescuers and held the angry crowd back from lynching the two fugitives.[26]

The assassins were taken away to Gerald Road police station for interrogation. Furious police, who had witnessed their comrades being shot, beat O'Sullivan unconscious and kicked and punched Dunne. A defiant Dunne smiled when told that Wilson had been killed, provoking another frenzied assault and graphic representations from his interrogators of being hanged. O'Sullivan gave his name as John O'Brien, the first name that came into his head. It was the name of his brother-in-law, based in Cork. When Dunne came around he gave his as James Connolly, the founder of the Irish Citizen Army and one of the leaders of the Easter Rising in 1916 who had been subsequently executed. Connolly was a famous republican martyr in Ireland, but the men's interrogators did not recognise the name.[27]

News of the shooting travelled fast. The terraces in Belgravia around Eaton Place were home to many MPs and members of the House of Lords, and some were on the scene minutes later. Lord Arthur Hill, a friend and neighbour of Wilson, arrived minutes after the shooting and gave a second-hand account that Wilson must have removed his ceremonial sword from its scabbard as it was held in place with a clip and could not have simply fallen on the ground. The story of the gallant soldier reaching for his sword to confront his slayers gained immediate renown.

Wilson was the first sitting MP to be assassinated since the prime minister Spencer Perceval in 1812, and the first senior politician to

5 Crowds gathered outside 36 Eaton Place at the corner with Belgrave Place. The front door and steps have since been moved around the corner to face into Belgrave Place

be assassinated in the United Kingdom[28] since the Chief Secretary for Ireland Lord Frederick Cavendish was murdered in 1882 in Phoenix Park, Dublin, by Irish republicans. 'We must not get ourselves back into that hideous bog of reprisals, from which we have saved ourselves,' Winston Churchill, the Secretary of State for the Colonies, wrote to his wife in February 1922.[29] But once again the issue of Ireland – for so long dominant in British political life – had returned just when the British political establishment believed it had rid itself of the problem. The creation of two polities, Northern Ireland in May 1921 and the Irish Free State in December of that year, was an attempt to reconcile the irreconcilable demands of a thirty-two-county all-Ireland republic for nationalists with Ulster unionist determination to stay out of such an arrangement.

Several MPs brought the melancholy news to Westminster. The press gallery was soon informed and a brief report prepared for the wires.

Scarcely an hour and a half had passed between the shooting and the widespread dissemination of the information. Lloyd George entered the House of Commons in a jaunty mood, but he was immediately accosted by Churchill and Austen Chamberlain, the leader of the Conservative Party. Eyewitnesses noted Lloyd George's demeanour turning to cold fury and perhaps guilt. In her diary Frances Stevenson, his secretary and mistress, noted that the Home Secretary, Edward Shortt, had alerted Lloyd George to the presence of dangerous IRA men in London, but he had ignored the warning, lulled into a false sense of security after the signing of the Treaty. 'Just heard the sad news about Henry Wilson – will the Irish troubles ever end?' she recorded in her diary.[30]

As Britain's wartime prime minister from December 1916, Lloyd George had absorbed much terrible news, but none had felt like such a personal affront as the assassination of a man whose counsel he had sought at a time of national peril. Wilson and he had endured the bitterest falling out over Ireland, but their partnership flourished during the First World War, when Lloyd George needed an alternative vision to the attritional slaughter espoused by Field Marshal Sir Douglas Haig and others. Lloyd George regarded most British commanders as a doltish, mediocre lot – but not Wilson.

A ghastly atmosphere pervaded the House of Commons chamber as a series of routine parliamentary questions were asked and answered while members sought to ascertain what had happened. All the while Chamberlain was attempting to find out the facts as they presented themselves in order to answer questions in the House about the assassination of a sitting MP. Former prime minister Herbert Asquith was the first to address the chamber. Speaking almost imperceptibly, he was told to raise his voice. Asquith recounted that he had known Wilson well, and so his death was especially shocking in that context. In reality, Asquith, prime minister from April 1908 until December 1916, despised Wilson and regarded him as a 'poisonous mischief-maker' and a 'serpent', but one does not speak ill of the dead at such a time:[31]

Since I came down to the House, I have heard, and probably Hon. Members may have heard, tidings of the most terrible character affecting this House, namely, the death – the murder, I must call it – of a gallant soldier, one of the great figures in the war, who, though only recently elected a member of this House, already possessed in a high degree its esteem, and, indeed, its affection. I should like to ask the Leader of the House if he can give us any exact information as to the circumstances of this appalling event.[32]

It was left to Chamberlain to give what details he could. 'My information is imperfect,' he told the House. This was true. He assumed Wilson's residence had been broken into and three police officers shot. Chamberlain counted himself as a friend of Wilson. His delivery was matter of fact, but he became increasingly emotional. He stuttered and struggled to retain his composure:

> And I think that every Member of this House who remembers his great career elsewhere, who welcomed him here, and who had listened to him, will feel with me that this is not only a national, but, for us in the House of Commons, a personal tragedy. I believe that it will be the general wish of the House – precedent notwithstanding – that in the sad circumstances of this case, and as a mark of our profound respect for our colleague, and of our deep sympathy with his widow, the House should adjourn. I, therefore, beg to move, 'That this House do now adjourn'.[33]

The unnamed *New York Times* correspondent in the press gallery noted Lloyd George 'had the look of a man who had been cut to the heart. He was physically suffering and for once seemed quite cast down.'[34] He had to be steadied, and leaned on the arm of Sir Robert Horne, the Chancellor of the Exchequer, as he left the chamber. Asquith departed in tears.

In the House of Lords, Lord Edward Carson, the Dublin-born leader of Ulster unionism, asked if the news was true. He had heard different accounts. The normally voluble Carson listened with his head in his hands while the Lord Chancellor Frederick Edwin (F. E.) Smith, also known as the Earl of Birkenhead, recounted what he knew of the shooting. Wilson was indeed dead, shot by two men from the IRA. The Lord Chancellor had been a kindred spirit of Wilson in his opposition to Irish nationalism, yet, unlike Wilson, had drafted much of the Anglo-Irish Treaty and was a British signatory to it. Smith is famous in Irish history for his comment to Michael Collins, the best known of the Irish negotiators, after the Treaty was signed: 'I may have just signed my political death warrant,' to which Collins responded only half in jest and with chilling prescience, 'I may have just signed my actual death warrant.' Smith was a target of Wilson's vituperative criticism of government policy on Ireland, a fact he was not going to gloss over even in this shocking moment:

> Forty years have passed since he transferred from his original battalion into the Rifle Brigade – forty years crowded with adventure, with active service, and with brilliant contributions to the military operations of this country. Everyone knows that a part which had always been distinguished became almost decisive in the last few years of the war, but only those who were at that time members of one or other of the Governments which were responsible for the fortunes of the war know the full extent of the debt which this country owes to the ingenious resource, the imaginative capacity and the soldierly science of the late Sir Henry Wilson. I sincerely hope that the fact that the gallant field marshal differed, and even differed profoundly, from some of the views and recommendations for which this Government have made themselves responsible, will not be held a sufficient cause for repelling them or me from the expression, however inadequate, in this House of the heartfelt grief which we feel at his loss and the sympathy which every one of us must feel for the bereaved lady who mourns that loss today.[35]

*

The threat of assassination was ever present in the nineteenth and early twentieth centuries. The Russian Czar Alexander II, who emancipated the serfs, was killed by anarchists in 1881. In 1894 Sadi Carnot, the president of France, was also a victim of anarchists, as, four year later, was Empress Elisabeth of Austria, the wife of the Emperor of Austria Franz Joseph I. In 1900 King Umberto I of Italy was murdered, while in 1908 King Carlos I of Portugal and his eldest son Luís Filipe were shot dead by Portuguese republicans. Three American presidents were assassinated in less than forty years – Abraham Lincoln (1865), James A. Garfield (1881) and William McKinley (1901). 'We are all constantly in danger of death. One must simply trust in God,' said a fatalistic Archduke Franz Ferdinand, the heir to the Austro-Hungarian throne, before his assassination in Sarajevo on 28 June 1914 plunged Europe into the greatest war in history up to that date.

Germany's defeat in this war created a generation of vengeful ex-servicemen who sought to blame someone, anyone, for their country's defeat. The politicians who led the Weimar Republic were targeted. The Minister of Finance Matthias Erzberger, who negotiated the Armistice, was shot dead in 1921 by a right-wing paramilitary group, one of 350 political figures in Germany assassinated in the years following the conflict.[36]

These assassinations took place in countries riven by factionalism and instability, not in one with an unbroken tradition of parliamentary democracy stretching back centuries. Assassination was un-British and so the Irish problem had come home, said the Marquess of Salisbury, the leader of the House of Lords:

Here, in the middle of our own metropolis, he has been murdered. This crime cannot but bring home to us the circumstances in which we live, and in which another part of the United Kingdom has been plunged for so many months. I think we owe it to ourselves, we owe it to the other House of Parliament, to say what we feel in a formal manner, and to show the country how deeply we detest the horrible crime which has been committed.[37]

The Bishop of Norwich, who had been present at the ceremony in Liverpool Street Station, quoted Virgil. Those who are entitled to the Elysian Fields had *quique sui memores alios fecere merendo* ('built their own memorial by the services they have rendered').

Both houses adjourned until just after 4 p.m.[38]

* * *

On hearing the news King George V sent his equerry Colonel Arthur Erskine to Eaton Place to convey his sympathies to Lady Wilson. His eldest son, the Prince of Wales, the future King Edward VIII, who would abdicate in 1936, had arrived back in Plymouth the previous day from an eight-month tour of India and Japan. His visit to India, as the 'Empire's ambassador', was ostensibly to thank the Indian people for their service in the British armed forces during the First World War, but it was also an attempt to shore up waning allegiances in a subcontinent demanding more freedoms in the post-war world. The visit was boycotted by Indian nationalists led by Mahatma Gandhi and there were riots in Bombay (Mumbai). Thousands gathered in Plymouth when HMS *Renown* arrived into port; thousands more lined the stations along the route as the royal train made its way from Plymouth to Paddington Station in London. There to greet the prince at Paddington were his father and mother, the prime minister and his daughter, the Archbishop of Canterbury, Randall Davidson, and other significant luminaries in British society. The tour was regarded as a success thanks to flattering press coverage. The prince was a popular figure then and a long way from being the post-1936 pariah in the royal family.

The celebrations were intended to continue on the night of the 22nd, which was the eve of the Prince of Wales's twenty-eighth birthday. The king cancelled the party with sixty guests at Buckingham Palace. Having often sought Wilson's counsel during the war, he let it be known that he would not even contemplate holding a dinner in such circumstances. Nor was it to be a postponement. It was cancelled. The event found its way into Ernest Hemingway's novel *The Sun Also Rises*, in which the rakish ex-soldier and serial bankrupt Mike Campbell conveys his disdain for the paraphernalia of medals and titles. Campbell has never applied for the medals he is entitled to as a result of his war service. He finds himself invited to Buckingham Palace for the prince's birthday. He dashes off to a tailor, who procures him some medals for the occasion which he shoves into his pocket. 'Well, I went to the dinner, and it was the night they'd shot Henry Wilson, so the Prince didn't come and the King didn't come, and no one wore any medals, and all these coves were busy taking off their medals, and I had mine in my pocket.'[39]

That evening Lloyd George wrote a post-haste letter to Michael Collins, now the chairman of the newly established Provisional Government. Known in Ireland as 'the Big Fellow', Collins had been a prime organiser of the guerrilla war which confounded Lloyd George's often repeated assertion that Britain would treat Ireland like the Union treated the Confederate states. Collins was the most infamous man in Britain, turned famous by virtue of his presence, reluctant though it was, at the peace negotiations that concluded in the Anglo-Irish Treaty signed the previous December. Prior to the Truce of July 1921, which ended the Irish War of Independence, he was regarded in Britain as a brigand, the leader of a gang of murderers, a shameless gunman, yet evasive. Who was this man bringing the Empire to terms in Ireland? Why had he never been caught? His fugitive status burnished the myth. 'The elusive IRA chief in the open,' the *Illustrated London News* declared on its front page in September 1921, as if he were some rare bird of paradise found in a remote jungle.[40] The headline was accompanied by a full-page picture of Collins addressing a rally in County Armagh. The paper continued: 'There was a time not so long ago when Michael Collins was regarded almost as a myth, so elusive was he in escaping capture.'

6 Michael Collins in 1922

After the Truce he was the focal point of public attention during the Treaty negotiations, more so even than the prime minister, Churchill or Chamberlain. The *Hull Daily News* commented:

> Here we have a modern outlaw, an Irish guerrilla chief upon
> whose head a price had been fixed by the lawful authorities.
> Mr Michael Collins, motoring up to the residence of the
> Prime Minister of England and, under the guardian eyes
> and escorting hands of the Metropolitan Police, entering
> the Cabinet chamber at 10 Downing Street to confer with
> statesmen representing the British Empire. Surely there is an
> element of old romance about this episode? And it is romance
> quite in the most approved manner of the best sword-and-
> cloak drama too.[41]

The Treaty negotiated by Collins and the other members of the Irish delegation granted the twenty-six counties of Ireland Dominion status on a par with Canada and Australia, which amounted to self-governance within the Empire. The Treaty brought about the Irish Free State, but how free was this state, Collins's swelling band of detractors at home were asking, when it swore allegiance to a foreign king?

> I [name] do solemnly swear true faith and allegiance to the
> Constitution of the Irish Free State as by law established,
> and that I will be faithful to His Majesty King George V,
> his heirs and successors by law in virtue of the common
> citizenship of Ireland with Great Britain and her adherence to
> and membership of the group of nations forming the British
> Commonwealth of Nations.

Every word of it had been parsed and debated beyond endurance. Who was the oath of allegiance to? Collins said it was to the Irish constitution and not King George V. Fidelity was to the king as the head of the Commonwealth and not as British monarch. Besides, why did it matter? According to Collins, the British were leaving the twenty-six counties of Ireland and taking their army with them. There would be an Irish army, and the Border Commission, as agreed in the Anglo-Irish Treaty, would in time reduce Northern Ireland to a rump polity. The Treaty, Collins famously opined, was not the 'ultimate freedom that all nations desire and develop to, but the freedom to achieve it'.[42] Those against the Treaty said they had already taken an oath to the Irish republic, and a republic couldn't have a foreign monarch. It was not a matter of words, but a fundamental principle. Who was authority vested in – the British monarch or the Irish people?

The IRA had been the revolutionary guerrilla army of the underground Irish state that had fought the British to a stalemate during the War of Independence. It was an irregular army with the ranks and command structure of a regular one. Officers were elected. The smallest unit was a company based on the parish. Companies were organised into battalions, battalions into brigades and brigades into divisions. Its nominal strength during the Truce period was 115,000 men, but many of these were disparagingly known as 'Trucileers' or 'sunshine patriots', who had joined up when the fighting was over. The number of active volunteers was significantly smaller.

By 1921 the British forces fielded roughly 55,000 troops in Ireland, armed with the first-class weaponry that had won the Great War. By July 1921 the IRA was down to 2,000 active fighters, according to some estimates, and had only 569 rifles, 477 revolvers and 20 bullets per rifle.[43] It was a pitiful arsenal to bear against an empire, and there were many within the British security establishment, Wilson among them, who believed that one more push would silence the 'murder gang' once and for all. It was not an even fight, but the IRA had the support of the majority of the people; the Crown forces did not. Coupled with that was a war-weariness and a realisation that Ireland was more trouble than it was worth, and so the British government wanted the issue done with once and for all, as Churchill admitted in the House of Commons. 'It is a curious reflection to inquire why Ireland should bulk so largely in our lives. How is it that the great English parties are shaken to their foundations, and even shattered, almost every generation, by contact with Irish affairs?'[44]

The IRA was answerable to Dáil Éireann, the Irish parliament, and to the underground government set up after the British general election of December 1918, the so-called 'Khaki election', when Sinn Féin won 73 of the 105 seats in Ireland on an abstentionist platform promising to use 'any and every means available to render impotent the power of England to hold Ireland in subjection by military force or otherwise'. Civilian control of the IRA often proved problematic. There were tensions between the civilian government, the general headquarters (GHQ) and individual units, which often took their own initiative in launching attacks on the British. Communication was often poor or nondescript. This highly decentralised army split after the Treaty, and a substantial number of officers and brigades refused to accept the Provisional Government set up under the Treaty.

On 26 March 1922 IRA leaders hosted an army convention in defiance of the Provisional Government and voted to repudiate the Treaty and the authority of Dáil Éireann. There were now two armies in the Irish Free State, each disputing the other's right to exist. The first Irish state in history, the one desired for centuries by generations of Irish nationalists, was threatened with stillbirth.

The government, the first in the country's history as a modern state, was memorably described by Kevin O'Higgins, its justice minister, as:

> eight young men standing amidst the ruins of one administration with the foundation of another not yet laid, and with wild men screaming through the keyhole. No police force was functioning through the country, no system of justice was operating, the wheels of administration hung idle, battered out of recognition by the clash of rival jurisdictions. A people emerging from a period of revolution were thrown upon their own resources, unaided by any fabric of administration for the maintenance of order and the decencies of life.[45]

The *Irish Times* observed a month later, 'The situation is preposterous. The existence of a Provisional Government is an administrative necessity; but, at a time when it is confronted with the gravest problems, it has no roots in the soil, no authority from the people, no material forces for the execution of its decrees.'[46]

The Constitution of the Irish Free State was released on the day before the election and published in the newspapers on 16 June, the morning of the election. Any hope it could form the basis of an agreement between the Treaty and anti-Treaty factions was extinguished. Attempts by the Irish side to draft a republican treaty were rejected by the British side. The oath remained. The king's representative had the power to summon and dissolve parliament, and all legislation had to receive the Royal Assent through him. It was, however, enough for the Provisional Government to claim that all 'legislative, executive, judicial and governmental powers are declared to be derived from the people'. The election saw candidates who were pro-Treaty or neutral achieve almost 80 per cent of the vote. It gave the Provisional Government an expectation of finally having a mandate to rule, but now, after the assassination, it faced renewed external threats from the British, as well as a new one – republicans determined to oppose the Treaty at any cost, including war. As far as the Provisional Government was concerned, the Treaty now had a triple democratic lock, having been passed by the cabinet, four to three, in December 1921; by the Dáil in January 1922 by sixty-four votes to fifty-seven; and now in a public vote by proxy in the general election of 1922.

In April 1922 anti-Treaty republicans occupied Dublin's Four Courts, the centre of legal life in Ireland, hoping a confrontation with the newly established National Army of the nascent Irish state would provoke a British intervention and violate the Treaty. The Provisional Government, sensing a trap, refused to oblige and a strange impasse followed. Anti-Treaty supporters wandered in and out of the Four Courts unmolested, and both sides fraternised with the other. It was a phoney war, but an uneasy one where there was no meeting of minds, despite the bonhomie between erstwhile brothers-in-arms.

The pro- and anti-Treaty Sinn Féin factions agreed an election pact in May 1922 to stave off the looming prospect of civil war. They would form a peacetime government after the election, but the British were furious at the prospect that anti-Treaty politicians would be in government, in contravention of the Treaty.

Lloyd George now seized his chance. He told Collins that documents had been found on one of the men (Dunne, as it turned out) linking him with the anti-Treaty IRA. The 'documents' turned out to be a copy of *An tÓglách* (*The Volunteer*), the IRA newspaper that could be bought at newsstands in Ireland. Whether Lloyd George truly believed it or not, he now had a pretext to act. He wrote to Collins:

The ambiguous position of the Irish Republican Army can no longer be ignored by the British army. Still less can Mr Rory O'Connor be permitted to remain with his followers in open rebellion in the heart of Dublin in possession of the Courts of Justice, organising and sending out from this centre enterprises of murder not only in the area of your government but also in the six northern counties and in Great Britain. His Majesty's government cannot consent to a continuance of this state of things, and they feel entitled to ask you formally to bring it to an end forthwith. I am to inform you that they regard the continuous toleration of this rebellious defiance of the principles of the Treaty as incompatible with its faithful execution. They feel now that you are supported by the declared will of the Irish people in favour of the Treaty, they have a right to expect that the necessary action will be taken by your government without delay.[47]

From the Cabinet Office, Churchill sent a telegram to Ireland summoning General Sir Nevil Macready to London. Macready was the General Officer Commanding (GOC) British forces in Ireland during what the British considered an insurgency by militant republicans in Ireland between 1919 and 1921, but what the Irish regarded as the War of Independence.

'I loathe the people with a depth deeper than the sea and more violent than that which I feel against the Boche,' Macready confided to a friend about the Irish. But it had not stopped him reaching the conclusion that the British, outside their loyal north-eastern redoubt in Ulster, no longer had any business in Ireland.

At 6 p.m. on the evening of 22 June Macready reached his headquarters at the Royal Hospital Kilmainham. Under the terms of the Treaty, the British retained a garrison in Ireland to protect the settlement and the army was due to stay a year. Macready did not share in the collective shock of Wilson's assassination. He had realised Wilson was a marked man and told him so. Wilson was a scapegoat, he believed, for the excesses of the Ulster Special Constabulary (mostly the B Specials), set up in 1920 as a state militia and blamed for vicious pogroms against Catholics in Ulster. Macready warned Wilson to carry a concealed pistol with him. Now it was too late. An hour after receiving the news, Macready was summoned to London. There he found the British cabinet in a 'state of suppressed agitation' and spoiling for revenge. Churchill was charged with a 'feverish impetuosity'.[48]

Lloyd George and Churchill had no doubt the anti-Treaty agitators in the Four Courts were to blame. No evidence other than an educated hunch was advanced for this conclusion, but Macready was told to prepare his troops to storm the building beside the River Liffey in Dublin city centre. This was a militarily straightforward operation, Macready concluded, but politically disastrous. It would risk Britain being sucked back into the quagmire of Irish politics at a time when it had extracted itself at a great cost of both men and reputation. Such an attack would unite the pro- and anti-Treaty factions against the same foe they had faced in the war, which had ended in July of the previous year with a truce and an uneasy peace.

Macready travelled back to Ireland and was told to await further instructions. He hoped the brief hiatus would stop the Lloyd George government from acting impetuously in a manner it would regret. The prospect of Britain breaking an internationally recognised treaty would sully the country's reputation, already battered by the behaviour of its forces during the Irish conflict. The Lloyd George government, Macready concluded, had been 'accounted for by a bad attack of nerves'. On arriving back in Ireland, Macready anticipated that cooler heads would prevail, but they did not. Another telegram arrived ordering that his troops attack the Four Courts a day later. Macready realised that many British troops stationed around Ireland would be vulnerable to attack in the event of hostilities recommencing. Moreover, he believed that, if the anti-Treaty forces were responsible for Wilson's assassination, the British could be walking into a trap. He recalled in his memoir *Annals of an Active Life*:

> The few senior officers to whom I unfolded the scheme were unanimous in their agreement that it could have but one result, the reopening of hostilities throughout Ireland. It can only be supposed that panic and a desire to do something, no matter what, by those whose ignorance of the Irish situation blinded them to possible results, was at the root of this scheme.[49]

If the British attacked the Four Courts garrison, it could have the effect of uniting pro- and anti-Treaty elements against a common enemy, 'a call which would have been answered by a majority who would have claimed that the British had broken the Truce'. Macready sent his general staff officer General Sir John Brind to London to make the British cabinet aware of the possible unintended consequences of its plan. He was not the only one playing for time. Lloyd George's ultimatum arrived while Collins was in Cork dealing with an allegation of electoral fraud. The Provisional Government asked for the evidence associating the anti-Treaty side with the two assassins, promising to bring it up at the first meeting of the new Dáil, which was scheduled for 1 July 1922, an eternity away given the pressing nature of the moment. In Collins's absence Diarmuid O'Hegarty, the secretary to the Provisional Government, wrote back making anguished protestations about the shooting while requesting the information the British claimed they had that suggested the anti-Treaty side was to blame. Churchill responded by stating that the information was of a 'highly secret character and cannot be disclosed'.[50] In haste he proposed to send Royal Navy ships to Dublin with reinforcements and weaponry for the British garrison. The Treaty would be declared invalid. Wiser counsel prevailed and the proposed British attack was postponed. Nevertheless, in the House of Commons four days after the shooting, Churchill said in public what he had told the Irish in private – they would act against the anti-Treaty rebels if the Provisional Government did not.

> The time has come when it is not unfair, not premature, and not impatient for us to make to this strengthened Irish Government and new Irish parliament a request – in express terms – that this sort of thing must come to an end. If it does not come to an end, if either from weakness, from want of courage, for some other even less creditable reasons, if it is not brought to an end, and a speedy end, then it is my duty to say that we shall regard the Treaty as having been formally violated.[51]

The Wilson assassination had brutally clarified matters. The British government was no longer going to tolerate the ambivalence shown towards the anti-Treaty rebels in the Four Courts. Fortunately for the British, the Provisional Government had reluctantly come to the same conclusion.

In March Collins and the Northern Ireland prime minister Sir James Craig had agreed a pact to halt the terrible sectarian violence in the North, which had claimed more than 450 lives between July 1920 and March 1922. Craig said he would work to ensure Catholic workers expelled from their jobs in the ship-yards in Belfast could return, while Collins called off the so-called Belfast Boycott of goods and services from that city to the South. The anti-Treaty side refused to abide by it. On 26 June a party of anti-Treaty IRA men attempted to raid Ferguson's garage in Dublin's Lower Baggot Street, which had sourced its cars from Belfast. The raid was pre-empted by National Army forces that surrounded the would-be thieves and arrested them, including Leo Henderson, their commanding officer. In retaliation, the anti-Treaty forces kidnapped Lieutenant General J. J. 'Ginger' O'Connell, the deputy chief of staff of the National Army. O'Connell was extraordinarily lax in his personal security at such a fraught time and was picked up while walking from his girl-friend's home back to barracks.

There was no more vacillation or equivocation towards erst-while comrades. On the evening of 27 June the Irish cabinet met and decided to act. The Provisional Government now had a pretext that did not involve appearing to do the British govern-ment's bidding. It was time to get on with the task of saving the Free State:

> Since the close of the general election, at which the will of the
> people was ascertained, further grave acts against the security
> of persons and property have been committed in Dublin
> and some other parts of Ireland by persons pretending to
> act with authority. It is the duty of the government, to which
> the people have entrusted their defence and the conduct of
> their affairs, to protect and secure all law-abiding citizens
> without distinction and that duty the government will
> resolutely perform. Yesterday one of the principal garages in

35

the metropolis was raided and plundered under the pretext of a Belfast boycott. No such boycott has any legal existence and, if it had, it would not authorise or condone the action of irresponsible persons in seizing private property. Later in the same evening Lieutenant General O'Connell, deputy chief of staff, was seized by some of the persons responsible for the plundering of the garage and is still in their hands. Outrages such as these against the nation and the government must cease at once and cease forever. For some months past all classes of business in Ireland have suffered severely through the feeling of insecurity engendered by reckless and wicked acts which have tarnished the reputation of Ireland abroad. As one disastrous consequence unemployment and distress are prevalent in the country at a time when, but for such acts, Ireland would be humming with prosperity. The government is determined that the country shall no longer be held up from the pursuit of its normal life and the re-establishment of its free national institutions. It calls therefore on the citizens to co-operate actively with it in the measures it is taking to ensure the public safety and to secure Ireland for the Irish people.[52]

Collins clarified that it was not just about the Treaty. It was about who governed Ireland. 'We have borne with extreme patience the illegal and improper conduct of certain elements in our midst since the signature of the Treaty with Great Britain and its endorsement by the supreme authority of the nation – Dáil Éireann,' he told the international press agencies.[53] He tasked the National Army's director of military operations, Major General Emmet Dalton, with procuring field guns from the British – the Provisional Government had none of its own.

Dalton, who had gaelicised his first name from Ernest to Emmet, was another British army veteran of the First World War. He, like Dunne and O'Sullivan and thousands of other Irishmen, had switched sides afterwards. Despite his elevated rank, Dalton was only twenty-four, the same age as Dunne. At the Battle of the Somme he had witnessed the death of Lieutenant Tom Kettle. Kettle, a former Irish Party MP and great hope of constitutional Irish nationalism, was felled by a bullet at Ginchy on 9 September 1916 while serving with the Royal Dublin Fusiliers.

Commandant General Tony Lawlor, who had served with the Royal Flying Corps in the war, knew how to operate the 18-pounder guns. At a minute to midnight on 27 June the two artillery pieces were handed over to the National Army and taken from Marlborough (McKee) Barracks. The guns were placed either side of the two bridges that flanked the Four Courts on the opposite side of the River Liffey.

It was midsummer and a soft rain was falling. The tramp of army boots followed by the rumble of armoured cars woke many residents and drew them to their windows. Two military ambulances followed on behind. An *Irish Times* correspondent looking from his window surmised 'dire events were toward in the Irish capital'.[54]

At 3.40 a.m. on the morning of 28 June Tom Ennis, the National Army commander, issued the Four Courts garrison with a warning to leave within twenty minutes:

> I acting under orders of the government hereby order you to evacuate the buildings of the Four Courts and to parade your men under arrest without arms on the portion of the quays immediately in front of the Four Courts by 4 a.m. Failing compliance with this order the building will be taken by me, by force. You will be held responsible for any life lost.[55]

37

No response came from inside the Four Courts. The Provisional Government cut the power to the building and the lights went out on any chance of a peaceful resolution. At 4 a.m. the 18-pounder located at Winetavern Street fired its first shell. It crashed into the metre-thick walls of the Four Courts at near point-blank range. The kinetic energy of the shell and its impact smashed windows in shops in the vicinity of the Four Courts and roused the people of Dublin for miles around.

The Irish Civil War had begun.

2

Henry Wilson – The Early Years: 'I am an Irishman'

Two kilometres outside Ballinalee in north County Longford, about 115 kilometres north-west of Dublin, down a single-lane track lined by rhododendron bushes that bloom lilac and pink in the summertime lies the townland of Currygrane.

Its primary feature is Currygrane Lake, a lough of eighty acres in size, fringed by reeds and lined with stones, and lying beside woodlands of larch and birch trees. A slipway and a boathouse lead to a restored small stone cottage, once the herdsman's, which is rented to anglers who come here for the coarse fishing, in particular for pike, bream, roach, perch and tench.

A kilometre away is a large, L-shaped, two-storey outbuilding next to a private house. It stands beside a large horse chestnut tree, of a kind which are plentiful on the estate. Its slate roof had fallen in and weeds grew from the crevices in the 200-year-old white-washed rubble stone walls, but it has now been restored. This is all that remains of the Currygrane estate, where Henry Hughes Wilson was born and raised. That, and three faded, rounded limestone headstones with a concrete base remembering three dogs on the estate: 'Barney, 1895–1901', 'A Faithful Companion; Pat, 1901, Always a Rifleman' and 'Scraps, 1897–1907, A Great Companion'. Henry Wilson inherited the family devotion to dogs and had a few of his own in his lifetime.

There was a big house on the site as far back as 1813. Currygrane House, owned by the Wilsons, was built in the 1830s for a local landowner, William Lloyd Galbraith, a member of the Orange

7 Currygrane House, County Longford

Order in the county. It was then bought by the Bond family, followed by the Wilsons in 1860. The lands were owned by a colourful figure named Samuel Wensley Blackall, a former MP for Longford, who sold up and moved to become a colonial governor in Queensland, Australia. New works on the house began in 1864.[1]

Currygrane House sat on the crest of a hill, with a large lawn in front. No trace of the original house remains. In its place now are two houses owned by the Brady family, who have lived in the townland for seventy years. 'The house of the planter is known by the trees,' the poet Austin Clarke once observed, and Currygrane House was surrounded by mature horse chestnut trees, copper beeches and laurel bushes that remain from the Wilsons' time. A solitary trace of Ireland's British past remains on the perimeter wall of Noel Brady's home. The post box retains the symbol of the Crown. When the Irish Free State came into being, the post boxes were simply painted over from red to green.

Halfway between Currygrane House and the lake is a high ridge planted with trees and bushes called Bridget's Hill or Miss Bridget's Plantation, named after Henry Wilson's niece Bridget, who was born in 1903.

Stone houses were provided for fourteen families on the Currygrane estate, who, as tenants, provided some income for the Wilson family. The estate was sufficiently well run for Wilson's father James to spend much of his time on committees deliberating about the things that interested him most, namely the fate of unionism and Anglicanism in Ireland. His wife, Henry's mother Constant Grace Martha Hughes, from Stillorgan near Dublin, was known locally as the 'good lady' and ran both the estate and the household. She married her husband, eleven years her senior, on her eighteenth birthday in 1861. The couple had seven children, Henry being the second eldest of four sons.[2]

The Wilsons did not consider themselves a rich family in comparison with many of their Anglo-Irish peers. In response to a proposal by the Land Commission in Ireland to reduce the rents of tenants in 1897, James Wilson Sr wrote to *The Times*:

> I had to deal with the excessive hardship which the present reductions of rent by the Land Commission is to bring down upon the smaller landlords. The general opinion I'm afraid is that Irish landlords are a comparatively rich class and that a man who has £10,000 a year can get on very comfortably even if his rent be reduced to £6,000 or £7,000

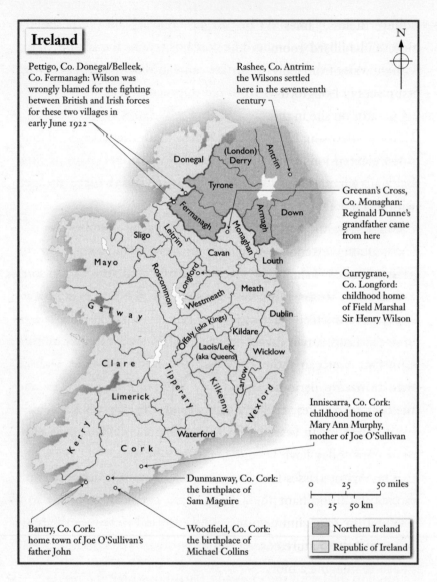

Ireland

Pettigo, Co. Donegal/Belleek,
Co. Fermanagh: Wilson was
wrongly blamed for the fighting
between British and Irish forces
for these two villages in
early June 1922

Rashee, Co. Antrim:
the Wilsons settled
here in the seventeenth
century

N

Donegal

(London)
Derry

Antrim

Tyrone

Fermanagh

Down

Armagh

Monaghan

Greenan's Cross,
Co. Monaghan:
Reginald Dunne's
grandfather came
from here

Sligo

Leitrim

Cavan

Louth

Mayo

Roscommon

Longford

Currygrane,
Co. Longford:
childhood home
of Field Marshal
Sir Henry Wilson

Westmeath

Meath

Galway

Offaly (aka Kings)

Dublin

Kildare

Laois/Leix
(aka Queens)

Wicklow

Clare

Tipperary

Kilkenny

Carlow

Limerick

Wexford

Inniscarra, Co. Cork:
childhood home of
Mary Ann Murphy,
mother of Joe O'Sullivan

Kerry

Waterford

Cork

Dunmanway, Co. Cork:
the birthplace of
Sam Maguire

0   25   50 miles

0   25   50 km

Bantry, Co. Cork:
home town of Joe O'Sullivan's
father John

Woodfield, Co. Cork:
the birthplace of
Michael Collins

Northern Ireland

Republic of Ireland

a year, though it may be he is treated unjustly. Alas! This is
not true for although there are a few well-known rich Irish
landlords, there are very many of small means on whom
these reductions are falling not only unjustly but with cruel
hardships.[3]

Nevertheless, James Wilson added an annexe with a smoking room and billiard room to the original house. A pump system brought water from Currygrane Lake, and the house was one of the first places in Longford to get electric light, which was provided by a generator on site in the 1890s. The estate was inherited by James Wilson's eldest son, James Mackay Wilson, known as Jemmy.

More extensions were carried out in 1916 and 1920, by which time Currygrane House was a mansion with fourteen bedrooms, a smoking room, office, drawing room, library, five servants' bedrooms, a servants' hall and a kitchen with sculleries and pantry. The building extended to 165,000 square feet (15,300 square metres), all kept in 'apple pie order'.[4]

The 1911 census indicated a prosperous and thriving estate. There were thirteen stables, two coach houses, four cow houses, three calf houses, two dairies and a barn. It was good pastureland. Jemmy was both an antiquarian and a naturalist, and would often write to nature periodicals with the first sightings of swallows, cuckoos, corncrakes, chiffchaffs, spotted flycatchers and willow wrens. 'After thirty years of careful observation of bird life here, never until today have I seen a Jay. I had him under observation with my opera glasses for at least a quarter of an hour and could not mistake his brilliant plumage,' he observed in December 1918.[5]

When the sun glimmers off the lily pads that fringe the lake and reflect the mature copper beech trees on the opposite side, it is hard to imagine a more tranquil place.

'I am an Irishman, born in County Longford, and can say for about fifty years before Mr Birrell came into power in 1906, the front door of my home was never shut by day or night,' Henry Wilson declared in a speech at Caxton Hall in London in May 1922. He was accused of anti-Irish bias, when to him it was about the difference between 'right and wrong' and England having to rule for the sake of the '99 out of 100 decent, quiet, peaceable folk in Ireland'.[6]

Augustine Birrell was the Chief Secretary for Ireland from 1906 until the Easter Rising of 1916, after which he resigned. Birrell was a reforming and generally popular Chief Secretary whose brief it was to prepare Ireland for the modest measure of self-government, as envisaged in the home rule settlement. The Wilsons regarded home rule as an affront to the established order, where everybody knew their place. Wilson detested politicians, especially Liberal ones.

Outside Ballinalee is a memorial which remembers the Clonfin ambush during the War of Independence, when men from the North Longford flying column ambushed two lorry loads of Auxiliaries, killing four and injuring eight, on 2 February 1921. The IRA commander that day was Seán Mac Eoin, known as the Blacksmith of Ballinalee. A bronze memorial to him in the town centre depicts him with a copy of the Anglo-Irish Treaty in one hand and the other resting on an anvil modelled after the one he used in his forge at the family home, Rose Cottage. He is forging a new state as assuredly as he forged hot metal into shape. Mac Eoin was Wilson's neighbour.[7]

Although their politics were at odds with those of most of their neighbours, the Wilsons were not unpopular landlords. Mac Eoin had himself threatened to burn Currygrane House to the ground during the War of Independence in 1921 if reprisals by Crown forces against local people did not stop. He told Jemmy to tell his brother to call it off. Jemmy protested that he had no such influence.

'Well,' I replied, 'in that case it will be too bad for Currygrane and for you.' I added that, should he attempt to leave

Currygrane, I would have him executed before he had reached Edgeworthstown or Longford.[8]

The reprisals did stop. Jemmy reciprocated the gesture when Mac Eoin was sentenced to death by the British after being captured in March 1921, urging his brother to intervene and reprieve him. As it happened, Mac Eoin was saved by the Truce that ended the War of Independence in July 1921. Currygrane House was also saved, albeit temporarily. It was burned to the ground by the anti-Treaty IRA in an act of tribal spite in August 1922, less than two months after Henry Wilson was assassinated, the same faction that had been blamed, erroneously as it turned out, by the British government for the killing.

Mac Eoin had a grudging respect for Jemmy, who had 'great courage' and cleaved to his unionist convictions with sincerity. Writing in the 1960s in the *Evening Herald*, Mac Eoin recalled that Henry Wilson's youngest brother Arthur set up a home industry with his wife Alice for girls in the district to earn money doing crochet and lace work. The Wilsons made no monetary gain from the enterprise, but their activities enabled 'many girls, Catholic, Presbyterian and Protestant, to marry and save good dowries to settle them in life. They, the Wilsons, were a fine family and were popular in the country and in Ballinalee in particular.' He regretted not being in a position to save Currygrane House from being destroyed by fire.

Following on from Mac Eoin's praise, an anonymous letter writer to the *Evening Herald*, who signed himself as 'Longfordman', was also complimentary of them. 'The Wilson family were popular in County Longford. They were very good employers and contributed generously to all charities, irrespective of class or creed. Ireland is the poorer today through the loss of such families over the last forty years.' That 'Longfordman' declined to reveal his real name indicates that such a viewpoint would not have been universally well received in Ireland.

There is no evidence, however, that the family was unpopular locally. They do not appear on the Land League's list of rogue landlords who had exploited their tenants. In 1880 a 'nefarious document' was sent to James Wilson and universally condemned by his tenants, who praised him for having provided them with 'handsome slated cottages and comforts they were heretofore unaccustomed to in the manner of living'. A certain sycophancy might be expected from his tenants, given his authority over them, but the parish priest Father Martin Monahan was moved to state that he 'never heard an unkind word spoken of Mr Wilson'.

* * *

Henry Wilson was born at Currygrane House on 5 May 1864. Daniel O'Connell once said of the Meath-born Duke of Wellington that 'just because you are born in a stable does not make you a horse.' O'Connell's jibe was intended to suggest that the Duke was not Irish despite having been born in Ireland. Wilson, though, saw himself as Irish. Others did too, attributing his general garrulousness and vivaciousness to his nationality. Wilson was happy to play along with it when it suited him, but he never identified as an Irish nationalist. In the nineteenth century, being an Irish unionist was not regarded as a contradiction in terms.

He never identified with his birthplace nor with his neighbours. Unlike Jemmy, whose worldview was tempered by his engagement with local people, Henry Wilson had little to do with Longford in his adult life and formed the perception of an outsider about the people he grew up around. 'I think we can safely say that the

Persians are an absolutely rotten people, far more rotten than even the Poles or the South-country Irish and that puts them pretty low,' he wrote in a letter to his good friend Sir Henry Rawlinson in June 1921.[9] Wilson's critical biographer Bernard Ash observed of his subject:

> When personally involved with them – as he was for much of his younger life – he mingled with them quite unaffectedly, could even jest uproariously with them, but when confronted with them as a nation instead of as human individuals he regarded their national aspirations as a plain instinct for murder and classed them all as corner boys and layabouts.[10]

When he stopped being a soldier in February 1922 and could speak freely, Wilson made clear his views that the Wilsons were an Ulster family, their roots in Longford were shallow and he had spent little time there. Instead, the Wilsons had spent 'something like 250 years in County Antrim', he declared in April of that year, after being elected as MP for the staunchly unionist North Down constituency. Wilson identified himself as a unionist, and just as importantly, was identified by Ulster unionists as one of their own. His identification with the cause of unionism and specifically with the creation of Northern Ireland in May 1921 made him a hate figure for republicans; although some were shocked by his death, few were outraged. As for the unionists, Northern Ireland's first premier, Sir James Craig, declared on hearing the news: 'Sir Henry Wilson has laid down his life for Ulster.'[11]

Wilson inherited a unionist sensibility that was impervious to rising nationalist expectations. Unionism, landlordism and the Protestant faith were the Holy Trinity of the Wilson family. His father, who died at the age of seventy-four in 1907, was a graduate of Trinity College Dublin, then a bastion of Anglicanism and imperialism in Ireland. James Wilson was a member of the Irish Landowners Convention and served on its executive committee. The convention was a conglomerate of landlords who frequently opposed or sought to water down British government legislation redistributing the land of Ireland back to the nationalist majority. He was a member of the General Synod of the Church of Ireland and held every position in the Church that a layman could hold. He was also a member of the Irish Unionist Alliance (IUA), an all-Ireland unionist party founded in 1891 to oppose plans for home rule, and the forerunner of the Ulster Unionist Party (UUP).

Jemmy went further than his father and stood in the North Longford Westminster constituency as a unionist. In 1885, as an Irish Conservative, he achieved just 6 per cent of the vote in a two-horse race against the Irish Party candidate. Undeterred by this electoral chastening, he stood again in the general election of 1892, this time for the IUA, and won the same share of the vote. Such devotion to a cause that those around them had so emphatically rejected was a characteristic of the Wilson family that Henry shared. A lack of popular support for their ideals never deterred the Wilsons from pursuing their opposition to home rule for Ireland. Jemmy eventually took up the position of land agent in County Longford, his duties requiring a great deal of office work, drawing up agreements with tenants and receiving rents.

He wrote regularly to newspapers in Britain and Ireland about the issues of the day, usually to express his incredulity at the prospect of home rule and concessions by British politicians to that end. In 1901 he wrote a letter to *The Times* about the Irish land question and the attempt by the Chief Secretary for Ireland, Gerald Balfour, to bring forward legislation to resolve the issue once and for all. 'The English people do not understand Irish affairs,' Jemmy wrote, a time-honoured refrain even from those Irish people well disposed towards the Union.[12]

In 1908 he entered into an extraordinary public correspondence with Balfour's successor but one, Walter Long, about the nature of home rule. Having heard of the formation of an 'Imperial Home Rule Association', Jemmy protested that the concepts of imperialism and home rule were 'utterly incompatible – how imperialism and home rule could ever go hand in hand is beyond my comprehension'.[13] By 1914 he had reached the conclusion that no compromise was possible in relation to home rule. It was either unionism or home rule, two mutually incompatible points of view that no amount of 'conferences, congresses, conciliation, committees and all the rest' could reconcile.

'There are only two schools of thought in Ireland deserving any attention,' he added in his letter to the *Irish Times* in June 1914, 'those who desire to uphold the union intact and believe wholeheartedly in the beneficence of that splendid Act [the Act of Union] and those who really in their hearts, no matter what they say, are devoted to the idea of "Ireland as a nation".'[14]

Henry Wilson shared his brother's disregard for the wishes of nationalist Ireland that never accepted and never would accept that the Act of Union was an act of beneficence. Jemmy was right, though, that there could be no compromise and partition would maroon Southern unionists in a nationalist state, as he wrote to *The Times* in 1914:

I believe I can speak for the great majority of unionists in the three southern provinces when I say that they are entirely hostile to any move which the government may make to exclude the northern province. Unionists in the south and west have from the beginning of this great controversy of home rule in 1886, been definitely engaged in the one supreme object of maintaining the Union between Great Britain and Ireland intact and they cannot conceive at this crisis that any such policy as the exclusion of Ulster is feasible. It has not been easy for unionists in the south and west (in many places groaning under the intimidation exercised by their opponents) to give frequent and loud expression to their views, but, writing as an individual who knows something of the feeling in these districts, I can say that the last thing desired by at any rate the thinking section of the community is that this country should be dismembered in the way that rumour has it the government may propose to do.[15]

The roots of the Wilson family's uncompromising unionism stem from their origins among the English and Scottish settlers in Ireland in the seventeenth century. Henry Wilson was part of the seventh and last Wilson generation in Ireland. The original Irish Wilson was an Englishman, John Wilson, who is said to have arrived in the vanguard of King William III ('King Billy') in 1690, the most glorious year for the unionist tradition in Ireland. William's defeat of the Catholic King James II, who had the support of most of his co-religionists in Ireland, secured the Protestant ascendancy in Ireland. The date is as much symbolic as actual. The Wilson family's desire to be associated with King Billy's victory at the Battle of the Boyne is as important as the historic veracity of those claims.

Longford historian Dr Eileen Reilly-Prunty's study of the family, however, reveals there was already a Robert Wilson living in Rashee, County Antrim, in 1662, who is listed in the Connor (County Antrim) Diocesan Administrations, but it is John Wilson who is named in Arthur Young's *Fighters of Derry* as having fought at the Battle of the Boyne. He received a grant of land at Rashee for his services and the family remained there for many generations.[16]

His great-grandson Hugh made the family's first fortune in shipping in the late 1770s while retaining the land at Rashee. He bought a substantial property in Belfast and died in 1805 a wealthy man. His son William, Henry's grandfather, continued in the family tradition and made a fortune in the shipment of salted pork. He bought a house in Wellington Place, where many of Belfast's most prosperous merchants lived. William Wilson had enough money to send four sons to Trinity College Dublin, including Henry's father.

William took advantage of the chaos and penury of the Irish famine to buy large swathes of land from encumbered landlords. He purchased 17,500 acres in 1849, at a time when many in the Irish landlord classes were bankrupted by the famine. William moved the seat of the family south to Dublin in 1850 and prospered further during the Crimean War (1853–6), supplying provisions to the British army.

James, as the youngest of the five sons, inherited the smallest portion of the land, some 1,200 acres in the counties of Longford and Westmeath, and the lease on a holiday home at Frascati in Blackrock, County Dublin, the former home of Lord Edward Fitzgerald. Fitzgerald, a tragic figure in Irish history, was one of the instigators of the United Irishmen movement and the most wanted man in Ireland before his death in 1798 at the age of just thirty-five. His republicanism was anathema to the Wilsons.

Currygrane was a substantial estate in itself and placed the Wilsons among the most privileged families in Ireland, but their status as arrivistes made them minor rather than major gentry in the hierarchy of the Protestant ascendancy. Henry Wilson was born in the twilight world of that ascendancy, which had dominated Irish life for 200 years. Though representing just 7 per cent of the population, they once owned 95 per cent of the land of Ireland. They built big houses, many bigger than Currygrane, and kept townhouses in London. They produced some of Ireland's greatest patriots, writers, scientists, inventors and soldiers, along with some of the greatest scoundrels, traitors and eccentrics.

Until the election of Daniel O'Connell as the first Catholic Irish MP in 1828, they had a monopoly on Irish political representation at both national and local levels. Before the advent of democratically elected county councils in Ireland under the 1898 Local Government Act, families like the Wilsons were the high sheriffs, the bailiffs and the king's representatives in their respective counties. Wilson's father served as a justice of the peace, district lieutenant and high sheriff for Longford.[17]

In Henry Wilson's lifetime everything changed. When he was three, the Fenians staged an uprising in Ireland. The 1867 rebellion, the last before the Easter Rising of 1916, was a farcical affair that was easily dealt with by the British government, but it was a timely reminder of the enmity held by many Irish nationalists towards the British and those who regarded Wilson's class as the 'English garrison in Ireland'. The Fenian Proclamation, a forerunner of the Easter Rising Proclamation of 1916, declared:

> We have suffered centuries of outrage, enforced poverty, and
> bitter misery. Our rights and liberties have been trampled
> on by an alien aristocracy, who treating us as foes, usurped
> our lands, and drew away from our unfortunate country all
> material riches. The real owners of the soil were removed
> to make room for cattle and driven across the ocean to seek
> the means of living, and the political rights denied to them at
> home, while our men of thought and action were condemned

to loss of life and liberty. But we never lost the memory and hope of a national existence. We appealed in vain to the reason and sense of justice of the dominant powers. The soil of Ireland, at present in the possession of an oligarchy, belongs to us, the Irish people, and to us it must be restored.[18]

Such sentiments would appear and reappear throughout Wilson's life. The issue of land became the dominant one in late-nineteenth-century Ireland. The 1870s and 1880s were punctuated by rising demands from Irish tenant farmers, sporadic violence, coercion and reforming legislation. In Wilson's lifetime, the deference, some of it genuine, some of it born out of fear, afforded to families like his disappeared, to be replaced in many cases by a militant hostility. A succession of land acts brought forward by British governments, both to placate nationalist Ireland and right a historical wrong, saw the gradual handover of the land from the Protestant ascendancy to their former tenants. In 1870 3 per cent of Irish farmers owned 97 per cent of the land. By 1929 that ratio had been reversed, with 97.4 per cent of land owned by farmers who were previously tenants.[19] In tandem with the land issue was the desire of nationalist Ireland for greater autonomy from the UK. In 1800 Ireland's short-lived parliament, known as Grattan's parliament, which had been established in 1782, was dissolved and the last vestige of Irish autonomy disappeared with the Act of Union. Irish affairs were subsumed into the Westminster parliament. O'Connell had campaigned without success for the repeal of the Act of Union and the restoration of an Irish parliament.

In 1870 the home rule movement was founded by Isaac Butt, a Protestant lawyer who represented the Fenians at their trials.[20] He, and many like-minded Irish nationalists, sought the restoration of the Irish parliament and Irish control over domestic affairs. Their demands were couched in moderate terms. They did not seek an independent Irish state, instead pursuing autonomy within a federalised United Kingdom. Home rule, Butt suggested, was 'equally essential to the safety of England and to the happiness and tranquillity of Ireland. I was sure that it would meet with the approval of many persons in both countries who would not support a measure which would simply repeal the Act of Union without making some provision to secure the united action of the two countries in all matters that can concern them as an imperial state.'[21]

Even the moderate demands of the home rule movement were too much for Irish unionists who wanted no loosening of the bonds with Westminster. Unionists constituted 25 per cent of the population of Ireland, but a slim majority in the province of Ulster. In four counties, Antrim, Down, Derry and Armagh, they represented a majority. 'Home rule is Rome rule' was the oft-repeated slogan, which encapsulated the fears of unionists that their religious freedoms and liberties would be threatened by a Catholic-dominated Ireland. The introduction of the first Home Rule Bill into the British parliament in 1886 was defeated by a revolt from prime minister William Gladstone's own Liberal Party MPs, but the most vocal opponents were Ulster unionists and their Conservative Party backers. 'Ulster will fight and Ulster will be right,' declared Lord Randolph Churchill, the father of Winston, in 1886. Throughout the whole of his public life Henry Wilson made common cause with Conservatives and Unionists over the issue of home rule. The unionist tradition and the Protestant faith were the lodestars of the Wilson family. This confluence of land and nationalism would have devastating consequences for the family, costing Henry his life and Jemmy his home.

Henry Wilson had an upbringing typical of his class, but untypical of those around him. He was separated at the earliest age from local children. Rather than being sent to a local school, he was educated at home by a governess who taught him fluent French, a valuable asset in the monoglot British army and society. His life-long Francophilia would find its perfect application in his role as a conduit between the French and British at critical stages in the First World War. At the age of thirteen Wilson was sent to Marlborough, one of England's best-known public schools, named after an earlier martial hero, the Duke of Marlborough, and founded in 1843 by the Church of England primarily for the education of the sons of the clergy. Wilson spent just three years there, not enough to make an impact. He was brought home at the age of sixteen to study for the army. The preponderance of those of an Anglo-Irish background in the British armed forces has often been remarked upon. Even for Wilson, a member of what passed for the 1 per cent in Irish society in the nineteenth century, the options were limited. The estate had been inherited by Jemmy. Henry could have been a clergyman, a lawyer, an antiquarian or an academic, but given his notably adventurous manner and lack of formal education, the armed forces were an obvious option. 'When I was a little boy in Ireland,' he once declared, 'who could tell what would become of me? One way (crescendo) Field Marshal – Privy Council – GCB – all the rest of it: the other way (diminuendo) just a little bit of bog-cotton.'[22] His brother Cecil also joined the British army. Curiously, Wilson's wife and brother had the same first name.

Wilson's elevation to the role of Chief of the Imperial General Staff (Britain's top military advisor) was noteworthy for its inconspicuous beginnings. He crammed for the army exams with the help of tutors who arrived at Frascati, but none could inspire him to pass. He failed Sandhurst three times and Woolwich twice. Biographers have speculated as to why Wilson, a born soldier, could have been so poor academically. Wilson's streak of individuality and his sense of mischievousness may have militated against the strictures of rote learning, but he demonstrated throughout his career a great aptitude for soldiering, for logistical planning and original thinking. His sympathetic biographer and friend, General Sir Charles Callwell, posited that it was only a lack of effort that held the young Wilson back:

> Few, suffering under no disability in respect of birth or
> fortune, or education, from amongst that select band who
> had reached the highest grade in the British army, can have
> experienced greater difficulties in getting into that army than
> did the future commandant of the Staff College and Chief of
> the Imperial General Staff. His discouraging succession of
> failures can only, indeed, be attributed to a lack of application,
> a lack of application of which there was to be no indication
> when, a few years later, he had made up his mind to win his
> way into Staff College as a first step towards rising high in
> his chosen profession. He used often to laugh over the early
> educational mishaps of his, when the time came for him to
> hold prominent appointments in the army that were largely
> concerned with the supervision of military studies.[23]

Wilson's military career began in the Longford militia. Most of the Irish militias were attached to the eight Irish regiments based in the country, but there were exceptions and the Longford militia was one of them. It was attached to the Rifle Brigade and, at the age of eighteen, Wilson was gazetted to its 6th Battalion as a lieutenant in December 1882. Over the next two years he trained with them, and he retained an affection for the regiment for the rest of his life. He sat the army examinations in July 1884, passing out as 58th on the list, an unremarkable result. He was gazetted to the Royal Irish Regiment based in County Tipperary and then back to the Rifle Brigade. Shortly after graduating from Staff College in July 1884, he was shipped off to India.

At the time Britain was extending its empire in south-east Asia into Burma and encountering considerable resistance. Wilson experienced his first combat situation in Burma during the Third Anglo-Burmese War of November 1885. The British had conquered Burma in 1824 and absorbed it into the Empire, but their hold on this country, with its mountains, dense jungles and sweltering climate, was always tenuous.

Wilson was put in charge of a detachment of mounted cavalry to deal with dacoits, or local bandits. The war was short, but the aftermath was bloody and protracted, as guerrilla warfare continued for the next decade. It was during an encounter with some dacoits in late 1886 that Wilson was slashed in the face with a *dal*, a traditional Burmese long, sharp jungle knife used for cutting bamboo shoots. The wound left a permanent scar over his right eye and caused him pain for the rest of his life.

He went back to Ireland and spent more than a year there between November 1887 and December 1888. His lack of physical vanity might be a consequence of his long and happy marriage to Cecil Mary Wray, who was also from an Irish Protestant ascendancy family like his own, although in her case the family fortunes in County Donegal were on the slide. He met her at a regatta in Kingstown (now Dún Laoghaire) while at home on convalescence, and the couple were married in Kingstown on 3 October 1891. She would turn out to be his most redoubtable champion, even to the considerable detriment of his posthumous reputation when she commissioned Charles Callwell to write his biography, published in 1927. The two-volume book, based heavily on Wilson's indiscreet diaries, served only to damn its subject's reputation as an intriguer and gossiper.

On his return from Burma in 1887, Wilson spent the next thirteen years being steadily promoted. He was appointed a staff captain at Staff College, where he first won a reputation for being an excellent communicator as a lecturer. In 1894 he had a chance encounter with a champion whose intervention would be critical in his career progression. Unlike Wilson, Lord Frederick 'Bobs' Roberts was neither born nor brought up an Irishman, but he, like Wilson, considered himself to be Irish. His father, Sir Abraham Roberts, was born in Waterford. The Roberts family owned estates in the county, and one of their ancestors, John Roberts, was the architect of both the Anglican and Catholic cathedrals in Waterford city. Bobs had just returned as Commander-in-Chief in India, his reputation enhanced by that role.

Wilson very much feared being returned to India and was relieved when it did not happen. He was turned down on medical grounds, but he did not want to go anyway. Quite why is not clear, but, as a newly married man, he may have demurred at leaving Cecil so soon. A less benign interpretation is the idea that being in Camberley, so close to many senior officers, would enhance his chances of promotion. In 1894 he became the youngest staff officer in the army at the age of thirty on his appointment to the Directorate of Military Intelligence. With the exception of the Boer War and a brief spell as a brigadier general in the First World War, Wilson spent the rest of his career as a staff officer.

In 1897 Wilson was promoted to brigadier major of the 3rd Brigade of the 2nd Division at Aldershot. It was in this position that he was to have his second and most significant posting overseas, as brigadier major of the 4th or Light Brigade in October 1899, bound for South Africa. Of his introduction to the Second Boer War, he wrote: 'It's exactly two months tomorrow since we came here. In those two months we have lost heavily, fought heavily, marched heavily and are no nearer Ladysmith.'[24]

The Boer War shook Britain's military establishment. It had anticipated a quick victory over a poorly armed, numerically inferior enemy, but the Boers proved to be resilient fighters. They had much support in nationalist Ireland, and liberal opinion in Britain – epitomised most famously by David Lloyd George – was against the war.

Half a million British troops were needed to bring about a victory which, it had been anticipated, could have been achieved with a fraction of that number. Reputations were broken in South Africa, but others were enhanced. Fortunately for Wilson, his was one of the latter. He was mentioned four times in despatches, promoted to brevet lieutenant colonel and earned the Queen's Medal with five clasps.

After South Africa, Roberts was made Commander-in-Chief of the British army and promoted to field marshal. He took Wilson with him to England and made him his assistant military secretary. Wilson's gift for strategic friendships, which enhanced his career, was never more evident than with Roberts. Bobs lost his only son Frederick in the Boer War and treated Wilson as a confidant. Callwell observed, 'Wilson had been fully in the confidence of the field marshal almost from the day when he had joined army headquarters at Pretoria and he had come to be an intimate friend, not only of the field marshal himself, but also of the whole Roberts family.'[25] For the next four years, from 1903 to 1906, Wilson was assistant adjutant-general at army headquarters for military education and training, holding the post of assistant director of staff duties during the last three years. He was appointed the head of the Staff College in Camberley on 1 January 1907. 'The officer who is taking my place is even uglier than I am,' Wilson told his friend Sir Henry Rawlinson. 'Oh, I hope not, sir,' Rawlinson replied.[26]

Wilson was noted as an engaging lecturer who was able to put complicated tactics into plain language. His gift for communicating difficult ideas and his clarity of thought were already apparent.

Wilson's modernising instincts were in vogue when Richard Haldane took over as Secretary of State for War in 1905. Haldane was a reforming minister who recognised that Britain's Victorian army needed overhauling. The question of conscription proved to be a vexatious one in the years before the First World War. Advocates included Lord Roberts, Wilson and Rudyard Kipling, the bard of Empire. On the other side were the British government and most of the British public, who did not see the necessity for such a drastic move and considered it an affront to the spirit of volunteerism that had characterised the British armed forces in the nineteenth century. When Roberts was elevated to the Lords, he made speeches warning against the German menace and called for conscription. These speeches were prepared for him by Wilson.

In 1910 Wilson was promoted again, this time to Director of Military Operations, a post he held when the First World War broke out and which demonstrated his gifts as a military strategist. In that year too he met his French counterpart Ferdinand Foch, with whom he forged a close friendship. Wilson's opening question to Foch framed Britain's preparedness for a continental war that many thought might happen, but others felt was too horrible to contemplate. 'What would you say was the smallest British military force that would be of any practical assistance to you in the event of a contest such as we have been considering?' Foch replied with a suggestion that six divisions might suffice.[27] Six divisions it would be when the war commenced in late July 1914. Wilson bent his organisational skills to the formation of the British Expeditionary Force, even breaking off his continental holiday before the war to reconnoitre the 'fatal corridor' of

8 General Wilson and Marshal Foch, the *Illustrated News*, 1 July 1922

the Flanders flatlands through which armies have marched into France over the centuries.

The Agadir Crisis of 1911 convinced Wilson that a European war was imminent, a war for which the UK was blithely unprepared. This largely forgotten incident demonstrated how the despatch of a German gunboat, the SMS *Panther*, to threaten French colonial rule in Morocco almost brought the European powers to war three years earlier than in fact happened. Talk of war consumed the chancelleries of Europe. Wilson had been warning of war against the Germans when nobody in Britain wanted to know. Lord Esher wrote of Wilson in *The Tragedy of Lord Kitchener*:

> When others prattled of peace, he prepared their souls for war; not for an indefinite war, as men barricade their doors against imaginary thieves, but for a specific struggle with the German nation, the early stage of which he foresaw in detail with a soldier's prophetic insight.[28]

The British, Wilson concluded, were not ready, confiding in his diary: 'It seems possible though I think not by any means certain that we shall have a European war this next year. And in spite of all I have written and worked during the whole year, we are not ready. It is disgusting and scandalous.'[29]

In 1911 Wilson was invited to brief the British cabinet on how Britain might respond to a German invasion of France. Wilson spoke for an hour and a half, deploying all his skills of lucidity and directness to telling effect. Churchill, then First Lord of the Admiralty, recalled the briefing ten years after the event in his book *The World Crisis*:

> Standing by his enormous map, specially transported for the purpose, he unfolded, with what proved afterwards to be extreme accuracy, the German plan for attacking France in the event of a war between Germany and Austria on the one hand and France and Russia on the other. The plan involved six British divisions deploying on the left of the French army. It was a small force by the standards of the other opposing armies, but its effect on morale would be great.[30]

The European crisis and the fate of Ireland dominated the last decade of Wilson's life. Two indecisive elections in 1910 left

John Redmond's Irish Parliamentary Party as the kingmaker in the British parliament. They forged a coalition with the Liberal Party, and the price for coalition was home rule. The Home Rule Bill passed through the House of Commons in 1912. The Liberal government and its Irish allies had also dismantled the power of the House of Lords to veto legislation passed by the House of Commons, a critical stumbling block to previous attempts to introduce home rule. The bill allowed for an Irish parliament based in Dublin to have control over matters of exclusively Irish interest, such as health and education, but there would be no Irish army or navy. Ireland was to remain within the United Kingdom and, crucially, its legislature was subservient to the imperial parliament in Westminster.

Even such a modest level of self-government was too much for unionists, more than a half million of whom signed the Ulster Covenant in 1912. Signatories pledged 'to stand by one another in defending, for ourselves and our children, our cherished position of equal citizenship in the United Kingdom, and in using all means which may be found necessary to defeat the present conspiracy to set up a Home rule Parliament in Ireland'.

The Ulster Volunteer Force (UVF) was founded in 1913 to oppose home rule, by force if necessary. Wilson was an enthusiastic supporter of the Ulster cause. There was a binary choice on offer from the British government: home rule or continued direct rule from London. Wilson saw the fate of Ireland in the same terms: unionists were loyal, nationalists treacherous and the British government untrustworthy. He never wavered in his belief that home rule would be a disaster for Ireland, although his principal concern was for the integrity of the British Empire. Wilson was an imperialist above all. Lose Ireland and you lose the Empire, he reasoned. He took a keen interest in the attempt by Ulster union-ists to arm themselves in opposition to home rule. Roberts sug-gested to Wilson that he become the UVF's chief of staff. Wilson declined but offered instead to work behind the scenes to advance Ulster's resistance.[31]

The preponderance of Anglo-Irish soldiers in command posi-tions in the British army and their adherence to unionism was exemplified by the Curragh Incident (also known as the Curragh Mutiny) of March 1914, by which time Wilson was sufficiently senior to influence events from behind the scenes. This unedifying episode greatly aggrieved the armed forces' commander-in-chief, King George V, and convinced Irish nationalists that the British army could never be relied upon to enforce the Home Rule Act, which was due to come into effect in 1914.

In the fraught atmosphere of March 1914, Ulster Unionist leader Edward Carson left Westminster with a pledge to declare an independent Ulster state if necessary. Churchill, a late convert to the cause of home rule, warned unionists that the British gov-ernment would put the 'issue to the proof' if they resisted by arms. There were fears in the British government that unionists would raid the armouries in Ulster, so in such an atmosphere cool heads were called for. These were conspicuous by their absence in the Curragh Incident.

The trouble arose out of a promise by General Sir Arthur Paget, the officer commanding in Ireland, that Anglo-Irish officers would be exempted from any attempt to coerce Ulster into accepting home rule. This pledge pertained to most of the officer class based in Ireland and many high-ranking officers in Britain. Paget had no authority to make such a pledge, and the Liberal government was aghast that elements in the army could be perceived to be disloyal. Wilson was kept informed of developments throughout the crisis and covertly supported the potential mutiny. He thought it mad that the government would attempt to bring in home rule against the wishes of unionists and a large section of the army. His private diary entries for these dates showed his loyalties were with the UVF and not the government he served:

> The arrangements of the Ulster Army are well advanced and there is no doubt of the discipline and spirit of men and officers. That they have bumped up against 100,000 men who are in deadly earnest and that, as neither the Cabinet nor Englishmen are ever in earnest about anything, Ulster was certain to win.[32]

Wilson, like his brother Jemmy, believed the British government did not understand the seriousness of the situation from an Irish unionist point of view. Wilson's contempt for the Liberal government was never more apparent than during this crisis. He coached the Conservative leader Andrew Bonar Law on baiting prime minister Herbert Asquith in the House of Commons. Wilson went to lobby Sir John French, the then Chief of the Imperial General Staff, telling him in apocalyptic terms that the passage of the Home Rule Bill would pit the British army against the people of Ulster. Even French, who had unionist sympathies, 'agreed with very little that I said', Wilson wrote in his diary.[33]

Wilson found common cause with the Gough brothers, Hubert and Johnnie. Hubert commanded the 3rd Cavalry Brigade at the Curragh in County Kildare; Johnnie was chief of staff to Lieutenant General Sir Douglas Haig at Aldershot Command. Johnnie and his father John Gough Sr were the first father and son to win the Victoria Cross. John Sr was awarded his in 1859 for four separate acts of gallantry during the Indian Mutiny. Johnnie won his in 1903 during the Third Somaliland

Expedition in modern-day Somalia. The family had estates in County Wexford.

Johnnie Gough told Wilson that he and his brother were prepared to resign their commissions rather than take up arms against Ulster. Wilson counselled them out of it, still believing that the 'Frocks', as he contemptuously called politicians, would never countenance a British civil war in Ulster. Wilson was informed by Hubert that fifty-six of the sixty cavalry officers attached to the 16th Lancers based at the Curragh had opted for dismissal. Wilson's intriguing did not stop there. He went to see John Seely, the Secretary of State for War. 'He opened the talk by thanking me for the way I have behaved during a trying two years because he knew my sympathies were with Ulster and so forth, and he consequently wished to thank me as S of S. I replied that no thanks were required as I had only done what I considered right.'[34]

What followed was the so-called 'peccant paragraphs' row. Seely secured a document from the cabinet acknowledging that the incident had been a misunderstanding and it was 'the duty of all soldiers to obey lawful commands'. That would have been the end of the matter had Seely not added two paragraphs that stated the government had 'no intention whatsoever of taking advantage of this right to crush political opposition to the policy or principles of the Home Rule Bill'. Johnnie Gough added a note to state that he understood that paragraph to mean troops would not be called upon to enforce home rule on Ulster. French, fatally for his position as Chief of the Imperial General Staff, also initialised the document with the words, 'This is how I read it.' Seely went well beyond his brief in including the two paragraphs. When they were repudiated in the House of Commons by Asquith, French and Seely resigned. Wilson, who had a key role in the putative mutiny, remained in post, but he was a 'marked man', according to Bernard Ash.[35] Although he would eventually rise to the top of the British army, his elevation was delayed by the resulting distrust in him. Wilson wrote in his diary that he thought about resigning, despite lacking the financial means to quit the army.

In any case the UVF smuggled in twenty thousand German-made rifles and millions of rounds of ammunition to Larne on 25 April 1914.

Wilson and his co-conspirators won, but at a considerable cost to their reputations, and Asquith never forgave Wilson for his involvement in the Curragh Incident. Thousands joined the Irish Volunteers, the nationalist counterpart to the UVF, following the Curragh imbroglio, but it strengthened the will of unionists to hold out against the imposition of home rule. In July 1914, at Howth in north Dublin, the Irish Volunteers smuggled their own guns and ammunition into Ireland. There were now two armed militias with opposing views on the future of the country.

The roots of partition stemmed from the decision by Irish nationalist leader John Redmond to reluctantly concede home rule as a temporary expedient for a set period of years. Sir Edward Carson wanted it to be made permanent and likened any time delay to a stay of execution. King George V's attempts to act as an honest broker by summoning unionists and nationalists together for the so-called Buckingham Palace Conference in July 1914 ended without agreement. The Home Rule Act was given the King's Assent in September 1914, but the cataclysm of the First World War intervened. It was agreed that the act's implementation would be suspended for the duration of the war. Redmond encouraged Irish nationalists to come to the defence of little Belgium and to go 'wherever the firing line extends in defence of right, of freedom and religion in this war'. In the vacuum created by the suspension of the Home Rule Act, a group of Irish separatist republicans staged the 1916 Easter Rising.

In the meantime, the outbreak of war saved the careers of many of those involved in the Curragh Incident. French was immediately reinstated as the Commander-in-Chief of the British Expeditionary Force and Johnnie Gough went to France as a brigadier general. Like many in the 'Old Contemptibles', the small army that Britain sent to the front in August 1914, he was killed in the opening months of the war. His brother Hubert went on to command the Fifth Army, but his record was poor and he was eventually removed from his command in 1918.

The war's commencement brought to fruition Wilson's plans to deploy the BEF in aid of the French. It was a close-run thing. In the years preceding the war he had reconnoitred the western frontier between Germany and Belgium, even though Belgium was a neutral country at the time and the assumed wisdom was that Germany would attack France across the German–French frontier. As far back as 1911 Wilson planned for an expeditionary force to deploy on the left of the French army. Given the enormous size of both the French and German armies, it was expected that the British presence would be small, but the boost to French morale would be enormous. This, by and large, is what happened.

Wilson sailed to France and impressed everybody with his cheery demeanour during those dreadful opening weeks of the war, when 'all the resources of courage, good sense, singing wit and uproarious Irish mirth of which he was possessed had been placed torrentially in the service of the army and its chief,' according to French's biographer Lord Esher.[36] After a month of war Wilson correctly analysed that the Germans had pushed too far too quickly, overrun their supply lines and were fatigued by their rapid progress. This presented an opportunity for the French and British to strike back. The First Battle of the Marne in early September 1914 was the decisive battle of the First World War and the whole conduct of the war from that date flowed from it. It prevented the Germans from occupying Paris in the early months of the war and thus winning an early victory. The Marne ended the war of movement and hastened the beginning of trench warfare. The stalemate was only broken by the German Spring Offensive, which started in March 1918.

Wilson, not a man to hide his light under a bushel, claimed some credit for the battle's success. Being an optimist, he had believed the war would be over in February or March of the following year, and found that it wasn't 'owing to nothing but absolute incompetence and want of regimental officers. We have lost the finest opportunity of the war and are now being thrown on the defensive. Maddening and perhaps disastrous.'[37]

Wilson might have hoped his prescience in readying the BEF for embarkation would lead to promotion, but his attempts to become Chief of the Imperial General Staff foundered on the opposition of Asquith, who described him as 'that poisonous tho' clever ruffian Wilson'.

French admitted in his valedictory autobiography *1914* that Wilson had been his choice to replace the invalided Archibald Murray as Chief of the Imperial General Staff, 'but owing to his candid expression of opinion in the Irish imbroglio he had many enemies and his appointment was vetoed. It was this bad luck alone which prevented his valuable services then being used for his country's benefit in the best direction and in a position for which he was better qualified than anyone else.'[38]

Instead, Murray was replaced by Sir William Robertson, as taciturn as Wilson was talkative. Wilson was made a liaison officer between the British and French armies, a role that suited his linguistic and personal skills. He remained underpromoted until after David Lloyd George became British prime minister in December 1916.

In May 1915 Sir John French was replaced by Sir Douglas Haig as Commander-in-Chief of the British army, and Wilson was given command of IV Corps. Reflecting on the tempestuous year of 1915, Wilson regretted he had not been promoted, and yet 'the command of a corps of four divisions is a fine command and I shall enjoy it immensely.'[39]

The divisions were the 1st, a regular pre-war division, the 15th (Scottish), the 16th (Irish) and the 47th, a division made up of ex-Territorial soldiers from London. Wilson had a low opinion of his fellow Irishmen, who were from a predominantly nationalist background, dismissing them as 'Johnnie Redmond's pets' and 'whiskey-sodden militia men'.[40]

Wilson was at home on furlough in England when the Easter Rising broke out in Dublin in April 1916. Nothing could have been a greater affront to Wilson's worldview than an Irish uprising supported by Germany against British rule in the middle of a continental war. The 1,200 rebels who occupied the General Post Office and other strategic buildings in Dublin initially represented nobody except themselves. They were, in the words of one commentator, a 'minority of a minority', but they set nationalist Ireland on a trajectory away from incremental constitutional change towards violent revolution. The small coterie of Irish Volunteers present at the Easter Rising swelled over the coming five years into the IRA, a volunteer army of 130,000 men that included Wilson's assassins.

Bonar Law wanted Wilson to go to Dublin to handle the Rising but 'agreed my Ulster record made it impossible', Wilson wrote in his diary.[41] Instead, General John 'Conky' Maxwell was sent to Ireland to deal with the aftermath of the rebellion and effectively given the status of a military governor. The execution of sixteen leaders of the rebellion and the imprisonment of thousands of Irish nationalists, some of whom had nothing to do with the rebellion, had a galvanising impact on Irish public opinion, which had initially been ambivalent towards the rebels. The response of the British government, adopting a military strategy when a carefully calibrated political one was required, was blamed on Maxwell. Given Wilson's subsequent record on Ireland, it is hard to believe he would have acted any differently.

In the hiatus before the Battle of the Somme, Wilson's IV Corps saw little action except for an unfortunate incident on 21 May 1916, when the Germans infiltrated the corps line below a ridge in Arras. Wilson was not a success as a frontline commander, but he was not long enough in the role to be judged as a failure either. His true strengths lay in the development of strategy and in his relationship with the French. In that capacity, the end of Asquith's premiership and the beginning of Lloyd George's in December 1916 marked a change in his fortunes. Lloyd George and Wilson eventually fell out over Ireland, but their wartime relationship proved to be of mutual benefit. Lloyd George despised Haig and Robertson and despaired over the colossal loss of life at the Somme. He found in Wilson another maverick soul and original thinker.

Despite his role as a sounding board for Lloyd George, Wilson was unemployed and at a loose end at the beginning of 1917, after IV Corps was transferred to General Sir Hubert Gough's reserve corps. It was at this stage that friends approached him about becoming an Ulster Unionist MP. He mentioned to Haig that the devil makes work for idle hands to do, 'So I told him that I should probably get into mischief.' Wilson once again demurred, admitting to himself that should he become an MP, a drop in salary from £3,000 to £600 was not one he could bear.[42]

Wilson returned to frontline military affairs when he was sent by Lloyd George to Russia in February 1917 to shore up a wavering eastern ally. The visit occurred just weeks before the overthrow of the Romanov dynasty and its replacement with a moderate provisional government, only for that government to be overthrown during the Bolshevik revolution of November 1917. Wilson was not the only western observer to badly misjudge Russia. He thought the country was sound and would remain in the war. His misjudgement did not cost him Lloyd George's trust. On the contrary, Lloyd George told him: 'The whole future of the war rests on your shoulders. You must get us out of the awful rut we are in. I don't like your politics but I do like and admire you as a man and as a soldier.'[43]

In April 1917 Wilson visited Ireland for the first time since before the war. He travelled to Galway city, only to find a lot of Sinn Féin flags around. 'We went to the old fishing village of Claddagh, which is intensely loyal and has all its men either in the Navy or the Army. I had a talk with some old men. We were mobbed by women shouting, "Long live the King; Long live England." A curious experience in Galway.'[44] He went on to Belfast to meet Unionist leaders and was promised a seat in the North Belfast constituency should he stand, but Wilson believed his business with the war was not finished. Towards the end of 1917 he resumed his role as the liaison officer between the French and British commands, and in February 1918 he left that job to be appointed Chief of the Imperial General Staff.

Within a month he was assailed by the biggest challenge that the British army had faced in the war to date. The German Spring

Offensive began on 21 March 1918, breaking three and a half years of stalemate on the Western Front. Using elite forces and with the benefit of surprise, poison gas and flamethrowers, the Germans smashed through the Allied lines. The attack brought two problems for Wilson. The first was the immediate strategic situation; the second was manpower. At an emergency cabinet discussion, Wilson suggested that all men up to the age of fifty should be conscripted – and by 'all men' he meant every available Irishman too.

Conscription had not been introduced into Ireland in February 1916 as it had in the rest of the United Kingdom. This was a tacit acknowledgement that Ireland was a place apart within the kingdom, but it stuck in Wilson's craw. Why should the Irish be exempt when the rest of the nation was doing its bit? The presence of so many Irishmen of military age was a source of perpetual irritation to Wilson and a political embarrassment to the British government. The cabinet continued to demur on introducing conscription in Ireland in 1916 and 1917, but the Spring Offensive forced its hand. The bill proposing conscription for Ireland was passed with predictable consequences. It provoked a general strike and the Irish Party withdrew from Westminster. Conscription was never introduced in Ireland. By the time it came to be implemented, the emergency on the Western Front had passed, but the boost it provided to the separatist tradition in Ireland, namely Sinn Féin, was incalculable. Irish restiveness played out against the much greater drama of the war. The Spring Offensive illustrated the difficulties of having separate commands against a common foe.

The Supreme War Council was founded in November 1917 but gained its greatest iteration with the appointment of Wilson's friend Marshal Foch as Allied Supreme Commander in March 1918.

The Spring Offensive was the closest the Allies came to disaster, with the Germans only being halted outside the vital railway junction of Amiens. Wilson's diaries exhibit rare moments of despair. His great contribution to the Allied victory was his work to create a unified chain of command between the Allies. He was one of the few who predicted the Allies could win the war in 1918. Many expected it would be 1919 before the weight of American men and materiel could make the decisive difference.

Wilson was the right man at the right moment, Churchill recalled years later. 'The War Cabinet found for the first time an expert advisor of superior intellect, who could explain lucidly and forcefully the whole situation and give reasons for the adoption or rejection of any course.'[45] Wilson's diary shows his obsession with conscripting Irishmen continued right up until the Armistice of November 1918, long after the idea was even practicable or necessary. 'If we conscript Ireland, thus showing our determination to "go all out", the Boches will agree to my terms of disarmament,' Wilson wrote in his diary just three weeks before the end of the war.[46]

On 11 November 1918 Wilson attended cabinet and afterwards went to a reception in Buckingham Palace, a 'little informal ceremony', he wrote in his diary. That evening, on walking back from Downing Street to Eaton Place, he encountered a woman sobbing on the streets. Wilson reportedly heard her say, 'I am crying, but I am happy, for now I know that all my three sons who have been killed in the war have not died in vain.'[47]

Wilson had played his part. The Armistice brought with it honours and acclaim, but also new responsibilities. The mass demobilisation of Britain's biggest ever army consumed much of his time in the immediate aftermath of the war. The post-war world was deeply troubled. A month after the Armistice, Britain went to the polls, re-electing the coalition government under Lloyd George that had seen the war through to its end. In Ireland, though, the Irish Parliamentary Party was vanquished by Sinn Féin.

Writing on the last day of 1918, Wilson reflected: 'What is the outlook for 1919? Lloyd George ought to last out a year. Clemenceau won't. President Wilson will be discredited. We shall have serious troubles in Ireland and many wars in many parts; and Bolshevism frightens me. The Bolshevists are approaching Reval, Riga and Vilna, and will soon get Poland. I don't like it.'[48] Having been on the winning side in the biggest war in history to that date, Wilson would find himself confounded by a small but decisive war in his own country.

3

Wilson – The Post-war Years: 'Never daunted, never dismayed'

Field Marshal Sir Henry Wilson's mind turned immediately to administering the peace, even while he attended dinner on Armistice evening with David Lloyd George, Winston Churchill and F. E. Smith, the Attorney General. The conversation was dominated by the subjects of the general election (there had not been one since 1910), the fate of Kaiser Wilhelm II, who had fled to the Netherlands, and the threat of Bolshevism at home and abroad. The general election was set for 14 December, and Wilson found little urgency in the British cabinet for the huge job of demobilising seven million men in uniform. Politicking got in the way of pragmatism. The 'Khaki election', as it was known because of the number of soldiers who voted, was held on a hugely expanded franchise that included for the first time all men over the age of twenty-one, as well as women, albeit only those over thirty who met a property qualification.

The general election returned the wartime coalition of Liberals and Tories with a huge majority, but the real victors were the Tories, who won 379 of the 707 seats, enough to form a majority government on their own. This did not signify great public enthusiasm for the Tories, who won just 38.4 per cent of the vote, but the UK's first-past-the-post electoral system allowed them to take advantage of a split electorate forced to choose between the pro-Lloyd George and pro-Herbert Asquith wings of the Liberal Party. Lloyd George's party divided into those who supported the continuation of the coalition government with him at its head (famously described as a prime minister without a party) and those led by Asquith who wanted out. The Liberals would never again hold the same pre-eminence in British politics.

The approved Liberal candidates, known as 'coalition coupon' candidates, won 127 seats, while Asquith's independent liberals won just thirty-six. Lloyd George prevailed on a bellicose platform summed up by the phrase 'Hang the Kaiser', an empty promise as Wilhelm had fled to the Netherlands and would not be handed over to the Allies. The outcome of the general election in Ireland, where the separatist Sinn Féin party won 73 of the 105 seats (on a 47 per cent share of the vote), did not much trouble Lloyd George's government, which now had a whole world to reorder.

Wilson shared a fear of Bolshevism with many on the right of the British political spectrum. Communism in Britain was a minority pursuit, but the Bolshevik revolution and the Kiel Mutiny of November 1918 by German sailors, which prompted a socialist revolt and ended in the abdication of the Kaiser, were a terrifying reminder of the fragility of nation states in the aftermath of the Great War.

In early January 1919 a group of British soldiers refused to return to France and demanded another week's leave. Men who had survived the greatest conflict in world history to that date had reasonably expected an immediate return to civilian life. Wilson blamed Lloyd George for promising too much too soon. Lloyd George's 'homes fit for heroes' rhetoric created unreasonable expectations. The soldiers had no such homes to go to, and Wilson was not impressed. 'We have turned the period of the Armistice from a period preparatory to demobilisation into the demobilisation itself. Result – chaos.'[1]

At the same time Wilson was faced with the contradictory demands of demobilising Britain's largest ever army while providing cover for the multiplicity of new demands occasioned by the Allied victory in the war.

Wilson needed to find troops to occupy territory on the west side of the Rhine, which the Germans had been ordered to evacuate. There were also continuing commitments in Russia. British troops were first sent to Russia in March 1918 following the signing of the Treaty of Brest-Litovsk, which amounted to a capitulation by the Bolsheviks, despite Wilson's firm belief a year earlier that the Russian Empire would stay in the war. Wilson was unenthusiastic about the presence of 70,000 British troops in Russia, concluding that it was a hopeless endeavour in a huge country in support of allies who hated each other almost as much as they hated their adversaries. Wilson was fearful too that the prospect of individual soldiers being sent to Russia was adding to the gathering restlessness in the army.

On Russia's southern borders the British army was expected to keep order in a swathe of land reaching from Egypt to India, including mandates in Palestine and Mesopotamia, left ungoverned by the defeat of the Ottoman Empire, and oil interests in Persia. This amounted to an arc of responsibility from Egypt to Burma. Yet it was the fate of Egypt, conquered by the British in 1882, and the British Empire's older colonies of Ireland and India that most preoccupied Wilson.

On 21 January 1919 absentee Sinn Féin MPs, elected in the British general election, set up Dáil Éireann, an Irish parliament in Dublin. They declared an independent Irish state, nominated four delegates to the Paris Peace Conference (they were not allowed to address it despite fervent lobbying) and sent a message to the 'free nations of the world . . . to support the Irish Republic by recognising Ireland's national status and her right to its vindication at the Peace Congress'. The unilateral declaration of an Irish parliament was not taken seriously by the British. 'The end of it will be that these seventy-three devils will very soon go bag and baggage over to Westminster,' declared the Lord Lieutenant John French, the former commander of the British Expeditionary Force at the start of the First World War.[2] Like others in the British government, he believed the Irish were only playing at nationhood. How could a parliament with no legislative powers, no money and no international recognition survive?

On the same day two Royal Irish Constabulary (RIC) constables were shot dead in County Tipperary while escorting a cart of gelignite to a quarry. This rogue action by men attached to the 3rd Tipperary Brigade of the Irish Volunteers was widely condemned in nationalist Ireland, which wanted to be taken seriously as a nascent nation, and is regarded as the start of the Irish War of Independence (1919–21), although it scarcely constituted a war in that first year.

Ireland was a mere irritant for Britain, which was faced with the demands from peoples all over the world for greater autonomy. Putative nations from the ethnic patchworks of eastern Europe, Arab tribes and colonised people from the furthest reaches of the Empire all came to Paris believing they had a special case for nationhood.

Between January and the signing of the Versailles Treaty, Wilson spent four months in Paris as chief military advisor to the British government. It was for him the culmination of a life's work, the most important British military advisor at the most important peace conference of them all. Wilson loved the intrigue and the horse trading. He proved to be excellent company, and his indefatigable wit and stamina were in demand. He also had his portrait painted by his fellow Irishman Sir William Orpen, a childhood acquaintance. The mischievous painting was not much liked by Wilson but was admired by those around him. 'I gave Orpen an hour's sitting for my portrait. Result clever but appalling!' Later he recorded in his diary, 'I gave Orpen another hour's sitting. His picture is very clever, but it makes me look an awful blackguard. There are going to be two bidders – one is Scotland Yard; the other is Madame Tussauds.'[3]

He urged the British and French governments to treat the Germans with leniency, surmising that 'Bolshevism was a bigger threat than the Boche.' Wilson was fully engaged in the negotiations that led to the signing of the treaty on 28 June 1919. He was not impressed with the signing ceremony. 'The room was much too full, a crowd of smart ladies, a constant buzz of conversation, the whole thing unreal, shoddy, poor to a degree. The fountains played and some guns fired, and we went away. Considerable but very undemonstrative crowds. And the thing was over. It only took forty-five minutes from 3.10 to 3.55 p.m.'[4]

Only after the conference did Wilson turn his attention to Ireland. He was first informed of the situation when he visited Trinity College Dublin in early July 1919 to receive an honorary degree. Wilson travelled to Ireland with his wife Cecil and his mother-in-law, staying with John French in the Viceregal Lodge (now Áras an Uachtaráin, the residence of the Irish president). Dinner guests included the Anglican Archbishop of Dublin Dr John Bernard and Sir Charles Barrington of Glenstal Castle in Limerick. After receiving his honorary degree, Wilson and French visited Alexandra College on Earlsfort Terrace, another loyal (and Protestant) educational institution. Wilson kept within the circle drawn from Protestant loyalists who shared his outlook on Ireland.

Both men were appraised of the true feelings of nationalist Ireland when the students of University College Dublin, the nationalist counterpart to Trinity, opposite Alexandra College, roundly booed the pair as they left the ceremony at the school. French, who saw himself as a 'quasi-military governor', had much of the Sinn Féin leadership arrested in May 1918 on a trumped-up charge of conspiring with the German government. The German Plot, as it was known, made him a hate figure among separatists and he was also targeted for assassination.

'Coming away in the motor, Johnnie got booed and hissed by students in the National College opposite – a most disgraceful thing,' Wilson wrote in his diary.[5] Wilson paid a flying visit to see his brother Jemmy in the old homestead in Currygrane. The place looked so well, he remarked, and the whole visit had been 'just like old times'.[6] It was his last ever visit to Currygrane and the last year in which the professional head of the British army would be able to drive in relative safety through the countryside in Ireland.

July 1919 was a good month for Wilson. He was made a field marshal, the highest rank in the British army, at the age of fifty-five, the youngest since the Duke of Wellington. The *Irish Times*, then the voice of Southern unionism, noted he was following in the footsteps of other illustrious Anglo-Irishmen who had received the field marshal's baton – Wellington, French, his former mentor Lord Roberts and Lord Kitchener among them.[7]

Field marshals usually command great armies in the field, but Wilson's service at the front during the war did not merit such an honour in itself. It was given to him for his organisational skills in having the expeditionary force ready in 1914, for ensuring good Anglo–French relations during the war and for the smooth transition to the Supreme War Council, which won the war in one hundred days. Wilson's place in the British establishment was confirmed when 200 MPs and lords attended a dinner in his honour on 24 July 1919. In the guest room of the House of Commons Lloyd George paid the greatest tribute to Wilson: 'Never daunted, never dismayed, never despairing, never down-hearted, calm, courageous, full of resolution, full of fortitude and encouraging everybody to do his work.'[8]

Mellifluous flattery came easily to Lloyd George, less so to Wilson as a recipient. Though not a man coy about his own abilities, he found it all a bit much, as his diary entry testifies. 'It is very touching and it all makes me feel I want to hide. The same in the War Office, and I cannot realise that I am a field marshal.' Later Wilson reflected on how he and his great friend Ferdinand Foch stood in front of King George V as 'marshals of England'.[9]

Still the demands for troops kept coming. Eleven battalions were requested to police Upper Silesia, an area of the old German Reich with a mixed population of German and Polish residents. A plebiscite had been called for 1921, and the British were asked to keep order in the interim.

A month later Wilson travelled to Belfast to attend a passing-out parade of many of Ulster's war veterans. Despite the flattery, the public acclaim and the imprimatur of the British establishment, Wilson was becoming estranged from British government policies on Ireland.

According to Callwell, the estrangement began in the autumn of 1919. The introduction of home rule, given the king's assent in September 1914 but suspended for the duration of the war, was unfinished business. The government was mandated to introduce home rule whether the Irish wanted it or not, and the views of northern unionists had not changed. They wanted nothing to do with it. Lloyd George appointed Walter Long, a former Chief Secretary for Ireland and Southern unionist MP, to chair a committee on the future of Ireland. In November 1919 the committee agreed to a proposal for two parliaments, with a Council of

Ireland to discuss issues of mutual interest with a view to unity sometime in the future.

A month later the committee proposed a parliament for the whole of Ulster, but this was immediately opposed by unionists who did not want the counties of Donegal, Monaghan and Cavan, where nationalists had a clear majority. Unionists never wanted home rule or any separation from the imperial parliament but, when informed there was no going back on home rule, they decided to embrace a parliament of their own for six counties, with an assumption that a two-to-one population ratio of Protestant British to Catholic Irish would ensure a perpetual majority.

Throughout the autumn of 1919, as Long's committee continued its deliberations on the future of Ireland, Wilson fretted about the issue. His emotional attachment to Ireland's place within the United Kingdom meant he was incapable of either rational or detached analysis of the problem. Callwell observed:

> Bitterly opposed to the principle of home rule as he was, he observed with concern the gradual acceptance of that principle by unionist members of the cabinet, who in former times had been utterly opposed to granting independent government to his native land. From this autumn dates the beginning of an estrangement from many of his best friends holding high positions in Whitehall which grew more and more marked up to the time of handing over the responsibilities of CIGS to his successor in February 1922.[10]

In the autumn of 1919 the British administration in Ireland banned a slew of nationalist organisations, including Dáil Éireann, a democratically elected assembly, and Sinn Féin, the most popular party in Ireland. The decision was in response to a series of 'outrages', most notably the first attack on British soldiers since the Easter Rising. On 7 September 1919 Cork No. 2 Brigade of the IRA ambushed a detachment of men of the King's Shropshire Light Infantry on their way to church in Fermoy, killing twenty-year-old Corporal William Jones. It was the first engagement by the Irish Volunteers against the British army since the Easter Rising. In response the soldiers ransacked the town.

The IRA's chief of staff General Richard Mulcahy was coy about a full-blooded military campaign, surmising that the Irish people had to be 'educated and led gently into war'.[11] British policy in Ireland made that transition easier. At every turn the chance of a peaceful settlement arising out of the unilateral declaration of independence by Dáil Éireann diminished. In December 1919 a group of Irish Volunteers came close to assassinating Wilson's old friend Lord French. A shaken French concluded that they were dealing with more than a rag-tag bunch of militants. As Wilson surveyed the end of the year, he saw only trouble ahead:

> I pointed out that though Lloyd George paid attention to me as a soldier, he paid no attention to me in other matters. Witness his futile and childish proposals for home rule. At the same time, I would do all I could and I might be able to influence matters by my war-game. And so we left it. If England goes on like this, she will lose the Empire. There is absolutely no grip anywhere. I propose, after the New Year and after I have had a holiday, to take a rather active part in matters – even in some (like Ireland and Egypt) which are not solely military. We are certain to have serious troubles in Ireland, Egypt and India, possibly even with the Bolsheviks.[12]

The situation in Ireland began to deteriorate in 1920. Having engaged in sporadic violence in 1919, the IRA began the widespread and co-ordinated burning of RIC stations around Ireland at the start of the following year. Attacks on the demoralised police force continued. The RIC, drawn mostly from Catholic families, was ostracised, boycotted and, as the violence continued, attacked. The government recruited temporary constables to deal with the unrest from the ranks of ex-servicemen in Britain. The Black and Tans, as they came to be known, were sent to Ireland to do the policing the RIC could no longer do. They were followed by the Auxiliaries, recruited from the ranks of the officer classes and paid £1 a day for their services, the highest such fee in the world at the time. In addition to the military campaign, Sinn Féin had set up a parallel administration, parallel local authorities, courts and police. This shadow administration commanded widespread public support.

Lloyd George's government struggled with a coherent approach to the escalating violence in Ireland. The IRA framed it as a war against the British state. The government could not bring itself to dignify the IRA campaign with the word 'war' and so treated it as a security situation to be dealt with by the police. The Black and Tans and Auxiliaries became notorious for the reprisals they took against the civilian population. Wilson sensed from the beginning that this was the wrong course:

> I can't imagine what sort of officers and NCO we can get. I can't imagine what sort the men will be, no-one will know anybody, no discipline, no esprit de corps, no training, no musketry, no mess, no nothing. I don't like the idea . . . Then to make matters worse Macready proposes to draft these mobs over to Ireland at once and split them up into lots of twenty-five to fifty men over the country so there would be no hope of forming and disciplining this crowd of unknown men. It is truly a desperate and hopeless expedient bound to fail.[13]

Fighting an unconventional war by unconventional means against an invisible enemy would always be morally ambiguous. Wilson understood this, but the alternative he proposed, amounting effectively to a declaration of war against his own country, was unpalatable. The government should go all out to crush the rebellion, but a 'cabinet of cowards' was in residence in Whitehall, he believed.

In advance of a cabinet meeting in May 1920, he sought to lobby the Conservative leader Andrew Bonar Law, whose family like himself was from Ulster, and who was a strong opponent of home rule.

> He was deploring the dreadful state of affairs – there were four
> more police killed yesterday – and I told him as I have often
> told him before, that he had not begun his Irish troubles yet.[14]

Macready demanded more troops for Ireland, but Wilson continued to fret over the competing demands for a rapidly shrinking army. The decision was taken to allocate eight battalions but hold them back until they were absolutely needed. Wilson saw in Ireland an inspiration for anti-imperial causes everywhere. A rebellion next door could act only as an inspiration for rebellions further afield:

> Macready is not fighting Ireland, for in reality he is fighting
> New York and Cairo and Calcutta and Moscow. Who are all
> using Ireland as a tool and lever against England and nothing
> but determined shooting on our part is of any use. As usual I
> found the Cabinet hopeless. They are terrified about Ireland
> and, having lost all sense of proportion, thought only of that
> danger and completely forgot England, Egypt, India, etc in all
> of which we are going to have trouble – and serious trouble.[15]

The Irish quest for independence was popular in Ireland, among liberal opinion in Britain and internationally, especially in the United States. President Woodrow Wilson (Henry Wilson referred to him sarcastically as 'my cousin') saw it as an internal British matter, but the House of Representatives supported Irish independence by a huge margin of 216 votes to 41 in March 1919.[16] Many senators supported the cause of Irish independence, and Woodrow Wilson was constantly pressured by his Irish-American personal secretary Joseph Patrick Tumulty about the issue.

Lloyd George believed that an open policy of shooting IRA suspects would be unpopular in the US, which had become, as a result of the war, Britain's greatest creditor. Instead, his cabinet settled on a covert policy of retaliation, mostly against the civilian population. The towns of Balbriggan, Tuam and Mallow were burned, and creameries, the critical industry in rural Ireland, destroyed. IRA suspects were targeted and occasionally assassinated.

Wilson did not approve of these tactics. His fidelity was to the rule of law, and the rule of law meant never apologising or hiding when taking on the 'murder gang'. 'It was the business of the Government to govern. If these men ought to be murdered, the Government ought to murder them,' he confided to his diary.[17]

> I told him [Lloyd George] that it seemed to me to be an odd
> way of easing his conscience – by the murder of loyal Irish
> policemen; that, if he would state a figure of the number
> of policemen who must be murdered before his conscience
> was made easy, we might hurry up the process and get the
> lot murdered in a few days, instead of prolonging the agony.
> Marvellous people, the English.[18]

Wilson believed the British public would stomach a campaign of open assassination against the IRA, telling the Anglo-Irish peer Lord Duncannon that he would, if elected MP, march down to Lloyd George and tell him:

> You have two courses open to you. One is to clear out of
> Ireland and the other is to knock Sinn Féin on the head. But,
> before you do the latter, you must have England on your
> side and therefore you must go stumping around the country
> explaining what Sinn Féin means. If you get England on your
> side – and you can – there is nothing you can't do. If you don't,
> there is nothing you can do.[19]

Tell the British people the truth about what was happening in Ireland, get them on your side, flood the countryside with troops, crush Sinn Féin or lose Ireland and then the Empire – Wilson repeated the same sentiments to anybody who would listen to him for the rest of his life.

Wilson continued to chafe against the restraints imposed on the British government by public opinion. He detected an unwillingness to do what was necessary to defeat the IRA by legal means, but he had lost touch with the reality that the British were not just facing the IRA, but the bulk of nationalist Ireland. Train drivers refused to carry Crown forces; dockers refused to unload military materiel; shopkeepers would not serve policemen or soldiers.

In July 1920 the situation in Ireland had deteriorated markedly. The RIC had been driven from rural barracks, ceding large sections of the country to republicans, and republican courts and police were introduced. The apparatus of British rule in Ireland was collapsing. The IRA wished to make Ireland ungovernable for the British; the British wished to make support for the IRA so unpalatable that popular enthusiasm for the cause of Irish independence would wane sufficiently for the British to regain control of Ireland. Lloyd George saw the political difficulties of a modern liberal democracy engaging in open assassination, especially given the international media interest in Ireland at the time. Wilson had no such scruples. Why shouldn't the government exercise authority in its own country? Why resort to murder illegally when you can do it legally? Wilson thought this kind of assassination was beneath an imperial power of Britain's stature and told Lloyd George as much:

> But he reverted to his amazing theory that someone was murdering a Sinn Féiner to every loyalist the Sinn Féiners murdered. I told him that, of course, that was absolutely not so, but he seemed to be satisfied that a counter-murder association was the best answer to Sinn Féin murders. A crude idea of statesmanship, and he will have a rude awakening.[20]

Much of Wilson's attitude to Ireland can be gleaned from his regular correspondence with his friend Macready, who was appointed General Officer Commanding in Ireland in April 1920. 'My dear, you are an old friend and I am very sorry for you and I think you are unaware to take this job, but, however, there it is and you will find nothing but friends in the G.S. [General Staff] and all the help we can,' he wrote to him.

The two fell out later over the conduct of the war in Ireland. Wilson believed in the mailed fist or, as he put it, 'nothing but determined shooting on our part is of any use.'[21] Macready did too on principle, but in practice saw it as a counter-productive measure. In the Wilsonian choice between governing in Ireland or getting out, Macready was on the side of getting out. 'Your country suffers from a cancer,' he bluntly told Wilson, 'a disease that is rarely eradicated, and though you may operate severely upon it, it grows again in a worse form later.' What is the point of trying to coerce a whole people when they have turned against you?

I do not believe that the killing of Michael Collins and say 50 of his next best men will improve matters to any appreciable degree. Practically the whole manhood under the age of about 25 of the country except Ulster are, so to speak, fanatically patriotic according to their lights.[22]

Two events occurred in the autumn of 1920 that would damn Wilson as a villain in the eyes of nationalist Ireland. On 25 October 1920 Terence MacSwiney, the Lord Mayor of Cork, died on hunger strike in Brixton Prison. He had been arrested by British soldiers in August of that year on a charge of sedition and sentenced to two years' hard labour by a military court. MacSwiney went on hunger strike in protest at the absence of due process. The British calculated that they would find a way to end his hunger strike as they had done with others previously, but they had not reckoned with MacSwiney's single-minded determination nor the fact that he would linger as long as he did – seventy-four days in total, when the conventional medical wisdom was that he would last scarcely a month. His death did more to focus attention on Ireland's plight internationally than anything else.

'It is not those who can *inflict the most* but those who can *endure the most* who will conquer.' MacSwiney's most famous utterance became an anti-colonial mantra far beyond Ireland. In New York longshoremen refused to unload British ships; in South America several countries called for the Pope to intervene; Paris theatres gave updates on his condition during intervals. His death made headlines around the world. *Le Petit Journal*, a mass-market Parisian newspaper, published a memorable cartoon showing a dying MacSwiney being comforted by a Catholic chaplain. 'Le

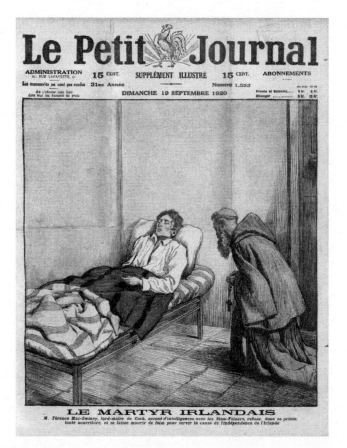

9 Terence MacSwiney on his deathbed, *Le Petit Journal*, 19 September 1920

Martyr Irlandais', the paper called him. In London 30,000 people filed past his coffin at St George's Cathedral in Southwark. Mock funerals were held in Manchester, Bradford and Newcastle upon Tyne. All this occurred before MacSwiney's remains had even left Britain. His family thought they had an agreement with the British that his remains would be taken by train to Holyhead and from there to Dublin. They were anxious that the people of Dublin could pay their respects, but Wilson was having none of it. The obsequies were stirring up the Sinn Féiners and embarrassing the government. They had to end:

I telephoned to Macready and told him that Hamar Greenwood [Chief Secretary for Ireland] told me last night that the government could not prevent the Lord Mayor's body being taken through Dublin, so all precautions must be taken. I then went to Winston [Churchill] and stormed about it to such an extent that he raced over to see the prime minister, with the result that the body will not be sent through Dublin but will be shipped straight to Cork. This is good. I telephoned to Macready and told him of the change.[23]

An ugly stand-off ensued at Holyhead between the family, who tried to protect the coffin, and police, who broke through the protest and seized it. It was placed on HMS *Rathmore* and taken straight to Cork, leaving the MacSwiney family behind, stranded on the quayside. They had to make their own way to Ireland. Wilson's actions ensured that any attempt by Britain to rescue a modicum of international goodwill from the public relations disaster of MacSwiney's death was lost.

Six days after MacSwiney's death, Kevin Barry, an eighteen-year-old medical student at University College Dublin was hanged in Mountjoy Prison. Barry was an IRA volunteer who had been involved in a raid on Monk's Bakery in Church Street, Dublin, which had ended in the death of three British soldiers. There were many calls for a reprieve, given Barry's youth. A photograph circulating of Barry in his rugby jersey made him look almost like a child, but Private Harold Washington, one of the soldiers who was killed, was just fifteen. Barry was sentenced to death by a military court, which he refused to recognise. The British authorities in Ireland felt that executing him was the lesser of two evils as it would stave off any desire in its forces to avenge the deaths of the three soldiers. Wilson was against the execution, but again not out of any humanitarian instincts. He wrote to Macready:

> I care neither for age, name or sentiment. Law is law and terrorists come under the jurisdiction of the law. What does worry me is your unenviable position in Dublin. If this fellow hangs we are in for a spate of real trouble over there. As much as I detest thuggery and sneaking terrorists, the balanced view in my opinion is to hold our hand in Dublin. It means that we shall have weakened our right there because of one man. But to execute is to invite the pot to boil over and we wouldn't control it.[24]

Nevertheless – and this would be a pattern with Wilson – his private utterances stood in contrast to the public perceptions of his actions. Four days after the execution, a letter appeared in the *Irish Independent* newspaper written by Ernest Albert (E. A.) Aston. Aston, as he made clear, was no Sinn Féiner and detested violence. He had been a prominent advocate of the proportional representation system, partially to curb the dominance of Sinn Féin, and was a supporter of the Irish Labour Party. He had agreed to travel to London as part of a delegation seeking a reprieve for Barry, as Barry's sister worked for him. His letter was all the more powerful for not coming from a known republican:

> In March 1914 a military officer of high rank, a member of a distinguished Irish family of extreme Unionist reactionaries – acted as chief technical advisor to the Ulster Volunteers. In that capacity he organised the holding up by force of coastguards and policemen so that his friends might

obtain arms with which to defy British law, and to defeat
the constitutionally obtained liberty of the overwhelming
majority of his fellow countrymen. The officer is now Field
Marshal Sir Henry Wilson, military chief of the British
army, and as I propose to show, supreme dictator of the Irish
government. In September 1920 Kevin Barry, an eighteen-
year-old boy modelling his conduct precisely upon that of
Sir Henry Wilson at Larne, set out to obtain arms for an
exactly similar purpose. Not having the co-operation of
highly placed politicians and officers he and his friendship
sought to procure them by the only means in their power,
viz, by forcible seizure. The force employed most deplorably
involved the death and wounding of British soldiers – and
finally the execution of Kevin Barry. On Wednesday of last
week I learned by accident that the cabinet has decided
upon Barry's immediate execution and at once proceeded
to London with a friend to seek by any means to secure a
reprieve. It is sufficient for the moment that I should state
categorically the information which I obtained during my
visit to London and since my return, leaving proof of my
statements to be supplied later if their accuracy is challenged.
The facts in my possession are:

1. That the Prime Minister clearly stated his personal wish and
   intention that the sentence should not be carried out.

2. That Sir Hamar Greenwood personally disapproved of the
   execution.

3. That no single leading official of the Irish Government was
   opposed to reprieve.

4. That Sir Nevil Macready on Saturday and Lord French

on Sunday declared that they had no power to alter the sentence.

5. Where, then, was the power which tied the hands of the prime minister, chief secretary, Lord Lieutenant and Irish commander-in-chief and forced them to become parties to the blackest crime and the most brutal blunder in the Anglo-Irish relationship? One word from any member of the Carson–Wilson–Bonar Law gunrunning junta would have stopped the execution. Mr Lloyd George was threatened with the resignation of Sir Henry Wilson if a reprieve was granted. To that threat, Mr Lloyd George yielded and replied to the 11th hour appeal of the Lord Mayor of Dublin that the law 'must take its course'.[25]

This letter contains two of the most serious allegations that could be made in public against a serving soldier. It is true, as we have seen, that Wilson was a staunch supporter of militant Ulster unionism, but there is no evidence that he personally intervened to ensure that the Ulster Volunteer Force could illegally import guns at Larne in April 1914. Similarly, the notion that it was Wilson who intervened to ensure that Barry was hanged is at odds with his private correspondence with Macready.

Aston's letter was reprinted in much of the nationalist press in Ireland, but Wilson made no reply. Perhaps he did not see it; maybe he did not care what his fellow countrymen thought of him; maybe he felt, to paraphrase Franklin D. Roosevelt, 'They are unanimous in their hatred for me and I welcome their hatred.' He should have been paying attention. It was shortly after Barry's hanging that he became a target for the IRA.

In 1921 the British began to get the measure of the IRA. In May the Dublin IRA attacked the Custom House in the biggest

95

assault of the war. The attack on the centre of local government administration in Ireland was a propaganda victory but a military fiasco, and a hundred IRA men were arrested.

There were 3,000 IRA men in jail and the organisation was desperately short of arms, while the British army fielded sixty-eight infantry battalions in Ireland by the time of the Truce, amounting to almost 60,000 troops. Wilson proposed another surge for the autumn, with an additional 20,000 to 30,000 men.

Yet the country was not quiescent and the British military establishment had concluded that nothing other than saturating the country with more troops would do. This the government was not prepared to contemplate. The Government of Ireland Act 1920 set up home rule parliaments for the six counties of Northern Ireland and the twenty-six counties of Southern Ireland. The unionists in the North accepted their own parliament with alacrity as a means of guaranteeing their status within the Union; the home rule settlement for Southern Ireland was rejected, as the government knew it would be, but that was not the point. One part of the two-headed hydra that was the Irish problem was dealt with in the settlement with Ulster. Now the cabinet, shorn of its greatest opponents to home rule – Andrew Bonar Law was ill and Edward Carson had retired – was prepared to offer nationalist Ireland more generous terms. Wilson was horrified. He and his family would be among the 400,000 Southern unionists stranded on the wrong side of the border by partition.

On the day of the Custom House attack, the British cabinet met. Macready spelt it out in stark terms. The situation would have to be brought to a conclusion by October, he stated, or else the troops that were there would have to be replaced. Either seek peace or prepare for perpetual conflict. 'Now it must be peace or real war and no fooling,' Viscount FitzAlan, the Lord Lieutenant of Ireland, declared.

Three days later the first substantial meeting between the British and Sinn Féin took place. Patrick Moylett met General Brind, Macready's general staff officer, in the Shelbourne Hotel. On the following day Moylett met Andy Cope, the senior civil servant and Assistant Under-Secretary for Ireland. Moylett's recollection of the meeting included an extraordinary admission by Cope:

> We are willing to acknowledge that we are defeated. There is nothing else for us to do but to draft 400,000 men and exterminate the whole population of the country.[26]

We only have Moylett's word for it as recounted many years later in his Bureau of Military History statement, but it chimes with many pronouncements made by other senior British figures and with what Macready told Wilson in January. A truce was called for 11 July 1921. Wilson was beside himself with rage. He hoped that the Truce would break down; many on both sides did not believe it would last, but it did. He hoped the government would use the Truce period to prepare for a resumption of hostilities. He wanted a special enlistment of 40,000 men from the infantry to do one year of service within the United Kingdom, which then included Ireland. 'I think that we shall want 100,000 to 200,000 men and one or two years to stamp out the murder gang and re-establish law and order and the King's writ,' he declared in his diary in September 1921.

He wanted nothing to do with the negotiations and refused many entreaties to meet his fellow Irishmen who were negotiating the Treaty. 'We do not speak to murderers,' he told an exasperated Lloyd George. 'Oh nonsense,' Lloyd George responded, 'in public life we must do these things.' The Anglo-Irish Treaty was signed on 6 December 1921. It granted the Irish Free State Dominion status within the British Empire, the same as Canada. This was a huge advance on what had been offered through home rule. The twenty-six counties would no longer be part of the United Kingdom. The Irish Free State would have its own police force and its own army. At the same time Ireland would remain within the British Empire and members of Dáil Éireann would swear an oath of allegiance to the king. The Irish negotiators, led by Arthur Griffith, the founder of Sinn Féin, and Michael Collins, were told bluntly that Ulster was not up for discussion. Instead, the issue of partition was dealt with in Article 12, which stated:

> A Commission consisting of three persons, one to be
> appointed by the Government of the Irish Free State, one to
> be appointed by the Government of Northern Ireland, and
> one who shall be Chairman to be appointed by the British
> Government shall determine in accordance with the wishes
> of the inhabitants, so far as may be compatible with economic
> and geographic conditions the boundaries between Northern
> Ireland and the rest of Ireland, and for the purposes of the
> Government of Ireland Act 1920, and of this instrument,
> the boundary of Northern Ireland shall be such as may be
> determined by such Commission.[27]

Wilson's response to the Treaty was, as it had always been when it came to Irish matters, an emotional one. It was, as his diary attests, an

> abject surrender to murderers. It gives complete independence
> under the guise of Dominion home rule. It gives army, police,
> judiciary, fiscal autonomy, taxation, agriculture, education,

etc. In short, Ireland is gone. There is not one word about the loyal people of the south and west. So, Lloyd George is getting on fast with the ruin of the Empire. We shall incidentally lose our sixteen Irish battalions and have to withdraw altogether from Ireland. It is quite impossible to see what all this means.[28]

Wilson left no entry in his diary for New Year's Eve 1921. In early January 1922 he suggested to the cabinet that the government move ahead with withdrawing its troops from Ireland. He argued, accurately as it turned out, that the British army could find itself called upon to intervene on one side or the other:

What is going to happen in Ireland, goodness knows. It will be great fun if they start pistoling each other instead of pistoling us. But if they do start a form of murder government, I am most anxious that we should get our troops out before one set of murderers call on the British troops to shoot another set of murderers.[29]

For once the cabinet agreed with Wilson, and British troops started returning home after the formal handing of power to the Provisional Irish Government at a ceremony laden with symbolic significance in Dublin Castle on 16 January.

Wilson visited the Irish Free State a day later, passing through Dublin on his way to Belfast. He told FitzAlan that no 'sane man can imagine that Collins and Co., who none of them ever administered a typewriter, can be expected to keep law and order over three millions of people who have now no sense of either and this without either any army or police, simply passes any comprehension'.[30]

Much to everybody's relief, most notably his own, Wilson's tenure as Chief of the Imperial General Staff came to an end on 19

February 1922. In four years everything had changed. Germany had been beaten; the First World War won; the British had gained commitments it was struggling to keep. Above all, as Wilson had prophesied, Ireland had been lost as a united and indivisible part of the United Kingdom, and Wilson had failed to keep the South in the United Kingdom. He would devote the final months of his life to ensuring the same fate did not befall Northern Ireland.

4

Henry Wilson and Ulster: 'The Orange Terror'

Three days after Wilson retired as Chief of the Imperial General Staff he was elected unopposed as an Ulster Unionist MP for North Down. Prior to his retirement, Wilson's support for the cause of Ulster unionism was an open secret, especially when a letter he sent to the Northern Ireland prime minister-elect Sir James Craig was intercepted, most likely by the IRA in London, and published in the *Irish Bulletin*, the propaganda sheet of the underground Irish government, in June 1921.

The letter revealed that Wilson had turned down an invitation from Craig to attend the state opening of the Northern Ireland parliament on 22 June, on the basis that any invitation for him to attend would have to come from King George V. In response to the invitation, Wilson elaborated that he expected to presently send over troops to 'bring the Sinn Féin rebellion to an end . . . I think it would bring politics into the army if as a preliminary to ordering thousands of troops over to crush the rebellion in the south and west, I was seen to take part in the opening of the parliament in the North.'[1]

In declining the invitation, Wilson made clear that his opinions on the 'Irish question are fairly well known . . . I have an unlimited belief in our corner of Ireland, in fact so much that I often tell these unfortunate English fellows that when they have made a hash of the Empire we Ulster boys will take over the show for them and let them see how to run a real Imperial idea!'

The letter demonstrated a lack of tact and discretion for one

10 Wilson declined to attend the state opening of the Northern Ireland
parliament on 22 June 1921 as he was a serving soldier

in such a senior position, and caused no little embarrassment. A
few days later Wilson wrote to the Secretary of State for War,
Laming Worthington-Evans, setting out how he saw the question
of Ireland:

> For the last two years I have always thought and openly said
> that we have only two courses open to us in Ireland. One is to
> crush out the murder gang with a ruthless hand and restore
> law and order and the King's writ and the other is to clear out
> altogether, i.e. grant independence. But although I believe this
> to be proper, and indeed the only course to pursue if we want
> to keep our Empire, I have always said that it is an impossible
> course and one which should never be attempted unless Great
> Britain is wholeheartedly in favour of it. Now as regards the

grant of independence, I am quite clearly of the opinion that this will mean that we shall have a hostile Ireland in our rear and right athwart all our trade routes.[2]

His viewpoint is striking for a number of reasons. First, there is no acknowledgement in his letter that home rule was already agreed British government policy going back to 1914, had been given royal assent, was the law of the land and had to be implemented. Second, Wilson gives no consideration at all to the desire of the Irish people for more autonomy from Britain, going back to the Act of Union of 1800. Last, Wilson appeared capable of seeing British government policy on Ireland only through the prism of its impact on Britain and the Empire. The considerations of the people in Ireland did not figure in his calculations at all. In the same letter Wilson had the self-awareness to acknowledge that powerful forces in Britain were against coercion in Ireland, but that this could be overcome:

> I am one of those who believe that if Great Britain was really told of the appalling state of Ireland and of the savage, cruel murders perpetuated every day, she would not only approve of any measures, no matter how severe, she would cry out for them.[3]

His faith that the British public would support a policy of further coercion in Ireland was not shared by the British government. In November 1921 Wilson unveiled the Ulster Tower on the site where 2,000 men from the 36th (Ulster) Division were slaughtered in northern France on 1 July 1916, the first day of the Battle of the Somme. In tandem with the Battle of the Boyne, the Somme was emblematic of the 'blood sacrifice' unionists had made for Britain. It was the first memorial to be put up on the

Western Front and its erection was a political imperative for the Northern Ireland government. The Somme region was still in a state of desolation three years after the war had ended, and the countryside would take generations to repair. 'To right and left, before, behind, everywhere so far as the eye can see, there is a vast sea of black despair,' wrote the unnamed *Irish Times* reporter who attended the unveiling. 'A few gaunt skeletons that once were trees stick crazily out of the pock-marked earth. The earth is littered with barbed wire, old helmets, bits of broken tanks, even bones obstruct the feet and a frosted November sun smiles on this withered land as if to enhance its heart rendering misery.'[4]

Conspicuous by their absence were Sir James Craig and Sir Edward Carson. Craig was ill with influenza, Carson was just ill. His hard-man image was at odds with his status as a hypochondriac or, as he put it himself, 'a dyspeptic pessimist'. He was frequently missing from important events with some ailment or another. Wilson's presence as CIGS was as far as he could go at the time in publicly showing solidarity with the cause of Ulster unionism.

Wilson travelled across to Ulster on 19 January 1922 to unveil a statue in Lisburn of Dublin-born Brigadier John Nicholson, who was killed in 1857 during the Indian Mutiny. Nicholson, like Wilson, was a Southern Irish unionist and British imperialist. He had dealt with the mutineers ruthlessly. When he heard that barrack cooks had poisoned the food intended for his soldiers, he had them hanged on the spot. Nicholson became a posthumous hero in Victorian Britain but was described recently by the Indian-based author William Dalrymple as an 'imperial psychopath'.

Later, Wilson unveiled a roll of honour in Queen's University Belfast to students who died in the Great War, and Craig declared there was no better Ulsterman than Wilson and no better man to aid Ulster in its hour of need. A month later Wilson's four-year term as CIGS came to an end. There was no question of him being reappointed, even if he had wanted the job. Nor did he play any role in the appointment of his successor, another Anglo-Irish choice, the Earl of Cavan.

Wilson had not attended cabinet for eight months and would only deal with Lloyd George through intermediaries. Senior figures in the British government, who depended on him for advice during the war, now chose to ignore him, surmising that his uncompromising views on Ireland made him more trouble than he was worth.

Wilson was found a safe seat in North Down after the sitting MP Thomas Watters Brown became a judge of the High Court of Justice in Northern Ireland. Wilson was returned unopposed on 22 February 1922, now free of the constitutional and professional need as a soldier to keep his thoughts to himself. His intriguing and contempt for the 'Frocks' and his private fulminations, once confined to the privacy of his diary, were now on display for the world to see. His bitterness towards the government that he had served was expressed with the unvarnished candour of a soldier, not a politician or statesman. Nor did he make any attempt to conceal his partisan view of the Irish situation, with his support for Ulster unionism matched by his contempt for Irish nationalism. As a retired senior soldier, Wilson might have been expected to bring his professional judgement and a cool head to calm the fraught situation in Ireland. Instead, Ireland brought out his most partisan instincts.

His pro-imperialist, pro-military and anti-Irish nationalism views were in tune with the views of the right wing of the Conservative Party, known as the Diehards, who were opposed to the coalition government led by Lloyd George. The *Manchester Guardian* speculated soon after his election as an MP that Wilson was a natural leader of the Diehards, who lacked an effective mouthpiece. 'Sir Henry Wilson has a national reputation and a flair for effective and pungent speech. Far more important in a leader, he has knowledge of the inner secrets both of this government and of certain continental governments.'[5]

Wilson became an MP at a fraught time in Irish politics, when the two political entities created as a result of partition, Northern Ireland and the Irish Free State, were riven by strife and beset with internal enemies. In doing so he pitched himself into the most serious and prolonged bout of violence in Ulster for centuries. In the two years between July 1920 and July 1922, 680 people died in political violence in the North, 498 in Belfast alone. In the years between 1969 and 1995, 3,526 people were killed as a result of the Troubles. Had the same intensity of violence as occurred between 1920 and 1922 recurred during the Troubles, that figure would have been closer to 8,500. The violence of 1920 to 1922 was the original Troubles, pitting nationalists against unionists, republicans against loyalists and republicans against the British state.

Catholics were disproportionately killed. They represented a third of the population of Belfast yet constituted two-thirds of those who were killed. Thousands of them were driven from their jobs and tens of thousands from their homes by loyalist mobs, many fleeing south across the border in scenes that eyewitnesses compared to the evacuation of French and Belgian villages during the First World War. The IRA was ruthless in targeting the security forces, but each act of violence prompted a disproportionate response.

The killings of those years ensured that the newly created Northern Ireland was born in an atmosphere of mutual distrust and recrimination. Catholics never accepted the state and never expected it to protect them. Protestants never trusted Catholics, and after a brief flurry of North–South co-operation in early 1922, occasioned by the intensity of the violence in the North, relations between the two political entities were frozen until 1965.

The whole period is known colloquially in the North as the 'Belfast pogroms', though they were not confined to Belfast and the name is disputed by unionists. The genesis of the violence of those years came in 1912 with the passage of the Home Rule Bill through parliament. It prompted the setting up of the Ulster Volunteer Force in 1913 in opposition to home rule, and the importation of arms at Larne in 1914. The Irish Volunteers (later to become the IRA) was set up in reaction to the UVF in November 1913 and it smuggled arms into Ireland at Howth in July 1914. In the summer of 1914 many, not least the British government, feared civil war would break out, with elements of the army siding with the UVF.

The outbreak of the First World War postponed the problem. As the Foreign Secretary Sir Edward Gray exclaimed in his famous speech to the House of Commons on 3 August 1914: 'The one bright spot in the whole of this terrible situation is Ireland. The general feeling throughout Ireland – and I would like this to be clearly understood abroad – does not make the Irish question a consideration which we feel we have now to take into account.'[6]

The Easter Rising of 1916 did not affect Ulster directly, and the Irish War of Independence initially had a low profile in the province. Constitutional nationalism was stronger in Ulster than in the South. The Irish Party won five of its six seats in Ulster in the 1918 general election, though they were outpolled two to one in the rest of Ireland by Sinn Féin. The most popular nationalist politician in the North was 'Wee' Joe Devlin, the MP for West Belfast, who outpolled Éamon de Valera by two to one in the Belfast Falls constituency.

In the January 1920 local elections, nationalists won twenty-three local authorities to the unionists' twenty-two across the nine counties of Ulster. Nationalists captured Derry City Council for the first time. The fall of the province's second-largest city to a nationalist majority increased unionists' sense of insecurity. The city had seen clashes between nationalists and unionists in the aftermath of the First World War. Stones turned to bullets on the evening of 23 June 1920, when shots were fired into a nationalist crowd from the Protestant Fountain area of the city. In response the local UVF mobilised and the IRA brought in guns from Donegal.

Howard McKay, the son of the governor of the Apprentice Boys in the city, was shot dead by republicans. Derry was 'like a town on the Western Front' and 'a powder-mine', wrote local republican Charles McGuinness in his memoirs. The *Irish Times* suggested in an editorial dated 23 June that 'a match thrown into it from either camp was bound to produce a general explosion.' In one week in June twenty people were killed.[7]

The violence became more widespread a month later. On 12 July Sir Edward Carson made an irresponsible speech to 25,000 Orangemen at Finaghy, outside Belfast. 'We must proclaim today clearly that come what will and be the consequences what they may, we in Ulster will tolerate no Sinn Féin – no Sinn Féin organisation, no Sinn Féin methods . . . And these are not mere words. I hate words without action.' Carson went further, targeting not only nationalists but 'men who come forward posing as the friends of labour' whose real object was 'to mislead and bring disunity amongst our own people; and in the end, before we know where we are, we may find ourselves in the same bondage and slavery as is the rest of Ireland.'[8]

Five days later the IRA in Cork shot dead Lieutenant Colonel Gerald Bryce Smyth, the divisional commander of the RIC, who had been sent from London to stiffen the resolve of the force in dealing with the IRA. Smyth made a notorious speech at Listowel police station in County Kerry on 19 June in which he exhorted the men to shoot suspected republicans on sight. The speech was circulated to the nationalist press by RIC officers, who mutinied rather than enforce his will. The most notorious lines, disputed by Smyth himself, came when he told the assembled men, 'You may make mistakes occasionally and innocent persons may be shot, but that cannot be helped and you are bound to get the right persons sometimes. The more you shoot the better I will like you; and I assure you that no policeman will get into trouble for shooting any man.'

Smyth was born in India and brought up in England, but he was buried in his mother's home town of Banbridge, County Down. No train driver would transport his body across the border, reinforcing the perception among unionists that there was, to quote a more contemporary phrase, a 'pan-nationalist front' conspiring to threaten the unionist way of life. For nationalists Smyth was a villain who was paid back in his own coin; for unionists he was a martyr who had sought to uphold the rule of law and their way of life against a republican murder gang. His funeral on 21 July 1920 was one of the biggest ever seen in Banbridge. Afterwards the town's Protestant majority targeted Catholic businesses. Over a three-day period, shops were destroyed and many Catholic families driven from their homes.

On the same day an organisation calling itself the Belfast Protestants' Association summoned 'all Unionist and Protestant workers' to a meeting at lunchtime in the Harland & Wolff shipyards. The majority Protestant workforce passed a resolution stating they would not work alongside 'Sinn Féiners'. Eight thousand Catholics and approximately two thousand 'rotten Prods', those from a trade union or a perceived left-wing background, were expelled from the shipyards, foundries and factories. Catholics, considered to be disloyal, were thrown into the River Lagan and pelted with rivets and bolts, known as 'Belfast confetti'. 'Disloyal' workers were expelled from other prominent factories in the city. The offices of the Independent Labour Party were burned to the ground. Irish republicanism was associated with Bolshevism and socialism. Rioting spread from the Protestant Shankill Road to the Catholic Falls Road. Ten people, six Catholics and four Protestants, were killed on Kashmir Street.

The IRA took their assassination campaign north when they shot dead District Inspector Oswald Swanzy on 22 August as he left a church service in Lisburn. The killing was in revenge for the assassination of the Lord Mayor of Cork, Tomás Mac Curtain, in March of that year. An inquest into Mac Curtain's death held Swanzy directly and Lloyd George indirectly responsible for the killing. Michael Collins sent four of his best men from Cork to the North to carry out the hit, and Swanzy was killed in a symbolic act of revenge using Mac Curtain's revolver. Swanzy's death provoked a ferocious backlash against the Catholic population. Catholic premises were burned and families forced to flee the town. Those who left by the road to Belfast were further targeted and many fled with their belongings over a mountain pass. The violence again spread to Belfast. Twenty-two people were killed in the week after the Swanzy killing.

Sir James Craig, then a junior member of the coalition government and soon to be the first prime minister of Northern Ireland, persuaded the cabinet in October 1920 to set up the Ulster Special Constabulary (USC) as an auxiliary to the Royal Irish Constabulary. These were a counterpart to the Black and Tans and the Auxiliaries in the South, which were then assisting the RIC. Neither force operated in the six counties. The Specials were composed, not of recruits from Britain, but of local loyal-ists. Wilson later became associated with the worst excesses of the Specials, but he was not responsible for setting them up.

There were three classes of Specials. A-Specials were full-time uniformed officers who worked alongside the Royal Irish Constabulary (soon to be the Royal Ulster Constabulary); the B-Specials were armed part-timers and had their own command structure; and the C-Specials were older men who guarded instal-lations and were generally unarmed. The British government agreed to the establishment of the USC on the basis that it could not spare any more men for Ireland.

In early 1921 a younger, more aggressive IRA active service unit began killing policemen in the North, leading to a series of tit-for-tat killings through the spring and summer of that year. As the conflict in the South of Ireland wound down, the violence got progressively worse in the North.

On 10 June IRA volunteers shot three RIC officers, killing Constable James Glover. Fourteen people were killed in the fol-lowing days. The violence reached another climax just as the Truce was imminent in the War of Independence. On Bloody Sunday, 10 July, seventeen people died, eleven of them Catholics. Homes were destroyed in mixed areas. The Truce announcement in the South on 11 July was only the start and not the end of a renewed period of violence in Belfast – twenty-eight people were killed or fatally wounded in Belfast that week. The commandant of the IRA's 2nd Northern Division, Eoin O'Duffy, was sent to Belfast by the organisation's leadership in Dublin to liaise with the British authorities there and try to maintain the Truce:

> I found the city in a veritable state of war. The peal of rifles
> could be heard on all sides, frenzied mobs at every street

corner, terror-stricken people rushing for their lives, and ambulances carrying the dead and dying to hospitals.[9]

There was a temporary lull in the violence until August, when three days of fighting saw the loss of another twenty lives. Both sides were capable of indiscriminate attacks on each other. On 22 November a grenade was thrown onto a tram carrying Protestant workers from the shipyards. Three were killed. Two days later a second bomb attack on a tram killed four people.

After the signing of the Anglo-Irish Treaty in December 1921 and the handover of power to the Provisional Government on 16 January 1922, Sir James Craig and Michael Collins agreed the first Craig–Collins pact. Their attempt to end the violence raised unrealistic expectations of North–South co-operation. Craig pledged to 'facilitate in every possible way the return of Catholic workmen without tests to the shipyards as and when trade revival enables the firms concerned to absorb the present unemployed'.[10]

Collins agreed to end the Belfast Boycott, a boycott of goods and services instigated in August 1920 by Dáil Éireann as a protest against the shipyard expulsions. Both consented to scrap the British representative on the Boundary Commission as set out in Article 12 of the Anglo-Irish Treaty. Instead, they would appoint their own representatives to mutually agree on the boundary between the Irish Free State and Northern Ireland. They further agreed to dispense with the Council of Ireland as outlined in the Government of Ireland Act 1920 and opted to deal with issues of mutual concern between the two of them and their officials.

The prospect that the two political entities set up on the island of Ireland could live in peaceful co-existence was swiftly shattered by Craig's declaration three days later that there would be no territorial concession to the Irish Free State. Nationalists had reluctantly accepted the Anglo-Irish Treaty on the basis that the Boundary Commission would cede nationalist majority areas to the Free State, including Tyrone, Fermanagh and south Armagh, making the rest of Northern Ireland only a rump enclave, or so they expected.

The uneasy peace of 1922 was broken in mid-January, when five members of the Monaghan Gaelic Athletic Association team were arrested on their way to play Derry in the Ulster Senior Championship in Dromore, County Tyrone. Some of them were also using the match as cover to spring three colleagues from Derry Jail who had been sentenced to death. On 7 February the IRA responded by kidnapping forty-two prominent loyalists in Fermanagh and Tyrone and holding them as hostages across the Border.

Four days later a party of eighteen armed B-Specials, travelling by train from Belfast, stopped at Clones railway station in County Monaghan en route to Enniskillen. The IRA rushed to the train station and called on them to surrender, but they responded by shooting dead the IRA commander, Matt Fitzpatrick. The IRA opened fire on the train, spraying the carriages with a blizzard of bullets. Four B-Specials were killed and others injured. By the time the train arrived in Enniskillen, the carriages were a mass of blood. The Clones Affray, as it became known, was a serious incident that prompted the British government to temporarily suspend its troop withdrawal from Ireland. Over the next three days thirty-one people died in Belfast. The worst atrocity occurred at Weaver Street on 13 February, when loyalists threw a bomb into the middle of a group of children playing at a street corner. Six children were killed and seventeen injured – all of them Catholics. The barbaric nature of the killings caused universal shock, Churchill stating: 'It is the worst thing that has happened in Ireland in the last three years.'[11] Craig's response to the bombing was more equivocal. In a statement drafted in his name and read out by Churchill in the House of Commons, Craig remarked on

[. . .] the indiscriminate throwing of bombs over a wall into Weaver Street, a Sinn Féin area, which resulted in the death of two children [the other children died afterwards] and the wounding of fourteen others. These outrages are greatly deplored by my Government, especially the latter dastardly deed, involving the lives of children.[12]

Indiscriminate throwing of bombs by whom? Craig did not name the culprits but the juxtaposition of 'indiscriminate' and 'Sinn Féin' suggested he believed republicans to be responsible. His vague response cemented the belief among nationalists that he was indifferent to violence against their community. That night 148 Catholic families in the area around Weaver Street were forced to leave their homes.

Wilson became actively involved in Northern politics in March 1922, a month that saw the worst atrocities of this period and the deaths of fifty-three more people. His appointment as military advisor to the Northern government was announced in the Belfast parliament by Sir James Craig, at the same time as he announced the Civil Authorities (Special Powers) Act (Northern Ireland), better known simply as the Special Powers Act.

This was based on the Restoration of Order in Ireland Act, which was used during the War of Independence. The Special Powers Act empowered the Minister for Home Affairs to 'take all such steps and issue all such orders as may be necessary for preserving the peace and maintaining order; and to make laws without reference to parliament'. It allowed for the prohibition of public meetings, the closure of newspapers, the imposition of curfews and the flogging of those caught with unauthorised fire-arms. Internment (detention without trial) was also provided for, as we will see later, with devastating impact.

The legislation was brought forward by the Minister for Home Affairs, Dawson Bates, a prominent member of the Ulster Volunteer Force. Staunch defender of Ulster as he was, Wilson was enamoured by neither Craig nor Bates. The former was 'a very second-rate man' and Bates a 'small man in every way'. Wilson did not draft the wording of the Special Powers Act, but he was associated with it from the beginning. The degrading use of the whip, even in the 1920s an anachronistic form of punish-ment, came to symbolise the humiliating nature of the legislation, as nationalists saw it.

The *Freeman's Journal* declared 'Wilson the dictator' and blamed him for the legislation: 'Yesterday the Belfast parliament initiated a measure to place the cat-o'-nine-tails in the hands of Sir Henry Wilson to flog Northern nationalism into submission.'[13]

The worst atrocity of this terrible time was the massacre of five members of the McMahon family, along with a barman, Edward McKinney. Owen McMahon was a publican who lived in a Victorian house in Kinnaird Terrace, north Belfast. He was a nationalist, a good friend of Joe Devlin, but not a republican and had no links to the IRA. He appears to have been targeted simply because he was a successful Catholic in a predominantly Protestant city.[14]

At 1 a.m. on 24 March 1922 five men burst into the McMahon home, using a stolen sledgehammer to break the door down. There were eleven people in the house at the time: eight men (Owen McMahon, his six sons and McKinney) and three women (McMahon's wife Eliza, her daughter and her niece). The men

11 The Belfast IRA kept a handwritten list of those who had been killed in the
Belfast pogroms between 1920 and 1922. Listed here in the killings of March
1922 are the five members of the McMahon family

were lined up in the living room and shot. One son hid and another, John, was shot but survived by playing dead. He left Belfast a short time afterwards and lived out his life in London. The perpetrators of the massacre were never found, but they were named in a Free State government report as twelve RIC policemen led by Detective Inspector John Nixon, a unionist from County Cavan.[15]

The McMahon shootings and incidents like it had a profound impact on many Irish nationalists, Reggie Dunne among them, as his father recounted:

> He is intensely religious and since he came back from France he had read deeply in the papers about his co-religionists and the pogroms in Belfast, and I have seen the tears run down his face as he has been reading this.[16]

The McMahon shootings led to a second Craig–Collins pact, signed six days later. This one was much more comprehensive than the first, and Churchill declared with characteristic bombast, 'Peace is declared today.' The pact recognised the difficulties nationalists in the North had with the new state. Catholics were to be actively recruited into the Ulster Special Constabulary and there was to be a special police force in mixed areas of Belfast that would include equal numbers of Catholics and Protestants. The IRA agreed to release the loyalists it held captive, and the Northern authorities those republicans who were currently in jail. The British government provided funding for relief work for any workers who had lost their employment. In addition, a number of committees were established to oversee and attempt to conciliate disputes, grants and employment. The problem for both Craig and Collins was that the hardliners on both sides were determined to scupper the agreement. Within hours of its signing the IRA killed two children in a sectarian attack on Brown Street, Belfast.

This was followed by ambushes on special constables in Newry and Belfast that left two more people dead.

In retaliation the police rampaged through the Stanhope Street and Arnon Street areas of Belfast on 1 April, beating down doors. Five Catholics were shot dead in a frenzy of shooting that became known as the Arnon Street massacre. The police did not even bother to conceal their own identities. The pact was still-born, prompting de Valera to state a day later that it was merely a 'piece of paper'.[17] Collins, even while he publicly advocated peace and supported the Anglo-Irish Treaty he had signed, sought to undermine the Northern Ireland state. He set up a secret Ulster Council composed of the seven divisions of the IRA operating in the North or along the border. He hoped that the setting up of an Irish army would one day allow him to 'march on the North', but in the meantime he thought destabilising Northern Ireland would be a useful distraction from the disastrous split over the Treaty.

In April Collins reached the conclusion that the pact was use-less, hence his decision to set up the Ulster Council in defiance of the Treaty. The pro- and anti-Treaty forces had their well-aired differences, but undermining the new Northern state was something that motivated all republicans. On 21 April 1922 the Council agreed a joint offensive in the North involving local and Midlands divisions of the IRA. They were to be supplied with guns by the Provisional Government, until it became apparent that these guns, which had been supplied by the British, could be traced. A swap was done with old guns held by the anti-Treaty side. Even while the pro- and anti-Treaty sides threatened war against each other, they were prepared to unite to foment another civil war in Northern Ireland.

The Northern Offensive in May 1922 was, as the local historian Patrick Concannon put it, a 'dismal failure'.[18] How it could have been a success is hard to conceive given the disparity in forces: 27,563 Specials constables and 5,000 British soldiers against approximately 8,500 IRA men. 'It is unclear if the offensive was actually intended to produce a military success and the ultimate aim of the attack is obscure,' the military historian Matthew Lewis concluded.[19] The chances of bringing down the Northern administration were minimal, but the IRA might have hoped to make the North ungovernable for the British, as they had done in the South. The offensive might have had more to do with Southern politics than its Northern variety, restoring unity and common purpose in the IRA at a time when it was sundering as a result of the Treaty.

Michael Collins was front and centre of the approach to it. 'I understood from Frank Aiken that Michael Collins was the inspiration for the general offensive,' recalled Padraig Quinn, the quartermaster of the Fourth Northern Division of the IRA.[20] It began on 2 May 1922, when the Second Northern Division attacked the RIC barracks in Bellaghy and Draperstown in County Derry, killing one RIC man and injuring another, but they were quickly overwhelmed. The Northern advisory committee of the Provisional Government met at the Metropole Hotel in York Street on 15 May and urged the Provisional Government to wage war against the Northern government. Approximately one hundred hardcore IRA activists moved north to participate in the offensive. A new start date of 19 May was given, with a proposed raid on the Musgrave Street RIC barracks in Belfast, but the attack went awry. The Fourth Northern Division under the command of Frank Aiken, who went on to become a prominent minister in the new Irish state, did not rise as planned on 22 May for reasons that are still not understood.

On that day the IRA assassinated William Twaddell, a Unionist MP in the Northern Ireland parliament. Twaddell was a prominent Orangeman and a leader of the Ulster Imperial Guard, one of the largest paramilitary forces that formed a significant proportion of the Special Constabularies. The killing of Twaddell shared many of the details of the Wilson shooting exactly a month later.

Twaddell's assassination served no useful purpose and enraged the Northern government, which immediately deployed the Special Powers Act and arrested 350 IRA men, interning them without trial. An IRA Belfast Brigade report concluded: 'Under the present circumstances it would be impossible to keep our military organisation alive and intact as the morale of the men is going down day by day and the spirit of the people is practically dead.'[21]

The last act of this spiral of violence was the Altnaveigh massacre in south Armagh on 17 June, just five days before Wilson's assassination. In response to the killing of two republicans near Camlough, County Armagh, and a sexual assault on a Sinn Féin councillor's wife, six Protestant civilians were killed and many families burned out of their homes.

From his election as an Ulster Unionist MP in February 1922 to his death in June of that year, Wilson firmly took the side of the Northern government, to the detriment of his reputation, and this eventually cost him his life. He set the tone for his engagement in the North with a notorious letter to Sir James Craig, written on 17 March 1922:[22]

> You have asked me for my opinion and advice on the present and the future. Here they are. Owing to the action of Mr Lloyd George and his government, the twenty-six counties of south and west Ireland are reduced to a welter of chaos and murder, difficult to believe, impossible to describe. A further consequence of the course pursued by Mr Lloyd George is seen by the state of unrest, suspicion and lawlessness which has spread over the frontier into the six counties of Ulster.

The dangerous conditions which obtain in the twenty-six counties will increase and spread.

1. A man in those counties rises who can crush out murder and anarchy and re-establish law and order. With a thousand years of Irish history to guide us, it is safe to predict that this will not happen: and unless

2. Great Britain re-establishes law and order in Ireland. Under Mr Lloyd George and his Government this is frankly and laughably impossible because men who are only capable of losing an Empire are obviously incapable of holding an Empire and still more incapable of regaining it.

In the fact of such a state of affairs, what is my advice?

3. Get Great Britain warmly on your side. There never was a more fair-minded, more generous people, than the men and women who live in England, Scotland and Wales. Get them on your side. Tell them and get others to tell them, the real truth of what is now going on in the south and west and what is really passing in Ulster. Get those splendid Britons on your side for with Great Britain with you – there is nothing which can't be done, as witnessed by the last Great War, whilst on the other hand, with Great Britain indifferent, lukewarm or hostile, there is but little that can be done.

4. And when you are laying your case before Great Britain, while I have been greatly impressed by the magnificent manner in which the citizens generally have enrolled in the Special Constabulary, and the way in which they have met the serious situation up to the present, I suggest you should make:

5. Considerable alterations in the command and administration of all your armed force RIC, A Specials, B Specials etc.

6. Re-class and re-adjust the various categories of your police and greatly strengthen some of them.

7. Re-draft your laws for the carrying of arms.

8. Take increased powers for rapid and drastic action against the illegal importation and carrying of arms, bombs etc.

On these points, I am submitting separate and detailed proposals for your consideration. With Great Britain in active sympathy with you in your efforts to maintain law and order and with the great addition in strength which I hope my proposals will give you, I think that in the very near future you will see a wonderful recovery in a situation which, at the moment, must cause you grave anxiety.

Yours sincerely, Henry Wilson MP.

In a separate and secret memorandum to the cabinet, Wilson said firearms should only be carried by individuals who took an oath of allegiance to the state and, if not a member of His Majesty's Forces, were a member of some class of the Ulster Constabulary and of 'sufficiently good character to be admitted'. A whole-time policeman or a B-Special should be allowed to carry a firearm at all times. Wilson urged a new proclamation should be issued, calling all inhabitants of the six counties to join this force:

[...] irrespective of class or creed, emphasising the determination of the Government to stamp out murder and other forms of crime and to restore settled conditions in the Six Counties. Encouragement should be given to Catholics to join equally with other religions. The result of such a step would be to secure that those who were loyal and wished to see settled conditions in the Six Counties would be given the opportunity of declaring their willingness in stamping out crime and once it was realised that this Government were in earnest in carrying out their proposals, a good number of those who are refraining might come to their side.[23]

Wilson's private exhortation to the Northern government that Catholics should be allowed to join did not appear in his public pronouncements, and once again the impression was given that Wilson was a shameless partisan whose real aim was the maintenance of Orange supremacy, not the restoration of law and order.

Outside Ulster, Wilson's letter to Craig drew universal condemnation. Even the *Morning Post*, the mouthpiece of the Diehards, baulked at the notion of a reconquest of the South.

> It reminds Sir James Craig and his colleagues that a war
> with the South would be no small matter whatever the
> outcome may be. We regret that Sir Henry Wilson was not
> more careful and temperate in his letter to Sir James Craig
> accepting the position of quasi-military advisor.[24]

The reaction in the South of Ireland was unequivocal, most notably from the people he came from – the Southern unionists. The Earl of Mayo, a prominent Southern unionist who accepted the new Irish state with enthusiasm and served in the Irish senate, penned an open letter to Wilson refuting his suggestion that the South was in a state of chaos:

> This is not true and requires at my hand instant refutation.
> In the south and west the plough and the harrow are at
> work and the agriculturists, rich and poor, are taking every
> advantage of the fine and dry spring. The season of fox-
> hunting, hare-hunting and stag-hunting is drawing to a close
> – one of the best season's sport we have experienced in the
> south and west. Racing is being carried on in the south and
> west. I read of successful meetings of sportsmen and point-to-
> point races; in fact, high and low are taking their pleasure in
> a legitimate manner. History tells us that when a revolution

is ending there is always an aftermath of crime and disorder; but to state in the press that the twenty-six counties of the south and west of Ireland are reduced to a welter of chaos and murder is not correct. Let me say in conclusion that I also read in the Irish as well as the English press of bad work going on in Belfast. I would humbly suggest that with your great military knowledge this bad work should be dealt with at once and by yourself remembering the words in the New Testament. Physician heal thyself.[25]

The *Irish Independent* editorial of 20 March was devastating in its denunciation of Wilson. 'He is telling England what he would have her believe and telling exactly what one would expect him to tell in view of his record as a bigoted partisan who has long been on the side of Orange domination.' The most significant denunciation, however, came from Michael Collins. He penned a furious open letter to *The Times*, describing Wilson as a 'violent Orange partisan':

Anyone who would read this would fancy that a state of anarchic barbarity prevailed in the twenty-six counties while blissful happiness and peace reigned in the six Northern Counties. What are the actual facts? From the 11th February last to the 6th March, thirty-nine people were murdered in Belfast and those murders are continuing daily. Of those thirty-nine victims, twenty-two were Catholics and eleven Protestants. When it is remembered that in the city of Belfast there are 92,245 Catholics and 294,704 non-Catholics, that, in other, words, the Catholics are only 24.1 per cent of the entire population, this proportion of Catholic deaths is very high indeed. During the same period in all the rest of Ireland there were only seven violent deaths and none of them caused by sectarian motivations.[26]

Collins went on to criticise the Special Constabulary officers as 'open members of the Orange Society and fanatical partisans'. He added that the Special Powers Act with its provision for flogging was not intended as a means of restoring law and order, but to flog 'unfortunate nationalists and Catholics' to death.

Wilson attended the Northern cabinet meeting at the end of March and urged the executive to act impartially. According to Callwell, the private and the public Wilson were at odds at this time. 'In London he was a black Ulsterman and anti-papist. In Belfast he preached moderation.'[27]

Privately, Wilson despaired of the sectarian nature of the Specials, writing in his diary: 'The Specials are now all Protestants. The whole of this miserable affair will go straight not only into civil war, but into religious war. It is heart-breaking.' Callwell commented:

Wilson's dejected reference in his diary to the development of an untoward form of religious warfare in Ireland, which is quoted above, is highly significant. His lament was indeed most fully warranted by the condition of affairs that was growing more and more alarming as the tale of acts of violence mounted up. If the activities of Roman Catholics of pronounced Sinn Féin sympathies were at the root of the grave unrest that prevailed, those activities were being countered by uncompromising reprisals on the part of Orangemen [. . .] An impression, moreover, undoubtedly existed and this not only in Ireland as a whole, but also among those of the public in GB who interested themselves in Irish affairs that the Field Marshal himself was taking a far more prominent part in the carrying out of the executive functions of the North Ireland Government than was actually the case. He had urged the vital importance of effectual steps being taken to preserve law and order impartially in the six counties, but he was not responsible for the manner in which the constabulary performed their duties nor was he concerned in the executive measures that were actually being taken in hand by Sir J. Craig and his colleagues to address disorder and to stamp out crime.[28]

Whatever private reservations Wilson had about the nature of the sectarian violence in Northern Ireland, his public pronouncements continued to be partisan and did nothing for his reputation. In Oldham at the end of April, he compared Collins and de Valera to Bolsheviks, a risible comparison given the two men's innate social conservatism.[29] De Valera would have found the reference to him being a Bolshevik amusing, later admitting that 'every instinct of mine would indicate that I was meant to be a dyed-in-the-wool Tory, or even a bishop, rather than the leader of a revolution'. These sentiments were echoed by the first Minister for Justice, Kevin O'Higgins, who once observed: 'We are the most conservative-minded revolutionaries that ever put through a successful revolution.'

Wilson addressed the Liverpool Ulster Association at the end of May 1922, stating that the situation had got so bad that either Britain should 'come clean out and let Ireland rip or govern Ireland. If you come out and leave Ireland an enemy right across your trade route, then the British Empire is gone.'[30]

Tension along the border erupted into open warfare between British and Irish troops in late May and early June 1922 in the Pettigo–Belleek triangle, a portion of land along the shores of Lough Erne between Donegal in the Irish Free State and Fermanagh in Northern Ireland. Pettigo is mostly in Donegal, though parts of it are across the border in Fermanagh. It was predominantly a Protestant town, whereas Belleek is in County Fermanagh and was nationalist.

A mixed force of National Army and anti-Treaty volunteers occupied all of Pettigo and the village of Belleek in contravention of the Treaty. A group of Ulster Special Constables arrived by pleasure steamer, the *Lady of the Lake*, to take Belleek, but were driven back by about a hundred IRA men. Prisoners were taken on both sides and the inhabitants of both villages evacuated. In London, Collins was negotiating the terms of the Free State constitution with Churchill when news came through of the fighting. Craig demanded that the British intervene. Churchill was incensed and ordered the British army into the area with heavy artillery and a thousand men. It was overkill, but intentionally so. Churchill wanted to teach Collins the lesson that no Free State adventurism across the border would be tolerated.

On 4 June the British took Pettigo using howitzers to shell the Irish garrison guarding the bridge, which marked the boundary between the two jurisdictions. Three IRA volunteers manning a machine-gun nest were killed. The British occupied Pettigo until January 1923. The battle, the last time British and Irish armies faced off against each other, is largely forgotten now, but it caused profound angst on both sides of the border at the time.

Although Wilson had nothing to do with the use of British forces, he was blamed for it. The actions of the British army in invading and holding Free State territory was regarded as a provocation resulting from Wilson's talk of re-invasion. The *Freeman's Journal*, normally a moderate nationalist newspaper, did not hold back:

Sir Henry Wilson has scored even beyond his expectations and he can be relied upon to leave nothing undone to improve his advantage. Already he and his fellow conspirators are protesting that the mouthful bitten out of Free State territory is not nearly large enough and it may be taken for granted that they will employ their own methods of creating border incidents which will furnish excuses for a further advance. The object of the Orange fanatics is avowedly to create conditions in the disputed areas which will enable them to be effectively cleared and thus present the Boundary Commission with a fait accompli which will free the Northern Government from the necessity of backing its case by argument. Sir Henry Wilson and his fellow conspirators made no concealment of their purpose. Partition, they recognise, is impossible as a political device and the only hope of evading a working arrangement with the South is to secure the re-imposition of the Act of Union by a renewal of the Anglo-Irish War.[31]

In an interview with the *New York Herald* published on 11 June 1922, Collins blamed the clashes at Belleek and Pettigo on Wilson and his supporters:

> These unprovoked attacks by whomsoever ordered are carrying out directly the policy of Sir Henry Wilson and other prominent advisors of Sir James Craig. These men quite avowedly want to destroy the position created by the Treaty and want to pave the way through a boundary situation on the north-east border for the return of the British troops and thence the ultimate re-conquest of Ireland. The whole object of the Belfast Government and their advisors was to deflect world attention from the worse than Armenian atrocities that are of daily occurrence in Belfast and concentrate it on their border in the hope that a situation would arise such as may confront us any day now.[32]

The liberal-minded *Westminster Gazette* concurred: 'The danger has been greatly influenced by Field Marshal Sir Henry

Wilson's incendiary speeches and by the fact that a good many British officers are in sympathy with his desire to scrap the Treaty and carry out the re-conquest of Southern Ireland.'[33]

Six days before Wilson was shot, Collins accused him and Wilson's hand-picked henchman Major General Arthur Solly-Flood of 'bringing the mentality of the *Morning Post* which was the mentality of the British army and navy' to the North. Their goal, Collins believed, was to restore their ascendancy over all of Ireland and restore the Act of Union.

Wilson kept up his criticism of British public policy in Ireland until the end of his life. Armistice Day had been the greatest day in the history of the British Empire, when it had 'stood higher probably than it ever stood before. Every man, woman and child in the Empire was proud to belong to it.' Now look at it, he told readers of the unionist *Newsletter* in an article published on 19 June. 'One part of the Empire, of the United Kingdom, in fact has been surrendered to murderers and revolutionaries and there are other and greater parts of the Empire threatening to break away.'[34]

The coalition government had been engaged in a 'policy of surrender' in Ireland, he suggested. 'Ireland, as a direct result of the Government's surrender to murderers, is rapidly degenerating to the same condition of anarchy and economic ruin as Russia.' Two weeks before he died, the *Daily Mail* asked Wilson for a 'few plain words' about Ireland. Wilson responded:

> The situation in Ireland is indeed grave, but nothing to what it will be later if the present government is allowed to remain in power. No self-respecting citizen of the twenty-six counties will have further communications with the Imperial government except to dictate and impose terms. A little later and our Government will be alone and we shall have

gone back to 1798. What a tragedy! And all from ignorance, incompetence and various forms of cowardice. You ask for plain words to the Irish nation. Alas there is no Irish nation, nor has there ever been one and so there is no address to which one can post a few plain words.[35]

5

Reginald Dunne:
'The blood that's in them'

Reginald William 'Reggie' Dunne, also called Dunn, was old beyond his years. His intense personality, deep faith and intellectual sensibilities are apparent in the correspondence he left behind him. He had the worldview of an English Catholic intellectual, not an Irish revolutionary.

Dunne was extraordinarily well read by the standards of the time. He immersed himself in the lives of Cardinal (now St) John Henry Newman, the great English convert from Anglicanism to Catholicism, St Ignatius of Loyola, the founder of the Jesuit order, and Alphonsus Liguori, the founder of the Redemptorists. His Catholic faith helped him to endure the twin ordeals of the First World War and his incarceration after the Wilson shooting. He was thoughtful, unworldly, chaste, given to worrying about his weight, but not one for grumbling. 'I have never allowed myself to become what is known as "windy". Lack of cheerfulness is due largely to a lack of self-control,' he wrote to his mother while awaiting trial. 'I have slept through air-raids, shellfire and many other annoyances and the present circumstances do not tend to counteract that.'[1]

He appears to have had no interest in women, given his admission to his mother, 'You may know, mother, that my lips have never kissed any woman in love. You were always sufficient for me in spite of my queer ways.'[2] He would not fit the criminal profile of a man who might pull the trigger on the former head of the British army.

*

Dunne was born on 27 June 1898 in an army barracks in Woolwich, south-east London, where his father Robert was stationed.[3] He was an only child, born to a father who was forty-seven and a mother who was eleven years younger than her husband. Dunne's Irish ancestry on his father's side is uncertain. Robert Dunne claimed to be a descendant of a Lord Dunsander from County Galway, whose Protestant son had married a Catholic woman and was disinherited. In the 1930s Robert Dunne made a claim on the estate but found that there was a descendant closer to Dunsander still alive.[4] Reggie Dunne's mother, Mary Agnes Dunne, *née* Greenan, was born in London in 1872, her father having emigrated to London from County Monaghan in 1839. The couple married two years before their son was born. They were devoted to him and he to them.

Reggie Dunne and Joe O'Sullivan were part of the large Irish diaspora living in Great Britain. Due to the proximity of the two islands, there had always been population movement between Britain and Ireland, but mass migration to Britain did not begin until the Great Famine between 1845 and 1851. By 1861 more than 600,000, or 3 per cent of the population of England and Wales, were Irish-born. 'The Irish people who came to Britain during the half-century before 1871 were mainly reluctant immigrants, even more so than those who settled in America or Australasia,' the historian David Fitzpatrick has suggested.

> Many stayed in Britain just long enough to earn their
> wherewithal to ward off destitution or else to pay for
> their passage to the New World. For those who lingered,
> transience within Britain was encouraged by the virtual
> exclusion of Irish immigrants from secure employment and
> housing . . . Irishmen were concentrated in the most menial,
> casual and impermanent sectors of manual employment.[5]

In 1871 the Irish-born population of England and Wales was 566,540. The Irish percentage of the population declined in absolute and relative terms in every census after that. In 1871 2.49 per cent of the population, or one person in forty in England and Wales, was born in Ireland. By 1921 the numbers had dropped to 364,747 and just under 1 per cent of the population (0.96 per cent). Irish-born people were far more numerous in relative terms in Scotland, where the numbers peaked at 207,770 in 1871 (6.18 per cent of the population) but fell to 159,020 (3.26 per cent of the population) in 1921. Irish emigration to Scotland led to a great deal of sectarian tension and resentment from the host population.

In the twentieth century there was again mass migration from Ireland to Britain, especially after the Second World War, but prior to the First World War Britain was a destination for only a fifth of Irish emigrants (the United States accounted for 50 per cent). Between 1841 and 1921 the population of Ireland almost halved, from 8.2 million to 4.4 million.[6] This population drain, unprecedented in European history, created a huge Irish diaspora across the English-speaking world, and this diaspora, nursing current and historic grievances against Great Britain, amplified the case for an independent Ireland.

Many Irish-born emigrants were radicalised in London, most famously Michael Collins, who lived in the city from 1906 to 1916. The teenage Collins expressed a desire to 'live in the biggest city in the world' and, even for those from an Irish nationalist background, London was a place of opportunity for the ambitious. Collins was evidently an exceptionally bright student who, at the age of sixteen, became a clerk in the Post Office Savings Bank at Blythe House in west London. Afterwards he worked in a stockbrokers and then a bank, later putting his experience to good use as the chief organiser of the Dáil Loan, which funded the underground Irish government from 1919 to 1921. The Gaelic Athletic Association (GAA) was another organisation that provided a gateway for Collins to the Irish nationalist movement. It was set up in 1884 to foster the development of the uniquely Irish games of Gaelic football and hurling, and as a counterpart to the so-called 'foreign' or English games of soccer, rugby and cricket.

Through the GAA he met his great mentor Sam Maguire, who, it has been claimed, swore Collins into the Irish Republican Brotherhood (IRB), and also Liam MacCarthy, a London-born Irish nationalist. The most famous trophies in Ireland, the All-Ireland senior football championship and the All-Ireland senior hurling championship cups, are named the Sam Maguire Cup and Liam MacCarthy Cup respectively.

Collins spent nearly a third of his life in London, leaving in 1916 to fight in the Easter Rising and to avoid conscription in Britain. Though ostensibly equal citizens of the United Kingdom, nationality and religion made the Irish a people apart. Old stereotypes about the Irish being feckless, irresponsible and violent emerged during the Victorian era and persisted into the twentieth century. A school textbook written in 1911 by Rudyard Kipling and the Oxford academic C. R. L. Fletcher observed:

> So Ireland never went to school, and has been a spoilt child ever since; the most charming of children, indeed, full of beautiful laughter and tender tears, full of poetry and valour, but incapable of ruling herself, and impatient of all rule by all others.[7]

Collins felt the sting of anti-Irish sentiment in London, as he recorded in a Dáil debate in early 1922:

I know very well that the people of England had very little
regard for the people of Ireland, and that when you lived
among them you had to be defending yourself constantly from
insults. Every Irishman here who has lived amongst them
knows very well that the plain people of England are much
more objectionable towards us than the upper classes. Every
man who has lived amongst them knows that they are always
making jokes about Paddy and the pig, and that sort of thing.[8]

This perception bred a degree of insularity in the Irish community in London, as Collins recalled in an interview with the
American journalist Hayden Talbot:

I had Irish friends in London before I arrived, and in the
intervening years I had made many more friends among
Irishmen resident in London. For the most part we lived lives
apart. We chose to consider ourselves outposts of our nation.
We were a distinct community – a tiny eddy, if you like, in
the great metropolis. When wonder is expressed as it often is,
that I could have lived eight years in London, and still have
been so little known that 120,000 British troops and Black and
Tans could not find me in four years of hunting me in Ireland,
I can only attribute it to that policy of voluntary isolation we
all observed in London. And, after all, Michael Collins, junior
bank clerk, could hardly be expected to have attracted any
notice.[9]

Music brought Reggie Dunne into the Irish community in
London. Robert Dunne played the trumpet, his wife the piano
and young Reggie the violin. On his way home one night,
Reggie heard music and dancing come from the branch of the
Gaelic League near his home in Stamford Hill. A family friend,

Mary MacGeehin, gave a vivid account of his conversion to Irish nationalism:

> He became interested at once and went in. He was amazed
> to find a large crowd of people organised for the fostering of
> Irish culture, and he was immediately interested in the dancing
> and music and asked to be allowed to join the club. From that
> time onwards he never severed his connection with the Gaelic
> League. He or his family had known absolutely nothing of
> Ireland or the Irish language although Reggie spent some time
> in Dundalk, as his father was a bandmaster in the British Army
> all his life. He had retired a good while before 1916 and was
> at Reggie's death in receipt of a pension of £120, which the
> British continued to grant until his death.[10]

Dunne retained his love of traditional Irish music all his life. While awaiting execution, he requested that his fiddle should become a trophy to be competed for in the annual Gaelic League féis (festival). One of the test pieces was to be 'The Coolin', but his violin disappeared after his death. Dunne also had a highly developed knowledge of the classical music canon and, like many musicians, could mentally play music without need for instruments. In this way he whiled away his hours in Brixton Prison while awaiting trial for the murder of Wilson:

> I have just had a silent mental operatic concert and have
> enjoyed it thoroughly. The big idea is quite simple – just
> concentration on favourite arias, duets etc and imagining a
> rendering which accords with my taste. Nobody is disturbed
> and I am decidedly the better for it. I am reserving Wagner
> for a separate concert, but I've just been indulging in Verdi,
> Meyerbeer and Puccini, the last whom the critics are calling

vulgar, possibly because he is a millionaire. My father will doubtless understand the enjoyment I get from a mental concert. Let him come with me through the first movement of Schubert's *Unfinished Symphony*, starting off with that poignant, troubled, slow melody in the bass which is B natural. Schubert was indeed in the dumps when he wrote this. We pass on through the agitated string passage with its undercurrent melody until we come to that soothing passage from the cello which is never out of reach of my brain.[11]

In the late nineteenth and early twentieth centuries a cultural movement known as the Gaelic Revival would have a profound impact on the Irish at home and abroad, and Dunne would be among them. The Gaelic Revival sought to resurrect the Irish language, music, games and literature. The notion that a colonised people could rise up and take pride in their own identity presaged the political nationalism of the second decade of the twentieth century. The Gaelic League was a critical part of the Revival, and in the development of Irish-Ireland, a cultural and political movement succinctly described by Patrick Pearse, one of the leaders of the Easter Rising, as an Ireland 'not merely free but Gaelic as well'. The Gaelic League was established in 1893 by Eoin MacNeill, who also founded the Irish Volunteers, which became the IRA.

The League's first president was Douglas Hyde, a Protestant from County Roscommon, the neighbouring county to Wilson's. He was a relation by marriage of the French family, which included Sir John (later Lord) French, the Commander-in-Chief of the British Expeditionary Force at the start of the First World War, who was appointed Lord Lieutenant of Ireland in 1918.

Hyde, like Wilson, was home-schooled, but his education brought him closer to his neighbours, not more distant. He delighted in the idiomatic use of the Irish language among local people and became its most passionate and articulate advocate, the more so for coming from a class associated with all things English. He crystallised his thinking about the relationship between Ireland and England in an essay, 'The Necessity for De-Anglicising Ireland', delivered in November 1892 to the National Literary Society in Dublin. Hyde addressed the paradox of so many Irish people ostensibly claiming to hate the English but seeking to ape English culture. Irish people had 'ceased to be Irish without being English':

> It is a fact, and we must face it as a fact, that although they adopt English habits and copy England in every way, the great bulk of Irishmen and Irishwomen over the whole world are known to be filled with a dull, ever-abiding animosity against her, and – right or wrong – to grieve when she prospers and joy when she is hurt.[12]

It was not enough, Hyde stressed, to be anti-English; one must be pro-Irish, embracing the country's struggling native language and customs.

Like many in the League at the time, Hyde was fixated on bringing back a sense of national pride and interest in the Irish language. The Gaelic League was set up as an apolitical organisation, though it could be argued that its aims were inherently political as well as cultural. The movement espoused a series of dichotomies that would influence the thinking of Irish nationalists for generations afterwards. The British were degenerate and materialistic, the Irish pure at heart and non-materialistic; the British imperialistic, the Irish nationalistic; the British Protestant, the Irish Catholic.

The Gaelic League of London was formed in October 1896 in Southwark, south London, and at its peak in 1913 had 2,000 members. It was more than just an Irish-language organisation; it organised dance and musical entertainments and ceilidhs, and advocated a 'buy Irish' policy and cultural separation from the host population. Its separatist tendencies were advocated in the nationalist newspaper *An Claidheamh Soluis* (*Sword of Light*), edited at the time by Patrick Pearse. He declared in 1908, 'We can sing and dance and have fun without our English friends around us. It is not often we can escape from them – like the poor they are always with us.'[13] *An tÉireannach* (*The Irishman*), an Irish-language publication based in London, sought to emphasise that Irishness was a state of mind as much as it was a place of birth:

> One may be born in London, or Dublin, or Limerick and develop into as good a Gael as if one had been born in Cois Farraige [beside the sea]. It is a question of blood, brains, study, spirit and other things. The real Gaedhealtacht [Irish-language-speaking areas] like the Kingdom of Heaven is within. Everybody can be a Gael if he tries.[14]

Dunne and O'Sullivan embraced these exhortations. Despite being born and raised in England, they identified as Irishmen. Dunne went further, describing Britain, where he as well as his parents were born, as 'the enemy country'. In many ways it was not Ireland he and O'Sullivan loved, but the ideal of Ireland as represented by the Gaelic Revival. As David Fitzpatrick has pointed out:

> Romantic Ireland had particular appeal for better educated expatriates and their children, providing an attractive image of the Irish past which was not (as in Ireland) seen to be painfully at odds with the drab materialism of the Irish present.[15]

The Gaelic League in London was more than just a place to learn the Irish language. Dunne was not much interested in the Irish language, as many of his contemporaries observed, though he did sign his name in Gaeilge (Irish) as R Ua Duinn, ceann catha Óglaigh na hÉireann (Reginald Dunne, IRA commandant). It was the music and the dancing that attracted him, and the opportunity to meet like-minded people.

In the early years of the twentieth century the pursuit of Irish independence by violent means was embraced by only a fringe minority. Most Irish nationalists were fixated on the limited form of autonomy offered by home rule, which would see the Irish take care of internal affairs but remain part of the United Kingdom. Home rule clubs were also common in the Irish community in Britain.

The Irish Volunteers was founded in November 1913 as a nationalist counterweight to the UVF and to protect the promise of home rule. Companies were formed in several British cities in the first flush of enthusiasm that followed the Volunteers' foundation, but as the historian Peter Hart attests, they 'dwindled into nothingness' at the outbreak of the First World War.[16] The few men that remained true to the cause emigrated to Ireland when conscription was introduced in Britain – though not in Ireland – in February 1916. Approximately seventy of them participated in the Easter Rising and became known as the 'Kimmage garrison'.

Before he became a commandant in what he called the 'army of the (Irish) Republic', Reggie Dunne was a British soldier. When he joined the British army in September 1916 at the age of eighteen, he was following his father, who served in the 3rd Dragoon Guards and was for thirty years bandmaster of the regiment. Dunne senior retired from the army in 1905 at the age of fifty-three, on a pension of £123 5s 6d per annum, his discharge notes recalling 'exemplary' service and the award of six good-conduct badges.[17] The Dunnes' peripatetic lives, the lot of the British soldier, included a time in the Curragh Barracks in County Kildare when Reggie was a young child. In his final letter to his father, written before he was executed, Dunne recognised their common military bond. 'We two have been soldiers. You and I must not grouse when it comes to enduring discipline because we are good soldiers and Catholic Irishmen.'[18]

The Dunnes formerly lived at 24 Crookston Road, Eltham, but moved to 90 Lealand Road, a narrow street of Edwardian houses in Stamford Hill, as Reggie's school was nearby. This part of north London was countryside until the arrival of the railway in the 1870s and a tram system that enabled the suburbanisation of the area. A large immigrant population settled into what was then the outer fringes of London. The Jesuits, who would play a critical role in Reggie's life, moved into the area in 1892, and St Ignatius Church on Stamford Hill High Road was built between 1903 and 1911.[19]

Dunne attended the Jesuit primary school, followed by St Ignatius College, then attached to the church but now based in Enfield. The school was founded in 1894 with just forty-six pupils and four Jesuit priests. By 1907 it qualified for state funding, further evidence of the integration of Catholicism into mainstream life in the UK. Dunne attended between 1910 and 1915, an exemplar of the old Jesuit adage: 'Give me a child until the age of seven and I will give you the man.' In his final letter, Dunne named four Jesuit priests as among those to whom he wished to send his regards.[20]

One of Dunne's contemporaries at St Ignatius was the film director Alfred Hitchcock, who came from a Liverpool Irish family. Hitchcock's film version of Sean O'Casey's *Juno and the Paycock* was produced in 1930. It was an early talkie and cleaved heavily to the stage play. According to Hitchcock's biographer Patrick

McGilligan, the story of Dunne's radicalisation and execution had a profound effect on the director's work. Many of Hitchcock's films revolve around sabotage, espionage or assassination. His villains in these stories tended to be ideological fanatics turned traitors or terrorists. McGilligan believes the portrayals of Johnny Boyle in *Juno and the Paycock* and Abbott, played by Peter Lorre, in *The Man Who Knew Too Much* were influenced by Dunne's life and death.

For the director it was his first opportunity to explore how politics has corrupted history. His characters tended to be ideological fanatics turned traitors or terrorists. Just as Hitchcock had a specific real-life case that haunted him when dealing with marital murders (to paraphrase George Orwell), the director's political films were shadowed by the true story of Reggie Dunn [*sic*].* Dunn was no 'wrong man', he was a resolute killer and another notorious criminal the director knew firsthand. During his time at St Ignatius, Dunn had been one of the most popular, athletic boys at the school. After World War One, however, Dunn grew embittered about the policy of the British Government towards Ireland. He joined the IRA and volunteered to become an assassin. He and an IRA comrade shot down the former Chief of the Imperial General Staff, Field Marshal Sir Henry Wilson, in London in 1922 – the same year Edith Thompson was alleged to have plotted her husband's murder. Like Thompson, Dunn was caught and executed (unlike her, he proudly admitted his guilt). The character of Johnny would be a stand-in for Dunn and *Juno and the Paycock* would be the first Hitchcock

---

* The name Dunne derives from the Gaelic word '*donn*', which means brown. Reggie was known in his lifetime as either Dunne or Dunn. For the purposes of continuity I will use the more common and modern form of the name – Dunne.

film to establish the theme that he carried over to later work – of ideological extremism as a spreading stain that distorts idealism and destroys innocents. This was also O'Casey's theme and so the director (half Irish, after all, and his own mother a Juno of the Hitchcocks) felt completely in sync with the play – if not the playwright.[21]

Recalling his own school days, Hitchcock spoke about a lingering sense of religiosity that permeated his upbringing. 'I was born a Catholic, I went to a Catholic school and I now have a conscience with lots of trials over belief.' Catholic schools in England have traditionally been the preserve of the recusants (old English Catholic families who did not convert to Protestantism) and immigrants, usually Irish.

St Ignatius College was a progressive, liberal-minded school with a broad curriculum encompassing Latin as a mandatory subject, rote learning of English, the classics and science. Above all, boys were taught to be observant Catholics. Daily Mass was offered, and those who showed an inclination towards a religious vocation were sent to a Jesuit seminary. Supporters of Dunne and O'Sullivan stressed their religious faith as a counterpoint to the public view that they were common murderers.

The prolific use of the cane was recalled by another famous alumnus of the school, Cardinal John Heenan, though he qualified that by stating 'stupid boys in those days were beaten in every type of school almost as a matter of routine'.[22] Dunne appears to have been an impressive pupil, winning a gold medal in his final year for English essay-writing, a medal that his mother kept after his death.

The Easter Rising in 1916 had a radicalising effect on Dunne, as it did on many Irish nationalists. The Rising during Easter week was the first armed rebellion against British rule since the Fenian rebellion of 1867. The rebels, approximately 1,200 in all, occupied many buildings in Dublin. They held out for six days, by which time much of the centre of Dublin had been reduced to ruins, and 485 people were killed, the majority of them civilians. The rebellion was not initially popular, but the execution of its leaders, sixteen in all, enraged the Irish public and inclined them towards complete separation from Britain.

Dunne was particularly exercised by the actions of Captain John Bowen-Colthurst, a deranged British officer from County Cork who ordered the summary execution during the Rising of the pacifist Francis Sheehy-Skeffington and two journalists, Thomas Dickson and Patrick McIntyre, none of whom had anything to do with the Rising. Bowen-Colthurst, whom Dunne would later plot to kill, was declared insane and later emigrated to Canada. Yet just five months after the Easter Rising, in June 1916, Dunne joined the Irish Guards, a few weeks before his eighteenth birthday in order that he should not be conscripted.[23]

The Irish Guards regiment was founded in 1900 by a grateful Queen Victoria in recognition of the gallantry of Irish regiments in the Second Boer War. It mainly recruited from Ireland and from those of Irish ancestry in Britain. The regiment had a minimum height requirement of 5ft 9in, height indicating better nutrition in the early part of the twentieth century. It was then – and remains – an elite regiment within the British army and survived the cull of Irish regiments in 1922. The current Duke of Cambridge, Prince William, the honorary colonel of the regiment, was married in its uniform.

The records of those who served in the Irish Guards during the First World War survived the bombing in 1940 of the War Office repository in Arnside Street, London, which destroyed the records of millions of British servicemen in that war. The copy of the Irish Guards' records was kept in Wellington Barracks in central London and was transferred in recent years to the Army Personnel Centre in Glasgow. Dunne's record, however, does not survive. His medal index card states in red ink that his file was destroyed on 31 October 1930.[24] By whom? It does not say. His medals were destroyed five years after the war ended as they were never collected. One of Dunne's last requests was that all trace of his involvement with the British army in the war be destroyed. Could it be that the record-keepers in Wellington Barracks wanted to remove all evidence of Dunne's records, given his notoriety at the time, or did they accede to Dunne's last request and destroy them?

According to Robert Dunne, his son served with the 1st Battalion of the Irish Guards and was wounded during the German Spring Offensive of March 1918. The regimental historian Rudyard Kipling – his son John was killed serving with the 1st Irish Guards in 1915 – recounted that the battalion faced a tense time 'waiting for a certain blow to be dealt with at a certain time'.[25]

The offensive began on 21 March. The Germans broke through the British and French lines, and their rapid progress caused panic among the British. The Irish Guards battalion retreated six miles south of Arras, where they had been billeted. Rumours reached the camp that the battlegrounds of the Somme, won for the Allies with such a grotesque expenditure of human lives, were taken in a couple of days. There followed a lull as the breathless German advance outpaced its supply lines, but the attack was renewed on 30 March. A relentless barrage of all calibre of German guns fell on the Irish frontlines. The attack lasted almost two hours, and forty-two men were injured, among them, presumably, Reginald Dunne.

Dunne was wounded in the knee at Arras and sent to Erskine Hospital, a dedicated facility in Glasgow for war veterans, from where he was invalided out on 15 July 1918.[26] He had reached the rank of corporal. 'Dunne bore a very good character in the army,' Metropolitan Police inspector Albert Burton noted in the file on Dunne and O'Sullivan, adding, 'He was underage when he joined voluntarily,' although this is unlikely to be correct as eighteen was the minimum age for enlistment. The two men's war service and their lack of a criminal record were both cited in their defence at their trial.

The shell that shattered Dunne's knee bone left him with restricted mobility. Those who knew him afterwards testified that he occasionally walked with a limp and carried a cane. He had a pension until 1920, so he probably regained mobility. In prison he noted that the pain had come back, meaning that it had dissipated at one stage.

His father would appear to suggest that he suffered from post-traumatic stress disorder as a result of the war. 'He has very fine feelings and he has seemed queer from the injuries he received in France,' he told Chief Inspector William Brown of Scotland Yard just four days after the Wilson shooting.

Reggie Dunne passed the Oxford local examination and went on to train as a teacher at Brook Green College in Hammersmith. The college, which changed its name to St Mary's and relocated to the pastoral setting of Strawberry Hill in south London in 1925, was founded in 1896 to produce teachers for the growing Catholic population in Britain. By the time Dunne joined in September 1918 it had more than a hundred teachers on its books and was run by the Vincentian order.

His father noticed Reggie's mental deterioration in the three years he spent at the college, before he left in June 1921. 'My son

12 Snapshot of Reggie (left) with three friends at St Mary's College,
Hammersmith, 1920. All were in the IRA

was at the college for three years. During the first two years my
son's nerves were so bad that he used to come home every weekend and sometimes during the week and sleep at home.'

There seems to have been an IRA cell in the college. The photograph above shows him with Lieutenant Séan Phelan, who was
later killed in the disastrous IRA Upton train ambush in February
1921, Volunteer J. O'Sullivan (not Joe O'Sullivan) from Killorglin,
County Kerry, and Volunteer Tom Monaghan, who served in the
Irish Guards with Dunne during the war. Dunne never qualified
as a teacher.[27]

After the Easter Rising thousands of Sinn Féiners, as they were
called, were arrested and sent to prisons in Ireland and Britain.
In March 1918 British proposals to introduce conscription into
Ireland gave a fillip to the separatist cause and rejuvenated the
Irish Volunteers following the reversals of the Easter Rising and
its aftermath. The end of the First World War and Sinn Féin's
resounding victory in the December 1918 British general election created a new dynamic for Irish nationalism. The unilateral

declaration of an independent Irish state on 21 January 1919 hastened a military conflict between Britain and Irish separatists.

In 1919 the Irish Volunteers was reorganised into the army that became known from August of that year as the Irish Republican Army. Eventually Irish Volunteers/IRA companies were formed in Birmingham, Liverpool, Newcastle, Manchester, Sheffield, Glasgow, Edinburgh and London. The historian Peter Hart estimates there were perhaps a thousand volunteers in Britain of varying levels of commitment and ability who served during the War of Independence. Their numbers were small, but their importance to the campaign for Irish independence has only recently been acknowledged.[28]

Dunne's journey from British army veteran to active Irish republican began as he convalesced from his war wounds. He joined the IRA in September 1919 in Arthur 'Art' O'Brien's offices at 3 Adam Street, off the Strand in London. O'Brien was described as the 'God of our little world' in London. He was an unlikely ardent Irish nationalist. His father came from County Cork but was a British army officer; his mother was English and from a prosperous music publishing family. O'Brien began adult life as an electrical engineer and joined the Gaelic League at the relatively late age of twenty-seven. A disappointed bachelor with much time on his hands, he devoted the rest of his life to the promulgation of Irish freedom, often to the detriment of his financial and personal reputation. In 1919 he was appointed as the first envoy of the Irish Republic to Britain, an unofficial role for an unofficial state. O'Brien had been sworn in to the Irish Republican Brotherhood, a secret oath-bound organisation set up in 1858 to overthrow British rule in Ireland by force if necessary. A secret cell within the IRB, a 'minority of a minority' as they were described, staged the Easter Rising in defiance of the leadership of the organisation, who were not informed in advance about it. The IRB was organised into 'circles' – semi-autonomous groups of up to a dozen individuals that operated independently of each other to lessen the prospect of infiltration by spies.

At that meeting in O'Brien's offices were Sam Maguire, the Cork-born Protestant who was head of intelligence in London and worked in the central sorting office of the London post office at Mount Pleasant in Clerkenwell, along with the London-born brothers Denis and J. J. Carr, two British army veterans turned IRA volunteers.

According to Denis Carr, Dunne was not enrolled in the IRB at the meeting but remained outside the room while the meeting was going on to receive his instructions afterwards. Dunne was unanimously chosen as the officer commanding (O/C) of London operations, given the rank of commandant (the equivalent of major) in the IRA and then sworn in to the IRB. In a guerrilla army like the IRA, ranks were given by consent.[29] Dunne's status as a British war veteran would have been no bar to leadership in the IRA. His military experience and evident seriousness were invaluable to an organisation where few had any formal training or understanding of military discipline.

Maguire, as the head of the IRB in London and a close friend of Michael Collins, gave instructions to Dunne as head of the IRA in London. There was much overlap in membership between the IRA and the IRB, but critically the IRA was an open organisation that did not try to conceal its activities from the public, while the IRB operated in secret. These distinctions caused a great deal of animosity in republican circles among those who believed there was no place for a secret society in a movement openly trying to overthrow British rule in Ireland. They are also crucial to our understanding of the Wilson assassination.

Initially, a single company of the IRA was founded in London and then as men joined it became four companies, A, B, C and D, divided into quadrants in north, south, east and west London. Men were drilled in Blackfriars Road and at a hall in Underwood Street, Whitechapel. Along with being O/C for London, Dunne had direct command of the men in south London. The IRA in London consisted initially of 120 men, rising to 200 in 1920, a small number relative to those in service at home, but its effectiveness was disproportionate to its size.[30]

From the 1860s, Irish republicans had pondered the usefulness of acts of violence and sabotage, concluding that nothing brought home to the British public the gravity of the Irish situation as much as acts of violence on British streets. This was particularly true of London. The nexus of political, military and media centres in London made it a prime target for attention-seeking acts that garnered much publicity but caused little in the way of damage or loss of life. In the 1880s the Fenian movement carried out bombing attacks in London over a four-year period. The campaign was led by Irish-Americans but garnered little support among the Irish in Britain. One civilian and three bombers were killed. It was not a success and alienated public opinion in Britain.

Dunne was, according to Mary MacGeehin, a 'born leader and both boys and girls would have done anything for him and were very loyal to him and very fond of him. He was not a bit conceited and at the meetings on Monday nights avoided attracting any special attention. I cannot remember any special incident in which he was concerned.'[31]

Dunne's first engagement as commanding officer was organising the Irish Volunteers to protect Irish demonstrators outside Wormwood Scrubs prison in Hammersmith, west London, in the spring of 1920. When 217 republican prisoners in Ireland

went on hunger strike because they had been sentenced without trial, the British moved them to London out of fear that
their hunger strike would become a focal point for attention in
Ireland.[32]

The newly formed Irish Self-Determination League (ISDL),
set up in 1919 to lobby British civil society for the cause of Irish
independence, mobilised the Irish community in support of the
prisoners. Within days thousands gathered outside the prison.
They waved tricolours and carried banners as the republican
prisoners watched from the windows. Exhorted by Irish priests,
they said the Rosary and sang patriotic songs. The gatherings also
attracted a hostile crowd of anti-Irish agitators. The police too
turned against the Irish demonstrators and beat them off.

Dunne was there every day. He was armed, but wisely baulked
at the idea of using his concealed pistol. Stones and bricks were
thrown, and Dunne was hit over the head with a piece of iron.
Frequent melees ensued between local people, incensed at what
they saw as the veneration of terrorists, and the protesters. Some
agitators simply turned up in search of a ruckus. Frank Lee, a
London-born piano player who would become one of Dunne's
greatest posthumous defenders, recalled 'warding off gangs of ruf-
fians who were attacking our people'. Lee blamed 'the criminal
hooligan element which was being imported in increasing numbers every evening'.[33] Even though the IRA men wore steel helmets, Dunne received an injury to one of his eyes.

The violence got so bad that the ISDL feared somebody would
be killed and called the protests off in May 1920. The prisoners were then released, but English nurses would not treat them,
so the women of Cumann na mBan (the Women's Council) did
so instead. Cumann na mBan was the female auxiliary of the
IRA and a significant organisation in its own right. It played a

prominent part in the Irish revolution and had a role in Dunne and O'Sullivan's decision to shoot Wilson.

The Wormwood Scrubs demonstrations were a useful rallying cry for the IRA in a city whose size was overwhelming. With only rudimentary communications and a small group of committed volunteers, the IRA in London could not congregate in numbers and had to watch their step constantly. Men lived in digs, and at the time very few people had access to a telephone. Sometimes they did not turn up at the appointed time, got lost or were otherwise delayed. Many found it difficult to hold down a full-time job and be an IRA volunteer. There was the persistent fear of being captured in enemy territory. 'You have to be careful in London. I would never leave anything in my pockets at night,' William 'Billy' Ahern recalled. Cork-born Ahern moved to London in 1918 to work and joined the IRA in the city:

> We had to be careful about every little detail, meetings, friends for communications purposes. Every man worked as an individual and we never discussed any business with each other unless it definitely concerned the job we were doing.[34]

Ahern got a job in Knightsbridge Barracks but failed in his attempt to poison the Household Cavalry horses in advance of the state opening of Parliament, one of many madcap schemes tried by the IRA.

The IRA in Britain was initially formed to remedy the urgent need for weapons in Ireland. Volunteers in Ireland had only a few thousand Mausers, German cast-offs captured from the Russians in the First World War. Irish republicans raided the big houses and barracks at home, purloining shotguns and revolvers from gun safes and lofts, including an old shotgun they took from Henry Wilson's brother Jemmy, but they also needed high-velocity rifles such as the Lee-Enfield .303, the standard-issue British army rifle of the First World War that could cut a man in two from a distance of one mile. They also needed ammunition, revolvers, explosives, detonators and machine guns. The post-war world was replete with a surfeit of munitions and grudges, both personal and ethnic, yet getting arms to Ireland under the noses of the Royal Navy was always difficult.

The Carr brothers were the prime movers in the supply of weapons. Their father, a successful road contractor from County Tipperary, was a member of the IRB and encouraged their interest in Irish affairs. They began by sourcing small amounts of weapons from ex-servicemen, but nothing that satisfied demand in Ireland. Then, with finance from the IRA in Dublin, they extended their net into the London and Birmingham underworld. They negotiated with the Titanic gang of Hoxton, a gang mixed up in drug smuggling and illegal bookmaking; the Sabinis of Clerkenwell, a gang of Italian origin; and – shades of the BBC hit series *Peaky Blinders* – the 'Birmingham mob'.

Through these Denis Carr was able to make contact with a major arms dealer in Hackney and purchase a vast supply of ammunition and weapons, from revolvers to machine guns. The Carrs set up seven dumps across London. The locus of this clandestine operation was a house at 1 Morteyne Road in Tottenham, lived in by Agnes Browne, the sister of Joe Good, who had been involved in the plans to kill members of the British cabinet during the conscription crisis of 1918.

The house in Tottenham was used as an arms dump from early 1919. The IRA also used the Good's family home in Chelsea. Agnes Browne transported guns between her house and the family's home, and made dozens of trips to the London docks, sometimes carrying revolvers in shopping bags overlaid by vegetables.

Browne's husband, Martin Browne, who was also involved in clandestine activities, was transferred to Belfast in July 1921, just as the War of Independence ended in the Truce. There was so much weaponry in the house that a horse-drawn cart had to be commandeered to remove the arms. Billy Ahern was another who sourced guns from two Jewish dealers, one called Fingers, the other a gunsmith in Hackney Road 'who sold us any amount of stuff, Webleys and any amount of .303 and .45 ammunition'.[35]

In 1888 the sociologist Beatrice Webb noted that 'Paddy enjoys more than his proportional share of dock work with its privileges and miseries. He is to be found especially among the irregular hands as a result there.'[36] Getting the guns to Ireland tested the ingenuity of the IRA in London, but the preponderance of dockers of Irish extraction, as Webb noted, helped greatly. Friendly stevedores and ships' crews were sworn in to the IRA by an Oblates priest based in London. The Rev. Joseph O'Gorman was parish priest of the Church of the English Martyrs in Prescot Street, Whitechapel, and he allowed his presbytery to be used as an arms dump.

Twice a week, guns and ammunition were loaded on board B&I (British and Irish) vessels plying their trade between London and Dublin. One consignment consisted of fifty .303 Lee-Enfield rifles and three sacks of small arms and ammunition. Sympathetic sailors carried weapons in their kitbags while reporting for duty. The Carr brothers set up a picture-frame shop in the Docklands as a front to dump and collect arms. Such was their success that IRA brigades in Ireland sent across men to buy guns from the same sources, but these men were betrayed by their Irish accents. Denis Carr said he and his brother got away with it because of their English accents, but those coming from Ireland were 'naturally marked down as Irishmen and, given a free hand, would have seriously impeded and jeopardised our organisation'. They were intercepted by Sam Maguire and Dunne, who organised their return to Ireland. Dunne was front and centre of these gun-running operations.[37,38]

Martin Walsh joined the IRA in September 1919. He was a checker on the Surrey Commercial Docks in London and his home was in close proximity to the docks:

> After attending some drills, I was approached by Comdt Reg Dunne who requested me to get in touch with the Brothers Carr for the purposes of helping them in their work of handling munitions for HQ supplies. Usually, two boats were loaded weekly. This work continued throughout this entire period.[39]

IRA activity increased with the arrival of Rory O'Connor as O/C Britain in August 1920 with the intention of taking the war to the British in Britain. O'Connor was the IRA director of engineering and, like Dunne, a Jesuit boy, having attended Clongowes Wood College in County Kildare, known as the Eton of Ireland. His plans were ambitious. In September he called a summit of all the IRA commanders in Britain, including Dunne. They were to target the Liverpool docks, a power station in Manchester and timber yards in London and Manchester. The plan was to create maximum damage with minimum loss of life and therefore bring home to people in Britain what was being done in their name in Ireland by the Black and Tans and the Auxiliaries.

These plans for the IRA in Britain were captured and publicised by the authorities, giving the inadvertent impression that the IRA was a more sinister and omnipotent organisation than it actually was. The plans were hair-raising in their ambition and scope. Six men were detailed to hold up workers in the Stuart Street power station in Manchester, which powered the tramway system and the coal mines in the vicinity. They intended to destroy the building or engine room and the turbines. Another sixty-five men were to target the pumping stations at Clayton Vale. The crank would be stuffed with 50 lbs of gun cotton.[40] Fortunately for the people of Manchester, the attack never came off.

A document was seized detailing IRA plans to use germ warfare against British soldiers based in Dublin by introducing typhoid fever bacteria into their milk supply. Similarly, republicans intended to poison British army horses by introducing a horse with the highly infectious disease glanders into their stables. These threats were deemed so outlandish as to be dismissed as British propaganda even in Britain. The boys had cried wolf too often. The document, in this case, was real. It was put forward by a Sinn Féin TD (member of Dáil Éireann) and medical doctor, Dr Pat McCartan, in a memo to Michael Collins in which he advocated growing bacterial cultures in a laboratory. 'I know of no ordinary disease that would be spread among them [British troops] with safety to the rest of the population,' he wrote. McCartan's proposal never went any further.[41]

The Sinn Féin typhoid plot was mentioned on the floor of the House of Commons by Sir Hamar Greenwood, the excitable Chief Secretary for Ireland, on 18 November 1920, but the furore quickly dissipated because of the events of Bloody Sunday two days later, when thirty-one people, including fourteen British agents, were killed.

On the night of 27 November the IRA in London sought to burn a timber yard in Clerkenwell, but was thwarted at the last minute. The following day coincided with the largest ambush of the War of Independence at Kilmichael in west Cork, in which eighteen Auxiliaries and three IRA men were killed. That night the IRA in England struck the Liverpool docks, burning twenty-three buildings and causing thousands of pounds' worth of damage. The attack garnered huge publicity for the IRA, and given that the police had boasted of thwarting previous efforts it was a great embarrassment for them.

Michael Collins understood the importance of successful operations being carried out in the capital of the Empire, and Rory O'Connor had big plans for London. He sought to purchase a lorry, pack it with a tonne of explosives and gas cylinders and detonate it outside the Houses of Parliament. He also planned to send men into the London Underground tunnels beneath the Thames and blow them up, paralysing public transport in the city. Some of his schemes were reasonable, others amounted to suicide missions. Billy Ahern recalled, 'Michael Collins was more for the publicity which our undertakings used to cultivate, but Rory O'Connor was more for the spectaculars and he did not care about human life.'[42] Other London-based volunteers doubted O'Connor's sanity.

In November 1920 barriers were erected across Downing Street to keep the expected crowds back during the unveiling of the Cenotaph in Whitehall, but they were retained afterwards because of the fear of republican attacks – a psychological victory as far as the IRA in Britain were concerned.

Life for those in the organisation in London was difficult. London-born recruits were often regarded with suspicion and hostility by their own families, who wanted nothing to do with a campaign for Irish independence that was of little interest to the average Briton. Irishmen in the London IRA were also treated as suspicious by the host population. Four IRA volunteers were arrested after one of them, Seamus Moran, returned from the burning of a timber yard and oil works wearing soiled clothes. His wary landlady contacted the police, and Moran and three others were jailed for ten years. The IRA burned the landlady's home to the ground in retaliation.[43]

Hayricks were a popular target for the IRA in Britain, and London volunteers began burning them in March 1920. They were easy, undefended targets, and the visual impact could be seen from miles around. In the north of England the IRA co-ordinated attacks on hayricks to create an impressive spectacle. The simultaneous burning of dozens of them in Cheshire made headline news in national newspapers, as Collins hoped it would.[44]

In February 1921 IRA volunteers in Manchester were caught trying to burn down Manchester United's Old Trafford stadium, and in April an IRA volunteer, Seán Morgan, was shot dead during a raid on the Erskine Street Irish club in Hulme, which police suspected was being used as a front for the IRA.[45] The burning of the main stand at Manchester City's then ground, Hyde Road, in November 1920 was blamed on a discarded cigarette, but newly released files from the Military Service Pensions Collection (MSPC) in 2019 reveal that it was carried out by six IRA volunteers as revenge for the death of Terence MacSwiney on hunger strike. 'It was not a raid. It was propaganda,' stated Thomas Morgan, one of those involved in the arson attack.[46]

When Manchester became too hot for the IRA, IRA officer William O'Keeffe fled to London. He was introduced to Dunne on his second day there. He remembers him as a 'tall stern-faced man who, I would say, was in his thirties. He carried a stick and walked with a limp from a wound received in the 1914–1918 war. I regret to say that was the only time I ever came into contact with Reginald Dunne, and if there were any meetings held we were not invited to them. We came to the conclusion that the London organisation was not equal to that which existed in Manchester.'[47]

The London IRA went on the offensive again in February 1921. Two farms on the outskirts of the city, one near Croydon and another near West Molesey, were burned in retaliation for the destruction of civilian property in Ireland. Over £3,000 worth of produce was destroyed. This was accompanied by similar attacks in Lancashire, with factories and mills burned, followed by more farms. The raids spread fear and panic in England, prompting Greenwood to warn the House of Commons that the 'Sinn Féin conspiracy has spread to England and I urge the House to remember that it will spread further'.[48] This was prescient, as a massive arson campaign took place during the following months in major British cities, with twenty attacks in March 1921, thirteen in April, ten in May and fifty-one in June.[49]

Beginning on 14 May 1921 the IRA in London and St Albans carried out attacks on the homes of British officers recruited to serve in Ireland (known as Auxiliaries). Five officers were shot and their houses burned, but fortunately nobody was killed. 'We were instructed, of course, not to kill,' Denis Kelleher remembered. Kelleher was another Cork-born IRA volunteer in London. He was from Macroom and had moved to London at the age of sixteen. By day he worked as a civil servant at the Board of Education, at night he sought to undermine the British state by acts of arson, destruction and gun smuggling.

In June IRA volunteers in London set fire to signal boxes in Barnes, Barking, Tilbury and Southend. A signalman was bound and gagged and the signal box burned along a stretch of line between Wood Green and Bowes Park. Telegraph poles became a favourite target of the IRA in Britain as they were isolated and easy to cut down, guaranteeing a huge amount of disruption. Hundreds were felled by the IRA on 15 June.[50]

The last major act of the London IRA during the War of Independence was an attempt to blow up the Ministry of Pensions building in Regent's Park. From then until the Truce of 11 July 1921 the IRA in London carried out sporadic acts of violence that made an impact in the newspapers but caused little in the way of damage or injury.

Many in the IRA, Dunne among them, believed the Truce that had been called between the British and the IRA would not last and hostilities would soon resume. In July 1921 an IRA bomb factory in Greenwich blew up and killed Tom McInerney, a volunteer who was working on explosives at the time.

Rory O'Connor toured English cities in September 1921 and found just 106 volunteers in London willing to carry on the fight. One of them, though, was Dunne, who told O'Connor that the 'number of intended operations is greatly increasing'. Later, Dunne wrote to him under the heading 'renewal of war'. This rare and valuable insight into Dunne's leadership qualities as a soldier, in which he emphasises 'strict discipline, secrecy, cheerful obedience to orders and punctuality', reveals his thinly veiled irritation at the perceived different treatment of volunteers in Britain:

> The army of the Republic whether in Dublin, Cork or London are equal in the eyes of the General Staff. They are all working towards the same end. Courage, fidelity and fearlessness alone will command special recognition. Men born in England whose parents reside there have more to lose than others and their devotion to the Republic is recognised and appreciated by the chief of staff. The army in Ireland may be relied on to defend the Republic as in the past. Their sacrifices and those of the women and children will be materially lightened if pressure be brought to bear on

the enemy in his own country. So, is there any chance of you returning here? The last time you met my officers they were not exactly prepared to give details of possible operations without reports in hand. They would be now in a somewhat better position. The number of intended operations is greatly increasing. In the event of a renewal of war I would like if possible some sort of address to be sent over which could be read to the rank and file. Your last visit had a splendid effect on NCOs. If you or the CS [chief of staff] could find time for some military exhortation to put on paper, a very useful purpose would be served. It could officially deal with difficulties which constantly crop up in spite of all efforts on my part. In an outpost such as London, there are men from all parts of Ireland. The men from each county hang together like freemasons. They think that the men of their city or county have won the war. Kerry men imagine they are the salt of the earth and so on. There is moreover a certain amount of scorn for men born over here. Some of these latter class have very little to interest them materially in our cause. They have everything to lose, on the other hand, and in many cases their own parents are against them. These men are fighting because of the blood that's in them. Many of them are sensitive about their London accents and manners. It would console them greatly if GHQ endorsed my views on this matter. I should not be surprised if this difficulty were to exist in other areas. A written address, something after the manner of the usual *An t-Óglách* front page then would be most welcome here.[51]

O'Connor passed on the note to General Richard Mulcahy, the IRA chief of staff in Dublin, whose cool and distant response said a lot about his indifference to the IRA in London. 'I would try my hand in the matter that you suggest, but it is very difficult to know what to say in the case of men about whom one knows absolutely nothing. I would be glad if you would suggest a few heads to go on.'[52]

The Truce of 1921 left many of the IRA volunteers at a loose end. Some had lost their jobs over their activities and were now penniless and restless. Having sacrificed so much, they were left with nothing. Dunne was incensed on their behalf and demanded a share of the proceeds of Irish fundraising events in London, as Sorcha McDermott remembered: 'I knew Reggie Dunne slightly. He praised the work I did but did not like me personally because on some occasions I refused to take his orders. On one occasion we held a ceili and he instructed me to hand over the money to him for the Volunteers and I refused.'[53]

Dunne also fell out with Art O'Brien over money and the status of IRA volunteers. O'Brien could be bumptious and did not like his authority being questioned. He was not enamoured of Dunne nor his efforts to make the London IRA a more credible force. O'Brien dismissed him as 'a young fellow with such muddled notions' and the London IRA as akin to a 'Gilbert and Sullivan opera'.[54]

The Treaty left Dunne in a tricky position. On the one hand was his loyalty to Michael Collins; on the other, most of London's republicans had rejected it, regarding it as less than the measure of Irish sovereignty that they had tried to achieve. So he tried to play for time, as he was desperate to keep the organisation together in London. Unlike in Ireland, where the majority of the people supported the Treaty, there was no one in London to lessen the anxiety of those like O'Brien who believed it was a sell-out. As we will see, Dunne, while O/C London, was fully involved in plans to assassinate members of the British cabinet and senior members of the security establishment, including Wilson.

After the signing of the Anglo-Irish Treaty, the barriers across Downing Street were lifted and the security detail surrounding ministers stood down. Most assumed the war between Britain and Ireland was over, but Dunne had other ideas.

6

Joseph O'Sullivan:
An Old Fenian Family

The town of Bantry in west Cork is blessed by geography and cursed by history. It lies in the bay created by the Beara and Sheep's Head peninsulas, which jut out like two wrinkled fingers into the Atlantic. These promontories have provided a landmark for centuries of sea travellers. Bantry Bay is deep, sheltered and protected from the Atlantic's most capricious ways by the presence of Whiddy Island, which provides a welcome windbreak. The seas around Bantry are rich with cod, mackerel and hake, and shipping and fishing have made and broken Bantry's fortunes over the centuries.

Bantry Bay is a key part of the tragic tapestry of Irish history. The longest and bloodiest conflict between the English and Irish was the Nine Years' War (1593–1602), the last stand by Gaelic chieftains against the encroaching power of Tudor England. The decisive engagement was the Battle of Kinsale in west Cork in late 1601 and early 1602, in which the English defeated a combined Irish and Spanish force and the northern chieftains retreated back to their own lands.

Despite the setback, Donal 'Cam' O'Sullivan, known as O'Sullivan Beara, held out against the encroachment of the English into his territory. O'Sullivan Beara's sept (or kingdom) consisted of the three peninsulas – the Beara, Sheep's Head and Mizen Head peninsulas – which mark the extremities of west Cork centred on Bantry. English soldiers laid siege to his castle and slaughtered its defenders. They also slaughtered three hundred of his tenants sheltered on Dursey Island and threw them off cliffs into the sea. On New Year's Eve 1602, O'Sullivan Beara led what remained of his supporters, four hundred men and six hundred women and children, on a long trek hoping to meet up with his fellow Gaelic chieftains further north, who were continuing to fight the English. Travelling in the depths of winter and consistently harassed by enemies, there were just thirty-five survivors by the time they reached County Leitrim sixteen days later.

In March 1689 a French fleet sailed into Bantry Bay with seven thousand soldiers, arms, ammunition and money for the Catholic King James II in his war with the Protestant William of Orange, only for most of them to return home in 1691, defeated and much diminished.

In 1796 Napoleon sent an invasion fleet to Ireland at the behest of the Society of United Irishmen, a society composed of Catholic, Protestant and Dissenter (Presbyterian) rebels opposed to British rule in Ireland. Inspired by the American and French revolutions, they sought a society based on republican values of equality and liberty. Napoleon reluctantly agreed to send a huge flotilla of ships and 15,000 men in December, with instructions to land in Bantry Bay and march south-eastwards on Cork city. The flotilla left Brest on 15 December and reached Bantry Bay on 21 December, but icy, gale-force winds made it impossible to land. Another proposed landing on Christmas Day was abandoned as the weather worsened. The forty-four-gun frigate *Impatiente* lost its anchor, was driven ashore and smashed on the rocks. All but seven of its complement of 550 men were killed. Twelve ships were lost and two thousand men drowned off Bantry Bay.

Wolfe Tone, the instigator of the expedition, recalled pacing the deck and being able to put his hands out and almost touch the soil of Ireland. So near and yet so far. On 27 January 1797 the order was given to abandon the attempted invasion, and the few remaining ships in the bay that were seaworthy sailed back to France.

The attempted Bantry Bay landings exercised the imaginations of generations of Irish separatists throughout the nineteenth century. Joe O'Sullivan's family were raised with the stories of what might have been, of British perfidy and doomed heroism. West Cork was the cradle and the cockpit of the Irish revolution, but the western seaboard of Ireland was particularly devastated during the Great Famine years, which lasted between 1845 and 1851. The Skibbereen Poor Law Union lost a third of its population during the famine. The town to this day remains associated with the famine, and the title of a popular ballad of the 1880s, 'Revenge for Skibbereen', became synonymous with the desire to right historical wrongs:

O father dear, I often hear you speak of Erin's Isle,
Her lofty scenes and valleys green, her mountains rude and
   wild.
They say it is a lovely land wherein a prince might dwell.
Oh why did you abandon it, the reason to me tell.

My son, I loved our native land with energy and pride,
Until a blight came o'er my crops, my sheep and cattle died.
My rent and taxes were too high, I could not them redeem,
And that's the cruel reason why I left old Skibbereen.

In March 1847 a *Freeman's Journal* correspondent noted: 'There is not a house from Bantry to Schull that, with scarce a dozen exceptions, does not contain either the sick, dying or the dead . . . none of the peasantry, for the world's wealth, would go near the bodies, such is their apprehension of contagious fever.'[1]

John O'Sullivan, Joe's father, was born in Bantry in 1858, just seven years after the famine ended, into a family of tailors. The O'Sullivan family started out at Caheragh, a townland in west Cork, halfway between Skibbereen and Bantry; they later moved to Bantry, at a time when it had seen better days. During the Napoleonic Wars Bantry had thrived, its port and fishing fleet supplying the British army in the Peninsular campaigns. Irish agriculture slumped after the wars and Bantry went into decline. In 1841, before the Great Famine, the population had peaked at 7,910. Forty years later it had fallen to 4,627 and kept falling throughout the nineteenth century.[2]

The southernmost extremity of Ireland was a stronghold of the Fenian movement. Michael Collins, one of the masterminds of the Irish revolution, came from near Clonakilty. His good friend Sam Maguire from Dunmanway was a Protestant but the most dedicated of separatists and a lynchpin of the national movement in London. Jeremiah O'Donovan-Rossa, known as 'O'Dynamite' Rossa, was born in Rosscarbery. He was jailed in the 1860s for treason felony (treason not punishable by a death sentence, but by transportation or a life sentence) and spent time in British jails before being released as part of the Fenian amnesty. He emigrated to the United States, from where he orchestrated a bombing campaign in Britain in the 1880s. When he died in August 1915 his body was brought back to Ireland, and the words spoken over his grave by Patrick Pearse, one of the leaders of the Easter Rising, resonated through the following tumultuous years: 'The fools, the fools, the fools! They have left us our Fenian dead and while Ireland holds these graves, Ireland unfree shall never be at peace.'

Tom Barry, like Dunne and O'Sullivan, was an ex-British serviceman turned Irish rebel and was also from Rosscarbery. As an IRA commander he inflicted the heaviest defeat of the War of

Independence on the British when sixteen Auxiliary policemen were killed at Kilmichael on 28 November 1920.

O'Sullivan's mother, Mary Ann O'Sullivan (*née* Murphy), was born in Inniscarra, west of Cork city. The Murphys too were a nationalist family. The O'Sullivans saw themselves and were seen by others as an 'old Fenian family', to quote Joe's brother Pat O'Sullivan, who also joined the IRA in London during the War of Independence and was vice-commandant to Dunne. John O'Sullivan's brother Eugene Sr was sentenced to a month in prison in 1879 for using threatening language to the local district inspector of the Royal Irish Constabulary, the pre-independence police force for Ireland outside Dublin. According to family relative Jim Barry (not a relative of Tom), this provided the impetus for both brothers to leave Ireland:

> Family lore has it that both brothers were regularly in conflict with the Peelers. Detective Inspector Leary in particular took great interest in their case. Such was the pressure on them that they had little option but to leave Bantry. It is said that both of them took some measure of physical retribution against their tormentors before leaving.[3]

John and Mary Ann O'Sullivan emigrated to London in the 1880s. In 1891 they were living, along with four other families, at 21 Clare Street in the parish of St Clement Danes, near today's Drury Lane. In 1901 they occupied three rooms at nearby 12 Stanhope Street, a property shared with about six other families. By 1911 they had moved to 21 Little James Street, occupying the house with the occasional lodger. Little James Street, now Northington Street, is in Holborn, a densely populated residential district a hundred years ago. It signified an improvement in the family's living circumstances, as they were no longer living in tenements.

13 John and Mary Ann O'Sullivan with their eleven surviving children, *c.*1902–3: (*standing, left to right*) Aloysius, Lily, Dennis, Catherine, John Jr, Eugene, Jane, Michael; (*sitting, left to right*) Patrick, John Sr, Margaret Mary, Mary Ann Sr, Joseph

The census of England and Wales for 1921 reveals that Joe O'Sullivan was still living at home at 21 Little James Street with his father (sixty-two), who is listed as a 'journey tailor' at Henry Corlett Tailor in London; his sister Catherine (thirty-three), a short-hand typist; and a Goysins O'Sullivan (twenty-seven), a sorter at the Royal Mail (Goysins may be a misspelling of Aloysius).

John Sr possessed a rebellious streak and became involved in trade union activity. He had enough money to raise a family but was not in good circumstances by the time of his son's execution, according to his application for an Irish military pension. His son Joe, as a lowly clerk, was earning as much as him at the time. The O'Sullivans were a republican family, their ardour for the cause not dimmed by living in the belly of the beast. They saw no contradiction between living in Britain and wishing to end British rule in Ireland. Living in England, though, did not make John O'Sullivan Sr enamoured of the English. Paul Raffield, whose grandmother was Lily O'Sullivan, recalled she was ostracised for marrying an Englishman:

> My grandmother was never forgiven by her father when she married my paternal grandfather, Arthur Raffield, an English non-Catholic, to the extent that he refused to attend their wedding in 1919. I don't think they were ever reconciled. When I visited the family home in Bantry Bay and introduced myself to my distant cousin, I told him that I was Lily O'Sullivan's grandson. He replied: 'Oh yes, the one who married the Englishman.'[4]

Steeped in Irish nationalist culture though they were, the O'Sullivan boys signed up to the British war effort during the First World War. Six of the seven brothers served in the armed forces and only Michael, born in 1892, did not join up. He was a street bookmaker who worked out of a pub in Camden Town, and it is not clear why he avoided military service. The family's involvement was referenced by the Home Secretary Edward Shortt when he erroneously and briefly stated in the House of Commons that Joe O'Sullivan was a Londoner and therefore not Irish, and that he had served king and country in the war, along with others in the O'Sullivan family. Moreover, Shortt added there was no evidence Dunne or O'Sullivan had ever been to Ireland. For a short time Shortt believed, as did Scotland Yard detectives, that the Wilson shooting had nothing to do with Ireland, until James Hyndman (J. H.) MacDonnell, well known for representing Irish republican prisoners, became Dunne and O'Sullivan's defence solicitor.[5]

Aloysius joined the same battalion, the 3rd (City of London) Battalion, London Regiment, as Joe. He was clearly an early enthusiast for the war, having joined up at the end of August 1914, but was discharged with shellshock in December 1916. Eugene, who returned home from South Africa in 1915, is listed in 1918 as a secret service agent in Barrow-on-Furness, and his family believe he was involved in K-class submarine sea trials. Dennis emigrated to Australia in 1912 and returned to fight in Europe with the Australian Expeditionary Force. He was hospitalised in England and returned to the front. John Jr served in the Royal Engineers, working on the railways in France and finished as a warrant officer. He was not demobbed until late 1919.[6]

Pat, who was two years Joe's senior, claimed he was forced to join as a result of conscription, introduced into Great Britain (but not Ireland) in February 1916. He served with the 6th Battalion, London Regiment, in France from September 1916 to December 1918. According to the O'Sullivan family, he was gassed during the war and left behind on the battlefield, before being saved by an Australian priest. He settled down in Mitcham, south London, after the war, cutting a debonair figure in a black homburg hat, black overcoat and a white beard. In a certain light you could see the tiny, iridescent fragments of shrapnel on his hands and face. He saw his British war service as ultimately a service to Ireland:

> At the time of conscription I had to enter the British army, but I made up my mind to put this service to good knowledge for Ireland's cause if ever the occasion arose. I was eventually discharged and started my business as a master tailor (my father was a master tailor). I built up a very good trade, everyone was needing suits and, as an ex-serviceman, I was

able to get in touch with many good contacts as soon as I had joined the IRA.[7]

He kept a tailoring business in Chancery Place, where he used to conceal arms and Mills bombs in 'gents neat suitings'. He was never suspected: 'I was born in London and I, of course, have an English accent. That was very useful to me in many's a tight scrap (this also applies to many of our London men).'[8]

By the time of Joe's birth on 25 January 1897, most of his siblings had left home. The family was sufficiently well off to send Joe to St Edmund's College, a private school in Ware, Hertfordshire, which he attended between 1910 and 1913. St Edmund's is now a co-educational public school and the longest continuously operative post-Reformation Catholic school in England. O'Sullivan appears to have made little impact and does not feature in any of its annual publications from that period. The only reference to his time there is in the school magazine, *The Edmundian*, from Easter 1919:

14 Joe in his First World War uniform

Joseph O'Sullivan lost his right leg at Passchendaele after war service (8th Royal Munster Fusiliers and the 3rd London Regiment [*sic*]). He was discharged on July 10th 1918 and applied immediately for a commission as a flying officer.

At the time the newly formed Royal Air Force was hiring ground staff and training technicians, jobs that would have suited a disabled serviceman like Joe, but he was unsuccessful in his application.

His war records were lost along with the records of millions of other British servicemen when the War Office repository in Arnside Street, London, was destroyed by a German bombing raid in September 1940, as noted in the previous chapter. What details we do have from his medal card reveal that he joined up in January 1915 on his eighteenth birthday, the year before conscription was introduced, so he was not coerced into joining the British army.

It was not unusual for those from an Irish nationalist background to serve in the First World War and join the IRA afterwards. These included Dunne, of course, the Carr brothers, as we have seen, and the aforementioned Tom Barry and Emmet Dalton. Another interesting individual was Martin Doyle, who won the Victoria Cross in 1918. Doyle had the double distinction of also winning the Military Medal. In August 1918 he led a group of his men to safety, prevented German soldiers from storming a tank and then single-handedly rushed a machine-gun nest, capturing three prisoners. Doyle 'set the very highest example to all ranks by his courage and total disregard of danger', read his citation for the Victoria Cross published in the *London Gazette*. In June 1919, and still dressed in his Royal Munster Fusiliers uniform, he received the Victoria Cross from King George V at Buckingham

Palace. A month later he left the British army after nine years. In June 1920 a photograph was taken of him at a garden party in Buckingham Palace for Victoria Cross recipients, but in October of that year he took up arms against Britain when he joined the IRA in East Clare, acting as an intelligence officer, and he would wander in and out of the military barracks in Ennis as befits a doubly-decorated war hero. A month later he was back in London representing the Royal Munster Fusiliers at the unveiling of the Cenotaph in Whitehall.[9]

Former British soldiers played a disproportionate role in a guerrilla army where few volunteers had any formal military training. According to historian Stephen O'Connor, at least twenty-four had senior positions in the IRA and seven commanded brigades.[10]

For many ex-British soldiers a radical conversion to Irish nationalism did not take place until after the war, as Tom Barry recounted in his introduction to his autobiography *Guerrilla Days in Ireland*, published in 1949:

> In June 1915, in my seventeenth year, I had decided to see what this Great War was like. I cannot plead I went on the advice of John Redmond or any other politician, that if we fought for the British we would secure home rule for Ireland, nor can I say I understood what home rule meant. I was not influenced by the lurid appeal to fight to save Belgium or small nations. I knew nothing about nations, large or small. I went to the war for no other reason than that I wanted to see what war was like, to get a gun, to see new countries and to feel a grown man. Above all I went because I knew no Irish history and had no national consciousness. I had never been told of Wolfe Tone or Robert Emmet, though I did know

all about the Kings of England and when they had come to the British Throne. I had never heard of the victory over the Sassanach at Benburb, but I could tell the dates of Waterloo and Trafalgar. I did not know of the spread of Christianity throughout Europe by Irish missionaries and scholars, but did I not know of the blessings of civilisation which Clive and the East India Company had brought to dark and heathen India? Thus through the blood sacrifices of the men of 1916, had one Irish youth of eighteen been awakened to Irish nationality. Let it also be recorded that those sacrifices were equally necessary to awaken the minds of 90 per cent of the Irish people.[11]

The Irish in Britain were assiduous in answering the call from Lord Kitchener for volunteers. The nationalist MP turned British army officer Stephen Gwynn observed in his book *John Redmond's Last Years*:

The Irish in Great Britain, always outdoing all others in the keenness of their nationalism, were nearer the main current of the war, and were more in touch with the truth about English feeling. They had a double impulse, as Redmond had; they saw how to serve their own cause in serving Europe's freedom; and their response was magnificent. Mr T. P. O'Connor probably raised more recruits by his personal appeal than any other man in England.[12]

The Liverpool Irish raised two battalions by October 1914, the London Irish Rifles three, but nowhere was the response more forthcoming than in the north-east of England, the Tyneside Irish community raising four battalions. The 1st, 2nd, 3rd and 4th Battalions of the Tyneside Irish were also known in the

British army list as the 24th, 25th, 26th and 27th Battalions of the Northumberland Fusiliers. They became the 103rd Brigade of 34th Division.

'Irishmen, to Arms!' the advertisement in the *Newcastle Evening Chronicle* exclaimed. 'The greatest fighting men of our time are Irishmen – [Lord] Kitchener, [John] French, [Horace] Smith-Dorrien and [Lord] Roberts.' Kitchener was the War Secretary, French the head of the British army, Smith-Dorrien the commander of I Corps, and Roberts, who had retired, was a former commander-in-chief. Inadvertently, the poster demonstrated the prominent position the Anglo-Irish had in the British army at the time. Three of the four – Kitchener, French and Roberts – were actively hostile to Irish nationalists. On the first day of the Battle of the Somme 103rd Brigade sustained 2,171 casualties, with at least 599 deaths, amounting to a 70 per cent casualty rate. Others would succumb to their wounds later.[13]

It has frequently been stated that Joe O'Sullivan joined the Royal Munster Fusiliers first. Given his family background, this would be understandable, but it is not borne out by what records remain. In August 1915 he was posted to France with the 3rd (City of London) Battalion of the London Regiment. The battalion served with the 167th Brigade and the 56th (London) Division. During his two years serving at the front, the 3rd London first fought at the Battle of Loos in September 1915. In 1916 it moved to the Somme sector, specifically to the Gommecourt salient in preparation for the Battle of the Somme. Gommecourt was the furthest position north on the first day of the battle and was intended as a diversionary attack. That day, 1 July 1916, was the worst in the history of the British army, with almost 20,000 dead. The battalion saw further fighting on the Somme in September.

In 1917 it participated in the initial attack at Arras, before moving to Ypres for the forthcoming summer offensive. The Third Battle of Ypres, better known as the Battle of Passchendaele, began on 31 July 1917.

There were some early successes before the rain started to fall. It did not stop falling and turned the battlefield into a glutinous quagmire. Shelling shattered the precarious drain structure and a ghostly tableau of blasted trees, craters filled with water and the decaying remains of dead soldiers made Passchendaele a hell on earth. The battalion moved into position between 13 and 14 August at Château Ségard, a stately home that had been cleaved in two by a German shell. The 3rd London was shelled heavily on the 14th as it massed for the attack. At dusk on the 15th the men gathered in their frontline trenches, and at 4.45 a.m. on the following day they went over the top. Their goal was to get through Polygon Wood, so named because of its shape, some six kilometres from Ypres. The twisted remains of felled trees made it a death trap for the Tommies. At 5.15 a.m. the assault was held up as the enemy shelled their front with 45mm and 75mm shells. The ground, as the battalion diary euphemistically reports, was 'impassable' and defended by snipers and machine guns. At 4 p.m. the Germans counter-attacked, regaining the territory lost earlier in the morning. The 3rd London lost its commanding officer when Lieutenant Colonel Percy Ingpen was badly wounded.

The diary was unsparing about what was a typically botched attempt at an assault, which characterised this phase of the Battle of Passchendaele. Preparations were rushed, communications failed and aeroplanes went missing overhead. German planes were able to fly over the attacking troops, strafing at will. 'This takes the heart out of the men and also discloses their positions,' the battalion diary states. In August the battalion lost twenty-eight men killed, with 250 wounded or missing. O'Sullivan was wounded and evacuated across the border to France on 21 August. O'Sullivan's battalion was withdrawn from the line after the 16 August assault. There are no extant casualty records from the period, but the incident in which he lost his leg is likely to have occurred on that day. The attack on 16 August was particularly bloody for the 16th (Irish) Division and 36th (Ulster) Division, which sustained 1,200 dead between them in a disastrous assault on Frezenberg Ridge.

O'Sullivan was sent back to Blighty, travelling on a Red Cross hospital train from the south coast into Waterloo Station. Coincidentally, a group of Irish Volunteers prisoners arrived from Lewes prison in the station at the same time. One of them was Gerard Doyle, who had been sentenced to death after the Easter Rising, but later had his sentence commuted and was released under a general amnesty in 1917. He recalled in a statement to the Bureau of Military History how the prisoners had arrived into Waterloo Station:

> On the centre of the platform was a Red Cross train which had just arrived before us and they were taking British and German wounded from it. As a result of the delay, we were kept in our carriages. The news of our release had got to the Irish circles in London and numbers were in the station to watch us. At this stage, I wish to record an incident which happened. Two Irish girls, Margaret O'Sullivan and Mary O'Byrne, had come to welcome the prisoners. They were standing at the platform where the Red Cross train had come in and were looking at the stretcher cases as they were carried by. Suddenly, Miss O'Sullivan recognised her brother, Joseph

O'Sullivan, as one of the stretcher cases. Both were shocked, as no information had been received at home that he had been wounded in France. A Red Cross attendant told them the name of the hospital to which he was being removed. This lad, Sullivan [*sic*], was later to take part in the shooting of General Wilson in 1922, with Michael [*sic*] Dunne, for which offence both were later executed in London. As the German prisoners were, however, carried along, some of the crowd began to boo and call names at them. As we watched the Red Cross train moving back out of the station, another train moved in beside us. From it, we could see Dev [Éamon de Valera], and about another 30 prisoners, forming up to march away. There was loud cheering, accompanied by some booing and I also believe that a few bottles were thrown at them. It then came to our turn to march down the platform where covered lorries awaited us to take us to Pentonville prison.[14]

This statement is significant because it demonstrates that members of the O'Sullivan family were involved in the Irish national movement *before* the First World War ended and not just afterwards. On being discharged from the army in 1918, O'Sullivan was employed by the Ministry of Munitions and, after the war, was transferred to the Ministry of Labour, where he worked as a messenger in Montagu House, beside Scotland Yard. At the time of his death O'Sullivan was earning £4 15 shillings per week and giving £2 15 shillings of it to his father.

Unlike Reggie Dunne, who admitted in his final letter that he had never kissed a girl, Joe O'Sullivan appears to have had a girl-friend. She called herself Posh and was from Wharncliffe near Sheffield. Her one extant letter to him, which is undated, suggests that he was a less than diligent boyfriend:

Dearest O'Sullivan,

Well, what has happened to you all this time? I am sure I
can't think why you have not written. Did you get my letter
I wrote you to Roehampton? I suppose now that you can get
about you find so much to do you can't afford much time for
letter writing but I really didn't think you would forget all
about it as soon, however one never knows does one? But of
course you remember me telling you. Now it's usual with the
bhoys [*sic*], out of sight out of mind. I had a long letter from
Sgt Bench some time ago (by the way I must answer it or
he shall be telling me off the same as I am to you now). He
was making great inquiries for you and wants your address
to write to you. He seems very well back at his old job and
quite enjoying life again. By the way what about my banjo? I
should very much like to have it back, you know you faithfully
promised to let me have it back. Well, what are you doing with
yourself still attending meetings or have you found a more
amusing thing to do? I should find that rather tame. Life is
plenty much the same here. Still the same old. It has started
to rain already and I expect we won't see any sunshine again
for a time. I shall be looking out for a letter from you so don't
forget when you have time. With love, Posh.[15]

The letter gives a significant clue as to O'Sullivan's rehabilitation. Roehampton refers to the Queen Mary Convalescent
Auxiliary Hospital, established in south London in 1915 to deal
with the war's amputees. Some 26,000 artificial limbs were fitted to
wounded servicemen during the war at the converted stately home.

It would appear from her letters that Posh was not aware of the
true nature of O'Sullivan 'attending meetings'. She would have
found his real activities far from 'tame'. Posh materialises again

when O'Sullivan is awaiting the hangman. Father Lancelot Long, who was at school with him, requested that he be permitted to visit on behalf of a 'girlfriend of his. I may add that I have no politics of my own. My only object is to do good and give some consolation to the lady who is broken hearted.'[16] The priest was told to write to the visiting committee of the prison, but there is no surviving correspondence to suggest whether or not he was successful.

From the beginning Joe O'Sullivan is listed as a 'committed volunteer' in the London activities of the IRA. The extent of his commitment is outlined in a testimonial from Seamus Lynch, a Cork volunteer. O'Sullivan travelled over to Cork with Lynch during the War of Independence. When the ferry arrived in Cork, a detachment of British soldiers asked O'Sullivan how he lost his leg. When O'Sullivan told them he was a British war veteran, they gave the pair a lift in an ordnance lorry to where his brother Pat was staying while fighting for the IRA. In his cork leg Joe O'Sullivan had concealed more than a hundred .450 cartridges for the IRA. The term 'cork' in this context is slightly misleading as artificial legs would have been made from wood and/or metal in 1917, with cork block only being used for end-bearing pads. Cork legs did, though, have hollow shins, with ample space for smuggling.

O'Sullivan is very much the silent partner to Dunne, who has left a considerable archive and was evidently the more vocal character. Only a couple of letters from O'Sullivan survive. Rex Taylor, the author of *Assassination: The Death of Sir Henry Wilson and the Tragedy of Ireland* (1961), who spoke to those who knew O'Sullivan, described him as a humorous, unassuming sort. Most of what we know about Joe O'Sullivan comes from other people.

Denis Kelleher lists O'Sullivan as having accompanied him when they burned haystacks and barns outside London in 1920 and 1921. Having concluded that burning houses in urban areas was problematic, they headed for remote countryside and targeted places they knew would be undefended:

Every haystack and house was reconnoitred. The idea was for us to pop up unsuspected now and then. The effect was good for the material damage was little. Our lads released cattle before they burned the outhouses. The work we carried out was by the select few.[17]

According to Seán Dillon, who was tailing Wilson for a while, plans to assassinate the British cabinet were made in Pat O'Sullivan's tailoring shop in Chancery Lane, and Joe O'Sullivan was in on them:

In December 1919 I was told I was required for intelligence work and reported at the offices of Mr O'Sullivan in Chancery Lane. There were almost nine or 10 present at the first meeting which was under the guidance of a Mr Fitzgerald. After two meetings Sam Maguire took charge. We were told that it was special duty and various jobs given to us. For the first few weeks I was told to knock about Whitehall and keep an eye out for Mr [Edward] Shortt [the Home Secretary]. After that I was offered the job of watching Lloyd George in order to obtain the number of his motor car and report all information. I continued this duty until after the death of Terence MacSwiney RIP and Downing Street was barricaded. In February 1921, I, along with Joe O'Sullivan and a fellow by the name of Mooney, were sent down to Chequers where Lloyd George had been bottled up for a long time with a view to ascertaining a good spot for an ambush on the London Road.

We know from Frances Stevenson's diary that Lloyd George was aware of threats to his life from Irish republicans and was less than phlegmatic about it. In May 1921 he was particularly rattled when he went for a walk on the Chequers estate and spotted four unknown men in its grounds. When they reached the Chequers pavilion, he and a walking companion found scrawled on the walls: 'Up the Rebels: Up Sinn Féin – IRA'. Lloyd George was furious at the security breach and summoned the Home Secretary, Edward Shortt, and Sir Basil Thomson, the assistant commissioner of the Metropolitan Police, to see him.[18] He was particularly exercised by the fact that the four men involved had been questioned and released without charge. Their identity has never been revealed. Lloyd George was often brave politically, as he demonstrated during the talks that led to the Anglo-Irish Treaty, but his physical cowardice was noted by many of his contemporaries. At one point, during a First World War Zeppelin raid, he was found under a table 'all of a tremble', according to his good friend and assistant cabinet secretary Tom Jones, and he frequently obsessed about his death.[19] Fears for his personal safety may well have played a role in his anxiety to get a settlement in Ireland.

Joe O'Sullivan was named by Rex Taylor as the man who shot the spy Vincent Fovargue. Fovargue was the intelligence officer of the IRA's 4th Dublin Brigade. He was captured by the British in 1920 and turned to become one of their agents. He escaped during a fake ambush on the South Circular Road in Dublin in February 1921. The British let him go and then claimed he was an escaped prisoner, but Michael Collins had a spy in Dublin Castle called David Neligan who identified Fovargue as a double agent.

Realising the danger, Ormonde Winter, the head of British intelligence in Ireland, sent Fovargue to spy on the IRA in London, but Collins had already been tipped off. Fovargue arrived in London and began to ask a lot of questions. On the night of 2 April he attended a ceilidh in Fulham High Street. He was asked to accompany a number of men to visit an arms dump. His body was found beside a bunker by the 14th hole of Ashford Manor Golf Club in Middlesex the following morning. Four spent cartridges were on the roadway opposite. He had a sign pinned on his chest: 'Let spies and traitors beware – IRA'. The death of Fovargue made a deep impression in Britain because his killing happened so far from the country lanes and small towns that were the battlegrounds of the war in Ireland. For the IRA it sent out the message that there was no hiding place for its enemies.

Who killed him? Dunne was named by David Neligan as the killer, along with Joe Shanahan, another IRA volunteer. 'Joe Shanahan and Reggie Dunne executed him at a golf course outside London. Shanahan told me this,' Neligan wrote in his autobiography *The Spy in the Castle*. In his application for a military pension, Shanahan states that he was involved in intelligence work in London from March 1921 under the command of Dunne and Sam Maguire, the IRA's chief intelligence officer in London, but he makes no specific reference to having been involved in the shooting of Fovargue. It is certain that the killing would have had to have been sanctioned by Dunne, but did he pull the trigger? Dunne and O'Sullivan took the secrets of the Fovargue shooting to their graves.

O'Sullivan was involved in the burning of the homes of Auxiliaries in Tooting, south London, in May 1921. At that time, he went by the name of Cunningham. The targeting of the homes of the Auxiliaries had a chilling effect on recruitment to the organisation, according to his companion that night, William Smyth:

> Over 5,000 men presented themselves for enrolment in the
> Auxiliary Police in a certain week in May 1921. The attacks
> on the homes were carried out on the night of Saturday of
> that week and the number who applied for enlistment in the
> Auxiliaries in the following week did not exceed a score.[20]

The O'Sullivan brothers and Dunne were able to use their status as London-born British army veterans to procure arms for the
IRA. The wound badges all three wore and their cockney accents
made them the least suspect of men, according to Pat:

> I was able to enter army barracks, demob camps etc. At the
> RAF depot at Uxbridge I had 'free entry' seeking orders for
> suits etc. I located the arms stores and we obtained a large
> number of revolvers from time to time and they were never
> missed and we were never suspected. Bear in mind, Dunne,
> my brother (who had lost a leg in France) and myself all were
> able to wear in our coats the wounded badge awarded by the
> British army and could mix freely without being suspect.[21]

Britain had more guns from returning servicemen than it knew
what to do with. There were millions of rifles, revolvers and
countless rounds of ammunition, grenades and shells surplus to
requirements. The materiel was brought out in store carts by a
sympathetic Irishman. The haul of guns Pat O'Sullivan claimed to
have purloined out of RAF Uxbridge was considerable – between
seventy-five and a hundred Lee-Enfield rifles, twenty to thirty
Webley service revolvers and between 3,000 and 4,000 rounds of
.303 and .45 ammunition.

He also made contact with London-Irish workers in the
Woolwich Arsenal, and they too were able to procure 'stuff' for

him, to use the IRA parlance of the time. He brought it to Ireland in August 1920, before he joined the IRA in Cork. Pat O'Sullivan and four other volunteers travelled to Ireland disguised as a golfing party. The guns were brought over to Ireland in golf bags with the clubheads sticking out and a travelling rug around them.[22]

Joe O'Sullivan did not live long enough to give an account of his activities in the IRA, but Pat O'Sullivan did, and we can glean much about Joe's services from his brother's application to the Irish state for a military pension. His tailoring business in Chancery Lane and the family home were put at the disposal of the republican movement, he recalled:[23]

> I enrolled my brother Joseph into the London battalion. He
> afterwards, as you are aware, was executed with the battalion
> commandant Reggie Dunne. My father was old Fenian
> stock and it was from him we learnt our love of Ireland and
> determination one day to fight her battles. Our house in
> London was always a place of call for any of the men on the
> run. Sam Maguire, Danny Healy, many others, food, letters,
> clothes, money always available to 21 Little James Street
> London. Why bring my family into it, not to boast, no, but
> to help you form a true picture. From 1919 on my whole life
> onwards was devoted to the fight for freedom; I will always be
> satisfied in my conscience that I did my duty for Ireland.[24]

Others were willing to vouch for the family's involvement in Irish republicanism. Art O'Brien said the O'Sullivans were well known in London and elsewhere for their 'continued and unselfish help to the Irish national movement'.[25] Bill Ahern said he knew Joe and through him got to know the family well. 'I cannot be too loud in my praise of the way in which the family helped in the IRA movement from 1919 to 1922 and onwards.'[26]

*

In August 1920 Pat O'Sullivan applied for permission to leave London and fight in Ireland during the Irish War of Independence, joining Cork No. 1 Brigade. He recalled that his former British army service and his English accent made his IRA comrades wary of him, but he turned these weaknesses into strengths. He took his British army discharge papers and presented them at Ballincollig Barracks to gain the trust of the British soldiers based there, then proceeded to steal revolvers, revolver ammunition and grenades from the barracks' arsenal. In December 1920 and February 1921 several consignments of rifles arrived at Bantry by rail for the IRA. The rifles were packed into cases and disguised as machinery for a local farm. These arms were sent from London on the instructions of Pat O'Sullivan.[27]

The early post-war years were traumatic for the O'Sullivan family. Mary O'Sullivan died in November 1920 at the age of sixty. Joe was clearly close to his mother, as is evidenced by his last letter:

> I had a letter from Sister Mary Raphael this morning and I'm
> sure she is right when she says my dear Mother's holy soul
> is hovering near us and I shall be ever so pleased to see her
> through the goodness of God. You know Dad that death is only
> a parting, sometimes it is harder than others, but it is an end
> we must all come to sooner or later and I can never thank God
> enough for giving one so unworthy as I such a happy death.[28]

Then in March 1922 John Jr died while working in Lincolnshire on a railway. He was engaged on the Great Central line at Keadby, examining the metal joints on a bridge, when he was hit by the guard's van of a passenger train and thrown onto the line. A verdict of 'death by misadventure' was recorded. The twin tragedies were on Joe's mind in his last letter as he exhorted other members of the family to always trust in God and be ready at any time to be 'with our dear mother and John and myself'.

The activities of the IRA were scaled down from early June 1921 as rumours of a truce began to circulate, and GHQ in Ireland did not want to antagonise the British government by staging incidents in their own backyard. After the Truce of 11 July which ended the War of Independence, Dunne and O'Sullivan went to Dublin on holiday and offered themselves to Michael Collins in the event that negotiations might break down, according to Seán MacCraith (also known as Seán McGrath), the secretary of the Irish Self-Determination League and an IRA activist. Collins told them to stay in London as they would be needed there. MacCraith's statement made to Ernie O'Malley in the 1950s is one that begs more questions than answers. Did Collins mention assassinating Henry Wilson at that meeting? O'Sullivan's father's application for a pension contains a startling admission that 'Michael Collins promised the two boys, my son Joseph and Reggie Dunne, that if anything happened to them that their parents would be looked after.'[29] This statement, if true, confirms that Dunne and O'Sullivan met Collins together some time before the shooting.

When the Anglo-Irish Treaty was signed, O'Sullivan took the anti-Treaty (republican) side, but appears to have been, like Dunne, more intent on preventing a split in the IRA ranks in London. 'Both of them were inclined to the Republican side when the Treaty was signed. Sam Maguire was neutral at first, then went Free State after a month. Dunne and Sullivan tried to keep the organisation in London neutral,' Kelleher remembered.[30]

One of the regular visitors to the Ministry of Labour, where O'Sullivan worked, was Field Marshal Sir Henry Wilson, who attended meetings about attempts to find gainful employment for millions of returned servicemen. O'Sullivan knew what Wilson looked like, and this would prove to be fatal for both of them. Photographs even of famous people were difficult to come by in the early 1920s. The British had no photograph of Collins prior to one taken in April 1919 of the members of the Dáil Éireann, and Collins had never wanted to be included in that photograph, for understandable reasons.

The O'Sullivans were a Catholic family, seeing in Joe's death a sacrifice for a country that they loved but where they no longer lived. They never doubted the rightness of the deed but railed against those who would deny they were not acting under orders. 'I feel you know of my loss for which I have no regrets as it was done for the love of his faith and for Ireland. You take it of course that I am alluding to my son Joe who gave his young life for the great cause,' John O'Sullivan wrote to the Irish Army Pensions Board years later. 'He removed a dirty Orange dog.'[31]

7

Planning: 'The Wilson job is on'

Political assassinations have been rare in modern British history. Since the Act of Union between Great Britain and Ireland in 1800 just nine serving MPs have been killed. Six of them were the result of Irish republican violence, the exceptions being the British prime minister Spencer Perceval, killed in 1812 by John Bellingham, a Liverpool merchant with a grudge; the Labour MP Jo Cox, who was killed by a far-right nationalist during the Brexit referendum campaign in 2016; and Tory MP Sir David Amess, killed by a radicalised British man of Somalian heritage, Ali Harbi Ali, in 2021.

The first Irish republican assassination was of the Chief Secretary for Ireland Lord Frederick Cavendish on 6 May 1882. A nephew by marriage of the British prime minister William Gladstone, and a political ingénue, Cavendish was brutally stabbed to death on his first day in the job while strolling through the Phoenix Park, Dublin, in the company of Henry Burke, the Permanent Under-Secretary for Ireland (the chief civil servant in Ireland). Both were victims of the Invincibles, an organisation within the Fenian movement intent on assassinating high-ranking British officials. The five men who carried out the killings – Tim Kelly, Daniel Curley, Thomas Caffrey, Joe Brady and Michael Fagan – were hanged in Kilmainham Jail.

The Invincibles had tried to kill Cavendish's hated predecessor William 'Buckshot' Foster on at least nineteen previous occasions but failed each time. Foster knew he was a marked man and varied his movements. In the days before telephones and booby-trap explosions, with inadequate and often inaccurate firepower, assassinating public officials was difficult.

The killings of Cavendish and Burke were universally condemned, not least by the Irish Parliamentary Party leader Charles Stewart Parnell and the Land League president Michael Davitt, the leaders at the time of nationalist Ireland. They addressed the counter-productive nature of the killings in a statement that could as easily have applied to the Wilson shooting forty years later. 'On the eve of what seemed a bright future for our country, the evil destiny which has apparently pursued us for centuries has struck another blow which cannot be exaggerated in its disastrous consequences.'[1]

The Phoenix Park murders cast the darkest of shadows on British–Irish relations and were cited many times after the Wilson assassination as evidence of the incorrigible Irish and their addiction to violence. Yet the period between 1882 and 1916 was a time of relative quietude in Ireland, with an ebb in revolutionary violence, the country becoming preoccupied with the peaceful and constitutional pursuit of home rule. The Easter Rising in 1916 changed all that.

Assassination as a tool of war was resurrected in the spring of 1918 and would be a key tactic of the IRA between then and the killing of Wilson in 1922. It was a dangerous, high-stakes pursuit that republicans hoped would concentrate the minds of the British government on a settlement in Ireland. Equally, assassination was an act that was more likely to alienate British public opinion and make a settlement harder. The republican leadership vacillated on the policy.

The conscription crisis of 1918 illustrated the chasm of misunderstanding between Britain and Ireland. The Military Service Act coming into force in February 1916 was the first time that conscription had been introduced in Great Britain. The Act specified that all unmarried men between the ages of eighteen and forty-one could be conscripted except those in reserved occupations. It was extended to married men in May 1916. As we've seen, Ireland was exempted from conscription, an explicit admission that one part of the United Kingdom was a place apart.

The German Spring Offensive that began in March 1918 panicked the British government and led to the Military Service (No. 2) Act, which extended conscription from forty-one to fifty and introduced it into Ireland.

Lloyd George was advised by those on the ground in Ireland that conscription in the country would be more trouble than it was worth and would need more men to enforce it than could possibly be gained by the measure. Lloyd George introduced the bill anyway, more as a sop to his critics than out of any conviction as to its merits. As a consequence of the decision, the Irish Party withdrew from Westminster, Sinn Féin was further emboldened and all strands of nationalist opinion were united against it.

The first plot to kill members of the British government arose out of the conscription crisis. In March 1918 the Irish Volunteers executive met and decided that if any attempt were made to introduce conscription into Ireland, members of the British cabinet would be killed. The most senior figures in the executive were all present at the meeting, including Éamon de Valera and Richard Mulcahy. The only absentee from the decision was Michael Collins, who was in jail at the time. Richard Walsh, a member of the executive, said that in the event of a successful assassination they would immediately claim responsibility:

The actual decision of the executive was that the most effective blow the Volunteers could strike in defence of their country to defeat conscription and the most destructive to the British was to make a personal attack on the lives of members of the British Cabinet, and to kill every one of them if possible. It was suggested that the most suitable place to carry out the operation and, at the same time, the most dramatic and accessible, was in the House of Commons in London. In the event of the House of Commons not being a feasible location, the Ministers were to be targeted wherever they were found. This order was not to be carried out until the actual proclamation for enforcing conscription in Ireland was issued. The publication would be necessary to show the world that the men who carried out the operation were acting on the orders of the only body that then had the authority to authorise such actions on behalf of the Irish people and that they were not just a crowd of gunmen acting on their own or taking orders from some unknown or obscure secret society.[2]

The instigator of the plot was Cathal Brugha. He was born as Charles William St John Burgess in Fairview, Dublin, to a Protestant father and Catholic mother. His attempts to become a medical doctor were cut short when his father, an art dealer, lost his business and could no longer pay for his son to attend university.

After finishing school, Brugha got a job in Hayes and Finch, a church supplies firm. A noted Anglophobe, Brugha quit his job in 1909 because his firm was English-owned and he became an early convert to the Irish-Ireland movement. He joined the Gaelic League in 1899, and it was then he gaelicised his name to Cathal Brugha.[3] He was also one of the early enthusiasts for the Irish Volunteers and led the plan to smuggle German guns into Howth in July 1914, the same guns that were used in the Easter Rising.

Brugha's one-man stand at the South Dublin Union against over-whelming odds personified the doomed heroism of the Rising. As the garrison fled the union buildings where many of the poor of Dublin were hospitalised, Brugha stayed behind firing his pistol through the window until, riddled with bullets, he was rescued and taken away. His shrapnel and bullet wounds were so extensive that many felt he wouldn't survive, but he did, albeit with a permanent limp.

Brugha agreed to lead the gang of assassins and persuaded a dozen volunteers to sign up in London. He was determined to lead by example, even if that meant certain death. The chances of a successful assassination were slim; the chances of escaping slimmer still. A narrative arose in the republican ranks from the beginning that these attempted assassinations would be veritable suicide missions but had to be done for the greater good.

The chief of staff of the Irish Volunteers, Richard Mulcahy, did not demur. 'Mulcahy gave me to understand that the chances of any of the party of Volunteers surviving subsequent to those executions would be one in a million,' recalled John Gaynor, who was only nineteen at the time he volunteered to go in the early summer of 1918:

> He also informed me that our dependants would be looked
> after and provided for by Volunteer headquarters. Mulcahy,
> without saying so, gave me the impression that I had the
> option of withdrawing from the venture should I wish to
> do so. Needless to say, I was appalled by the task we were
> expected to undertake but having volunteered I was not
> withdrawing. I was old enough to realise that this would be
> where I would say goodbye to this world. Having cautioned
> me that I was not to mention the matter to anyone, no matter

who they were, he told me he would send for me later when I would get full instructions.[4]

They were split up into different lodgings around the city. The dozen gathered together in London at a time when men of military age not in uniform were bound to arouse suspicion, with so many of them away at the front. Meetings were furtive affairs carried out on benches in public parks. On Hampstead Heath Brugha scattered his little band and visited them each in turn. 'We used to loll around in small groups of two or three at different points and Cathal would come round each group and have a chat and give us the latest information or surmise of what was going to happen,' Gaynor remembered.[5]

Nevertheless, they were all able to blend into the vastness of London and the Irish community was of sufficient size for the police not to suspect any of them. They were 'easily enough fooled. The police there were an extremely nice lot of fellows,' said Gaynor. It was, though, a dreadful time for the dozen, who had nothing else to do other than to hang around waiting for the summons that might or might not come, knowing it could become as much a death sentence for them as for their target. There were occasionally dances among the Irish community, but the time, as Gaynor remembered it, 'was terribly monotonous and trying':

Day after day and week after week without anything definite. You could see some of the lads beginning to look old and haggard under the strain, and I am sure many of them looked years older by the time they got back to Dublin. I lived up to the strain well. Probably my youth was an advantage. I was about ten or twelve years younger than the rest of the party. What annoyed me most was the want of something definite in the nature of work or something that would keep my mind occupied.[6]

Another would-be assassin was William 'Bill' Whelan from Bray, County Wicklow. Whelan was not impressed by Brugha's fanaticism, describing him as the 'most cold-blooded man I have ever met in my life', who even brought his children to Britain as cover. Brugha trusted Whelan enough to ask him to accompany him on a tour of the House of Commons. Brugha stuffed a Mauser C96, a clip-fed semi-automatic with ten rounds, down his trouser leg.

Serving and former soldiers were a common sight in the Palaces of Westminster, and Brugha looked like just another injured soldier shuffling his way around the corridors of power. Brugha told his friend and biographer John J. O'Kelly/Seán Ua Ceallaigh, known as 'Sceilg', that the police assumed he was a 'wounded soldier back from Flanders and he told me they did everything they could to help him'.[7] Whelan was unarmed and incredulous at the risk they were taking. As they took their place in the Visitors' Gallery, Whelan leaned across to Brugha and asked him sotto voce when he was going to start the shooting. Brugha's response was matter-of-fact:

No, I am not going to start. I only want to get the feel of this thing here in the gallery. If you can, shoot your way out. That is all I want you to do – keep the people away until I have finished the firing.[8]

The Mauser was known as 'Peter the Painter' after the Latvian-born anarchist who had fetched up in the East End of London. Peter the Painter, whose real name may have been Peter Piaktow, though his identity has never been definitively established, was reputed to have been involved in two shootouts before the war: three policemen were killed when they disrupted an anarchist assembly in Houndsditch in 1910, and the following year Peter the Painter reputedly escaped the Siege of Sidney Street in London's East End, in which two Latvian anarchists were killed. Historians dispute many of the details of Peter the Painter's life, but the weapon was undoubtedly named after him.

The 'Peter the Painter' which came with a detachable stock, used for greater accuracy, was used to deadly effect during the Easter Rising by Volunteer Michael Malone, who inflicted huge casualties on British troops at Mount Street Bridge in Dublin.

Joe Good was a London-born IRA volunteer who was part of the original dozen. During the First World War he had avoided conscription in Britain by fleeing to Ireland. He became part of the Kimmage Garrison, the second- and third-generation Irishmen who fought in the Easter Rising. He met Brugha and Mulcahy in an upstairs room in a gentlemen's club in Dublin. Good was probably the only volunteer unsurprised by this melancholy summons: 'I replied that I had already considered such a mission; it was only a matter of "who would bell the cat" and that, alas, I knew the terrain, so to speak.'[9]

Good had come to the same conclusion as Brugha and Mulcahy. The Irish Volunteers were in rag order after the Easter Rising. Many of the leaders had been in jail since the Rising, discipline had broken down and the organisation was short of weapons. It was in no state to resist by military means any attempt by the British to introduce conscription into Ireland. It made more sense, Good surmised, to cut the head off the snake than to take on the British military:

Mulcahy asked me who I had been speaking to, and I replied that I had been speaking to no one, but that I had been thinking over the matter for some time and thought that the British cabinet might be deterred if some of them were shot. Cathal Brugha then told me to consider the matter and if I was of the same mind I was to report in a week, or some such more precise date. I passed Bill Whelan in the hall on my way out and nodded to him as if to say, 'You have guessed right.'[10]

Whelan and Good were put up in the home of a sympathetic London-Irish family. 'The family with whom Bill Whelan and I stayed probably guessed that they risked severe sentences for harbouring us, but we were made welcome and fed on their limited rations, as we had no ration cards. I cannot speak too highly of their courage, hospitality and kindness.'[11]

When they met up, Brugha would pore over photographs of their assassination targets like a schoolboy examining football cards. 'He seemed to get the greatest pleasure out of discussing these people, much the same as some people look at photographs of film stars.'[12] The targets included newspaper owners who were hostile to Irish nationalism, especially the Irish-born Lord Northcliffe (Alfred Harmsworth), publisher of the *Daily Mail*.

At one point eight of them met in Regent's Park to plan the assassination. They could have been picked up there and then, Good recalled, but the police did not recognise them. They drew beads from a hat to decide who would shoot whom. Good drew Andrew Bonar Law, the Conservative Party leader, who had been the Chancellor of the Exchequer in Lloyd George's war-time government and a staunch supporter of Ulster unionism. Good often found himself in a cinema with Bonar Law. In a more innocent age, British politicians were careless about their safety as there had not been an assassination of a British politician for almost four decades:

> I had nothing against Bonar Law except that he was fond of matinées. I was several times close on Bonar Law's heels as he walked from Downing Street to the Houses of Parliament. I thought he was singularly incautious considering all he had done and proposed to do in Ireland. From day to day we expected orders to attack. It was very wearing.[13]

Good judged that the weapons assigned to the men for the job were inadequate for the task. The .38 revolvers were not deadly enough and would necessitate several shots to finish off the target. On several occasions they hung about Downing Street waiting for members of the British cabinet, but at the 'last moment we would be told "not today" . . . We would act tomorrow, and tomorrow, and then tomorrow.'[14]

Good was amazed that men like himself of military age were able to wander around London without being challenged, especially as four of them had London accents and were liable to be conscripted.

The British government never did introduce conscription into Ireland. By May 1918 the danger had passed. The Germans outran their supply lines and the pushback began, but the damage was done.

The closest that the IRA got to assassinating a member of the British government during the War of Independence was their attempt to kill Lord French, the Lord Lieutenant and Viceroy, on 19 December 1919. On the previous night a group of IRA men met at the Sinn Féin Club on North Summer Street, Dublin. The fire was roaring in the grate and there was much to discuss. There had been a marked escalation in activity by the IRA in the late months of the year and a subsequent repression by the British authorities.[15]

At about 9 p.m. Paddy Sharkey, a member of the 2nd Battalion of the Dublin Volunteers, told the others he was leaving. 'What's your hurry? Have you a date on or what?' inquired Vincent 'Vinny' Byrne, another member of Michael Collins's so-called 'Squad'. Collins had formed the Squad in 1919 from some of the most energetic and young members of the IRA, all of whom were asked at the initial meeting if they had any objections to shooting men in covert operations. Most did, and the conscientious objectors were sent on their way. The dozen that remained formed the basis of the Squad, and several of this group of assassins played key roles in a series of killings on the morning of 21 November 1920 – 'Bloody Sunday' – when fourteen suspected British agents were shot dead.

Sharkey told Byrne to get his father's basket – lunch provisions – ready for an early start. His father worked as a guard on the railways and was on his way down to Roscommon 'to bring ould French back to Dublin tomorrow morning'.

'Is that so?' Byrne said. French had become Lord Lieutenant in May 1918 and interpreted his role as being at the head of a quasi-military government.[16]

In September 1919 the Irish administration banned the Dáil and proscribed a slew of nationalist organisations, including Sinn Féin, the Gaelic League, Cumann na mBan and others. It was reported in republican circles around Armistice Day 1919 that French had addressed loyalist boy scouts and called Sinn Féin and its supporters 'vermin' to be eliminated. His actions made him a prime target for republicans, but he proved to be a maddeningly elusive quarry.

He rarely ventured out, and when he did, he frequently changed his route at the last moment. A group of would-be assassins assembled at Grattan Bridge in Dublin on one occasion with grenades primed, but they were rumbled by a spy and had to abort the mission. On another occasion the IRA planned to shoot French during the Armistice Day parade in 1919 but called it off fearing civilian casualties. Another plan to shoot French in the Viceregal Lodge was dismissed as a suicide mission.

Now, thanks to a fortuitous tip-off, there would be another opportunity to assassinate the head of the British government in Ireland. Byrne raced to the home of Mick McDonnell, the head of Collins's Squad, with the information. 'That's the best bit of news I've heard for a long time,' McDonnell said, and he worked through the night to assemble a team for the assassination attempt. Eleven men cycled from the North Circular Road in Dublin to Ashtown Cross the following morning. The would-be assassins entered the pub near the station, ordered some soft drinks and made chit-chat with the locals. 'We talked about cattle and markets and grazing, though some of our men knew very little about markets or livestock,' Dan Breen recalled in his bestselling autobiographical book *My Fight for Irish Freedom*.[17]

The train was due to arrive in Ashtown Station at about 11.40 a.m. The assassination attempt was a frenetic affair. A couple of volunteers spied a large cart in the vicinity of the pub and tried to drag it into the middle of the road to slow down the expected convoy. A policeman, who told them to desist as 'His Excellency' was on his way, was hit over the head by an unprimed grenade and knocked unconscious.

Moments later French's train pulled in to Ashtown Station, and he and his party transferred to three waiting cars. As his convoy approached, the volunteers crouched behind a hedge, weapons at the ready. After the dispatch rider passed, they opened fire on the first car, but assumed that French was travelling in the second one, as he usually did. A grenade was thrown at it, but it bounced off and exploded on the road. Marksmen in the third car returned fire. In the ensuing gun battle, Breen was shot through the leg and volunteer Martin Savage, a twenty-one-year-old shop attendant from County Sligo, was killed when a bullet entered his neck.

'How light-heartedly he had been singing and reciting poems about Ireland and the glory of dying for one's country as we rode out to Ashtown only one hour ago,' Breen remembered. 'Now he was breathing his last, meeting his death as he would have wished from a British bullet.'[18]

The assassination attempt had failed. It transpired that French had been travelling in the first car, which sped away quickly from the scene.

The response of David Lloyd George to the shooting was shockingly insouciant, according to the Chief Secretary for Ireland, Sir Ian Macpherson, who also feared that he himself would be assassinated. 'There was no expression of regret for my friend, nor was there expression of sympathy for us both in our difficult task,' Macpherson revealed. 'He simply said, "They are bad shots."'[19]

In the autumn of 1920, as the Lord Mayor of Cork Terence MacSwiney lay dying on hunger strike in Brixton Prison, Michael Collins renewed plans to assassinate members of the British cabinet. MacSwiney was close to Collins, and Collins took his suffering personally. He was enraged by the protracted nature of MacSwiney's hunger strike and the unwillingness of the British government to intervene. He dispatched four of his most trusted gunmen to London: Frank Thornton and Seán Flood, both members of the Squad, along with Shaun Cody and George Fitzgerald. According to Thornton, he and Flood could have changed the course of British and Irish history by a chance encounter. They were in Westminster Station when they discovered the lifts were about to close. 'I'll race you to the bottom down the runway,' Flood said. Flood immediately disappeared, and Thornton chased after him. From the top of the stairs, Thornton could hear the sound of two people colliding.

I fell over two men on the ground, one of whom was Seán Flood. We picked ourselves up and both assisted in helping to his feet the man whom Seán Flood had knocked down. To our amazement two other men who were with him ordered us to put our hands up. We more or less ignored them and started to brush down the man and apologise to him when to our amazement we discovered that the man we had knocked down was Lloyd George, the prime minister of England. The first act of Lloyd George was to tell his two guards to put their guns away, which they were reluctant to do, pointing out that from our speech we were evidently Irishmen. Lloyd George's answer to this was, 'Well, Irishmen or no Irishmen, if they were out to shoot me I was shot long ago.' Little he knew the people he was dealing with on that particular occasion but after a few muttered apologies on our part we went on our way towards the station.[20]

Collins also sent three Cork men: Jack Cody, Con Sullivan and Pat 'Pa' Murray. They were met in London by their fellow Cork man Sam Maguire, who put them up in digs. Maguire introduced them to Art O'Brien and Reggie Dunne. In turn Dunne introduced them to contacts he had in London in the police and the media who might aid their endeavours. The men tracked their targets every day, waiting for the order. Murray remembered:

Dunne and myself discussed the position in some detail, and he later arranged that I should inspect the different companies of the London Volunteers, under the guise of a GHQ officer. I did this and selected from the companies men whom I thought might be of use. I later met these men on different occasions and outlined a number of observers for different districts where the cabinet ministers, mentioned by Michael Collins, were living, whether in houses or flats. I also contacted a number of Irish newspaper men and, through them, I judiciously got particulars of ministerial functions, etc. Every day, Reggie Dunne collected these reports, and we carefully examined them, hoping that some measure of regularity might be discovered in the movements of the ministers.[21]

It was nerve-racking and dull work. Those involved knew their chances of success were slender, their chances of escape even more so. Collins could never make up his mind whether to go ahead with the plan. He was torn between striking at the heart of the British establishment and the realisation that he might eventually have to do business with the people he was trying to assassinate. Though then the most wanted man in Ireland, Collins travelled to Britain in October 1920 to familiarise himself with the work of his intelligence officers. He knew London well, having lived there for nine years, and he and his men walked around town, familiar-ising themselves with Scotland Yard and Whitehall. It was typical of Collins's chutzpah that the most wanted man in Ireland would stroll around central London.

As MacSwiney endured his hunger strike, the men tailing the cabinet members became impatient. The British secret service may have already been aware of the assassination plot as perman-ent barriers went up across Downing Street. Ministers varied their movements and the process became increasingly frustrating. 'We discovered, after a time, that the movements of the ministers were most irregular and uncertain and, for that reason, I was not able to devise any definite plan to carry out my objective, should the occasion arise,' Pa Murray recalled.[22]

Yet in October 1920 Murray would be another who came close to changing the course of Anglo-Irish relations. He had been tipped off that Arthur Balfour, the former Chief Secretary for Ireland and former British prime minister, was going to give a talk at Oxford. Balfour was then Lord President of the Council (the leader of the Commons), and therefore a member of the cabinet. Murray sought word from Collins over the weekend. Collins came back with a no, but Murray decided to go to Oxford anyway to see how accessible his quarry might be:

> I met and spoke to Mr Balfour on the street. I simply walked up to him and asked him the way to some of the Oxford colleges. He directed me and said, 'You are an Irishman?' I said, 'Yes,' and he walked a bit of the way with me. He did not appear to have an armed guard with him. I returned to Dublin on the following Thursday. Michael Collins told me he was sorry, but that he could not risk anything happening until Terence died. He also felt that the strain on us would be too much, if MacSwiney were to die while we were in England.[23]

George Fitzgerald's role was to tail Sir Hamar Greenwood, who was appointed in April 1920 as Chief Secretary for Ireland and was standing for re-election in his own constituency in Sunderland. Fitzgerald spent most of his life in the United States and had an American accent, so he was able to pass himself off as an American tourist and gain the confidence of Greenwood's election agent:

> He took me out to dinner the next day and told me practically all the information he had and which I wished to know about

Greenwood. He disclosed everything to me . . . I came back
to Dublin some ten days later and handed in this information.
This was immediately given to Collins. When Greenwood
took up his appointment in Dublin he brought with him the
car he used in Sunderland, together with one or two of his
escort cars. On the day following his arrival he was travelling
from the Viceregal Lodge to Dublin Castle. On the way he
was attacked by members of the Squad. I heard later that there
was great consternation over this with the Castle authorities
as they could not understand how Greenwood was identified
so quickly seeing that he had only arrived in the country the
evening before this attack was staged. I knew the answer.
Michael Collins had passed on my intelligence information to
the Squad.[24]

These attempted assassinations may have spread fear in British
government circles, but they were also a threat to the whole
movement for Irish independence as a successful assassination
might make a political settlement impossible. After returning to
Ireland, Pa Murray spoke to Cathal Brugha about how ill-advised
the whole project was. Brugha seems to have had a change of
heart about the practicalities of such high-profile assassinations.
'He [Brugha], personally, was of the opinion that the operation
should never have been even thought of, but he agreed that the
only way in which anything could be done would be by accident
more than by design, as might have happened in Oxford.'[25]

* * *

The next attempt to carry out a high-profile assassination came
in early 1921. Once again Reggie Dunne was involved, but poor

planning scuppered the IRA's chances of killing Lord FitzAlan, who had been appointed the first Catholic Lord Lieutenant of Ireland since the seventeenth century. FitzAlan was a son of the Duke of Norfolk, England's pre-eminent Catholic. His appointment was considered a sop to Catholic and nationalist Ireland, but the Irish public were now too far down the road of separatism to appreciate the concession. 'Ireland would as soon have a Catholic hangman,' the Archbishop of Armagh Cardinal Michael Logue caustically observed.[26]

The IRA felt much the same way and put forward an elaborate plan to shoot FitzAlan. The plan was for three men to travel to his home in Piccadilly, central London, disguised as police officers, tie his staff up, burn his house to the ground with petrol and hang him from the banisters. The assassination was planned for 10.30 p.m., when the crowds were spilling out of nearby cinemas and theatres and the volunteers could mingle with the throng.

The attack needed careful planning. Three men hijacked a taxi in Hampstead Heath near The Bishops Avenue, but the assigned driver did not know how to drive the car and accidentally put it into reverse. His botched attempt attracted the attention of locals and the three men had to make a run for it. Bill Ahern was supposed to meet Dunne in Highgate, but Dunne was unable to get a car and the operation had to be called off.

In March 1921 Brugha, then the Minister for Defence, appears to have had another change of heart about the merits of assassinating the British cabinet and revived his plans. He summoned Seán Mac Eoin to his Dublin office. After a circumlocutory talk in which Mac Eoin wondered whether he would ever get to the point, Brugha eventually said that the Black and Tans were causing havoc in Ireland, but even if they were all killed, others would take their place. It would be a more pointed lesson for the British if the men who had sent them to Ireland were killed instead. Mac Eoin protested that he was only a simple country fellow who had never been further than Dublin. Besides, he had his own command in Longford that he needed to return to. Brugha was having none of it. He told Mac Eoin he was to proceed to London two days later. Mac Eoin said he needed to go to fix things up 'before going on what might be my last journey in this world'.

'Nonsense,' Brugha shot back, 'no going home!'[27]

Mac Eoin went to see Michael Collins about Brugha and recounted Brugha's plan to Collins, assuming Collins was in on it. Collins listened with irritation and mounting incredulity.

> When I had finished, he said, 'You are mad! Do you think that England has only the makings of one Cabinet?' As his question invited argument, I tried to point out to him that, though she had the makings of Cabinets without end, the success of our scheme did not lie in just the removal of so many prominent men, but in the effect it would have upon those who succeeded them, upon England in general, and upon the world.[28]

Collins told Mac Eoin that the plan had been discussed by the cabinet and quickly dismissed. He sent Mac Eoin away with an exhortation to look after his own patch in Longford 'without thinking you are some vest pocket Bonaparte going over to conquer England'. The exchange is interesting in that Collins seemed to understand at this juncture that assassinating a member of the British cabinet was a counter-productive move. It also lays bare the level of enmity and distrust between Brugha and Collins.

It was during the MacSwiney hunger strike that Wilson became a target. According to Shaun Cody, Wilson, as Chief of the Imperial General Staff, was prioritised on the list, along with Lloyd George, the Home Secretary Edward Shortt, Greenwood

15 Cathal Brugha arriving by bicycle at a Dáil Éireann meeting in Dublin University, 1 December 1921

and Balfour, 'with strict instructions not to shoot till Terry [Terence MacSwiney] died and then to shoot the lot if we could manage it'.[29] Seán 'John' Dillon was detailed to follow Wilson around. Dillon was hardly an inconspicuous figure for the job. He was very short and of uncertain background, claiming to have been born in Australia, the son of an assistant to the Australian High Commissioner. He was a 'little lad about 3' 6" that looked like a boy', Bill Ahern remembered.[30] Dillon recalled trailing Wilson for six weeks near the end of 1920 but could get no fix on his movements. Wilson remained a target after that date, even while the prospect of a peace settlement that surfaced at the end of 1920 made assassination plans more problematic.

The evidence for this is substantial and from multiple sources. Cork IRA gunrunner Mick Murphy arrived in London in

December 1920 to procure weapons. He visited a safe house owned by Mary Egan, a Cumann na mBan volunteer who had been sent by her employers to London in 1919. Her house in Dalston was used for smuggling arms and as a safe house for IRA men on the run. Murphy recalled:

> On another occasion during my visit to London we made plans at her [Mary Egan's] house for the shooting of Sir Henry Wilson in 1921. Same did not come off at the time on account of a murder being committed in Wilson's area and the whole place was being held up and being watched for some time. Reggie Dunne and Joe Carr were also at this meeting, and Miss Egan was conversant with the whole proceedings.[31]

The letter from Murphy does not say whether the assassination was planned in her house before or after the Truce, which occurred in July 1921. However, Egan said in her own witness statement that she left London for Cork after the Truce.

The statement from Murphy is significant in that it shows Reggie Dunne was in on plans to shoot Wilson *before* the Truce. An uneasy peace existed between the British and Irish delegations during the Treaty negotiations, which lasted almost five months. Many in the IRA did not share Michael Collins's analysis that they lacked the men and the materiel to prosecute the war. On the British side there was a willingness to make a settlement, provided that it did not set a bad precedent for the rest of the British Empire.

The IRA continued to drill and organise during the Truce. There was no let-up on Dunne's part either. Just two weeks after the Truce came into effect, an explosion at an improvised munitions factory in Greenwich killed Michael McInerney, who had been born in County Clare but brought up in Fulham, south-west London. He was another veteran of the First World War.

Before the Truce, Wilson was targeted in his role as Chief of the Imperial General Staff. Although it was known that he was an opponent of Irish nationalism and a supporter of unionism, he was a target because of his role in the British establishment. It was only after the Truce that it became personal.

The Treaty split the IRA in London, as it did in Ireland. Those living in London were not imbued with the same level of war weariness as those at home, and they could take a more principled stance on it. Sam Maguire came out early in support of the Treaty and of his friend Michael Collins.

According to Seán MacCraith, after the Treaty was signed a meeting of the Irish Republican Brotherhood was held in Shaftesbury Avenue in December 1921, which Dunne as a circle leader in the Brotherhood attended.[32] There it was decided to 'sink our differences' over the Treaty and carry out the assassination of three people: Captain John Bowen-Colthurst, for his part in the Easter Rising; an unnamed woman from Cork who had betrayed IRA actions in the county; and Wilson. The fact that this was an IRB meeting and not an IRA one is critical. The IRA was bound by the terms of the Truce and the Treaty to the peace; the IRB, as a secret, unaccountable organisation, was not.

If Wilson was in the line of fire in December 1921, he was even more so in the spring and early summer of 1922. When he stepped down as CIGS, he immediately cleaved to the unionist cause and became associated in nationalist minds with the worst excesses of the Craig government in Northern Ireland. Collins was no respecter of either the Truce or the Treaty when it came to carrying out actions in support of the nationalist minority in the North. Three IRA prisoners were due to be hanged for an attempted escape from Derry Jail that had led to the deaths of RIC constable Michael Gorman and Special Constable William

Lyttle on 2 December 1921. The execution date for Thomas McShea, Patrick Johnson and the warder who helped them, Patrick Leonard, was set for 9 February 1922. Collins sent Joe Dolan to England with instructions to kill the hangman John Ellis. Dolan arrived at the appointed address in Rochdale and was let in by Ellis's wife, but the hangman had already departed for Ireland. The British government commuted the death sentences to life imprisonment for the three men and the danger passed. Ellis, as we will see, later hanged Dunne and O'Sullivan.

In 1922 Wilson remained a target, according to Denis Brennan, a London-born volunteer who became officer commanding south-west and west London before the Truce. The period after the Truce was one of 'intense activities', he remembered, as the London IRA readied itself for a resumption of hostilities if necessary. Brennan stated that Dunne had told him there had been opportunities to shoot Wilson three to four weeks before he was assassinated and therefore:

> There should have been no disclaimer after the shooting. Here it was thought that Dev [de Valera] said it was done by a couple of disgruntled ex-servicemen. The impression we had was that no one in Ireland wanted to have anything to do with the shooting. Reggie Dunne was a very careful planner.[33]

Similarly, Pa Murray, when he returned from the United States after killing an informer, said Dunne had told him a month before the shooting that he intended to assassinate Wilson. The months leading up to that incident were a fraught time for the republican movement in London. Many, like Sam Maguire, who was for the Treaty, and Art O'Brien, who was vehemently against, had taken sides. 'The feeling among the London crowd at that time was really bad – there was plenty of suspicion. Most of us thought we were being kept in the dark and bulldozed by one side or the other,' Brennan remembered.[34] Pressure came on Reggie Dunne to declare where he stood. Cumann na mBan was one of the few republican organisations that was almost completely against the Treaty, its members having voted 419 to 63 against it at a convention in Dublin in February 1922. The same anti-Treaty sentiments animated the organisation in London. They wrote to Dunne, asking him as O/C London where he stood on the issue, but got no response. Rumours abounded in London that Dunne had been to Ireland and had visited the Portobello Barracks, the headquarters of Provisional Government forces, and the anti-Treaty Four Courts garrison. Cumann na mBan sent him white feathers, the symbol of cowardice that women used to shame men who did not sign up to fight in the First World War. Dunne could not run with the hare and hunt with the hounds. Michael Cremen, who came over to Dublin on behalf of the anti-Treaty rebels to find out where the IRA in London stood, recalled:

> After the split took place the bulk of the London Cumann na mBan went violently republican, and as they did not know the feelings of the London I.R.A. they – the Cumann na mBan – refused to co-operate with them. The secretary of the Cumann na mBan informed the O/C Reggie Dunne of their attitude. As an instance of the Cumann na mBan's attitude, when Dunne inquired of the Cumann na mBan as to the identity of a person from Ireland who was looking for arms in London, he was told that they would give him no information. After this, in a letter written by Dunne to the secretary of the Cumann na mBan, Dunne asked the girls to have patience, that they would learn soon of his activities. This letter was written on the eve of the Wilson shooting.[35]

A meeting was held in Mooney's pub in High Holborn on the evening of 21 June 1922 to try to resolve matters. Cumann na mBan members attacked Dunne, and he responded by saying that he would do something. Somebody brought in an evening newspaper. Amid page after page of coverage of the return of the Prince of Wales from his tour of India and Japan was a single paragraph that amounted to a call to arms:

> A war memorial erected by the Great Eastern Railway
> Company in the main booking hall of Liverpool Street Station
> will be unveiled tomorrow by Field Marshal Sir Henry Wilson
> MP, the dedication service being conducted by the Bishop of
> Norwich. The booking hall will be closed to the public from
> 12.15 p.m. to 1.15 p.m.[36]

Dunne and O'Sullivan stared at the notice. Here was an opportunity to finally fell one of the greatest enemies of Irish nationalism. According to Liverpool IRB veteran Patrick Daly, who was at the meeting in Mooney's pub, Sam Maguire was there too, and when Dunne declared his intention to kill Wilson, they all repaired outside:

> I remember on the occasion of a visit to Sam Maguire in
> London we were standing outside Mooney's public house
> in Holborn when I saw Maguire in close conversation with
> a man of, I think, medium build. This man turned out to be
> O'Sullivan and Maguire remarked to me, 'This fellow is very
> keen on shooting Wilson.' Wilson was subsequently shot
> and the two men concerned in his shooting were Dunne and
> O'Sullivan.[37]

Con Neenan, a Cork volunteer, was in London around the time of the shooting. He said that in December 1921 Maguire had informed him that Dunne and O'Sullivan were keen to shoot Wilson. Neenan further revealed that he had been at a meeting in Mooney's pub in May 1922. In the company of Frank Thornton, Maguire is alleged to have told him, 'The job on Wilson is on.'[38] Perhaps Maguire had mentioned it to him a month before the shooting took place, but it is more likely that Neenan misremembered the month and it was actually the meeting which took place the night before the shooting.

The key figure in relation to the killing of Wilson is Denis Kelleher, the third man in the assassination. He was at the meeting in Mooney's pub, and when Dunne declared his intention to shoot Wilson at Liverpool Street Station, Kelleher advised him against it. The idea, he told him, was 'ridiculous'. Kelleher later revealed that he got a phone call at work just before 1 p.m. on 22 June, but he was not there:

> I was told there was a telephone call. I did not know what it was until the news came through that Sir Henry Wilson was shot dead. Dunne wrote me from the prison telling me that he had telephoned me about a quarter to one and could not find me. He made an appointment with O'Sullivan at Victoria Station, although Sullivan had only one leg.[39]

Kelleher told the Army Pensions Board that it was never intended that O'Sullivan would be involved in the Wilson shooting, and that he was to have been in on it instead. The obvious questions that the board should have asked are why did he not turn up to accompany Dunne in the task of shooting Wilson and why did he leave it to a one-legged man instead, thus ensuring the outcome was doomed from the beginning? Yet the board changed the subject, the questions were never put and Kelleher never revealed why he did not turn up as scheduled. Joe Dolan, who was

Patriot, public figure, Mr. D. P. Kelleher dies

THE death took place last evening at his home, Wynberg, Endsleigh Park, Cork, of Mr Denis P. Kelleher, a former town councillor and deputy Lord Mayor of Cork.

Born in 1901 at Coolavohig, Macroom, Co. Cork, the late Mr. Kelleher was educated at the local national school and later, at the North Monastery and at Mount Melleray.

On finishing his studies in 1917, Mr. Kelleher joined the British Civil Service and was posted to London. There, he became associated with the Gaelic League, the Irish Republican Brotherhood and the Old IRA.

Mr. Kelleher spent five years in London. During that time he became OC Old IRA, London Brigade. In his capacity as OC, Mr. Kelleher was extensively involved in smuggling guns for the Old IRA into this country.

He was one of the Guard of Honour at the Lying in State of Cork's Lord Mayor, Terence McSwiney, at Southwark Cathedral in October 1920.

Before the outbreak of the Civil War Mr. Kelleher was captured in London and deported to Dublin where he was imprisoned in Mountjoy Jail for some months. Then, on the outbreak of the Civil War, he took the Republican side.

CAREER IN ASSURANCE

In 1924 Mr. Kelleher took up a career with the Refuge Assurance Company. He was appointed district manager for Cork.

Mr. Kelleher's public career spanned 10 years in the early fifties, during which time he served on Cork Corporation.

In 1939, when many foreign assurance firms amalgamated to become "The Irish Assurance Company Limited", Mr. Kelleher became manager of the Cork branch, a position which he held until his retirement 12 years ago. He was also vice-president of the Insurance Institute in Cork.

A member of the Committee of Management of the North

16 The death of the third man, Denis Kelleher, merited an article in the *Cork Examiner* of 14 November 1971. Later in life he had become a respectable middle-class businessman and public representative

sent by Collins to London to rescue Dunne and O'Sullivan, may have had the measure of Kelleher when he arrived in the city. 'I formed the impression that Kelleher was not much of a gun man, not one to be relied upon in a dangerous undertaking such as the rescue we were planning.'[40]

Dunne and O'Sullivan left the meeting in Mooney's pub and proceeded to Liverpool Street Station. There they reconnoitred the station and realised that it would be impossible to shoot Wilson in such a confined setting. They parted. Dunne left via Shoreditch and arrived home at 1 a.m. O'Sullivan went home the short distance to Little St James Street. He would have work in the morning. They agreed to meet that afternoon. One wonders if either of them slept at all.

8

Aftermath: 'The assassination has horrified the whole civilised world'

The Conservative leader Austen Chamberlain arrived at 36 Eaton Place on the evening of the Wilson shooting and rang the doorbell. Chamberlain was a diffident man, shy and not given to hyperbole. He had an Edwardian sense of English propriety, as observed by Harold Macmillan, then a backbench Tory MP: 'His top hat, his eyeglass, his exquisite courtesy and his orotund oratory marked him out from his colleagues.'[1] By the time of Chamberlain's arrival the blood had been removed from the steps of Wilson's home, as well as the body of the slain Field Marshal, which had been taken to the city morgue for examination.

Chamberlain intended to convey his sorrow and that of the government at the shooting of Wilson. He was chosen as the person with the necessary tact for such a potentially fraught encounter. Lloyd George's government regarded Wilson's incendiary speeches since his election as North Down MP as an irrelevance at best and a provocation at worst, but the time-honoured principle of *de mortuis nil nisi bonum dicendum est* applied.[2]

Chamberlain was ushered into the drawing room and asked to wait. Moments later a niece of Lady Wilson entered the room. 'Who are you?' she asked peremptorily. There had been a lot of visitors all day and large crowds had gathered outside. Chamberlain, one of the politest men in British politics, took no umbrage at not being recognised. He told her who he was and the object of his visit. 'You are the last man who should be in this house today,' she told him.[3] She walked out of the room, leaving

Chamberlain on his own. Moments later he left too. As he did, he could hear a voice coming from the kitchen area shouting, 'Murderer.' It was Lady Wilson. Her disdain for Chamberlain's entreaties was both personal and political. As a Southern Irish unionist she shared her husband's politics and his contempt for the 'Frocks'. Lady Wilson pointedly reserved seats for Southern unionist refugees at her husband's funeral, and organised clothes and shelter for those left homeless after the Free State takeover. She too regarded the Anglo-Irish Treaty as a sell-out to murderers. Her belief that the cabinet had 'murdered' her husband was based on its decision to withdraw Wilson's police protection in January 1922.

The fury of Wilson's supporters was turned on the Home Secretary Edward Shortt, who was interrogated at length in the House of Commons about the killing. Why had he withdrawn police protection from a man who was an enemy of Irish nationalism? Shortt explained that a special officer was placed at the disposal of the War Office for the protection of Wilson when it 'was thought necessary'. Police protection, Shortt went on to say, had been withdrawn from all ministers and senior government figures in January 1922, following the implementation of the Anglo-Irish Treaty. This was a month before Wilson had stepped down as Chief of the Imperial General Staff. On resigning his position, he would not have qualified for police protection in any case. It was pointed out to Shortt, however, that Lord Carson, who lived not far from Wilson in London, had a policeman outside his door. Shortt responded that there was 'no reason to suppose the Field Marshal was in danger'. He made the startling admission that there may have been no Irish involvement in the shooting at all, stating that Dunne and O'Sullivan were English-born:

These two young men had not been sent from Ireland. They were both Londoners, people living in London; they were both ex-soldiers; one of them was a member of a family all of whose sons fought in the war. Both of them were living at home with their parents up till the time of the crime, and there was no evidence whatsoever that they had ever been in Ireland at all during their lives.[4]

'They have Irish names,' the Conservative MP Howard Gritten responded, to which Shortt replied, 'There are plenty of people with Irish names, many of whom have never been in Ireland.'

All police protection of ministers was stood down on 23 January 1922, with the exception of a three-day period when Winston Churchill, the Colonial Secretary, was thought to have been under threat. Churchill interjected in the debate to state that he supported the policy of standing down police protection. Moreover, it had been done on the recommendation of the Assistant Commissioner of the Metropolitan Police and head of Special Branch Sir Basil Thomson (himself a target for the IRA) and was universally supported. Churchill made it clear that removing police protection was the right policy, despite the Wilson shooting:

> We have enjoyed five months' complete immunity, so far as this country is concerned, and even if we look back to the worst period of the Irish trouble a year ago – two years ago – we see that there were hardly any political assassinations over here in Great Britain.[5]

Wilson would have been under threat in Northern Ireland when he chose to visit there, Churchill concluded, but no more so in England than thirty or forty other persons whose names came readily to his mind.

Lady Wilson's opposition to the government led to an awkward standoff after Chamberlain left. She let it be known through the pages of the *Morning Post* that she wanted the cabinet to stay away from her husband's funeral. Their presence would be 'distasteful' to her. This was a moment of acute embarrassment. Whatever their differences with Wilson, the cabinet's absence would overshadow everything else about the funeral. In the battle of public opinion, politicians could never win against the widow of an illustrious soldier gunned down outside his home. The cabinet response was judicious in the circumstances. The War Office, her husband's employer for decades, told her the king would not be pleased if the ministers of his government were excluded from the funeral of one of Britain's pre-eminent soldiers. 'The loyal widow of the most loyal soldier of the King could give but one answer. So, the ministers will follow the body of Field Marshal Sir Henry Wilson to the grave,' the *Morning Post* reported.[6]

Wilson's status as one of the government's most acerbic critics was forgotten about in the immediate aftermath of the shooting. The shock of his violent death eclipsed the more unhinged comments he had been making, especially on the issue of Ireland. King George V wrote, 'My dear Lady Wilson, I can find no words to express my feelings of horror and grief at the appalling tragedy which has robbed you of your beloved husband and the country of one of its distinguished soldiers.'[7]

Lloyd George's tribute focused on Wilson's prescience in judging, as early as 1911, that the German army would invade France through Belgium rather than directly across the French frontier. 'He was right and the French General Staff was wrong – disastrously wrong as it turned out.'[8]

Former Conservative Party leader Andrew Bonar Law, who had stepped away from public life because of illness and was closest to

Wilson's thinking on Ireland, said he was a man of 'exceptional intellectual ability' and a good friend. 'He died loved as well as admired by all who knew him most intimately.'[9]

The National Executive of the Labour Party at Edinburgh condemned the shooting, but it had been unsparing in its criticism of the government over its policy on Ireland and made it clear there was wrong on both sides:

> It deplores the policy of violence which continues in Ireland and against the Irish people against which British Labour has always protested and expresses the hope that the government will pursue a policy of bringing peace and goodwill into the relationships between the Irish and British people.[10]

The British press bristled with cold fury, blaming not just the killers, but Ireland and the Irish. Many newspapers had embraced the Anglo-Irish Treaty reluctantly on the basis that it would bring an end to the ancient quarrel between Ireland and Britain. Nothing confounded that expectation more than a sitting MP being gunned down on the streets of London. *The Times* did not hold back on the significance of the assassination:

> The thoughts uppermost in men's minds will be not the distinction of his military services, invaluable as they were to the country before and during the war, but the foul crime, the revolting mischance which has cut off so noble a character and so fine an intelligence while they were still at the height of their power. The assassination has horrified the whole civilised world. Whatever measures the Government and parliament may see fit to take, the responsibility for those measures must rest solely with the Irish nation. For months past that unhappy island has lain under the curse of Cain. Morally she

THE NEW FORCE.

IRISH GUNMAN. "SAINTS PRESERVE US! AN INFERNAL MACHINE!"

[It is to be hoped that the authority conferred upon the Provisional Government by the voice of the people, as expressed in the recent Elections, may bring to an end the campaign of murder—culminating in the brutal assassination of Field-Marshal Sir HENRY WILSON—which has disgraced the name of Ireland in the eyes of the whole world.]

17 An illustration in *Punch*, 28 June 1922. Many in the British press regarded the Irish as an incorrigibly violent race more interested in the gun than democratic politics

is an outlaw and there can be no hope for her regeneration whatever enactments statesmanship on either side of St George's Channel may ordain unless she can brace herself together to cast off the infection which at present threatens to drag her down into complete social anarchy.[11]

The *Daily Express* compared the impact of the shooting to that of the assassinations of Cavendish and Burke in 1882. 'Ireland's good name, her status as a civilised country, her whole future is imperilled by this dastardly political murder. The Phoenix Park outrage, never forgotten here, long cost Ireland home rule.'[12]

Few of Britain's major newspapers departed from the indignant tone, although the *Daily Mail* sought not to blame the whole Irish race. 'The cruel and cowardly murder of Field Marshal Wilson had sent a shudder of horror through the whole British community in which we include every decent Irishman.'[13]

The liberal *New Statesman* believed Wilson, with his 'inflammatory speeches', did more than any other man 'to promote that spirit of ruthless and stupid retaliation which has led to his own death'.[14]

The *Daily Telegraph* blamed the anti-Treaty rebels in the Four Courts. 'It was a gesture of mad defiance by the beaten extremists and an announcement of their determination to pursue the work of wrecking the treaty settlement by intensifying the attack on Ulster.' The paper added an anti-Irish rejoinder: 'The whole of Ireland is so saturated with lies and homicidal incitements that the present crime may fail to stir the conscience of the people in whose name it is perpetrated.'[15]

The *Morning Post* also warmed to the theme of the Irish as an incorrigibly violent race and blamed the shooting on the British government's appeasement of republicans: 'We do not fear to say that in surrendering the cause of law and order, Lloyd George, Chamberlain and Asquith all share in the murder of Field Marshal Wilson and are bedabbled by blood.' Their anonymous Dublin correspondent's views were not leavened by actually living in Ireland. If anything, it generated an even greater loathing:

> As far as the honour of this murder is concerned and as far as realisation of the added shame that it heaps on the already infamous Irish race is concerned, the vast bulk of Southern Irishmen from the Midletonian anti-Partitionists to the Rory O'Connor republicans are going about their business today as if the Empire's greatest soldier had been a blind beggar run over by a cab. The foul deed has not punctured their monumental satisfaction with themselves for the whole race is steeped today in the famous doctrine that killing is no murder when the victim is an Orangeman or a loyalist.[16]

The aforementioned Earl of Midleton, the most conspicuous Southern unionist and the nominal leader of the Irish Unionist Alliance in the South, was outraged by the suggestion and demanded a retraction from the owners of the *Morning Post*. When he was unsuccessful, he raised the issue on the floor of the House of Lords in exchanges that were extraordinary by the decorous standards of the time. There was much support and sympathy for Midleton in the House. His fellow Irish peer, the Earl of Donoughmore, visited Dublin the day after the shooting and observed:

> I have no hesitation in saying that this horrible murder was the one subject, if I may use a familiar phrase, in the mouth of the man in the street. It was the one subject of discussion and it met with universal condemnation.[17]

The Earl of Birkenhead, the Lord Chancellor, who was a Treaty signatory, condemned an 'insulting and vile association' between Midleton's name and that of Rory O'Connor and de Valera and their 'Four Courts friends'. There had never been an 'outrage so gross as is contained in the passage to which I have called attention'.

There followed a long exchange in the House of Lords between Midleton and Lord Bathurst, whose wife Lady Bathurst had inherited the *Morning Post* newspaper from her father. Lord Bathurst recalled that Midleton had turned up to the couple's home in an agitated state. He was seized with 'great indignation' about the slur.[18] Lady Bathurst said she was not aware of the article and, in any case, did not go through every article with the 'blue pencil'. Why, asked her husband, did Midleton not take it up with the editor? Midleton responded that he had been the subject of previous calumnies and the editor had ignored his entreaties. Midleton, evidently beside himself now, let slip an extraordinary admission about the substance of his conversation with Bathurst's wife:

> I did say, in order to bring it home to her, that if I had been dealing with Lord Bathurst, and he had made the statement, and if it had been a hundred years ago, I should have thought it my duty to call him out and endeavour to shoot him for saying that I was a party to, or in sympathy with, such an outrage as the killing of Sir Henry Wilson.[19]

The furore was eventually resolved when the *Morning Post* published a grudging acknowledgement of Midleton's concerns:

> We are of the opinion that our correspondent has been perhaps too general in his condemnation for he should have exempted Southern Loyalists and Ulstermen, but we are satisfied that he had grounds for the statements to which we

gave publicity and certainly we do not consider that Lord Midleton and Lord Desart [fellow Southern Irish peer] have any justification for thinking that our correspondent included them personally in the accusations of indifference to the shooting of Sir H. Wilson.[20]

Yet even the *Morning Post* diatribe was not the most objectionable article about the shooting. Brigadier General Cyril Prescott-Decie, a veteran of the Boer War, First World War and the Irish War of Independence, described Dunne and O'Sullivan as 'worthless members of the community', 'brutal and degenerate assassins' and the 'dupes and fools of cunning brains'. They were of a certain Irish type, the one, presumably Dunne, 'the burly ruffian type', the other, O'Sullivan, with his wooden leg 'a moral and physical degenerate'. These were the men the Black and Tans had to deal with in Ireland. Is it any wonder Crown forces behaved like they did when faced with people like this? Prescott-Decie suggested.[21] He had been divisional commander of the Limerick Division of the Royal Irish Constabulary and resigned his commission in protest after the Truce of July 1921, believing that Crown forces had the IRA beaten. The letter confirming his resignation after the Truce had been published in the *Morning Post*.

His comments about the Wilson shooting were made in *The Patriot*, a weekly subscription newspaper with a circulation of around 1,100 copies. The publication was of no consequence, but somebody sent Dunne and O'Sullivan's solicitor, James Hyndman MacDonnell, a copy – and he clutched at every straw he could, given the general hopelessness of the men's case. MacDonnell complained that his clients could not get a fair trial as a result of Prescott-Decie's attack. The case was the subject of a contempt of court hearing, but the judge concluded that both the newspaper's paltry circulation and the fact that it was mostly subscription-led and therefore preaching to the converted mitigated it being considered a threat to the impartiality of the jury.[22]

In Ireland the press worried about the impact of the shooting on the country's reputation abroad. The *Irish Independent* commented:

> The awful tragedy is bound to work untold harm to Ireland.
> Although strongly condemned in this country, it will but
> further inflame the passions of the north-east Ulster Unionists
> against the minority in their midst and against the people
> of the rest of Ireland. Already some British newspapers are
> laying the blame for the recent tragedy upon a large section
> of the Irish people. Abroad the effect will be almost as bad for
> Ireland's reputation.[23]

The *Irish Times*, the voice at the time of Southern unionism, was similarly fearful:

> Our whole country ought to be in mourning today, not only
> for the death of a great Irishman, but for the harm and shame
> which, as we must fear, the manner of it will bring to Ireland.
> Field Marshal Sir Henry Wilson was murdered yesterday in
> London and all the circumstances suggest that the crime had
> its origin in the bitter conflicts and hatreds of Irish politics.[24]

The *Freeman's Journal* had an interesting take on the shooting:

> It must be borne in mind that the British people have regarded
> Sir Henry Wilson as the mastermind which turned the cause
> of the Great War in Europe. The British are unimaginative
> and the idea that he was liable to assassination was, I believe,
> never thought of. Such being the conditions, the emotion was
> profound. The House of Commons was staggered.[25]

The *Belfast Newsletter* published two pages of tributes to Wilson from organisations across Ulster. Wilson was more than an honorary Ulsterman, the newspaper concluded, he was a martyr:

The assassination of Field Marshal Sir Henry Wilson in London yesterday by Sinn Fein emissaries will send a thrill of horror through the civilised world. Here in Ulster, which he loved so dearly, and in whose cause he has died as truly as if he had fallen on the field of battle, his loss will be felt as a personal bereavement by every local subject. He was ours in a peculiar and very near sense, ours by blood, ours by sympathy and by service. We gloried in the great reputation which he won as a soldier, we took pride in that in the height of his war achievements with honours thick upon him, he came to us in our need and placed at our new Government's disposal his services to defend us and his great abilities to support our cause in the British House of Commons. He died a martyr to the cause of the freedom and liberties of Northern Ireland.[26]

The French newspapers too were shocked by the killing of a man who was well known for being a Francophile, a friend of Marshal Foch and a prime mover within the Allied supreme command that cleared the Germans off French soil.

L'Écho de Paris suggested that without Wilson 'the triumph of the Allies in the Great War would very probably have been impossible. He was one of the strongest supporters of the Entente Cordiale. France will not forget.'[27]

The monarchist publication *Action Française* opined that the 'crime will not have the effect of making us sympathetic towards the Irish cause'.[28]

Le Gaulois newspaper similarly feared that the 'abominable and inexcusable crime will have the effect of making European opinion still less favourable to the Irish Republican cause'.[29] French republicanism had long been an inspiration to its Irish equivalent. There were deep political and religious ties between France and Ireland, but they were trumped by the bonds of blood forged between Britain and France in the First World War. The shooting of Wilson did not go down well in France, as one of the first Irish ambassadors to the country, Count Gerald O'Kelly de Gallagh, noted in 1930:

> I have found a great deal of goodwill towards Ireland in all grades of society. This goodwill is largely sentimental and traditional. At the same time I have noticed a tendency in a few cases to patronise. It will take time to destroy completely the effect of secular British propaganda. In some military quarters I sense a latent hostility, at the roots of which I believe to be:
>
> (a) the Easter rebellion, which was, of course, exploited to the full by the British at the time.
>
> (b) the assassination of Field Marshal Wilson, who was very intimate with Foch and his entourage.
>
> (c) the influence of the British Military on the French Senior Officers, who, though sometimes actually disliking a given British officer, have none the less what I would almost describe as a social inferiority complex towards British officers as a whole.[30]

Foch was reported to have broken down when the news was conveyed to him.

> He was a magnificent soldier of the highest intelligence – vigilant and a real patriot. We were old friends. I relied upon him and he never failed me during the war. He helped to avoid

friction and to preserve cordial relations between the staffs of the two countries. I am overwhelmed for I have personally lost a true friend.[31]

The Belgian ambassador to Britain, Baron Ludovic Moncheur, noted Wilson's role in the defence of Belgium:

We learn the news of the odious assassination of Marshal Wilson with an emotion which will be felt by the entire Belgian nation. Our army, which has the greatest admiration for this glorious soldier, will preserve a profoundly grateful memory of the marks of affection which he continually lavished on it in the course of the Great War. In asking you to interpret our indignation, we beg you to convey to the British Government and to the family of the illustrious marshal the heartfelt expression of our most sincere condolence.[32]

In the United States, General John Pershing, the commander of the American Expeditionary Force in the First World War, said the killing 'fills me with a sense of horror. To think that a man of his ability, who did so much in the world war, should be struck down by the hand of an assassin. It is terrible to contemplate. He was a personal friend and our associations were always most agreeable.'[33]

The shooting was the lead story on the front page of the following day's *New York Times*. It was another example of the 'malign fates which have historically pursued the cause of Irish self-government. It is up to the Irish people, who have just voted for peace, to show they have nothing but abhorrence for such a terrible crime.'[34]

The *Evening Star* in Washington, DC, said questions relating to the shooting were the 'most damaging demonstration against

18 Wilson's assassination made the front page of
the *New York Times* on 23 July 1922

the government that it has experienced, according to opinion in
the lobby. The view was expressed there that had it been possible
to debate the subject the existence of the government would have
been seriously in question.'[35]

Michael Collins had nothing to say in public about the killing, leaving it to Arthur Griffith, the president of the Provisional
Government, to respond. Griffith was genuinely horrified by
Wilson's assassination, but his response was tempered by his out-
right opposition to Wilson's political views and what he stood for:

> Whether the assassination of Sir Henry Wilson was an act of
> private vengeance or had a pseudo-political aspect I do not
> know, but it is a fundamental principle of civilised government
> that the assassination of a political opponent cannot be
> justified or condoned. Sir Henry Wilson's political views were
> opposed to those of the vast majority of his countrymen.

Nevertheless, I know that the vast majority will be unanimous in condemning and deploring this anarchic deed.[36]

Éamon de Valera stopped well short of condemning the killing, concluding archly:

Killing any human being is an awful act but the life of a humble worker or peasant is the same as the mighty. I do not know who shot Wilson or why, it looks as if it was British soldiers [the two gunmen were Great War veterans] but life has been made hell for the nationalist minority in Belfast especially for the last six months . . . I do not approve, but I must not pretend that I misunderstand.[37]

The Four Courts garrison enraged public opinion in Britain by denying responsibility for the killing but stating that they would have owned up to it had they carried it out. 'The death of Sir Henry Wilson is to be deplored not because it occurred apparently at the hands of Irishmen, but because he is a victim of the imperial policy pursued by the British Government in Ireland.' They continued:

There is no use in trying to saddle the responsibility on Ireland or any group of Irish people. Responsibility must rest where the inexorable finger of history will place it – on the Government that has tried to carry on the policy Britain has continually and consistently adopted in its relation with Ireland for centuries. The scenes of outrage and carnage in the North are the result of British instigation, British connivance and British duplicity. In all this Sir Henry Wilson played a part that time will define and he played it not for Ulster but for his imperial masters. It would be hypocritical to condemn such actions as the shooting of Sir Henry Wilson while the causes that provoke such deeds remain.[38]

* * *

Dunne and O'Sullivan were taken to Westminster Police Court about three hours after the shooting. An angry crowd had gathered outside and the prisoners were ushered in around the back. Both men had thick bandages around their heads and exhibited clear signs of having been roughed up in jail. O'Sullivan's eye was swollen and Dunne looked as if he had been hit on the chin.

Dunne looked around the court in a manner that court reporters suggested was insolent. The two suspects continued to give false names. The seriousness of the charges was indicated by the presence at short notice of Sir Archibald Bodkin, the Director of Public Prosecutions, and the Crown case was conducted by Travers Humphreys, who had previously acted both for Oscar Wilde in his disastrous libel action against the Marquess of Queensberry and for the Crown against Sir Roger Casement, who was hanged for his part in the Easter Rising.

Humphreys opened up: 'I am instructed to prosecute those two prisoners on charges, first of all, of the murder of Field Marshal Sir Henry Wilson; secondly, on a charge of shooting with intent to murder Police Constable Walter Marsh; further, with attempting to murder Constable Cecil Sayer and shooting with intent to murder Alexander Clarke.'[39]

Neither Dunne nor O'Sullivan made a reply to the charges, but Dunne inquired as to the well-being of the other men they shot. When told they were recovering, Dunne replied: 'I am glad to hear that.' The pair were remanded in custody for a week.[40]

In the days following the shooting, the Metropolitan Police arrested eighteen known Irish activists in an attempt to link others with the shooting. One of them was Seán MacCraith, the general secretary of the Irish Self-Determination League, who was arrested two days after the shooting at his offices in Shaftesbury Avenue by three Scotland Yard detectives. He was held for three days in dark cells without any ventilation and given dry bread and black tea. Another who was arrested was Katie Eadie, 'a lady of refinement', according to one newspaper, and the sister of Seán Connolly, the first rebel to die during the Easter Rising. Eadie was found to have been in possession of eleven incendiary bombs when police raided her flat in Bayswater following the Wilson shooting and was sentenced to two years' imprisonment.[41]

The Metropolitan Police arrested thirteen known republicans in total, according to Art O'Brien. It would have been fourteen had O'Brien not been in Ireland at the time Wilson was shot. Scotland Yard detectives also visited O'Brien's office in Holborn but did not search it. However, they arrested two of his staff: Charles Bertram (CB) Dutton and Fintan Murphy. This provoked a furious response from the bumptious O'Brien, who visited the Home Office and demanded to speak to the Home Secretary, Edward Shortt. O'Brien informed Shortt's secretary that he was the representative of Dáil Éireann in London and had accompanied de Valera to Downing Street the previous July to meet Lloyd George. It was, therefore, an 'unnecessary insolence' for Scotland Yard detectives to raid his office. Shortt's secretary, a Mr Maxwell, refused him access to the Home Secretary. O'Brien made a note of it on the spot. He left in a huff, empty-handed, and penned a furious letter to the Provisional Government's Minister for Foreign Affairs, George Gavan Duffy. Nothing came of the incident.[42]

Four days after the shooting the inquest was held at Westminster Coroner's Court in Horseferry Road. Before it began the jury were driven to 36 Eaton Place to view the body of the late Field Marshal before the casket was closed in preparation for the funeral.

Wilson's brother Major Cecil Wilson had identified the body. The subject of his brother's security had been mentioned in the past, Cecil Wilson told the coroner, but not recently. The taxi driver and a labourer both gave evidence. The taxi driver had not seen Wilson raise his sword; the labourer on the road outside had watched Wilson try to put his key in the lock before the final shots were fired. Wilson's maid said she had come on the scene after hearing the shots and saw his sword lying on the ground as if it had been drawn. None of the witnesses were named at the inquest or trial as it was thought that they might be subject to intimidation by Irish republicans.

Other witnesses, both civilian and police, gave evidence recounting in detail what had happened and how Dunne and O'Sullivan had been pursued by a crowd who had risked their lives to stop them. 'Law-abiding Englishmen saw murderers firing revolvers in the street, but they promptly took their lives in their hands,' the Westminster coroner Ingleby Oddie concluded. Wilson had been a 'truly great man, a brilliant soldier and a distinguished public servant . . . he was shot when his back was turned towards them as brave and fearless men are shot by assassins'. The inquest jury recorded a charge of wilful murder and put on record their admiration for those who risked their lives pursuing Dunne and O'Sullivan.[43]

* * *

The inquest coincided with Wilson's funeral, which took place in the late morning of 26 June. It was one of the biggest London had ever seen. Despite heavy rain and a high wind, thousands of mourners, at times ten deep, lined the route from Eaton Place to St Paul's Cathedral, many arriving hours before the funeral

19 Wilson's funeral was one of the biggest that London had ever seen

procession started. People stood in unbroken rows on both sides underneath the railway arch on Ludgate Hill and mounted police prevented the crowd spreading out over the roadway.

The parade was led by the Life Guards, Wilson's coffin following after, draped in the Union flag and borne on a horse-drawn gun carriage. A wreath of lilies from his wife rested on the front of the carriage; his plumed hat, baton and sword were placed on his coffin. The bearer party that walked alongside the coffin was from Wilson's old regiment, the Rifle Brigade.

Behind his coffin, poignantly, came his unmounted old grey charger, led by Wilson's manservant. Following on were seven officers wearing feathered plumes and long coats, carrying Wilson's honours. After that came Lady Wilson and Wilson's elderly mother Constant in a black brougham (a horse-drawn carriage). They were the only ones in the procession who did not walk.

His funeral was a gathering of those who had guided Britain to a bitter victory in the war four years earlier. Field Marshal Sir Douglas Haig, Wilson's good friend Field Marshal Sir William Robertson, First Sea Lord Earl Beatty, Lord French and Chief Marshal Sir Hugh Trenchard walked in the procession. General Sir Nevil Macready, who had succeeded in stopping a resumption of hostilities between Britain and Ireland and was a close friend of Wilson, was there too. The king was represented by his uncle, the Duke of Connaught.

The military procession was followed by a fleet of cars carrying wreaths from civil and political institutions across the world. The considerable police presence along the route demonstrated the residual fear after the shooting. The multitudes observed a 'reverent still which was eloquent'. The *Morning Post* correspondent thought the crowds represented the best of England:

We must add that with the sentiment of the crowd was mingled profound indignation sometimes expressed but for the most part unvoiced. The English are a silent people and their habit of reticence sometimes induces misunderstanding. They are the expression of the people – sensible, patient, good-humoured, disciplined, loyal and, underneath all, immovably resolute.[44]

The entrance to St Paul's Cathedral was sealed off with great wooden barriers painted purple, the colour of mourning. As the hearse arrived, the Irish Guards band, from the regiment Reggie Dunne had served in, played the 'Londonderry Air' ('Danny Boy').

Wilson's coffin was brought in through the great west door of the cathedral to its tolling bells and Chopin's 'Funeral March'. The cabinet were all in attendance, and Lloyd George's wife Margaret made a rare foray into public life. Among the titled aristocrats,

20 Lady Wilson is escorted down the steps of St Paul's by Marshal Foch

representatives of all the major powers and other notable guests were Lord Balfour and Lord FitzAlan, who had both been targeted for assassination by the IRA. Baron Carson was again conspicuous by his absence. He sent a representative.

There were twenty loyalist refugees from the Free State in attendance, hand-picked by Lady Wilson. They had either chosen or been forced to leave Ireland. The short service began with a lamentation by Canon Samuel Alexander from the Bible, 'Man that is born of woman has but a short time to live and is full of misery'. This was followed by the committal prayer and the hymn 'O God, Our Help in Ages Past', after which the Archbishop of Canterbury Randall Davidson pronounced the blessing. At the end the 'Dead March' from Handel's *Saul* was played, and then the bugles of the Rifle Brigade sounded the 'Last Post' and the 'Reveille'.

Wilson's body was lowered into the crypt of St Paul's and placed beside the graves of two other Anglo-Irish titans of the British military, his old friend Lord Roberts and Lord Wolseley, the Dublin-born veteran of many colonial campaigns, who had died in 1913. A slot in the crypt was held symbolically for the Kerry-born Lord Kitchener, who had drowned on his way to Russia in 1916 and whose body was never found.

* * *

It was a sullen and solemn House of Commons that debated the state of Ireland that evening. Churchill had to placate the Diehards and the sceptics within the Conservative Party who had never wanted the Treaty in the first place and saw Wilson's shooting as the inevitable outcome of parleying with the 'murder gang'. He laid the facts before the House.

When the British Government signed the Anglo-Irish Treaty on the night of 6 December 1921 it had done so in the belief that the plenipotentiaries nominated by Sinn Féin represented the Irish people and were therefore empowered to act on behalf of the Irish people in signing it. The Treaty had been passed by the Dáil in January 1922 by 64 votes to 57. This established the Provisional Government, but one which needed a democratic mandate to govern. The IRA was the only instrument available to the Provisional Government to keep order in the country, but it too was split over the Treaty and it was unclear if the government had any control over it.

Churchill then turned to de Valera, who had sought to 'weaken and discredit the Provisional Government, to create disorder throughout the country, and to embroil Southern Ireland with Ulster'. Two IRA divisions were located in Ulster and it was not clear who was organising them. They were carrying out outrages that were provoking retaliation in an 'equally combative, belli-cose spirit' by 'Protestant Orangemen of the North', and every Catholic outrage was 'repaid with bloody interest'. In the South a settlement was reached to 'end the historic quarrel between the two islands and to free our own good name from the reproach of being perpetually engaged in the coercion of a small people'. Nevertheless, the British government would have to act if the Provisional Government did not. That government now had an electoral mandate from the people. It was time to act. He finished with a clear warning:

> The ambiguous position of the so-called Irish Republican Army, intermingled as it is with the Free State troops, is an affront to the Treaty. The presence in Dublin, in violent occupation of the Four Courts, of a band of men styling

themselves the headquarters of the Republican executive, is a gross breach and defiance of the Treaty. If it is not brought to an end, and a very speedy end, then it is my duty to say, on behalf of His Majesty's Government, that we shall regard the Treaty as having been formally violated, that we shall take no steps to carry out or to legalise its further stages, and that we shall resume full liberty of action in any direction that may seem proper and to any extent that may be necessary to safeguard the interests and the rights that are entrusted to our care.[45]

The British newspapers were supportive of Churchill. The *Daily Mail* stated:

Ireland is rushing towards the precipice. Unless she pulls up sharply and acts sanely, the attempt to give Southern Ireland self-government will be a failure and Great Britain will have to reconsider the whole question. We approve heartily Mr Churchill's firm declarations concerning the headquarters of the Republican executive at the Four Courts, namely this sort of thing must stop. Mr Bonar Law's statement that he did not know whether he would have voted for the Treaty if he could have foreseen the position today is the sort of warning which the Government cannot afford to treat lightly.[46]

The *Daily Express* said Churchill's speech showed the 'policy of drift' towards matters in Ireland had now ended. 'Sir Henry Wilson's death and the feeling his murder has aroused have forced the cabinet to insist that the pro-Treaty leaders demonstrate their ability to maintain law and order and to govern.'[47] The *Daily Chronicle* had reservations about the tone but not the substance of Churchill's remarks:

Some will say that Mr Churchill's warning to the Southern Government would have been better expressed in the language of advice rather than of threats, but it amounts to much the same thing. Unless the Southern Irish Government puts down crime, the Treaty will lapse.[48]

At 11 p.m. on the night of the funeral anti-Treaty forces kidnapped Lieutenant General J. J. 'Ginger' O'Connell in Dublin. Despite the fraught nature of the current climate, O'Connell was captured unarmed while strolling back from a friend's house in Leeson Street to Beggars Bush Barracks, the headquarters of the National Army. Though just thirty-five, O'Connell was a well-respected figure in pro-Treaty circles. Critically, he had received formal military training while serving with the US army before the First World War.[49]

It was a grim meeting of the Provisional Government that took place the following morning. Many of its members had slept in their offices for fear of being kidnapped. It was only while the meeting was progressing that the cabinet received the text of Churchill's ultimatum. Far from strengthening their hand, the cabinet believed that conceding to the British government's demands would undermine them and make it look like they were operating at the behest of the British and not on their own behalf. Yet the desire to avenge the kidnapping of O'Connell trumped reservations about perceptions that they were being directed by London. In kidnapping O'Connell, the anti-Treaty side had kidnapped the wrong man. A worried cabinet was reassured by the National Army's Adjutant General Gearóid O'Sullivan that his men would be prepared to move against the anti-Treaty rebels. This was enough for the Provisional Government to act against the Four Courts rebels and assert its authority. It prepared the

Irish people for the worst in a statement issued on the evening of
27 June:

> For forty-eight hours the soldiers of your army have
> unflinchingly borne the brunt of battle against the forces
> of anarchy in your capital. Some of them have given their
> lives, and many others have been wounded in the defence
> of your rights as citizens. You are faced with a conspiracy
> whose calculated end is to destroy the Treaty signed by your
> representatives and endorsed by yourselves. Under that Treaty
> the Government and control of your own country and its
> resources have been surrendered back to you after centuries
> of usurpation. You are asked to reject this surrender and to
> engage in a hopeless and unnecessary war with Great Britain.
> The people in the Four Courts say they are fighting for a
> Republic. In reality they are fighting to bring the British
> back. Remember, we ask no man or woman to yield up
> any ideal or principle. Liberty will be secured to all under
> constitutional guarantees, but it will be constitutional liberty
> and no man shall be permitted to do violence to the views of
> his neighbours or to the will of the majority, least of all will
> the profession of ideals or principles be permitted as an excuse
> for undermining the people's rights, the security of the person,
> the security of property, and freedom to live their own lives in
> their own way as long as they do not trespass upon the rights
> of others. Fellow citizens! This is what your Government
> stands for, this is what your soldiers are fighting for. In this
> programme we do not hesitate to turn to you for support in
> any call which we may be compelled to make on you.[50]

* * *

On Saturday 1 July 1922 Dunne and O'Sullivan appeared at Westminster Police Court charged with the murder of Wilson and the shooting with intent to murder police constables Marsh and Sayer and the civilian Alexander Clarke.

Giving their real names, the pair also revealed that they were ex-soldiers. They looked a lot better than they had done when they appeared bloodied and dishevelled immediately after being caught. A new, unnamed eyewitness was called at this stage of proceedings, who said Wilson had got as far as reaching for his house keys when he was shot first by Dunne and then by O'Sullivan. Wilson had collapsed as he reached for his sword, the witness said. Constable Marsh had survived, even though the bullet had gone through his body and out the other side. Constable Sayer had been shot in the right ankle.

The delay in both men giving their full names had given some time for both sets of parents to burn any incriminating documents, yet when Metropolitan Police officers raided the O'Sullivan home, they found a cardboard box that contained six bandoliers, and in a cupboard six copies of *An t-Óglách* (*The Irish Volunteer*) and a letter from Carrigrohane, County Cork. The notepaper was headed 'The Irish Republic'. The author's name was not revealed in court:

> Things are very busy here, for we, who swore to maintain
> the Republic, intend doing so. I know, Joe, you are not a Free
> Stater. You could not be. You would never consent after these
> hundreds of years of fighting to Ireland becoming part of
> England. Now, Joe, we will have no Free State governor, no
> oath to the King and no Ulster cut off from the rest of Ireland.
> The fight must go on. Some good men have given way under
> the influence of Lloyd George. But we give no allegiance to de

Valera, nor to Collins, nor to Griffith. We are not politicians. We give our allegiance to the Republic and, if needs be, our lives.[51]

The tone of this letter is interesting. It is clearly from somebody on the anti-Treaty side. What does the author mean by stating, 'I know, Joe, you are not a Free Stater. You could not be'? Is he saying that he knows for certain, or is he assuming O'Sullivan would never join the Treaty side? It is unclear.

Dunne and O'Sullivan were brought from Brixton Prison in a covered motor car guarded by armed officers. Only witnesses and the press were allowed into court, and the day chosen for their hearing, a Saturday, was highly unusual, probably chosen at short notice for security reasons.

Crown prosecutor Travers Humphreys told the judge that the evidence against the two men was so clear that there was no reason for a preliminary hearing. Their trial date was set for 18 July 1922. This was evidently as open and shut a case of murder as ever had come in front of a jury. No plea towards a political justification could mitigate that fact under English law, nor could any defence barrister on Earth save them. But their erstwhile IRA comrades thought they might be able to.

9

Rescue:
Kidnapping the Prince of Wales

Michael Collins was in Cork when news came through of the shooting of Field Marshal Sir Henry Wilson. Collins had just become the target of a crude electoral fraud in which his enemies had sought to alter the first preference vote for him in the general election. He was standing in the Cork County constituency and the election count was done on the basis of proportional representation, a form of election brought in by the British government to curb the success of Sinn Féin. The system, still in use today, distributes seats in a fairer manner than the first-past-the-post system and allows the voter to list candidates in order of preference.

The Cork County constituency returned six candidates to Dáil Éireann. The county, the biggest in Ireland, had many offshore islands, isolated headlands and bad roads, which made the collection of ballot boxes at the time a major logistical exercise. As a result, Cork was the last county to declare, although the outcome of the national election was already certain. To hasten the count, the first preferences for each of the candidates were sifted into fifteen separate sealed ballot boxes and left overnight. The support for Collins in his native county was so enormous that four ballot boxes were needed to accommodate his vote.

When the returning officer arrived in the morning to open the ballot boxes, he found that papers in Collins's boxes had been tampered with and the No. 1s turned into 4s, 7s and 11s.[1] Evidently somebody had entered the hall overnight with the purpose of reducing Collins's vote, but who? This was a surprise to the local

247

police, who had been guarding the hall in Cork city and could find no evidence of a break-in. Collins was wired to come to Cork and did so immediately on the morning of 22 June, having been at General Seán Mac Eoin's wedding the previous day in Longford.

Collins need not have bothered travelling to Cork. His victory was so emphatic that the 210 or so ballots marked as having been interfered with made no difference to the final outcome.[2] He was three times over the quota for election, with 17,106 votes, more than twice that of his nearest challenger. However crude it might have been, the episode was a telling reminder that there were some in Cork who would stop at nothing to undermine Collins.

The news of the Wilson shooting was relayed to Collins at the county centre by a friend, Paddy O'Keeffe. 'I suppose these men will hang,' O'Keeffe suggested, to which Collins responded with a volley of swearing: 'And they bloody deserve it, they have got me in a fix.'[3] A short time later Collins arrived back in Dublin and declared to General Joseph Sweeney: '"It was two of ours that did it." That was his [Collins's] reply.'[4] Who did Collins mean by 'ours'? Was he referring to pro-Treaty or anti-Treaty IRA, or just to the IRA in general? Sweeney did not seek any clarification. Once again, as we have also observed with the way obvious questions were not asked by the Army Pensions Board, a lack of curiosity affected people's response to the shooting.

Sweeney observed that Collins looked more pleased that Wilson had been assassinated than at any time since news came through of the killing in June 1920 of Wilson's near-namesake Captain Percival Lea-Wilson in Gorey, County Wexford. Lea-Wilson had been witnessed abusing Tom Clarke, the oldest signatory of the Proclamation after the Easter Rising, and Collins had made a mental note to exact revenge at a later date. (The Lea-Wilson family were in the news many years later when Captain

Lea-Wilson's widow bought a painting she thought was the work of the minor Dutch artist Gerard van Honthorst. It turned out to be Caravaggio's presumed lost masterpiece *The Taking of Christ*. This stunning revelation was not made until 1990. The painting now hangs in the National Gallery of Ireland.[5])

Collins dispatched Liam Tobin and Tom Cullen to London to effect a rescue of Dunne and O'Sullivan. Cullen was his assistant director of intelligence and part of the counter-spy ring that had beaten the British at their own game in the War of Independence. The alacrity with which Collins went about trying to rescue the two men has often been cited as compelling evidence of his intriguing in the shooting of Wilson.

Another factor may have been the success the IRA had between 1919 and 1921 in breaking out of jails in Britain and Ireland. Florence 'Florrie' O'Donoghue, an IRA commander who later became a respected historian, reflected on the successes of those years in the preface to the book *IRA Jailbreaks 1918–1921*, written in 1971: 'In the more recent phase of the nation's struggle, from 1916 onwards, there was scarcely a jail or fortress in the country from which some Irishman, held there for his part in the fight for liberty, had not escaped or been rescued.'[6]

On 21 January 1919, the day the War of Independence started with the Soloheadbeg ambush, four prisoners escaped from Usk Prison in Monmouthshire, Wales. The four – Joe McGrath, George Geraghty, Barney Mellows and Frank Shouldice – had been arrested in March of the previous year as part of the so-called 'German Plot'. Their escape was marked by the dogged determination and enterprise that characterised so many republican jailbreaks. Three files and a blank key were baked into a number of loaves and brought into the prison. Geraghty was a stonemason able to accurately estimate the height of a wall, and they made a rope ladder with roller towels and ash splinters for the rungs. The men escaped from prison at a time when the Spanish flu was ravaging the world, and the prison break would have been even greater had so many men not been stricken with the illness. From Usk, the men got a taxi driver to take them to Shrewsbury. They took a train to Liverpool and were smuggled on board a boat to Ireland.[7]

The most famous escape of the War of Independence was Éamon de Valera's from Lincoln Prison in February 1919. This involved ingenuity and daring in equal measure, with Collins as organiser. While serving as an altar boy in the prison chapel, de Valera found some candle wax and made a wax imprint of the key to a door in the exercise yard. A fellow prisoner, Sean Milroy, drew the correct shape and size of the key on a humorous cartoon on the front of a Christmas card. A key was cut and smuggled into the prison in a cake. It took three versions of the key – and three cakes, the final one also containing a file so that the key could be modified if needed – to find the right one. On 3 February de Valera was sprung from the prison, with Collins waiting for him on the other side of the wall.

A month later Robert Barton, a future signatory of the Anglo-Irish Treaty, escaped from Mountjoy Prison in Dublin. He cut the bars of his cell with a saw that had been smuggled into the prison and lobbed a bar of soap over the wall to signal he was ready to escape. After scaling the wall with a rope ladder, he jumped down onto a thick blanket on the other side. Again, Collins was there to meet him. A month later twenty Sinn Féin prisoners escaped from Mountjoy after the inmates attacked the guards en masse and scaled the wall.[8]

In October 1919 six prominent republican prisoners were sprung from Strangeways Prison in Manchester. They attacked

The portrait of Field Marshal Sir Henry Wilson by his childhood friend
Sir William Orpen was painted during the Paris Peace Conference in 1919.
Wilson was not enamoured with it: 'It makes me look like an
awful blackguard'

Top: The memorial at Liverpool Street Station to the men from the Great Eastern Railway Company who died in the First World War was unveiled by Field Marshal Sir Henry Wilson MP on 22 June 1922

Bottom: The Northern Ireland parliament was opened by King George V on 22 June 1921, a year to the day before Wilson was assassinated

Top: The St Ignatius College cricket first XI from 1914–15 includes Reginald Dunne (front row, extreme right)

Bottom: Joseph O'Sullivan's last will and testament was acquired by the National Museum of Ireland at auction in 2014, along with that of Dunne. The papers had been in the possession of the men's solicitor, J. H. MacDonnell

Le Petit Journal

illustré

ABONNEMENTS

Trois mois Six mois Un an
FRANCE & COLONIES
4 fr.   7 fr. 50   14 fr
UNION POSTALE
6 fr.   12 fr.   22 fr.

PARAISSANT LE DIMANCHE

33ᵉ Année - Nᵒ 1645

On s'abonne dans tous
les bureaux de poste

Les Manuscrits ne sont pas rendus

Un assassinat politique

L'histoire du conflit entre l'Irlande et la Grande-Bretagne a toutes ses pages tachées de sang. — Un nouveau chapitre dramatique vient d'y être ajouté. A Londres, le maréchal Wilson a été assassiné à coups de revolvers par deux fanatiques Irlandais. C'est un brave soldat et un ami de la France qui vient de disparaître.

Wilson's assassination made the front cover of the leading Paris weekly
Le Petit Journal in the week after his assassination

Wilson's funeral was one of the largest London has seen, outside
of members of the royal family

Top: This memorial in County Kerry recalls the Ballyseedy massacre of March 1923, when nine anti-republican prisoners were tied to a landmine by National Army forces and blown up

Bottom: Michael Collins's death in an ambush on 22 August 1922 shocked the world and ensured he would forever be known as Ireland's great lost leader

Top: Currygrane Lake provided water for Currygrane House, the home of the Wilson family

Bottom: This small pet cemetery contains the remains of three dogs that lived on the Wilson estate: (from left to right) Barney, Scraps and Pat

Top: The inscription on the tomb of Reginald Dunne and Joseph O'Sullivan states in Gaelic (Irish) that they gave their lives for Ireland in England. Also remembered on the headstone is Michael McInerney, who died during the Truce period while preparing a bomb factory in Greenwich

Bottom: The memorial to Henry Wilson at Liverpool Street Station was erected a year after his death and is located underneath the one to the men from the Great Eastern Railway Company

the prison warden, threw a rope ladder over the ten-metre wall and scrambled down another rope ladder on the other side. The British newspapers were highly unimpressed. The *Pall Mall Gazette* observed:

> The story of the organised escape of the Sinn Féin prisoners is far from edifying and reflects gravely upon those in authority at the prison, from which it was so easy to escape. The departure of the little group of Sinn Féiners seems to have been arranged quite methodically and conducted with a calm contempt for the guardians of the law. The contempt was justified and we trust that the Home Secretary will take such action as shall render the prisons throughout the country less easy of egress.[9]

Between the Truce of 11 July 1921 and the Treaty on 6 December 1921 there were further high-profile escapes. In September fifty prisoners escaped from the Curragh Camp in County Kildare by tunnelling underneath the perimeter. A month later a group of female prisoners escaped from Mountjoy, as did seven male prisoners, disguised as Auxiliaries.[10]

The problem, though, for the would-be rescuers of Dunne and O'Sullivan was that these post-Truce escapes took place in Ireland, where friendly jailers were willing to turn a blind eye and the escapees had widespread public support. Since the escapes of 1919, jails in Britain had become much more vigilant. There was also a hostile population to contend with.

The difficulties surrounding a rescue in Britain were illustrated by the fate of Frank Carty, the commandant (major) of the 4th Sligo Brigade and one of the most energetic IRA commanders in the War of Independence. He was rescued from Sligo Jail in June 1920 but then rearrested. On 15 February 1921 he became the first prisoner to escape from Derry Jail. He managed to squeeze his 6ft, 15-stone frame through the sawed-off bars in his jail and scale down a 40ft wall with the aid of a rope, despite an injured wrist. Determined to carry on the fight, Carty was smuggled out of Derry in a fishing trawler, the *Carricklee*, which left for Glasgow. There, known by the name of Frank Somers, he set about reorganising the IRA in the city, though he was once again arrested and taken to Duke Street Prison, Glasgow.[11]

The prison is in the centre of the city. The IRA judged it impossible to spring him from jail a third time so they decided to target the prison escort carrying him from jail to the court. Carty was scheduled to be taken to the Sheriff's Court on 4 May 1921 in a Black Maria escorted by armed detectives. After a brief hearing, the prison van was attacked just two hundred metres from the entrance to the jail. The escort party was set upon by twelve IRA men, who approached the van from two sides. In the ensuing gun battle Detective Inspector Robert Johnston was shot dead. His colleague Detective Sergeant George Stirton, though wounded, managed to keep firing, thwarting the attackers. A bullet aimed at shattering the lock had the opposite effect and jammed it even tighter.

The shootout took place in full view of dozens of terrified onlookers and made national news headlines. Carty was sentenced to ten years' penal servitude, and the unsuccessful rescue was a military and public relations disaster for the IRA. Throughout the War of Independence, the IRA had largely managed to avoid fatalities in Britain. The killing of a police officer brought public opprobrium and heat upon the republican movement at a time when there was a growing degree of sympathy in liberal circles in Britain for the cause of Irish independence.

These considerations were at the forefront of Dunne and O'Sullivan's would-be rescuers when they arrived in London to formulate a rescue attempt. The two men were being kept in Brixton Prison, at the top of Brixton Hill. When it had opened a hundred years earlier it was in open countryside, but now it was in a built-up area. At the time of their remand, Dunne and O'Sullivan were the most notorious prisoners in Britain. It had been almost a year since the Truce had ended the War of Independence, and many of the republican prisoners jailed in Brixton who might have been of assistance in springing Dunne and O'Sullivan had been released under the terms of the Treaty.

'Our intelligence system had broken down,' recalled Billy Ahern, who was involved in the rescue attempt. 'There were now no friendly wardens in Brixton Prison and no informants in the prisons.'[12]

Cullen had come immediately to reconnoitre the rescue attempt but returned to Ireland before the Civil War broke out, leaving Denis Kelleher, who succeeded Dunne as O/C London, in charge on behalf of Collins. Unknown to each other, the pro- and anti-Treaty sides both had men in London willing to rescue the pair. Michael Cremen, who had been the liaison between the anti-Treaty IRA executive based in the Four Courts and the London IRA, was asked by the executive to look at the possibility of a rescue:

On my arrival in London I found the organisation of a rescue of the prisoners presented great difficulties. Because of my estimate of the calibre of the men comprising the London Battalion, I did not approach any of them regarding the projected rescue.[13]

Cremen sent two officers from the Liverpool battalion of the IRA, Paddy Fleming and Dan O'Malley, to ascertain if the pro-Treaty side were in earnest about the rescue:

I came to the conclusion that Cullen and his crowd could carry out the operation easier in the matter of available resources than we could. I then sent Fleming and O'Malley to a meeting which Cullen had called in connection with the rescue. Both of those men when they reported back to me, assured me of the genuineness of Cullen's intentions. I then returned to Dublin to report on the position, which I did to the Executive. The Executive approved of my report on the position as I saw it.[14]

Cullen had reached the same conclusion. Sam Maguire called both sides together. They agreed that the only way to rescue the pair would be to ambush the prison van on the way between jail and the court, but when?

Cremen asked Art O'Brien to get the information from Dunne and O'Sullivan's solicitor, James Hyndman MacDonnell, but he had no date for their trial hearing either.

Only overwhelming force could hope to prevail. Dunne and O'Sullivan let those on the outside know that they would rather die as soldiers in the rescue attempt than be hanged as criminals. The would-be rescuers reconnoitred the vicinity of Brixton Prison and found there were two exits, one leading to the centre of Brixton, the other in almost the opposite direction. Brixton Hill was a heavily populated residential area, and there were too many eyes and ears around to allow for proper planning. Keeping so many men in readiness from 6 a.m. to 10 a.m. day after day was bound to attract attention sooner or later.

'It would be almost impossible to do so without attracting notice in such a crowded and hostile district. The difficulties of the case seemed so insurmountable it was decided to call the job off and the Free State side seemed to be of the same opinion,' Cremen concluded.[15]

Ahern was equally pessimistic about their chances. 'There was no information as to when the prisoners were to be brought out from Brixton as we worked hard to conceal sixty men in a house. We had men from Liverpool, Cork, Dublin, Southampton. We had enough arms.'[16]

Ambrose Bettridge, an IRA volunteer based in Liverpool, said he and another unnamed volunteer were on stand-by to travel from Lime Street Station in the city, waiting for the summons to bring about the rescue. 'The only information I got was that Michael Collins was to supply machine guns and he did not.'[17]

Ten other Liverpool volunteers signed up for the rescue but they were not needed. There was no chance of a rescue. What other options were left?

Unknown to the would-be rescuers, the prison authorities were already on to them. Sir John Anderson, the Under-Secretary for Ireland, wrote to the governor of Brixton Prison, stating he had information from an informer that a rescue attempt would be made:

> The commissioner is satisfied that the precautions taken
> with regards to the prisoners' escort to court render it in the
> highest degree improbable that any such attempt at rescue
> should be made outside the Prison. There is, however, the
> possibility that an attempt might be made at the prison itself,
> as in the case of the prisoners. The governor, at Mr Wall's
> insistence, has already taken special precautions by placing
> one or two armed men at the gate. I think, however, that it
> would be advisable to have four or six armed uniformed police
> on duty day and night inside the prison. The presence of
> such a guard would render it very unlikely that any attempt
> would be made and impossible that any such attempt should

succeed. There are, I believe, two armed police patrols on duty outside the prison and possibly these should double. It has been suggested that the duty of guarding the prison should be undertaken by a military guard but it appears to be primarily a matter for the police. I entirely agree, we must be prepared for every contingency and no precaution should be neglected. The presence of police will not of course detract in any way from the responsibility of the governor and he will remain for all purposes the supreme authority within the prison.[18]

Scotland Yard assistant commissioner Colonel J. F. C. Carter told the Brixton Prison authorities that 'parties of bandits armed with Thompson sub-machine guns have crossed intending to rescue the Wilson murderers.' He did not believe the information he had received was reliable, but 'you will remember the determined attack that was made to rescue the prisoners at Glasgow when Inspector Johnston was shot.'[19]

* * *

The trial of Dunne and O'Sullivan took place at the Old Bailey on 18 July 1922, four weeks after the shooting. Public and press attention was focused just two miles away, where eight thousand people, including the king, queen and the Prince of Wales, attended the wedding of Lord Louis Mountbatten, the great-grandson of Queen Victoria, and his wife, the heiress Edwina Ashley, at St Margaret's Church in Westminster.[20] (Mountbatten's assassination in County Sligo by the Provisional IRA in August 1979, along with his fourteen-year-old grandson Nicholas Knatchbull, Nicholas's eighty-three-year-old paternal grandmother Lady Doreen Brabourne and Paul Maxwell, a fifteen-year-old boat boy,

21 The wedding of Lord Louis Mountbatten and Miss Edwina Ashley at
St Margaret's, Westminster, 18 July 1922

would be as shocking an event in his generation as Wilson's had been over half a century earlier.)

The prisoners had been carefully watched since their arrest, and their trial was equally well guarded. Plain-clothes detectives scrutinised would-be spectators and only a few were allowed into the public gallery.

Given the enormity of the offence with which the men had been charged and the international interest in the case, it was a trial distinguished by its brevity – it was all over within a day – and the unwillingness of the trial judge Mr Justice Sir Montague Shearman to consider a statement written by Reggie Dunne justifying the shooting of Wilson.

Dunne's Jesuitical reasoning and his command of the English language were deployed at the trial, in which he admitted shooting Wilson, but he would not enter a plea despite several probings by the Clerk of Arraigns.

'Are you guilty or not guilty of the murder of Sir Henry Wilson?'

'I admit shooting Sir Henry Wilson. This is all I can say.'[21]

The same question was put to O'Sullivan twice and he gave the same response. As neither man pleaded guilty to the charge, the trial judge entered a plea of not guilty.

The case was prosecuted by the Attorney General, Sir Ernest Pollock KC. The facts were not in dispute. The men had shot Wilson as he was entering his home at 36 Eaton Place. The wicked crime of murder, Pollock told the jury of ten men and two women, was not palliated by the position of the victim but, in killing such a distinguished soldier, the nation and the Empire were the poorer. Shortly before he was killed, Wilson had unveiled a war memorial tablet at Liverpool Street Station. He had been invited to discharge that function by reason of his great position during the war, which he had reached by a combination of industry and ability and the application of both. There was a bitter irony, Pollock continued, in Wilson, having played his part in saving civilisation, to be laid low by an act which was an affront to civilised values.

Major Cecil Wilson, who carried out a positive identification after the shooting, told the trial that his brother had been employed as a military advisor to the Northern government. This was vehemently denied later by Sir James Craig, who said Wilson's advice had been given freely and without payment.

The pathologist in the case was Dr Bernard Spilsbury, a man so famous at the time it was said he was as infallible to juries as the Pope was to Catholics. He recounted that Wilson had been shot six times. One bullet entered the left side of the chest, traversing both lungs and smashing his ribs. A second bullet entered by the left armpit and traversed both lungs. Either of those two bullets would have killed him, but he was shot a further four times.[22]

The jury were told that both men had served in the First World War. Dunne had joined the Irish Guards when he was eighteen and been sent to the front in France in January 1918. He was discharged, seriously wounded, in July of that year and was in receipt of a disability pension in 1920. He had been pursuing university studies in the hope of becoming a teacher. O'Sullivan had joined the army in January 1915 and was discharged in 1918, having lost his right leg up to his knee. He was employed by the Ministry of Labour. They were men of the highest character from good families and had not been in trouble with the law before.[23]

The court drama was reserved for the defence, which was conducted by Thomas Artemus Jones KC, a Welsh-born advocate and campaigner for the Welsh language. Jones asked the trial judge if Dunne could make a statement to the jury. Shearman asked to see the statement and was presented with it on blue headed paper. It was not a statement, the judge declared, it was an 'open manifesto on the right to kill. I cannot allow the court to be used as a means of anarchic propaganda.'[24]

Jones asked for an adjournment. He returned and told Shearman that the prisoners no longer wished to be represented by him. This was as a result of the judge's decision not to allow Dunne to read his prepared statement.

Shearman told the prisoners that they were now representing themselves. 'Having heard the evidence you are at liberty, if you think fit, to give evidence on your own behalf in the witness-box,' he told them.

Both declined to give evidence, but Dunne asked to address the jury. He did so in a way that accurately summarised the statement he had intended to give them, and his words would be published in the *Irish Independent* a month later. In the meantime, Dunne declared:

I suppose I must cut out the patriotic adjectives I feel inclined to use under the present circumstances, but I must state that I feel still, under these very same circumstances, proudly conscious that I am an Irishman. You have all heard the accounts from the Divisional Inspector who has been asked for accounts of my character and you will agree that this is the first time that I, and my friend, for that matter, have appeared in any criminal court. That I take a particular pride in, besides my national pride in being a member of the Irish race. I am sorry that you are denied the chance of hearing an Irishman's statement. Several of you, I have no doubt, endeavoured to do your best in the recent Great War. I also took my share in that war, fighting for the principles for which this country stood. Those principles I found, as an Irishman, were not applied to my own country and I have endeavoured to strike a blow for it. I received no money for this particular bit of business and I am no mere assassin. I wish to state that if, as I surmise, you will find me guilty, although some of you may have been my comrades in the late war, I trust that a higher court, the only court that matters will judge me by my actions in this world and consider the purity of my intentions.[25]

O'Sullivan declined to make a statement. Everything he had to say was in the statement the judge had declined to allow Dunne to read.

Dunne's eloquence made no impression on the jury. If anything, it seemed to have concentrated their minds on a guilty verdict. They took three minutes to find the pair guilty of wilful murder. The judge asked Dunne and O'Sullivan if they had anything to say for themselves before he pronounced the sentence of death.

Dunne: 'Yes, I have a few words to say. There exist and have existed certain living exceptions to this general rule of justice. Captain Bowen-Colthurst, who murdered Mr Sheehy Skeffington, Captain Hardy of Dublin Castle, who murdered Brigadier McKee of the Irish Army, and Peter Clancy . . .'

Shearman interrupted him. 'Now, listen to me, Reginald Dunne. You are asked the question whether there is any legal ground why judgement should be postponed. You are not at liberty to use this opportunity for a political address, and I shall not permit you to do so. You are not at liberty to address to me a political oration.'[26]

O'Sullivan's interjection was short and eloquent: 'All I have done, my Lord, I have done for Ireland and for Ireland I am proud to die,' which was greeted with a 'Hear, hear' from the back of the court.

Shearman put on his black cap to pass sentence on the two men. 'And may the Lord have mercy on your soul,' he told Dunne, who replied, 'He will, my Lord.'[27]

O'Sullivan responded: 'You may kill my body, my Lord, but my spirit you will never kill.'

It was a 'cowardly, useless and futile murder', Shearman told them by way of a parting comment, and he forbade that any sketches or photographs from the trial be published in newspapers lest they add to the condemned men's notoriety. Dunne and O'Sullivan shook hands as they left the court. The men were then taken away to Wandsworth Prison to await execution.[28]

* * *

Cowes in the Isle of Wight is a little town overlooking the Solent, with narrow, winding streets that lead to a spacious marina. It was discovered by the British upper classes as an ideal place for sea-swimming in the nineteenth century, the 'silvery Solent' also proving ideal for yacht racing.

The town's association with the royal family began with the inaugural regatta in 1816. Cowes Week, which actually lasts eight days, traditionally starts on the Saturday after the last Tuesday in July, which was 29 July in 1922. Since its inception in 1826 by the Prince Regent (the future George IV), the event has been associated with the royal family. In 1922 the king and queen proceeded by train to Plymouth and sailed on the royal yacht *Victoria and Albert* to Cowes to start the regatta. Major and minor aristocracy, the royal families of Europe and arrivistes of all hues in British society descended on Cowes for the week. 'The presence of Royalty at Cowes causes no stir; the people expect kings to visit them,' one visitor observed in the 1930s.[29]

The pleasure-loving Prince of Wales (and future King Edward VIII) was an annual visitor. He usually stayed at Nubia House, the home of Sir Godfrey Baring, a scion of the famous banking family,

22 Regatta Week, Cowes, in the 1920s

and his wife Eva Hermione. During Cowes Week they frequently entertained visiting royalty at their home, which had extensive grounds, a tennis court and a slightly bohemian tinge, where suppers were announced in a novel nautical manner: 'All hands fore and aft, both sides and amidships, get your suppers!'

In 1921 Wilson had been elected to the Royal Yacht Squadron during Cowes Week and had almost drowned when he fell overboard from his yacht, the *White Heather*, in rough seas. Wilson was wearing a mackintosh and a pair of gum boots when he got hit by the mainsail as it swung in the wind. He spent twenty minutes in the water before being rescued by a dinghy. News travelled fast around Cowes, and on the following day he was invited on board the royal yacht by the king and his uncle, the Duke of Connaught.[30]

A year later the fate of Wilson's killers was not on the minds of the yachting fraternity in Cowes. Time was running short and so

263

were options to rescue the men from the hangman. Denis Kelleher remembered, 'We hit on a plan that if it would be possible to get a high person [and] if we undertook negotiations with the British government it might be possible to have a remission in the case of these men.'[31]

John Joseph Carr, who along with his brother Denis had played such a critical part in smuggling weaponry to the IRA during the War of Independence, was in Ireland when the Wilson shooting happened. He was arrested when Free State troops stormed and destroyed the Hammam Hotel in O'Connell Street in early July 1922, during the Battle of Dublin. Carr fled the burning building with a dispatch for the rebel 2nd Western Division headquarters in Ballinrobe, County Mayo. Twelve hours later he was caught in Roscommon town by Free State soldiers and imprisoned in Athlone Jail:

> After being in the Athlone Jail for about two weeks, I hit on a plan for effecting my release without sacrificing my honour. This plan was communicated to my fellow prisoners and agreed worth trying. Major General [Seán] McKeown [Mac Eoin] periodically paid visits to the prisoners. During one of those visits I expressed the desire to speak to him and informed him that if he was detaining me as an enemy or possible enemy, I would give an undertaking in writing to leave Ireland by the first train and boat. This was agreed to and a written undertaking given. I did not state that this undertaking would prevent me from returning to Ireland which I did later.[32]

Carr agreed to help in any rescue attempt in exchange for his freedom. By the time he had returned to London, attempts to spring Dunne and O'Sullivan from the prison van had been called off and another tactic was needed. Carr borrowed £100 from his mother to buy a car and induced Jerry Leydon, a taxi driver who was not a member of the IRA, to lend his personal services. Collins sent Captain William O'Reilly from Portobello Barracks in Dublin to help out. The trio formulated a plan as foolhardy as it was ambitious. They would kidnap the Prince of Wales and hold him hostage. They reasoned that the British authorities would be so embarrassed at the kidnapping of the heir to the throne that they would deal in secret with the kidnappers' demands and quietly commute the death sentences of Dunne and O'Sullivan.[33]

Carr, Kelleher and O'Reilly proceeded to Cowes. However, their operation was quickly rumbled, as Carr recalled: 'Unfortunately, in making the necessary questions, Kelleher's accent was commented on by the policemen with the result that we considered the attempt jeopardised.'

Theirs was a wasted journey in any case, as a notice appeared in the British newspapers before Cowes stating the Prince of Wales would not be going there as usual. Instead, he spent the week at the home of Lord and Lady Wimborne, a hundred miles away. Coincidentally, Lord Wimborne had been Lord Lieutenant in Ireland during the Easter Rising. He had urged in advance that the leaders be arrested but lacked the authority to do it himself, and he'd had to wait for the Chief Secretary Augustine Birrell, who was in London at the time. The whole history of Ireland might have been different had Wimborne's warning been acted upon.

Kelleher sarcastically told the Bureau of Military History that the kidnapping plan was a 'bright idea' without acknowledging that, as the senior IRA officer in London (he succeeded Dunne as O/C), he was in charge of the operation. The kidnapping, he concluded, was 'utterly impossible'.[34]

The group then switched their attentions to the Anglo-Irish peer the Earl of Arran. Born Arthur Gore, Arran was also known as Viscount Sudley and was a minor figure who never attended the House of Lords, despite being a hereditary peer. He was to be held on a barge on the River Thames, and Carr was chosen as his jailer. That plan too failed when their taxi got lost in the fog. 'Due to unforeseen circumstances this attempt was abandoned within a quarter of an hour of its commencement,' Carr remembered.[35] O'Reilly was satisfied that they had done their best, but there was no gainsaying that the rescue attempts for Dunne and O'Sullivan were half-hearted in comparison with previous IRA attempts.

* * *

The trial judge's refusal to allow Dunne to read his prepared statement gave MacDonnell grounds for appeal in what would otherwise have been an open and shut case. MacDonnell lodged papers with the Court of Criminal Appeal stating that Shearman had erred in demanding that the statement that Dunne proposed to make should first be submitted to him. In telling the jury that the statement was an assertion of the right to kill or was intended to be political or anarchical in nature, the judge had deprived the jury of the right to hear why Wilson's actions in Ulster had provoked Dunne. It was up to the jury, not the trial judge, to decide if the provocation was justified, MacDonnell maintained. The jury members, therefore, had been deprived of an opportunity to consider Dunne's motives and state of mind. Lastly, MacDonnell contended that Shearman should have returned the statement to Dunne.[36]

Dunne and O'Sullivan's defence barrister Artemus Jones made the same arguments in front of the two judges at the Court of

Criminal Appeal, the Lord Chief Justice Charles Darling and Mr Justice George Branson. Dunne should have been allowed to read his statement, Jones argued. If the prisoner abused his privilege in straying from the facts of the case, the judge could find him guilty of contempt of court. Other than that, Dunne had the right to give his justification to the jury.[37]

Darling countered by stating that Dunne's motives in making the statement were political in nature. Neither he nor O'Sullivan were looking for clemency. Dunne was seeking a platform to justify the extrajudicial killing of a man. 'That was merely no law, but subversive of the very foundation of justice,' Darling declared. There were certain grounds on which killing a man was justified, but none that would allow a man to claim justification for a killing outside the law.

In dismissing the appeal, Darling made his contempt clear by dismissing Dunne's statement as 'merely irrelevant, purposeless and grotesque'.[38]

Undaunted, MacDonnell attempted to appeal to the House of Lords, the final court of appeal in Britain, but on 8 August 1922, two days before the intended hanging, Pollock, the Attorney General, refused to allow it.[39]

In parallel with the court appeal, MacDonnell circulated a public petition looking for a reprieve and commutation of the sentences of death. Dunne and O'Sullivan were men who 'had served as volunteers in the English [sic] army'. Both had been severely wounded and were men of unblemished record. On the completion of the case for the Crown, counsel for the defence had asked if Dunne might be permitted to make a brief statement to the jury, but Dunne was refused that privilege. The petition stated:

The judge, having read the document, pronounced it a
political manifesto and refused permission to have it read
in court. Every fair-minded person will regard this refusal
as a cruel injustice to two men on trial for their lives. The
document is now available for publication, and having
perused it, can any honest man say that the prisoners should
have been denied the right to read it to the jury? None
but the prejudiced will share the judge's condemnation of
the statement as 'anarchic propaganda'. These men are not
ordinary criminals. They had gone out to fight England's fight
for freedom, trusting to England's word. They came home
severely wounded to find their own country enslaved. They
found installed in the highest position in the army Sir Henry
Wilson, the reputed originator of the terror in Ireland and
who, rightly or wrongly, they believed to be the director of
the foul deeds of [Sir Hugh] Tudor and [Lieutenant David]
Rutherford and [Major Jocelyn 'Hoppy'] Hardy. One can
well imagine the feelings of these disillusioned young men.
They had given the best of their youth to fight for England.
England gives a free hand to Sir Henry Wilson to carry out a
campaign of wickedness to which no decent Englishman can
now refer without shame or regret. They saw in Sir Henry the
avowed enemy of their race and creed.[40]

The petition argued that there was no precedent for a trial
judge to refuse a man his right to address the jury. 'It is not unreasonable, therefore, to say that the public interests are seriously
affected thereby and the two conditions set out in the Criminal
Appeal Act are thus fulfilled.'

MacDonnell assembled an impressive number of high-profile
signatories. Three Labour MPs – Ben Tillet, James Sexton and

James Kiley – signed, along with the Liberal MP Josiah Wedgwood; Ernest Bevin, the trade unionist and future Labour foreign secretary; Henry William Massingham, the journalist and campaigner; and the Rev. Conrad Noel, the Christian Socialist Anglican priest. Prominent women who signed the petition included Charlotte Despard, the sister of Lord French; Hannah Sheehy Skeffington, the widow of Francis Sheehy Skeffington, who had been extrajudicially executed on the orders of Captain John Bowen-Colthurst during the Easter Rising; the novelist Katherine Tynan; and Mary Kettle, the widow of the barrister and politician Tom Kettle, who had been killed in the First World War. The number would have been much greater had the petition been circulated in Ireland. MacDonnell told the *Irish Independent* newspaper that several mayors in London, clergymen of all denominations and even ex-servicemen and ex-RIC men who had fought against the IRA in the War of Independence had signed it. Some 44,905 signatures seeking a reprieve were collected and delivered to the Home Office.[41]

Dunne and O'Sullivan's best-known champion was the Irish-born dramatist George Bernard Shaw. Shaw considered himself a moderate home-ruler, but, like so many Irish nationalists, his conscience was profoundly shaken by the Easter Rising in April 1916. He became an ardent Irish separatist following the execution of fifteen leaders of the Rising, a deed he felt was as stupid as it was cruel:

> An Irishman resorting to arms to achieve the independence of his country is doing only what an Englishman will do if it be their misfortune to be invaded and conquered by Germany in the present war . . . it is absolutely impossible to slaughter a man in this position without making him a martyr and a hero.[42]

His indignation spilled over into support for Sir Roger Casement, who was hanged in August 1916. Shaw argued unsuccess-
fully that Casement should have been treated as a prisoner of war,
not a traitor. He then lent his linguistic ability and high profile
to supporting Dunne and O'Sullivan too. Two days before the
hanging was scheduled, he penned a long and angry letter to the
Manchester Guardian, decrying what he saw as an obvious miscarriage of justice:

> It is impossible to allow the scandalous travesty of judicial
> procedure by which Joseph O'Sullivan and Reginald Dunne
> will be hanged on Thursday morning to pass without a
> vehement protest . . .
>
> In the case now under consideration there was no question
> of the fact at issue at all; the two men had deliberately and
> openly shot Sir Henry Wilson. Their only possible defence
> was justification of their action. And neither the judge nor
> anyone else had the right to call the defence a justification of
> murder until the jury had found, in spite of the defence, that
> they were guilty of murder. To rule out a defence because it
> might possibly be successful (an impossibility in this instance)
> is simply to rule out any defence whatsoever. If a fanatical
> English unionist were to shoot Mr de Valera or Mr Collins
> tomorrow on English ground he would be fully entitled to
> exhaust all the resources of patriotic casuistry in an appeal to
> a British jury to find him not guilty and nobody in Ireland
> or America believes that any English judge would attempt to
> silence him. A judicial mind is a very rare gift and in England
> it is so incomprehensible that it is difficult for anyone with
> a vestige of it to obtain promotion in a profession which is
> becoming more and more entangled in party politics.[43]

Shaw's plea made no difference. Neither did a last-minute intervention by Hugh Kennedy, the Irish Attorney General, who wrote to the Home Secretary Edward Shortt, 'The execution of these sentences is felt by the Provisional Government to be something well calculated to disaffect those who have shown a will to peace in the North notwithstanding terrible provocation and will in all probability help the intolerable aggravations of the present situation in the North-Eastern counties.'[44]

Shortt was unmoved. He wrote to MacDonnell stating there were no grounds which would justify 'his Majesty to interfere with the due course of law'.[45]

There was no hope for Dunne and O'Sullivan now. They would hang at 8 a.m. on 10 August 1922, seven weeks to the day after they had shot Wilson.

10

Execution: 'The felon's cap is the noblest crown an Irish head can wear'

Reginald Dunne and Joseph O'Sullivan spent their last days preparing for death and setting their affairs in order. Their wills, made on the day before they died and witnessed by their solicitor James Hyndman MacDonnell and the governor of Wandsworth Prison, reflect how they saw themselves and those around them. Unassuming to the last, O'Sullivan's single-page will, written in his expansive handwriting, left everything to his father, 'that he shall give certain of my effects to my brothers and sisters at his discretion'.[1]

Dunne, by contrast, left a detailed list of instructions parcelling out every possession. His violin, blackthorn stick, fountain pen, numerous books, photographs and religious items were all itemised for named individuals. He requested that all traces of his involvement with the British army during the First World War be destroyed and that 'Hail Glorious St Patrick' be sung as they were being hanged. Failing that, there should be a sung requiem Mass for the benefit of their souls. 'And if any good Catholic Irish singer would sing the "Ingemisco" from Verdi's *Requiem* as an offertory piece, I promise to remember him in my prayers.'[2] Dunne wrote regularly to his mother. He apologised on 3 July for not having written before:

> I requested you to leave the court because you would only
> have been distressed otherwise. The whole business must
> have been an intense shock for both my father and yourself

and I have been praying ever since that you will both bear up under the strain. So far I am very happy to state that I am proud of my parents because I know now that they understand me better than I imagined. I cannot find words to express my regret at the plight in which I have left you both. I am resolved that you shall not suffer unduly for my actions. I am rather worried as to whether you are receiving any abuse or persecution from neighbours etc. I know that you will bear them with dignity, but if you have any reason for alarm, consult my solicitor.[3]

His letters, written in a tightly controlled script, constantly exhorted his parents to pray for him, as he was praying for himself and deriving great consolation from his Catholic faith. He was most anxious that the public did not see him as a 'reprobate' and a positive reference from the priests at his teacher training college in Hammersmith provided him with great solace. The letters, which are kept in the National Library of Ireland (NLI), are all to his mother, who also seemed to be the conduit between Dunne and his father. 'I hope my father is keeping well,' Reggie wrote. 'I know that he will look upon things with great dignity and comprehension. If he will look up Spencer's *Historical Survey on the state of Ireland* he will notice he referred to us as the "great scorners of death".'

Later he wrote, 'I thought of my father on the 1st of July and hoped that everything would be all right. Presumably everything is all right with him or I would surely have heard . . . Does my father read as much as ever? I hope so. I do not want him to worry unduly on my account.'

It is clear from the statement Robert Dunne gave four days after the shooting that he had no idea what his son was doing. He thought his appearance at the Wormwood Scrubs demonstrations were for the 'charitable purposes of praying and singing to the prisoners inside'.

Reggie had been to Ireland the previous summer (1921), his father revealed, but came back when he ran out of money. Most of the time he stayed indoors, reading and writing and playing music.

> I never heard him speak of a political society. I had no
> knowledge of it if he did belong to [one] anyway. If I had
> I should at once have put my foot upon it. I have seen a
> photograph of O'Brien or Sullivan [*sic*]. I do not know him,
> nor have I ever seen him. My son never spoke of him and
> was too secretive to let me know anything of his friends, and
> my belief is that he was anxious not to cause us any anxiety.
> I have never seen my son in possession of a revolver of any
> kind, and so far as I know, there has never been [one] in
> the house. So far as I know he did not belong to the Irish
> Self-Determination League or any other like society. He
> sometimes used to go out of an evening, but invariably kept
> good hours. He was fond of going to the Albert Hall or the
> Queen's Hall to hear good music or operas. I read the account
> of my son's arrest on Friday, that was the first I knew of it,
> in fact I could not believe it was his photograph when I saw
> it. During the past several months my son has been leading
> the normal life of a good living Catholic boy and I cannot
> understand how he can have become mixed with anyone who
> would have brought him [to] the position he is in.[4]

Dunne's father gave an interview to the *Daily Express* two days later in which he articulated his despair about his son's actions and appeared to suggest he knew nothing about his activities:

The boy was all right till the war broke out. He was invalided out of the Army and granted a wound pension. It has nearly killed me. I cannot realise it, and I do not know what I am doing half the day – it's awful. I do not know if he had been to Ireland. The boy lived with me for a long time on and off. He served during the war in the Irish Guards.[5]

There was a revealing paragraph in the article that may explain his father's silence while his son was in jail and Dunne's guilt about the shock he visited on his family. At this stage the true name of Dunne was not known, and it would appear that his father did not seek to correct the reporter's perception that his son's name was Connolly.

Mr Dunne, weeping bitterly, closed the interview in a state of collapse. A friend of the family stated that for some months past Connolly had been a source of great anxiety to his parents who were unable to discover the reason of his frequent absences from home. It is certain they were unaware of his having sympathies with the Irish rebels.[6]

Dunne was heartened by the fate of the Victorian illustrator Aubrey Beardsley, who was only twenty-five when he converted to Catholicism, shortly before he died from tuberculosis in 1898. Beardsley was an acquaintance of Oscar Wilde and, like Wilde, a cultural provocateur. 'If I am not grotesque, I am nothing,' Beardsley declared. Dunne was contemptuous of the type of people who judged Beardsley as a degenerate while he was alive:

You know the class of people I am referring to, who call actresses low class women, soldiers, the scum of the earth, bank clerks, steady young men, municipal officers, good citizens, and myself a murderer. Beware the respectable majority and challenge them. Judge not that ye may not be judged.[7]

There is an element of forced jollity about Dunne's letters, as if he could not comprehend what was going to happen to him. His concern seemed to be for his parents and not himself:

July 4: I am sticking to my prayers and daily Holy Communion, so that life is far from being irksome.

July 8: I have just returned from Benediction and at the present moment all's right with the world.

July 10: There happens to be some things over which I have exercised some control and, as a result, I am more or less serene in my present outlook.[8]

'Things could be very much worse, couldn't they?' Dunne asked rhetorically, yet as the trial date approached he began to comprehend the enormity of what he was facing. He advised his parents not to attend his trial and suggested they read about it in the press instead, preferably *The Times* or one of the Irish newspapers:

I would prefer you to stay at home or go to Church and spend the day in prayer for me. I shall need your prayers very much on that day it is hardly necessary to state. You are, I am sure, fully aware how serious things are.[9]

He appears not to have written to his mother again on a daily basis after he was sentenced to death on 18 July, judging by the correspondence kept in the NLI, which stops after that date and only resumes with his final (and separate) letters to his parents.

Dunne and O'Sullivan faced death with a stoicism and a certitude that emanated from their faith and the conviction that, despite the avalanche of opprobrium visited on them and the withering words of the trial judge, they had done the right thing in shooting Wilson. They were not without their supporters:

Dear Cousin Joe,

I am proud of the honour of being a cousin of yours. It is with pride that I can hold up my head and say that I had a cousin who died for Ireland. It was a good day for Ireland the day yourself and your hero of a companion went out and laid the second Cromwell dead at your feet. You need not be afraid to meet your God for what you did. You did it for Ireland and your faith and when the time comes for you to perform the last good act for Ireland you need not be afraid, but that you have all the Irish Catholic nation praying for you. Well, dear Joe, I thought you would be coming over this year, but He who knows best what to do with his people has chosen you as another martyr for Ireland. I know you will answer the call willingly and cheerfully. Uncle Jim, Aunty Kitty, Annie, Willie and Jimmie all wish to be remembered to you and they are all praying for you. I must now close with fondest love from all in Bantry from your loving cousin.

Aod [*sic*].[10]

Dunne and O'Sullivan were animated by a sense of self-sacrifice that was universal at the time. The notion of the noble death and warfare as a sanctifying thing sent a generation of men to the slaughter of the First World War. They queued at the recruiting stations, left their studies and their workplaces, lined up behind the marching bands and piled into the trains heading for the front, determined to advance on 'the old Lie: *Dulce et decorum est / Pro patria mori*' ('It is sweet and fitting to die for the homeland'), as Wilfred Owen so bitterly called it.[11] Owen died a month before the war ended. Rupert Brooke wrote in the first flush of patriotism that followed the outbreak of war in August 1914:

> If I should die, think only this of me:
> That there's some corner of a foreign field
> That is for ever England.[12]

Brooke died the following year on his way to the front in Gallipoli. This wave of unabashed patriotism also influenced advanced Irish nationalists opposed to Irish involvement in the British war effort. Five months before the Easter Rising of 1916, Patrick Pearse, the first president of the self-styled Irish Republic, declared: 'The last sixteen months have been the most glorious in the history of Europe. The old heart of the earth needed to be warmed with the red wine of the battlefields. Such august homage was never offered to God as this, the homage of millions of lives given gladly for the love of country.'[13]

James Connolly, the founder of the Irish Citizen Army and a fellow signatory of the Proclamation, dismissed Pearse's musings as the rantings of a 'blithering idiot'. Connolly had a greater understanding of the reality of warfare, having been a British soldier earlier in his life.[14]

The notion of the blood sacrifice animated many of those involved in the planning for the Rising. In 1914 Seán Mac Diarmada, one of the prime movers of the Rising, prophesied that it would be necessary for 'some of us to offer ourselves as martyrs if nothing better can be done to preserve the Irish national spirit and hand it down to future generations'.[15]

Mac Diarmada went to his death serene in the belief that the example of his life would inspire future generations to seek Irish freedom. In his last letter to his family, he wrote in tones which apply equally to Dunne and O'Sullivan:

The principles for which I give my life are so sacred that I now walk to my death in the most perfectly calm and collected manner. I go to my death for Ireland's cause as fearlessly as I have worked for that sacred cause during all my short life.[16]

Mac Diarmada was shot by firing squad after the Rising, as were Pearse and Connolly. 'Well, Lillie, hasn't it been a full life and isn't this a good end?' Connolly said to his wife. He was wounded so badly in the Rising that he had to be strapped into a chair in front of the firing squad. The fifteen leaders of the Rising who were executed by firing squad in its aftermath were followed some months later by Sir Roger Casement, hanged for treason in August 1916. The very date of the Rising, coinciding with the death and resurrection of Jesus Christ, was not coincidental. It was intended to convey a sense of the Irish nation rolling back the stone of centuries of subjugation and rising again.

In September 1917 Thomas Ashe died on hunger strike in Mountjoy Prison after being force-fed. He too embodied and was imbued by the spirit of self-sacrifice, writing in one of his poems:

> Let me carry your Cross for Ireland, Lord!
> The hour of her trial draws near,
> And the pangs and the pains of the sacrifice
> May be borne by comrades dear.[17]

It was the death of Terence MacSwiney on hunger strike in October 1920 that had the most profound impact on Dunne. In his will he asked for a small piece of brown paper to be taken from his pocketbook and handed over to MacSwiney's sister Mary. It was a lock of her brother's hair. 'I had the inestimable privilege of supporting his head while he was being dressed for his last journey to Ireland.'[18]

The roll call of failed Irish rebellions had produced an inexhaustible list of those revered for having died for Ireland – the aforementioned men from the Easter Rising, the twenty executed during the War of Independence, and going back further, Wolfe Tone, Robert Emmet, the Manchester Martyrs, the Phoenix Park Five, Lord Edward Fitzgerald, Father John Murphy and many others.

Dunne was anxious throughout that the public not consider them to be common criminals. Divorced from their deed, their final letters are articulate expositions of two men facing imminent death. They expressed no remorse. On the contrary, the imminence of death strengthened them in the conviction that they had done the right thing, and those people who mattered to them understood that well.

O'Sullivan wrote to a 'Jack' (this may be Captain Jack Barry, who served with his brother in Cork No. 1 Brigade) on 1 August, stating that he was 'quite prepared for the end' and was comforted by the number of people in Ireland who were thinking and praying for him and Dunne. His family came to visit him in prison every day and he wished to see for one last time his brother and brother-in-arms Pat, who was in Ireland fighting on the anti-Treaty side:

> I can't call it a sacrifice for it is an honour to die for old
> Ireland, but of course we are all God's children and He has
> only put us on this Earth for a short time so that when He
> calls us back to Him, we should be happy to respond to the
> call . . . I should like to see Pat just once more but I suppose
> he has his share to do so I must be content to wait until we
> meet to part no more . . . So now dear Jack when you hear that
> we are no more on this Earth, remember to thank God for his

goodness in letting us die in this grace. Believe me to be dear Jack your brother in the cause. Joe[19]

O'Sullivan quoted the valedictory republican ballad 'The Felons of Our Land' to his father in his final letter:

Although I die in the eyes of this country a felon, remember the 'felon's cap is the noblest Crown an Irish head can wear' and how many of our noble countrymen have gone the same way as Reg and I. Tell Mrs Dunne when you see her how proud I am to be dying alongside of her son, for old Ireland never had a truer or braver son than he and give my love to all my friends. So be of good cheer and with God's help we will be united again, never more to part, but, in the meantime, keep praying that God will grant our dear country that unity and liberty which we all desire of her. Well, a happy farewell now to you, my best of fathers, and all my brothers and sisters and hoping through the goodness of God to see you all again in that happier land and may he bless and protect you all and the cause in which we die.[20]

Dunne and O'Sullivan were resigned to their fate and faced it with equanimity. Not for them the agonising death watch of hoping against hope for a reprieve. MacDonnell had appraised them of his grounds for appeal and of the petition, which was gathering signatures by the thousand every day. O'Sullivan was consoled by the fact that people cared about their fate, but his last letters admitted no earthly hope:

Thanks to all those who have been praying and having masses said for us and let them know that God has answered their prayers. I believe there was a petition signed by a great number of people for a reprieve for us, to whom I am very grateful. Well, God has given them more than they asked for. For is He not going to release us altogether from this land of suffering and death and take us where death is no more?[21]

It is remarkable how the two men, so different in many ways, were steeped in the same Catholic religiosity of suffering and redemption. Dunne told his mother that he had contemplated death for six weeks,

but I am not afraid because I have been given abundant grace. It is good to think upon the thirty-three years during which Our Lord contemplated his Passion in every detail, deliberately experiencing sensations of fear. Our Lady, however, has calmed my fears in her own gracious way and there is no desolation within me, but a longing for the presence of God and the society of My Heavenly Mother and the saints. Join with me in this prayer.

Dunne asked St Joseph, the patron saint of fathers, and St Michael, the patron saint of soldiers, to pray for his father. He compared the suffering of his mother to that of Mary as Jesus was dying on the cross, and he took consolation in the relic of St Philomena she sent him. He was pleased he would be dead by the time of the Feast of the Assumption (15 August), which marks Mary's Assumption straight into heaven after her death. Dunne expected to celebrate it in heaven as John Berchmans, the Jesuit saint, was said to have done when he died two days prior to the feast day in 1621.[22]

O'Sullivan compared his suffering to that of Jesus in the Garden of Gethsemane and the moment of mental anguish in which Jesus agonised over his impending death and his sweat fell like drops of blood on the ground: 'Father, not my will, but thine be done.' O'Sullivan reminded his father:

23 Extract from Reggie's last letter to his mother

The knowledge that we will have plenty of Masses is most consoling to me and makes matters very simple. I made my second general confession today and am feeling very well and happy. In a short time I am going to pay a visit to the Blessed Sacrament. This has been granted as a special request so I will remember everybody in my prayers. Fr Day, my chaplain, may call to see you. You will find him an excellent man, so treat him as one of my special guests. I don't think I have ever known what true happiness was before now, dear Dad, and I want to share it with you and all my loving brothers and sisters. I had a letter from Sister Mary Raphael this morning and I'm sure she is right when she says my dead mother's holy soul is hovering near me and I shall be ever so pleased to see her through the goodness of God. You know Dad that death is only a parting; sometimes it is harder than others. But 'tis an end we must all come to sooner or later, and I can never thank God enough for giving one so unworthy as I such a happy death. When I meditate on all the good people I know who have gone before and have had not half so happy a death as I it makes me cry out, 'The ways of God are wonderful and no man understandeth.' Well, fondest parent, I know you will always pray for my noble comrade and my poor self, but I would ask you also to have some Masses said in thanksgiving for the happy death God has granted us.[23]

O'Sullivan's last letter to his father was not just a private expression of filial fidelity but was also intended for public consumption. It was copied and disseminated widely in the newspapers in both Britain and Ireland following his death. Dunne's final letter comes with an expression of regret that his father will not be a grandfather. 'I willingly sacrifice this privilege for the cause in which I am going to die. Could you possibly wish a better death for me? Hold your head well up tomorrow because I shall have given you cause to be proud of me as a soldier.'[24]

He requested that his mother and father move to Ireland, projecting an idealised view of them living the rest of their lives in a country where their son's deed would be seen as a heroic act, not a cowardly murder. As we will see, the Dunnes made good on their son's request soon after his death.

I am intensely proud of you both and cannot sufficiently appreciate your heroic demeanour under the present circumstances. You will still keep to yourself, I know, but if any friends of mine call, you will take my place in their hearts. I have many friends who will do anything for you. Accept of their kindness with the natural dignity of your family and I will be greatly pleased.[25]

The letters written to and from both men were read by prison guards. The condemned men had regular visitors as they waited in their cells. O'Sullivan's father and sister came to visit, but another sister who came with her eight-year-old son was refused entry as children were not allowed into the prison. An unnamed sister told the *Irish Independent* that she had visited O'Sullivan a few days before he was hanged and he was 'better than I have ever seen him'.[26]

Three women – Mary MacGeehin, Rose Killen and Constance Burke, all involved in the Irish independence movement in London – came regularly to see Dunne. In his will he asked that they be left mementos.

He had expected that his solicitor MacDonnell would bring his mother to see him on the day before he was scheduled to be hanged and anticipated their final farewell would be like Jesus meeting his mother on the road to Calvary. 'However, I did not wish to go back on my former statements and such a meeting might have unhinged my mind and brought regrets. I had formerly dreaded it as being almost an occasion of sin.'[27]

* * *

On the morning of the execution, a special force of police were on duty outside the prison, but there were no disturbances. The early-morning and evening vigils for republican prisoners were a regular occurrence between 1916 and 1923.

The crowd gathered outside Wandsworth Prison were led by a man calling himself Layman O'Leary, an Irishman living in London connected with the Knights of the Blessed Sacrament. He had traversed the city through the night to be present outside the jail for the hangings. He wore a cassock and surplice, and walked around the kneeling crowd incanting prayers and hymns as if in a trance. 'These boys have fought and bled for this country. Don't think we are mixing politics with our Church, for these boys were

24 Relatives and supporters praying outside Wandsworth Prison before the
execution of Dunne and O'Sullivan. They included Layman O'Leary, who
dressed as a priest for the occasion (seen here in the foreground)

daily and weekly communicants,' he told the Press Association.[28]
The crowds would have been even greater had many people not
gathered outside Pentonville Prison in the mistaken belief that
the men were being executed there.

Inside the prison Dunne and O'Sullivan were pinioned in their
cells. This involved placing the men's legs and arms in leather
straps and tying their arms with a rope. Both men yielded to the
restraints, and the one-legged O'Sullivan was helped to the gallows by two assistants. A last request for Dunne and O'Sullivan to
meet face to face before execution was refused, but now they were
to be hanged together. They had behaved with serenity from the
time of their trial to the very end, trusting in God and their own
judgement.

Their executioner was John Ellis, the British hangman whose day job was as a barber and newsagent in Rochdale, Lancashire. He had previously hanged Sir Roger Casement, and as we saw in a previous chapter, Michael Collins had sent Joe Dolan to kill him. As a precaution, Ellis was put under special armed guard in advance of the hanging. The executions took place in the Shed, a two-storey building, with the platform and the beam on the first-floor level. The condemned cells were adjacent to the gallows. Hangings took place on the top floor and the trapdoor opened onto the ground floor, where the bodies were collected after the hanging.[29]

Dunne and O'Sullivan met their deaths 'with the same unflinching demeanour they manifested at the trial', according to an eye-witness reporter from the Press Association.

Shortly afterwards the prison bell tolled twice to signal their deaths. Major Edward Reade, the governor of the prison, declared that the executions had been carried out without a hitch. Allan Pearson, the prison medical officer, was present at the executions and observed that the men had died as a result of their necks breaking and death had been instantaneous. They had been of sound mind when they were put to death and, therefore, they had been legally executed.

The formal notice stating that the men had been executed in accordance with the law was posted on the prison door at 8.30 p.m. A woman approached, carrying the Irish tricolour, and dropped to her knees having read the notice. This brought the crowd to song and they sang 'Wrap the Green Flag Around Me'. It took another hour for the crowd to disperse.

* * *

Dunne and O'Sullivan's statement, which was disallowed in court, was smuggled out of the prison by O'Sullivan's sister Connie, given to the *Irish Independent* and published two days after the hanging.[30] It was a more considered exposition of why they came to assassinate Wilson, Dunne beginning with a bald statement of the facts. They had shot Wilson dead and were therefore guilty under the law of murder, but the other shots had been fired in their attempt to escape:

> My Lord and members of the jury. My friend and I stand here before you today charged with the offence of murder; and I have no doubt that, from the evidence placed before you by the prosecution, you will find us both guilty. With respect to the charges of attempted murder, we merely tried, as everyone must know, to try and escape arrest.[31]

Dunne knew that killing was a grave undertaking, but the pair had also signed up for that when they joined the British army during the First World War. Neither he nor O'Sullivan had a criminal record and they both had good service records:

> The offence of murder is a very serious matter; so much so, that any act which results in loss of human life requires very grave and substantial reasons. We have never until now been charged with any crime. As you have heard from the police officer, who gave evidence as to our character and our previous records, we have both been in the British Army. We both joined voluntarily, for the purpose of taking human life in order that the principles for which this country stood, should be upheld and preserved.

Dunne then reminded the jury of what the war had been fought for. The UK only reluctantly agreed to fight when neutral Belgium was invaded by Germany on 3 August 1914. The fate of Belgium, a small Catholic country like Ireland, was to the forefront of the recruitment campaigns in Ireland.

An appeal to gallant Irishmen!

Do you hear the voice of heroic Belgium calling for your aid? Will you answer it?

Do you know that cathedrals and churches have been violated in Belgium and that ministers of religion have been driven from their churches by the Germans?

Dunne also alluded in this passage to President Woodrow Wilson's championing of the principles of self-determination, which Wilson outlined in his Fourteen Points in January 1918: 'National aspirations,' Wilson stated, 'must be respected; people may now be dominated and governed only by their own consent.'[32] Dunne continued:

These principles, we were told, were self-determination and freedom for small nations. We both, as I have said, fought for these principles, and were commended for doing so; and I imagine that several of you gentlemen of this jury did likewise. We came back from France to find that self-determination had been given to some nations we had never heard of, but that it had been denied to Ireland.

Dunne then railed against the partition of Ireland that occurred as a result of the Government of Ireland Act 1920, which divided the island into two jurisdictions, Southern Ireland and Northern Ireland. Northern Ireland came into being on 3 May 1921. As we have seen in earlier chapters, the foundation of Northern Ireland coincided with an upsurge in violence from both the IRA and state forces – the Ulster Special Constabulary and Royal Irish Constabulary:

We found, on the contrary, that our country was being divided
into two countries; that a government had been set up for the
Belfast district, and that under that government outrages were
being perpetrated, that are a disgrace to civilisation – many of
the outrages being committed by men in uniform and in the
pay of the Belfast government. We took our part in supporting
the aspiration of our fellow countrymen, in the same way
as we took part in supporting the nations of the world who
fought for the right of small nationalities.

He now addressed the reasons why they killed Wilson. There
was more to the slain field marshal than his involvement in
the First World War. He was also involved in advising the new
Northern Ireland government. Dunne makes a factual error here.
Wilson did not raise or organise the Ulster Special Constabulary.
It was created in October 1920 as an auxiliary to the RIC in the six
counties. Dunne is correct in his suggestion, though, that Wilson
was the military advisor to the Northern government. This was a
matter of public record going back to March, when Wilson's letter to Craig was published. As such, Wilson was associated in the
public mind with the activities of the B-Specials, even though he
did not control them.[33]

Who was Sir Henry Wilson? What was his policy, and what
did he stand for? You have all read in the newspapers lately,
and been told, that he was a great British Field Marshal;
but his activities in other fields are unknown to the bulk of
the British public. The nation to which we have the honour
to belong, the Irish nation, knows him, not so much as the
great British Field Marshal, but as the man behind what is
known in Ireland as the Orange Terror. He was at the time
of his death the military advisor to what is colloquially called

the Ulster Government, and as military advisor he raised and organised a body of men known as the Ulster Special Constabulary, who are the principal agents in his campaign of terrorism.[34]

Dunne then references the Belfast pogroms. The source of his information may well have been the Dáil Éireann publicity department, which produced a regular bulletin about the pogroms in the North. The one issued on 5 June 1922 listed 423 people killed, 1,750 wounded, 8,150 Catholics expelled from work and 20,500 driven from their homes.[35] It also blames the Specials for the murder of a number of prominent Catholics and states that these murders were 'carried out by men who were then high in the service of the Government and who are now still higher. These facts are known to the members of the Belfast Government themselves. Catholics no more expect Craig's government to take action against the murderers than did the early Christians expect the Emperor to punish the mob who stoned and kicked St Stephen to death.'[36] In 1922 some 7,500 refugees from Belfast fled south. The anti-Treaty IRA in response occupied perceived bastions of British rule in Dublin, including Fowler Hall, the largest Orange lodge in the South, and the Kildare Street club.

> My lord and members of the Jury, I do not propose to go into details of the horrible outrages committed on men, women and children of my race in Belfast and other places under the jurisdiction of the Ulster Government. Among Irishmen it is well known that about 500 men, women and children have been killed within the past few months, nearly two thousand wounded, and not one offender brought to justice. More than 9,000 persons have been expelled from their employment; and

23,000 men, women, and children driven from their homes. All the big cities of this country and even those of Northern France are now receiving these refugees. Sir Henry Wilson was the representative figure and the organiser of the system that made these things possible.

He finally accused Wilson of being behind the notorious Civil Authorities of Northern Ireland (Special Powers) Act. The act was passed on 15 March 1922 and Wilson sent his advice on 17 March but had no part in drawing up the legislation. Dunne continued:

> At his suggestion and advice the Ulster Parliament passed an Act authorising the purging of political opponents and this power is now exercised and enforced by the Courts in Ulster. There is and can be no political liberty in a country where one political party outrages, oppresses, and intimidates not only its political opponents, but persons whose religious opinions differ from those of the party in power. The same principle for which we shed our blood on the battlefield of Europe led us to commit the act we are charged with.[37]

While he was resigned to the likelihood of being found guilty, he finished with an exhortation that sought to prick the conscience of the jury members:

> My lord and members of the jury, you can condemn us to death today, but you cannot deprive us of the belief that what we have done was necessary to preserve the lives, the homes, and the happiness of our countrymen in Ireland. You may by your verdict find us guilty, but we will go to the scaffold justified by the verdict of our own consciences.[38]

Dunne and O'Sullivan died in the belief that their sacrifice would be recognised by Ireland, and this would give consolation to their families. Their hopes were unfounded. The deed was too controversial and its consequences too dire. August 1922 would be the bitterest of months in Ireland.

11

The Irish Civil War: 'The madness from within'

The sequence of events that began with the assassination of Field Marshal Sir Henry Wilson caught both pro- and anti-Treaty forces unprepared for war. The glorious unity of the War of Independence, despite the egos and chaos inherent in a guerrilla campaign, was sundered within six months of the Truce that ended the war. There was much talk of war, but this very talk paralysed people against its eventuality. IRA commander Florrie O'Donoghue remembered: 'Despite six months of the talk of the possibility of civil war no one had allowed himself to believe it to be inevitable and no plans existed on either side for conducting it.'[1]

In March 1922 the political head of the anti-Treaty movement, Éamon de Valera, made a series of incendiary speeches to captive audiences of armed IRA men. In Killarney, County Kerry, de Valera warned that those who supported the Treaty 'will have to wade through Irish blood . . . the people never had a right to do wrong'.[2] This mixture of blood-curdling incitement and disdain towards the electorate brought the sharpest rebukes to de Valera from the pro-Treaty media and politicians. He repeated the assertion that the majority had no right to do wrong in a meeting with Irish Labour Party politicians a month later, when they begged him to avert civil war.[3] De Valera's belief that the Irish people did not know what was good for them was something he had in common with Wilson.

For all the talk, the anti-Treaty IRA was badly prepared for the confrontation with the Provisional Government that its actions had brought about. At the beginning of the Civil War the public were perceived to be pro-Treaty, but the majority of the IRA and its women's auxiliary (Cumann na mBan) were anti-Treaty. These were people who had taken an oath to the Irish Republic and wanted full independence from Britain, not the Dominion status of the Treaty. They had taken up the fight, risked their lives and their livelihoods. They were the ones who had lain in ditches and faced imprisonment or death while the rest of the population were, to use the dismissive parlance of republicans at the time, 'under the bed'. For many of them the views of the public were moot.

The provisions of the Treaty quickly split the IRA between those supporting the government and those who did not. In March 1922 the Provisional Government, established under the Treaty, banned a proposed IRA convention, contending that only it had the lawful authority to hold such a gathering.

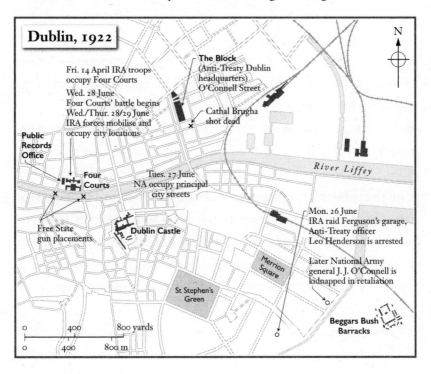

Dublin, 1922

N

The Block
(Anti-Treaty Dublin headquarters)
O'Connell Street

Fri. 14 April IRA troops occupy Four Courts

Wed. 28 June
Four Courts' battle begins
Wed./Thur. 28/29 June
IRA forces mobilise and occupy city locations

Cathal Brugha shot dead

Public Records Office

Four Courts

Tues. 27 June
NA occupy principal city streets

River Liffey

Mon. 26 June
IRA raid Ferguson's garage, Anti-Treaty officer Leo Henderson is arrested

Free State gun placements

Dublin Castle

Later National Army general J. J. O'Connell is kidnapped in retaliation

Merrion Square

St Stephen's Green

Beggars Bush Barracks

0   400   800 yards

0   400   800 m

Despite being banned by the Provisional Government, the convention went ahead on 26 March in the Mansion House, Dublin, although the men from the 1st Southern Division arrived in an armoured car expecting a fight. Predictably, the convention repudiated the authority of the Dáil.[4]

Three days later, anti-Treaty operatives wrecked the presses of the pro-Treaty *Freeman's Journal* and anti-Treaty volunteers of the 1st Southern Division seized the *Upnor*, a British tugboat that was transporting arms back across the Irish Sea. The massive haul included 266 cases of rifles and machine-gun parts, 1,500 cases of small-bore ammunition, 1,300 shell casings, 750 cases of fuses and fireworks, and 600 cases of small arms. This arsenal was brought ashore during the night at Ballycotton, County Cork, by several hundred men acting with complete impunity.[5] The challenge to the fledgling state grew more serious by the day.

A new anti-Treaty IRA was created. Rory O'Connor, the anti-Treaty IRA leader, hosted an infamous press conference in which he was challenged as to how they would respond in the event of the public supporting the Treaty.

They would not obey Arthur Griffith, the president of Dáil Éireann, or any Irish government supporting the Treaty, he said. 'Dáil Éireann has done an act which it had no moral right to do. The Volunteers are not going into the British Empire and stand for Irish liberty.'[6] O'Connor was asked if the people would be forced into accepting a republic even if they voted for the Treaty. 'That is a matter of policy for the executive of the army to consider.'

'Do we take it we are going to have a military dictatorship then?'

'You can take it that way if you like.'

'Then, no matter what the majority of the people decide as right, your intention is that what you think is right shall be enforced. If you do that, I think you are undertaking a terrific responsibility,' said an American journalist.

'It is a great responsibility, but it is no greater than the men took in 1916.'

When asked if the army would forcibly prevent an election from being held, O'Connor stated: 'It will have the power to do so.'

O'Connor concluded that 80 per cent of the IRA was anti-Treaty and 'of the other 20 per cent, we hope to get 19'. He was mistaken in those figures.[7] It was these extremist comments, coupled with the occupation of the Four Courts, which so alarmed the British government that Lloyd George directly cited O'Connor in his warning letter to Collins after the Wilson shooting.

A second convention met on 9 April and a new anti-Treaty IRA was created. The anti-Treaty IRA constitution was adopted, with a new leadership and general headquarters (GHQ). This sixteen-member executive would prosecute the Civil War against the government, and four days later occupied the Four Courts, the seat of law in Ireland, and turned it into its headquarters.[8]

Anti-Treaty forces began raiding post offices and banks on the pretext that funds promised for the IRA were being stopped by the Provisional Government. They gave receipts for the takings. They also renewed the Belfast Boycott of goods and services from the city, which had been suspended by the Provisional Government.

An editorial in the *Irish Independent* reflected on the seriousness of an army repudiating the government of a country. 'In all constitutionally governed countries, including republics, the army is the servant not the master of the civil authority,' it wrote,[9] to which de Valera responded that there could be no election while the threat of 'immediate and terrible war' hung over the Irish people.[10]

An oath in an age of deep religious faith was not entered into lightly or lightly renounced. The oath of allegiance to the British monarchy was famously dismissed in 1927 by Éamon de Valera as an 'empty formula' when his anti-Treaty Fianna Fáil party, established after the Civil War, finally entered the Dáil, yet it was considered a matter of life and death in 1922. Power was vested in either the people or the British monarch, opponents reasoned. It could not be vested in both. An oath of allegiance did not make the Irish Free State a free state.

The signing of an electoral pact on 20 May 1922 was a huge relief to the whole country and appeared to avert civil war. Collins and de Valera agreed to a list of candidates in proportion to the outcome of the Treaty vote in the Dáil. In a proportional representation system they encouraged the electorate to spread their preferences and ensure a Sinn Féin majority.

Under the terms of the Treaty the election had to go ahead by the end of June. It was agreed the election would not be regarded as a vote on the Treaty, but on putting together a unity government. 'Throughout the country relief was profound,' the anti-Treaty historian Dorothy Macardle recorded in her seminal work *The Irish Republic*, published in 1937:

> It was understood that the Treaty was not to be an issue in
> the elections decreed for June. Instead of being faced with
> the necessity of recording an immediate decision on this
> overwhelming question, the people were offered a chance to
> postpone their decision until the matter could be clarified and
> understood. Instead of being forced to choose at once between
> a government committed to empire and a government pledged
> to defend the Republic even at the risk of war, they were
> offered an opportunity of returning a coalition government

pledged to peaceful conservation of the present national strength.[11]

The British government, however, was not happy. Winston Churchill, then Secretary of State for the Colonies, declared that if republicans were to go into government without accepting the Treaty, the agreement would be forfeit. Article 17 declared that:

The British Government shall take the steps necessary to transfer to such Provisional Government the powers and machinery requisite for the discharge of its duties, *provided that every member of such Provisional Government shall have signified in writing his or her acceptance of this instrument* [author's italics].[12]

In the House of Commons Churchill sought to reassure the members, without much conviction, that the pact was the best chance for peace in Ireland. He added in the most euphemistic language he could muster that, should the Treaty be forfeit, 'the resources of our civilisation are by no means exhausted. Should the end be failure, this country would be in an immeasurably stronger position to resume the bloody struggle than it was before.'[13]

Wilson spoke in the same debate, while Collins and Griffith watched on from the Distinguished Strangers' Gallery. A few days previously Wilson had denounced the pact with characteristic hyperbole by suggesting the 'surrender of the Provisional Government to de Valera is one of the most pitiful, miserable and cowardly stories in history'. In the House of Commons he repeated his criticism of the government in the same uncompromising terms:

I would like also to ask the Colonial Secretary whether he can give any guarantee at all for the southern loyalists in the twenty-six counties? I am one of them. I do not ask him to give me any. I do not want to go into any military details. I do not think it wise in the face of the enemy to disclose these facts, but if serious trouble arises on the frontier between the six counties and the twenty-six counties, I hope that the Government will not restrain the military from crossing the frontier in their own self-defence. I wonder when the moment will come when the Government will have the honesty and truthfulness to come to this House and to say, 'We have miscalculated every single element in the Irish problem. We are exceedingly sorry for all the terrible things that have happened owing to our action. We beg leave to retire to private life, and never to appear again.'[14]

On 5 June de Valera and Collins made a joint appeal to the electorate on the basis that 'many of the dangers that threaten us can be met only by keeping intact the forces which constituted the national resistance in recent years'.[15]

All the while negotiations between the British and Irish over the Free State constitution were continuing in London. Lloyd George was outraged when the Irish side submitted a constitution that sought to repudiate the nominal authority of the king. With one of his theatrical flourishes he put blue pencil through several provisions of the Irish side. Collins was in London for the late drafting of the constitution and arrived back in Ireland two days before the general election was due to take place on 16 June.

On 14 June he made a speech in Cork urging the public to 'vote for the candidates you think best of, whom the electors of Cork think will carry on best in the future the work they want carried on'.[16] This was interpreted as a direct repudiation of the pact. Did

Collins know that the constitution would not bridge the divide between the pro- and anti-Treaty republicans?

On the same day attempts to unify the army were rejected by those still in possession of the Four Courts, who instead passed a resolution stating that negotiations with the Provisional Government on army unification should cease and that whatever action needed to be taken against British troops remaining in Ireland should be taken.

The constitution, published on the morning of the election, confirmed the oath of allegiance and the office of the governor-general as the king's representative in Ireland. The slim chances of agreement disappeared with its publication.

On 18 June, four days before the Wilson shooting, a third and last IRA convention was held in the Mansion House. It led to an extraordinary denouement. Thunderous denunciations of the Provisional Government were made. The emerging results of the election, a resounding victory for pro-Treaty and Treaty-neutral candidates, did not help the mood. Feelings were running high when Tom Barry declared it was time to give the British seventy-two hours to leave Ireland. Barry's stature meant his views were taken seriously. In a moment of high passion the motion was passed, but a recount was called for and the motion was lost.[17]

Rory O'Connor and Liam Mellows led a walkout, declaring, 'All those in favour of the Republic come to the Four Courts.' When Liam Lynch did not follow them, he was deposed as chief of staff and replaced by Joe McKelvey. Lynch and his other anti-Treaty officers left the meeting and set up their own headquarters in the Clarence Hotel across the river from the Four Courts. The Four Courts garrison issued an appeal to 'recreant Irishmen' to support the Republic and 'recognise that the resistance now being offered is but the continuance of the struggle that was suspended by the truce with the British'.[18]

The result of the election was interpreted as a victory for those who supported the Treaty, even though ostensibly it was not about the Treaty. Anti-Treaty Sinn Féin won just 21.26 per cent of the vote, less than the Labour Party (21.33 per cent), which accepted the Treaty and wanted to move on to address the serious issues of poverty and deprivation in the country. The Farmers' Party and independents also polled well. Despite the pact and the dominance of Sinn Féin over the previous five years, 40 per cent of the electorate voted for other candidates. There were many within the electorate who wanted to get on with things and were tired of the squabbling over the abstruse construction of the oath and the exact degree of Irish sovereignty contained in the Treaty.[19]

* * *

At the beginning of the Civil War, the anti-Treaty IRA had a numerical advantage in terms of men and munitions. It had a nominal strength of 12,000 men with 6,780 rifles, and was strongest in the south and west. The Provisional Government could only muster 6,000 men under arms and not even that number were fully uniformed or equipped. Most of its strength was put into the Battle of Dublin, which followed the shelling of the Four Courts on 28 June. The siege of the Four Courts lasted three days. The first day had an air of unreality. The 18-pounders were loaded with shrapnel shells and made little impact on the thick granite facade. One anti-Treaty garrison member sneered that the shells must have been bought in Woolworths, the cut-price store, such was their risible impact.[20]

Men from both sides sniped at each other to little avail, causing the Under-Secretary for Ireland, Sir Alfred Cope, to remark: 'Rory is in the Four Courts. Free Staters are in the houses opposite – each firing at the other hundreds of rounds with probably remarkably few hits. A hundred yards away people carry on their ordinary business.'[21]

The British, impatient at the hard work the gunners were making of the Four Courts, brought in a consignment of high-explosive shells and a breach was made in the facade. The siege of the Four Courts ended on 30 June with a catastrophic explosion that destroyed the Public Records Office and with it hundreds of years of documented Irish history. According to the author Michael Fewer, based on the latest research, the destruction of the Public Records Office was not caused by the detonation of explosives that the anti-Treaty side had stored, but by an explosion in the adjacent northern block of the Four Courts, where paraffin and petrol barrels were being kept with a view to setting

25 Free State forces, using British artillery, shell the Four Courts, where anti-Treaty rebels had been based for more than two months, in June 1922

the complex alight.[22] This was a reckless act, compounded by the risk that a stray shell could ignite an inferno. At approximately 11.30 a.m. the Public Records Office went up in a huge explosion that sent a dark plume of smoke hundreds of metres into the air. Ernie O'Malley, the anti-Treaty assistant chief of staff and a future chronicler of the conflict, noted that a 'thick black cloud floated up about the buildings and drifted away slowly. Fluttering up and down against the black mass were leaves of white paper; they looked like hovering white birds.'[23]

The explosion could be heard two kilometres away. It shattered windows in Grafton Street, Dublin's premier shopping street, scattered the ducks in St Stephen's Green and sent the populace scurrying for what shelter they could find. A member of the Public Records Office staff, S. C. Ratcliff, recalled a scene

26 On 30 June the destruction of the Public Records Office, where the munitions were stored, sent a huge cloud of smoke over Dublin city

of utter devastation afterwards. The glass and slate roof built in 1867 had fallen in and a huge crack emerged in one of the walls. The floor of the repository was piled up to five metres high with twisted ironwork and debris. The iron boxes containing many precious records had melted in the heat 'and the contents have been reduced in every case to a little white ash'.[24]

The census records for the whole of the nineteenth century, going back to the first in 1821, were incinerated. The records of those who had lived in Ireland before the calamity of the Great Famine were lost forever. Chancery records detailing British rule in Ireland going back to the fourteenth century and grants of land by the Crown were also destroyed, along with thousands of wills and title deeds. The records of various chief secretaries for Ireland, centuries of Church of Ireland parish registers, the Christ Church deeds going back to 1174, court records dating to the thirteenth century, military records of local yeomanry and transportation records to the colonies were also lost.[25]

The list of documents that were stored in the office's record treasury departments are contained in a single 300-page manuscript, which fortunately survived the fire. This unpublished book, compiled in 1919 by Herbert Wood, the deputy keeper of the Public Records Office, was described as the 'most depressing in Irish history' because it chronicles so many priceless documents that were incinerated.[26] The sense of national loss has prompted an international effort to recover what was destroyed. Beyond 2022, a project launched by the Irish state, involves the National Archives of Ireland, the UK National Archives, the Public Records Office in Northern Ireland, the Irish Manuscripts Collection and the library at Trinity College Dublin. They have teamed up to scour archives for duplicates of the documents that were lost, to be recreated in a virtual treasury for future generations.

Churchill, already a historian and author who would have understood the importance of archives, tried to console Michael Collins in a short letter: 'The archives of the Four Courts may be scattered, but the title deeds of Ireland are safe.'[27] It was a dreadfully inauspicious start for the new state, which had been founded on an acute sense of the preciousness of the past.

National Army forces completely surrounded the isolated garrison in the Four Courts, placing snipers at the rear of the building. Despite having had more than two months to prepare, the garrison inside had devised no escape route, and the tunnel leading from the Four Courts to the adjacent Patterson's Match Factory had not been completed in time. Writing years later, O'Malley reflected on the hopelessness of their position:

> It seemed a haphazard pattern of war. A garrison without proper food, surrounded on all sides, bad communications between their inside posts, faulty defences, girls bringing ammunition from attackers, relieving forces on our side concentrated on the wrong side of the widest street of the capital.[28]

O'Malley was referring to the republicans taking over the east side of O'Connell Street 750 metres away, when the logical position would have been to occupy the side closest to the Four Courts. The explosion concentrated minds and the Four Courts garrison surrendered. Approximately 140 dishevelled and disheartened men emerged from the ruins with their hands up. They were lined up against the wall in Chancery Place, the fit ones then taken to Mountjoy Prison, the wounded swept away in ambulances. Onlookers recalled the silence of it all after the continuous din of war. The chief organisers of the Four Courts stand-off, Mellows and O'Connor, were incarcerated by the state. They would never be seen in public again.

The battle moved right to the centre of Dublin. Anti-Treaty rebels captured a block on the upper east side of O'Connell Street of four hotels, the temporary General Post Office, relocated since it was destroyed in 1916, and the tramway office. The seizure was another military mistake and demonstrated they had learned nothing from the Rising. By occupying static and ultimately indefensible positions, the rebels made themselves easy targets for the 18-pounders, the walls of a city centre block proving highly porous to shells. Over the course of five days, from 1 to 5 July, the anti-Treaty rebels moved from building to building using an underground tunnel. The situation became hopeless, and Oscar Traynor, the Dublin No. 1 Brigade commanding officer, ordered a general evacuation to County Wicklow, just south of the capital.

Cathal Brugha and fifteen men agreed to remain to keep government forces occupied long enough to allow the rest to get away, but when their last holdout in the Granville Hotel was destroyed by shelling and set ablaze, Brugha ordered his men to surrender. He took their guns, emptied the bullets from the chambers and threw the weapons into the fire. But he refused to comply with his own order. The soldier, who had survived the Easter Rising and a visit to the House of Commons with a clip-fed semi-automatic pistol down his trouser leg, met his end down a laneway at the back of the Hammam Hotel. He emerged firing his pistol, dusty and shell-shocked, into the path of a National Army sniper and was felled with a single gunshot to the leg. Brugha, who later died in hospital from shock and blood loss from his wound, had shown a reckless disregard for his own safety – or preternatural courage, depending on your point of view – and became the first prominent fatality of the Civil War.[29] He left behind a widow and six young children. 'What was he

307

thinking?' his son Ruairi was asked in a documentary broadcast in 2003:

> I don't know. I said as much to my mother when she was dying. It wasn't right. It was a terrible pity. A great loss for his wife and children. My mother never talked about my father. It was probably too painful for her. All she said was that he died for Ireland.[30]

At the end of a week of fighting at least sixty-five people were dead, parts of the northern inner city were in ruins for the second time since the Rising and 280 people were wounded.[31]

There were many opportunities lost to 'stop the madness from within', as the Civil War was called by the Minister for Defence Richard Mulcahy. Liam Lynch, whose fanatical belligerence in the face of certain defeat did more than anything else to prolong the war, could have been arrested and detained on the day hostilities commenced. Lynch was avowedly anti-Treaty from the beginning. 'We have declared for an Irish republic and will not live under any other law,' he said within days of the Treaty being signed, when most people were keeping their counsel and seeing the way others were leaning.[32] Although only twenty-seven, Lynch had commanded the 1st Southern Division during the War of Independence in County Cork. In March 1922 he was elected chief of staff of the IRA at a stormy army convention at which the delegates refused to accept civilian control. Yet Lynch wanted to avoid a war and was not happy when the garrison occupied the Four Courts.

On the first day of the Civil War he and Liam Deasy, who would go on to be a prominent anti-Treaty commander, took a jaunting car – a two-wheeled horse-drawn carriage – from the hotel to nearby Kingsbridge (now Heuston) Station to get the train to Limerick. They were stopped along the way by Major General

Dalton, who recognised and then arrested them. Lynch was taken to Wellington (now Griffith) Barracks for interrogation. The Provisional Government assumed that the rift between Lynch and the Four Courts garrison remained, and that Lynch would use his influence to prevent war breaking out. Unknown to them, Lynch had patched up his differences in a meeting in the Four Courts on the night before it was bombarded. The deputy chief of the National Army, General Eoin O'Duffy, interviewed Lynch. According to O'Duffy, Lynch gave him an undertaking that he would take no part in any military offensive against the Provisional Government. Lynch claimed later he had given no such undertaking and bitterly complained when Free State propaganda accused him of being a liar who acted in bad faith. In any case, O'Duffy let both of them go, and Lynch and Deasy proceeded to Limerick, where they rallied the anti-Treaty side.[33]

Lynch envisaged a 'Munster Republic', a line between Limerick city in the west and Waterford city in the east, incorporating the

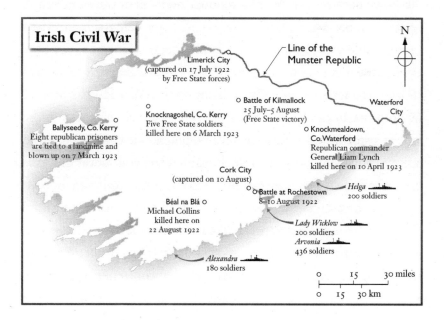

five southern counties of the province. It was to run at a slight diagonal and was 120 kilometres long, following the line of the River Suir in the east. This was not the First World War, where millions of men held an unbroken front from the North Sea to the Swiss border. The line was a notional one and existed more in the imagination of Lynch than it did in reality. He never had the men nor the resolve to hold it, and it was easily breached.

The city of Limerick had presaged the violence of the Civil War when clashes broke out in March, some of the most prominent guerrilla leaders of the War of Independence, pro- and anti-Treaty, facing off over the takeover of barracks the British were vacating. The republicans occupied the four barracks in the town, which became a stronghold of the republican movement. A ruthless commander might have sought to exploit the numerical advantage of the anti-Treaty side with its seven hundred armed men against the Provisional Government's four hundred, but old comrades were reluctant to turn their guns on each other. Lynch for the anti-Treaty side and the pro-Treaty Lieutenant General Michael Brennan and Commandant General Donncada O'Hannigan agreed a truce on 7 July 'in the interests of a united Ireland and to save our country from utter destruction'. The pact was reportedly made over the Blessed Sacrament.[34]

The truce lasted only four days, much to the detriment of the republican side, who lost both their materiel and tactical advantage. The Provisional Government told Brennan and O'Hannigan that under no circumstances should the accommodation be allowed to stand. The hiatus worked in favour of the government, which brought in reinforcements and artillery. Street fighting started on 11 July and lasted ten days. A convoy of Free State reinforcements finally made its way into the city on 18 July. Once again an 18-pounder gun was brought into the fight and eventually made a breach in the walls of the Strand Barracks, with at least twenty-three people being killed. The republicans fled the city, retreating south and west. On the same day as the republicans left Limerick, the Free State government captured Waterford city without much of a struggle.[35]

The fight now moved to rural County Limerick. Republicans occupied the neighbouring towns of Kilmallock, Bruff and Bruree in the east of the county to block the way to the counties of Cork and Kerry. The fighting lasted for eleven days, pitting committed but indecisive republicans against better-equipped National Army soldiers, who were a 'disgruntled, undisciplined and cowardly crowd', according to O'Duffy, their commander in the field.[36] The two sides faced each other across open fields and hedgerows, Irishmen killing other Irishmen in the Irish countryside. It took almost three thousand Free State troops to dislodge the republican defenders from the town of Kilmallock, by which time another front had opened up.

The National Army landed troops in Westport, County Mayo, on 24 July and then at Fenit near Tralee in County Kerry on 2 August. The latter landing by men from the Dublin Guard led by Brigadier General Paddy O'Daly later turned Kerry into a savage crucible of the Civil War, with republican forces barring the main roads and sabotaging the railways on the pretext that they carried National Army forces.[37]

Dalton decided to land troops by sea. This was potentially an extremely dangerous mission deep in enemy territory, but the alternative, travelling by road and rail with the potential of ambushes, was equally fraught. A sea landing was in nominal defiance of the Treaty, which forbade the Free State from having a navy and had even given the British access to three Irish ports. Yet, with the survival of the nascent state at stake, the British assisted the operation.

Two passenger steamers, the *Arvonia* and *Lady Wicklow*, left Dublin on 7 August. Many of the 636 recruits on board the vessels were so raw that their first experience of firing a weapon was after they had set sail. The captain of the Cork pilot boat told them they could only land at Passage West. The ships, carrying a pair of 18-pounder guns and three armoured cars, landed at 2 a.m., having been led by a Royal Navy escort through the minefield. Further down the coast 380 men were landed from the *Alexandra* and the gunboat *Helga*, which had achieved notoriety during the Easter Rising when it shelled rebel positions into oblivion.

The landing took the anti-Treaty soldiers by surprise. A detachment of republican sentries approached the *Arvonia* thinking it was the SS *Classic*, the steamship that sailed between Cork and Fishguard. They were on the gangplank before they realised it was the enemy they were engaging. They turned and fled.[38]

Among those on the republican side at Passage West was Joe O'Sullivan's brother Pat, who had joined an active service unit in Cork at the start of the Civil War. He recalled there were about thirty men opposing the landings. 'There was not a terrible lot of fighting . . . it was more of a retreat as a matter of fact from Passage.'[39]

Five hours later republicans blew the bridge up in Rochestown on the approach into Cork city and engineers improvised a wooden structure, while the men who crossed it joked about 'walking the plank'. Two days of heavy fighting followed in Rochestown and Douglas, leaving sixteen men (nine Free State and seven republicans) dead. The republicans had the aid of nine Lewis guns and it took considerable courage by National Army forces to drive the republicans out of Rochestown and then out of Douglas. Many of the National Army soldiers were exhausted and wanted to rest, but Dalton insisted they push on through to Cork city.[40]

On 10 August, the day Dunne and O'Sullivan were hanged, Treaty forces entered Cork city. The anti-Treaty forces fled the city, leaving a trail of destruction behind them. It did nothing to enamour them to a war-weary public unconvinced of the rightness of their cause. The fleeing soldiers burned an army barracks, a technical school, the offices of the city's two newspapers, the *Cork Examiner* and *Cork Constitution*, and attempted to destroy three bridges across the River Lee, without success.[41]

There was much cheering as Dalton's men paraded through the city. The fall of Cork city meant the end of conventional fighting with combatants facing each other in the open. It ought to have been the end of the war. Government forces had captured the cities of Dublin, Cork, Limerick and Waterford. A recruitment campaign bolstered the ranks of the National Army, many of them British army veterans of the Great War. The government had at its disposal an inexhaustible supply of munitions from the British, plus the support of the majority of the people, the trade union movement, the Catholic Church and the popular press.

On 11 August the *Irish Independent* juxtaposed the stories of the fall of Cork and the execution of Dunne and O'Sullivan on the same page, with the headlines 'Troops Advancing on Cork City' and 'Two Executions in London' appearing next to each other.[42] Photographs of the landing at Passage West and crowds praying outside Wandsworth Prison appeared in the following day's newspaper. Had the Civil War ended fifty days after the assassination of Wilson, it would have been remembered as a test of wills, a giant misunderstanding, an unfortunate and unnecessary confrontation, but one that decisively answered who would govern in the Irish state.

Rather than quit, the anti-Treaty side resorted to the same guer-rilla tactics as employed by the IRA in the War of Independence. Liam Lynch and his band of rebels retreated to the countryside and resorted to ambushes and material destruction. Both sides brought out the worst in each other. The horrors of the war were just beginning.

* * *

Two days after their execution, the suppressed statement by Dunne and O'Sullivan was published in the *Irish Independent*. Any impact it might have had was eclipsed by the death of Arthur Griffith, who had succeeded de Valera as president of Dáil Éireann. Griffith was just fifty-one. He had been seeing a doctor for tonsillitis, a poten-tially dangerous condition in the days before antibiotics, and was told to rest. With the Treaty settlement he had negotiated in daily danger, Griffith ignored the advice. He was bending down to tie his shoelace when he fell over, having suffered a cerebral haemor-rhage, and all attempts to revive him failed.

In a revolution driven mostly by people under the age of thirty-five, Griffith was the elder statesman of Irish politics. He would tell his younger, more hot-headed nationalist comrades that he was old enough to remember the failures of the Fenian move-ment, and that emotion and rhetoric alone would not win an inde-pendent Ireland. He originally proposed a dual monarchy, using Hungary as a model. Hungary had gained equal status with Austria within the Austrian Empire in 1867. They had the same head of state, but different parliaments. Griffith believed a similar model would work for Britain and Ireland. His vision of abstentionism from the British parliament and declaring a sovereign independ-ent state did not get widespread traction until the Easter Rising.

This was erroneously branded the 'Sinn Féin Rising', even though Griffith, who founded the Sinn Féin party in 1906, knew nothing about it in advance.

Griffith was an intellectual whirligig. Ideas poured forth from him incessantly, all of them exhorting Ireland towards a better future. According to William T. Cosgrave, the Irish Free State's first leader, he was 'the greatest man of his age, the father of us all'.[43] He was also a pragmatist who preferred to live for Ireland than die for it and was determined to work the Treaty as best he could, opining, as Collins had also done, that it was not the last word on Irish independence. 'It has no more finality than we are the final generation on the face of the earth.'[44] Although he died of natural causes, many would claim afterwards that the strain of the Civil War contributed to his premature demise. Certainly, Collins thought as much:

> Only those who have worked with him know what Arthur Griffith has done for Ireland; they can realise how he has spent himself for his country's cause and I have no shadow of doubt but that his end has been hastened by the mental anguish he has endured because of the actions of those who at this, the first time in the long and sorrowful history of our country when Ireland has the opportunity of becoming a nation, have acted as they have done and as they are doing still. The one bright spot in this fresh tragedy we have to endure would be for those who are against us and who realise as many of them I know do realise, what Arthur Griffith has done for Ireland, to be by his death brought to a better ideal of their own duty to the country which they profess to serve and love.[45]

Griffith was head of the Irish delegation during the Anglo-Irish Treaty negotiations. Although he and the other Irish signatories had reservations about the Treaty, he was determined to make it work. His death was a particular source of anguish to the British government, which accurately thought of him as the most reliable of the Treaty signatories. Griffith was genuinely horrified by the Wilson killing, in the same way that he had been horrified by the killing in Soloheadbeg, County Tipperary, of two Royal Irish Constabulary officers, Patrick O'Connell and James McDonnell, the action which started the War of Independence in January 1919. 'We would soon be eating one another,' he prophesied.[46]

Six days after the execution of Dunne and O'Sullivan, Currygrane House was burned to the ground. The Wilsons had left Currygrane for the last time in January 1921, bound for London. They intended to be away for only three weeks, but political circumstances prevented them from ever returning. It is a measure of their insecurity that not even the Truce nor the Treaty, which ostensibly ended the conflict between Britain and Ireland, and by extension between nationalists and unionists in the South of Ireland, could tempt them back.

There was no one living in Currygrane House when arsonists arrived at 1 a.m. on 16 August, although the steward and estate manager James Armstrong still occupied a dwelling adjacent to the main house. He asked if they intended to occupy the building. 'No,' came the reply, 'it is going up.' The blaze was so fierce that the house burned for two days. Even the timber in the walls went up in flames, and the roof was incinerated. The ruins were looted and silverware – antiques bearing the Wilson crest – were found in raids by the police a year later. It was never established who carried out the attack.[47]

James Mackay Wilson, Wilson's eldest son, claimed £50,000 (£1.75 million in today's money) for the damage. He was eventually

27 Currygrane outhouses, the only buildings still standing on the Wilson estate

awarded £12,000 (£720,000), following a protracted hearing at the Longford Sessions. Wilson was not present, but his lawyers argued that rebuilding Currygrane House was pointless as the location was remote and there was no 'fashionable crowd in Currygrane like in the adjoining counties of Meath and Kildare and no attraction for fashionable dwellers there'. Instead, he agreed to build eight houses in Castle Park Road in Dalkey, County Dublin, one of the most fashionable seaside suburbs of Dublin. The money had to be paid by hard-pressed Longford ratepayers, and the county council protested it would leave the county and bring no benefit.[48]

Henry Wilson's brother Jemmy never returned to live in Ireland and died in Gratwicks, Steyning, West Sussex, in 1933 at the age of seventy. In the years between the censuses of 1911 and 1926 (there was no census in 1921 because of the political unrest) the Protestant population of the twenty-six counties declined by a third from just over 10 per cent of the population to 7 per cent.[49] The reasons for this decline have been a matter of often fractious historical dispute ever since. Did the withdrawal of the British army play a role? Did the Protestant population leave for the same reason that many Catholics left – for better opportunities elsewhere? Was the notorious *Ne Temere* decree by the Catholic Church, promulgated in 1907, which insisted that the children of mixed marriages be brought up as Catholics, also a factor? Whatever the truth, it is undeniable that Southern unionist families like the Wilsons did not feel comfortable in the Irish Free State.

After his departure the lands at Currygrane were distributed through the Land Commission to former tenant farmers, among them James Armstrong, who was granted sixty-three acres.[50] His son Robert had served in the Irish Guards during the First World War, the same regiment as Reggie Dunne. Robert Armstrong joined the Imperial (now Commonwealth) War Graves Commission after the war, working as a gardener in France and Belgium. In 1940, after the Germans overran France, commission staff were evacuated to Britain, but Armstrong was allowed to stay because of his Irish nationality – Ireland being neutral in the Second World War. While tending to the graves of his fallen former comrades, Armstrong joined the French Resistance. He expressed no gratitude towards the occupiers. On the contrary, he needled them whenever he could. It was a dangerous game. Though too old to fight, Armstrong found another way to help the Allied cause. He joined the St Jacques evasion network, one of a myriad of networks set up to smuggle stranded Allied servicemen out of occupied Europe. He was arrested and sentenced to death for his Resistance activities, but his sentence was commuted by the German authorities to life imprisonment, thanks to the intervention of Seán Mac Eoin, who, as we have seen, had a long association with the Wilson family. Armstrong's health deteriorated in captivity and he died in Waldheim prison camp on 16 December 1944. Armstrong is now remembered with a plaque in his name at the Valenciennes (St Roch) Communal Cemetery in northern France. James Armstrong sold up his farm in Currygrane in 1950 and moved to Dublin, and the Brady family took over.[51]

The burning of the so-called 'big houses', the homes of the Anglo-Irish landed class, was one of the most unsettling episodes of the Irish revolution. Some 275 big houses were destroyed between 1919 and 1923.[52] They were perceived as belonging to the classes that had oppressed Ireland for centuries. Although there was some truth in that, the burnings were widely condemned and remain a source of embarrassment to nationalist Ireland. During the War of Independence they were burned in retaliation for the burning of the homes of republicans. Though morally dubious, there was at least a logic to the activities of the IRA in the War of Independence. No such logic attended the burning of 199 big houses during the Civil War, destroyed in retaliation for the executions of republicans. According to Liam Lynch, the homes of imperialists were legitimate targets, even if their owners had nothing to do with prosecuting the Civil War.

'All Free State supporters are traitors and deserve the latter's stark fate, therefore their houses must be destroyed at once,' Lynch declared after a number of anti-Treaty prisoners were executed.[53] Two days later the home of pro-Treaty Sinn Féin TD Sean McGarry was burned to the ground, and his seven-year-old son died in the blaze. William T. Cosgrave's home in south Dublin was burned out in January 1923. A Free State Army report from that month concluded: 'With depleted numbers, lack of resources and unified control and almost complete ineffectiveness from a military standpoint, their [anti-Treaty IRA] policy of military action is slowly changing to one of sheer destruction and obstruction of the civil government.'[54]

On 22 August Michael Collins was killed in an ambush at Béal na mBláth (the Mouth of the Flowers) in County Cork, on the road between Bandon and Macroom. Many had advised him not to go to west Cork, which was a stronghold of anti-Treaty rebels. He commented, half in jest and half in that mordant wit of his, 'Yerra, they'll never shoot me in my own county.'[55]

Collins embarked on a tour of the south on 20 August, secure in the knowledge that the major centres of population were in the government's hands. The convoy travelled to Limerick, where General Eoin O'Duffy told him the Civil War would soon be over. Collins continued on to Cork, where he met his sister and nephew. He also consulted with Major General Emmet Dalton, one of Collins's most senior men, a First World War veteran and the man in charge of the Four Courts bombardment that started the Civil War. Dalton told him that the whole of County Cork would soon be in government hands.

Collins's last journey has been freighted with portent. Every move he made in those last days has been analysed. Some say he was entering enemy territory to make peace; others that he went to rally the Treaty side and remind the public, whom he believed to be overwhelmingly pro-Treaty, that he appreciated their support. Before leaving for Cork, Collins had been told by Dalton that a 'committee of prominent citizens of Cork' had a proposition for a truce. No such meeting took place. On the day before he was shot, Collins met Florrie O'Donoghue, one of those who opted for neutrality in the war. Was Collins trying to put out peace feelers? Some believe he was, others that he was there to stiffen the spine of Treaty supporters.

On 22 August he was up and out at 6.15 a.m., with a busy schedule ahead of him. The party consisted of a motorcycle outrider, a touring car with Collins, Dalton and two drivers, a Crossley Tender (a light truck) and an armoured car, twenty-four men in all. It was not a large contingent to be venturing into enemy territory.[56]

The convoy criss-crossed the county, passing by many places Collins knew well. He passed by Béal na mBláth in the morning, where his convoy was spotted by a scout, Denis Long. He met Major Seán Hales, whose brother Tom had taken the opposite side in the Civil War. The convoy went through Crookstown, then to Bandon, then on to Roscarberry, where Collins paid a visit to his cousin Jeremiah's pub and talked of ending the Civil War and moving on to the North.[57]

On the way back, Collins's party passed by the remains of his childhood home, Woodfield, which had been burned down by the Essex Regiment in April 1921. Dalton noted that Collins was happy among his own people. 'He didn't say much as we travelled along the flat road towards Bandon, he appeared lost in the myriad thoughts of a crowded and successful day.'[58] After tea in Bandon, they headed back to Cork city via a circuitous route because so many of the roads had been blocked. As it was getting towards evening time, many of the ambushers had decided to clear off for the day, assuming Collins had gone back to Cork by a different route; a sizeable contingent of men remained, however, occupying a shaded area overlooking a continuous bend.

When the first shot was fired, Dalton ordered the drivers to 'drive like hell', but Collins insisted on engaging the ambush party. Dalton feared the worst. The ambush site had been perfectly chosen and there was no area of retreat. 'The only thing we could have done was drive on,' he remembered.[59]

Collins's death was all the more tragic for him being the only casualty of the engagement. He was hit while running from behind an armoured car to take aim at his ambushers. Some would claim later that his actions were a result of inexperience. 'If Mick had ever been in a scrap he would have learned to stay down,' Dalton said afterwards.[60] For all Collins's world renown as a guerrilla fighter, he had done little actual fighting. Others said he had been drinking during the day and the drink caused him to take unnecessary risks.

Dalton recalled that Collins 'had a gaping hole in the side of his head'. Dalton bandaged his wounds and O'Connell said an act of contrition. 'It could only have been a ricochet bullet or a dum-dum. He was either dying or dead when I got to him,' Dalton added.[61]

A mountain of speculation has produced a molehill of facts relating to the death of Collins. Over the last century there have been numerous books, academic papers and articles speculating on the identity of the person who fired the single shot that killed him. The man most widely believed to have been responsible was, like Dunne and O'Sullivan, an ex-British army Great War veteran. Denis 'Sonny' O'Neill from Timoleague, County Cork, had been wounded fighting with the British army in the First World War and joined the IRA in December 1918. Claims regarding his identity were strengthened in a 1990 documentary about Michael Collins entitled *The Shadow of Béal na mBláth*. Eamonn de Barra, an IRA intelligence officer at the time, suggested O'Neill never intended to kill Collins, but rather to fire a warning shot.[62] The bullet ricocheted off a lump of limestone. In his application for a military pension, O'Neill was described as having a 'very downcast appearance, hardly ever smiles, never looks a person in the face when speaking', though, significantly, he was also a 'first-class shot'.[63]

Art historian and performer Paddy Cullivan has, however, uncovered new evidence to suggest that Sonny O'Neill could not have been the shooter. According to Cullivan, there is no evidence that O'Neill ever operated as a sniper either for the British army or the IRA. Had he been a sniper, he would have been deployed as one in the War of Independence. Moreover, Cullivan has discovered documentation in the German archives that shows that when O'Neill was repatriated as a prisoner of war in 1918, he had a severe wound to his right arm, assessed later as constituting a 40 per cent disability.[64]

The careless and cack-handed way in which the Provisional Government handled the killing fuelled allegations of an official cover-up. No inquiry or inquest was ever carried out and no death certificate issued. The autopsy report carried out by Dr Oliver St John Gogarty was never made public and Gogarty was strangely reticent in speaking about it.[65]

The pro- and anti-Treaty supporters were briefly united in grief. Tom Barry, who had been captured while trying to come to the assistance of the Four Courts garrison, recalled the scenes in Mountjoy Prison:

> There was a heavy silence throughout the jail and ten minutes later from the corridor outside the top-tier of cells, I looked down at the extraordinary spectacle of about a thousand kneeling Republican prisoners spontaneously reciting the Rosary aloud for the repose of the soul of the dead Michael Collins. I have yet to hear of a better tribute to the part played by any man in the struggle with the English for Irish Independence.[66]

It was a useless death. Ireland's lost leader was just thirty-one when he was killed. In death Collins became a protean figure for people to imagine a better start to statehood than the desperate disappointments of the decades that followed independence. Collins would have been forward-thinking, outward-looking, prosperous, confident. He would have stood up to the Catholic Church, he would have ended emigration, he would have ended partition, he would have ensured that women were not second-class citizens in the new state. He would have made Ireland a success. Over the past century historians have trawled through Collins's book *The Path to Freedom*, published posthumously in 1922, to see what kind of Ireland might have emerged had he lived.

'It's my considered opinion that in the fullness of time history will record the greatness of Collins, and it will be recorded at my expense,' Éamon de Valera is reported to have said about him in 1966.[67] The quotation concludes Neil Jordan's 1996 film *Michael Collins*, which introduced a new generation to Collins, the revolutionary hero. Whether de Valera said it or not – and the quotation has been the subject of much dispute – it is certainly something many people believe. Collins's reputation has never been sullied by the messy reality of having to administrate an impoverished, pious state.

Dalton described Collins as a man of 'immense ability, untiring energy and thoughtfulness for others. He never had a free moment for himself. He was a patriot, a most courageous man and a great, great gentleman.'[68]

Kevin O'Higgins, the Minister for Justice, said Collins had framed the war as one of democracy against a potential dictatorship. 'Shortly before his death he told me that he regarded this fight [the Civil War] as a fight for the foundations of a State . . . but we could never make a start unless we had recognition of the basic principle of representative government – majority rule.'[69]

*

28 Harry Boland, Michael Collins and Éamon de Valera, 1 January 1920. Boland
and Collins were best friends and died on opposite sides in the Civil War

Collins's funeral cortège to Glasnevin Cemetery was one of the
biggest Dublin has ever seen. This was another chance to 'end
the madness within', but the conflict dragged on for another eight
ugly, bloody months. Without Collins to ameliorate the worst
excesses of the Provisional Government, its surviving members
passed the Army Emergency Powers Resolution in September,
which allowed for the execution of men captured bearing arms
against the state and aiding and abetting attacks on state forces.
The government had already adopted extrajudicial powers
through its Criminal Investigation Department, a police intelligence unit based at Oriel House in Dublin. It had been set up
originally by Collins and members of his Squad, and was implicated in the murder of many men, not all of them republicans.[70]

The first four anti-Treaty prisoners were executed on 17
November 1922, and a week later Erskine Childers, the English

gentleman turned Irish rebel, followed them. Childers was public school educated and the bestselling author of *The Riddle of
the Sands*, the spy thriller that highlighted the German threat to
Britain before the First World War. He had used his yacht the
Asgard to land guns for the Irish Volunteers in July 1914 and
promptly joined the Royal Navy during the First World War.

He was the secretary to the Treaty delegation and one of his
cousins, Robert Barton, was a reluctant signatory. Childers became
one of the most vocal opponents of the Treaty. His conflicted
nationality became a bête noire with the Provisional Government.
Griffith dismissed him as this 'damned Englishman'.[71] Churchill,
who once credited Childers's novel with waking Britain up to the
threat of Germany, described him as a 'strange being, actuated by
a deadly hatred for the land of his birth'.[72] Childers was a skilled
propagandist who continued to produce a newsletter throughout
the Civil War, when the media was overwhelmingly pro-Treaty.
It is clear from correspondence in Childers's military pensions
archive file that the Free State government was desperate to arrest
him and remove him from the scene, believing him to be one of
the prime military instigators of the Civil War, along with being
head of propaganda for the anti-Treaty IRA. In August 1922, just
two weeks before he died, Collins was told that Childers was in
Liverpool trying to organise rebels gathering in the city to attack
Dublin by sea while the National Army was engaged down the
country. It caused Collins to write to the Director of Intelligence,
'I should like to know if there have been any developments in the
Childers case. The idea that would be most suitable would be that
he should be arrested as a stow-away.'[73]

Despite his reputation as a renegade, the Free State struggled
to pin anything on Childers. The National Army's head of intelligence, Joe MacGrath, wrote a letter on 10 November to the

adjutant general in which he said, 'I am instructed to enclose your file and papers in connection with Erskine Childers and to state, that . . . neither the file nor the papers supply anything which would be the basis of a charge.' Yet that evening Childers was arrested at Barton's home in Annamoe, County Wicklow. He had been found in possession of a pistol, which he claimed was given to him as a present by Michael Collins. It was enough to pin a charge on him. He was transferred to Portobello Barracks and tried for 'being in possession of an automatic pistol'. On 19 November 1922 he was sentenced to death.[74] There are telegrams within the file pleading for clemency before he was killed, and others decrying the execution. One from the California branch of the American Association for the Recognition of the Irish Republic warned Richard Mulcahy that it would regard his execution or that of any other republican prisoner as 'murder'. *Sleep Soldier Sleep: The Life and Times of Pádraig O'Connor*, the memoir of a pro-Treaty officer, gives a detailed account of Childers's execution, which took place in Beggars Bush Barracks in Dublin. According to Captain Frank Holland, who had been guarding Childers, the man responsible for carrying out the execution ordered that only ex-British soldiers should be in the firing squad. The execution took place on 24 November. Fifteen men were selected for the job but only five had live ammunition. Childers is reported to have said to his executioners before he was shot, 'Take a step forward, lads. It will be easier that way.'[75]

On 5 December the bills giving effect to the Free State constitution under the terms of the Treaty received royal assent in the House of Lords. The Irish Free State came into being on 6 December 1922, one year after the Treaty was signed. The Provisional Government was now the government of the Irish Free State.

After seven hundred years of struggle the birth of the independent Irish state should have been a cause for national celebration, but the nation was not the state, six counties were missing, and a sizeable proportion of the population supported opposing that state in arms.

The *Irish Times* was downbeat: 'Freedom comes to us at the last, not blithe or smiling, but with a countenance severe and even tragic. Therefore, we greet her cordially, indeed, and hopefully, but without exultation. Whatever comfort her cornucopia may hold, she comes to a sad abode.'[76]

A day later republicans killed Sean Hales, a government TD, and badly wounded Pádraic Ó Máille, the Leas Ceann Comhairle (deputy speaker), as they left the Dáil. Liam Lynch warned that all those politicians who had signed the Army Emergency Powers Resolution were targets for assassination. The government acted swiftly. Dispensing with any pretension of following the rule of law, the Irish government's first significant act was to summarily execute the ringleaders of the Four Courts garrison – Rory O'Connor, Liam Mellows, Joe McKelvey and Richard Barrett – in revenge for the previous day's killings. In a proclamation the government described it as a 'solemn warning to those associated with them who are engaged in a conspiracy against the representatives of the Irish people'.[77]

The executions, according to the Labour leader Thomas Johnson, 'were murder most foul, bloody and unnatural'.[78] Cosgrave, the new state's first President of the Executive Council, was unrepentant. 'Terror must be met with terror,' he declared. He maintained, until the day he died, that he had done the right thing.[79]

At least seventy-seven republican prisoners were executed, although the total might have been as high as eighty-one – and those were only the official ones. Cosgrave insisted the end justified the means, declaring in March 1923, 'I am not going to hesitate if the country is to live and if we have to exterminate ten thousand Republicans, the three million of our people is bigger than this ten thousand.'[80]

The war dragged on into 1923. It reached a nadir of savagery that March in County Kerry, where a contingent of Free State troops from Dublin had been attempting to restore government control since July of the previous year. On 5 March five Free State troops were killed by a booby-trap mine in Knocknagoshel. In retaliation, nine republican prisoners were taken to Ballyseedy, outside Tralee, tied to a landmine and blown to pieces, with the exception of Stephen Fuller, who was blown into a nearby tree and survived. A day later at Countess Bridge four more republican prisoners were blown up by a mine, and on 12 March five were summarily executed by firing squad. These were atrocities perpetrated by government troops acting in the name of the Irish public.[81]

In April the noose finally tightened on the republican leadership. In early April prominent anti-Treaty IRA officers were captured in the Knockmealdown Mountains in south Tipperary and Waterford. On 10 April Liam Lynch was killed in the same mountain range, attempting to flee a Free State operation. With only a sidearm he could not possibly escape, but preferred death in combat to the certainty of execution. His replacement, Frank Aiken, called a ceasefire on 30 April. On 24 May he ordered the anti-Treaty fighters to 'dump their arms' and return home. Éamon de Valera concurred: 'Further sacrifice on your part would now be in vain and the continuance of the struggle in arms unwise in the national interest. Military victory must be allowed to rest for the moment with those who have destroyed the Republic.'[82]

The destruction of the Republic was in the eye of the beholder, but the anti-Treaty side almost destroyed the Irish state at birth.

They wrecked railway lines and roads, blew up bridges and torched some of Ireland's finest homes. The estimated cost of the war was £30 million, more than the Irish state collected in a calendar year in taxes at the time. The payment of compensation to those whose properties were destroyed during the war was a drain on the Irish state for years afterwards.[83]

The Civil War split the Irish nationalist movement in Britain too. Pa Murray, the man who could have shot Arthur Balfour, was sent to London by Liam Lynch to procure armaments but found that the Free State 'controlled all the original sources of supply and new contacts and lines have to be built up from zero'.[84]

Anti-Treatyites in London found themselves up against two formidable foes: not only the British intelligence network but also the Free State, which wanted rid of them. On 11 March 1923 the British police apprehended approximately 120 of the most high-profile anti-Treaty activists in Britain and deported them to Ireland. Among their number was Dunne's old mentor Art O'Brien, who had become one of the most trenchant and vocal opponents of the Treaty and had already been arrested in Dublin twice the previous year. The deportation was a highly irregular act. No extradition treaty existed between Britain and Ireland, but Kevin O'Higgins, the Minister for Justice, simply did not care:

> You had a country within a stone's throw of our shores – or
> at least a stone's throw for such a man as Finn MacCumhaill
> – used as a base, an arsenal, and an effective headquarters for
> a campaign against this State; not so much against the armed
> forces of this State as a brutal, cowardly campaign against
> the defenceless civilians who are citizens of this State. And
> we were to take no action! Afraid that we would lose our
> sovereignty, we were to take no action! People spin webs.

What fools we would be, conducting a fight for the very life and honour of this nation, not to accept the custody of those men and women. None of us lost a wink of sleep as to whether it was or was not a derogation of sovereignty. It was a thing that was not done of right, but as by agreement.[85]

O'Brien contested his detention on the basis that it was 'illegal to move his Majesty's lieges across the sea'. He won his case against illegal deportation and all the prisoners were released.[86]

At the remove of a hundred years, the passions of the Irish Civil War may seem alien. Both the pro-Treaty Cumann na nGaedheal (now Fine Gael) and the anti-Treaty Fianna Fáil, the two parties that emerged after the war to dominate the new state, dismantled the most controversial aspects of the Treaty without a shot being fired. They went into coalition with each other after the 2020 general election in the Republic.

The Statute of Westminster 1931 gave Dominions the right to make and repudiate international treaties. The oath of allegiance was abolished in 1933. The office of the governor-general was abolished in 1937, the same year the Irish Constitution came into being, and the Republic of Ireland Act 1948 severed the British connection entirely.

What had it all been for? The war pitted brother against brother, as evidenced by the Hales brothers. O'Higgins approved the execution of his best man, Rory O'Connor. Harry Boland, who shared a love interest with Michael Collins's fiancée Kitty Kiernan (played by Julia Roberts in the film *Michael Collins*), was shot dead in August 1922 by pro-Treaty forces. In September 1922 Brian MacNeill was killed, some believe summarily executed, by Provisional Government forces in County Sligo. His father

Eoin was Minister for Education in the Free State government. Another killed that day was Seamus Devins, an anti-Treaty TD. His widow Mary took her own life in 1936.

In a 1997 documentary to mark the seventy-fifth anniversary of the Irish Civil War, the writer Tim Pat Coogan, who has written popular biographies of both de Valera and Collins, described it as 'one of the most superfluous and wasteful conflicts experienced by man since the war between the Big Enders and the Little Enders that Dean Swift described in *Gulliver's Travels*'.[87]

The horrors which began with the Wilson shooting ensured that Dunne and O'Sullivan would never be spoken of in the same way as others in the pantheon of Irish martyrs. One group of determined campaigners would seek to remedy that fact.

12

Repatriation: 'The Irish Government's attitude is strictly illogical'

On 3 August 1929, in the republican plot in Deansgrange Cemetery, south Dublin, a Celtic cross was unveiled in memory of Dunne and O'Sullivan. Symbolically, the limestone cross was erected over an empty grave. The cross and the plot around it are looked after in perpetuity by the National Graves Association (NGA). The NGA was founded in 1926 to tend to the graves of the Irish republican dead, going back to the 1798 rebellion. Unlike the Imperial (later Commonwealth) War Graves Commission, the NGA is a voluntary organisation and receives no state funding.[1]

For some years the remains of both men remained in a corner of Wandsworth Prison, along with those of others who had been executed there. The request by their solicitor, James Hyndman MacDonnell, that the two men be reburied in Ireland was turned down by the prison authorities. In 1924 the Tipperary-born MP Jack Jones, who represented a London constituency, wrote to the then Home Secretary Arthur Henderson asking for the remains of Dunne and O'Sullivan to be buried in Ireland. There was another refusal.[2]

On the Sunday closest to the execution anniversary of 10 August every year, friends and family of Dunne and O'Sullivan would host Mass for them in Corpus Christi Church in Maiden Lane, off the Strand in London. There seemed no prospect that the British government would break its long-standing policy of burying executed prisoners in prison grounds into perpetuity.

They had not reckoned with Joe O'Sullivan's brother Pat and a small coterie of London-Irish IRA veterans, mostly comrades of Dunne and O'Sullivan, who sought vindication and recognition for the two men.

After the shooting, the IRA's chief of staff Richard Mulcahy denied that Dunne and O'Sullivan had been members of the IRA. This was not true. They were members, but Mulcahy knew nothing about the shooting and did not approve of it. He threatened to resign over it – surmising, accurately, that it had created another huge problem for a beleaguered Provisional Government.[3]

As the anti-Treaty side also denied being involved, the implication was left to linger that Dunne and O'Sullivan had acted of their own accord and were therefore not entitled to be remembered among those who had died on active service. This was a slur, according to their supporters, who maintained they had acted on orders and, as soldiers of the Irish Republic, deserved to be remembered among the honoured dead.

A month after the executions, the Dunnes fulfilled their son's wishes by moving to 8 Florence Road, Bray, in County Wicklow. It was a place where they sought solace after the trauma and shock of their son's death.

'This house we have is very nicely situated. It is about a minute and a half from the church and the same to the Carnegie Library,' Mary Dunne wrote to Art O'Brien in London. 'We have the sea and station within three minutes' walk, Bray Head about ten minutes away, we have the sea and the mountain air. The scenery around here is very nice.'[4]

A year later Liam Tobin and Tom Cullen visited the house. They apologised that nothing could be done formally by the new Irish state for the Dunnes, but they handed the couple the deeds to the house and told them it was theirs. Yet the Dunnes found it hard to settle anywhere in Ireland.[5] Robert Dunne died in 1934 and his heartbroken widow moved from house to house. She had never got over the death of her only child, as her good friend Mary MacGeehin told the Bureau of Military History in 1953:

Poor Mrs Dunne's mind was practically unhinged by her loss and one of the effects was that she could never settle for long in one place. During the seventeen years that she lived she never ceased talking about Reggie. She never got over the tragedy. She was a very beautiful woman with the fairest skin, pink colour in her cheeks and white hair that made a perfect frame for her face. We used to call her the Gainsborough. She had had beautiful bronze hair, but she told me that she had got white in one night at the time of Reggie's arrest. They were all very good practising Catholics and now the parents got their only consolation from prayer. She told me once three or four years after Reggie's death, when she was still mourning his loss as keenly as the first day and I think maybe her mind was in a precarious state – that she had a dream that she saw Reggie grown up and turned to profligacy. He had joined a band of something like tramps or tinkers and nothing was too hot or heavy for him. His appearance was evil. She thought she must die of sorrow when she saw him like this and suddenly he changed back to the boy she knew and he spoke to her, saying: 'Mother, you have been grieving too much for me. After all death is preferable to an evil life and imagine now that if I had lived I might have turned to evil.' This dream consoled her immensely and she felt that the message came from him. She always felt that he was still very close to her and never ceased to speak of him.[6]

One of the first acts of the Free State was to offer pensions to IRA and National Army veterans who had seen service during the revolutionary years (1916 to 1923). In some cases financial compensation was offered to their dependants. Over the next twenty-five years the categories were expanded to include anti-Treaty veterans and women involved in the Irish revolution. Critically, pensions did not come with service, as they did in most regular armies. An applicant had to prove 'active service' – to demonstrate they had put themselves in harm's way for Ireland. This amounted, effectively, to staring down the barrel of a British gun. The ancillary and often highly dangerous activities of spying, dispatch carrying, gunrunning, road trenching and scouting were not considered activities worthy of a pension. This parsimonious attitude was summed up by William Cosgrave, the Irish state's first leader. 'There would be no soft pensions,'[7] he declared. The result was, as the historian Diarmaid Ferriter put it, a 'chronicle of disappointment', with less than one in five applicants (15,700 out of 82,000 people) receiving a pension from the state.[8] The application process was cumbersome and exhausting for those involved, and left a deep well of anger and resentment. In many cases the sums involved were derisory, but, in the desperate economic conditions that followed independence, they were the difference between destitution and a modicum of comfort.

The pension process also left, however, one of the most comprehensive records of any revolution in history, with millions of pages of documents detailing the service of veterans, some of them well known, others forgotten by everybody except their own families. Since 2014 the Irish Department of Defence has been digitising and putting the records online. Among them are Mary Dunne's application for a pension for her son's service, John O'Sullivan's application for a pension in relation to Joe O'Sullivan, and Pat O'Sullivan's application in his own right for a pension from the Irish state.

Mrs Dunne first wrote to the Army Pensions Board in September 1934, after her husband died. 'I am left alone and would like to hear from you if I am entitled to anything. I have been advised to inquire if I am entitled to a small pension on account of my son's brave deed done for Ireland.'[9] She was turned down on the basis that she was not entitled to a pension under the legislation.

By this stage Mrs Dunne was living with Mary MacGeehin, who wrote a poignant letter to the Pensions Board. 'Since the death of her husband last September Mrs Dunne is finding it very hard to procure even the ordinary comforts of life. She is absolutely alone in the world.' Mrs Dunne was also estranged from her own sister because of her late son's activities.

MacGeehin said she could not provide for her friend and was loath to start a subscription, 'as we feel sure the state will recognise the services and sacrifices of her only child by granting her a pension in due course'.[10]

The correspondence reached Éamon de Valera, then the President of the Executive Council (prime minister), in March 1937. Another family friend, Kathleen Whelan, wrote to him suggesting that Dunne and O'Sullivan had been on official business when they shot Wilson: 'I am presuming that all the facts relative to Reginald Dunne's official services to the Government of Saorstat Éireann (Free State Ireland) are known to you and I feel that the Government of Saorstat Éireann have a certain moral responsibility in this matter.'[11]

The correspondence was also directed at Frank Aiken, the Minister for Defence, who said there was no provision for Mrs Dunne and no money either. Mrs Dunne would not let the matter rest. 'Reginald was my only child. If he was alive now he would be my support. Ireland deprived me of that support. I claim I have the right to Ireland's bounty and I look to you to see that I get it,' she declared.[12]

Aiken referred the matter back to the Army Pensions Board, who determined that Mrs Dunne had been a dependant of her son but was not entitled to a pension under the terms of the act. In 1937 she was eventually awarded a risible gratuity of £6 10 shillings per annum (€350 per year). Mrs Dunne died in a cottage in Howth in May 1939, penniless and alone, though de Valera did send a member of his government, Patrick (P. J.) Little, to represent him at the funeral. No relative of hers attended the funeral, nor were any identified afterwards despite many searches.

Until the end of her life she hoped the Irish government would recognise her son's sacrifice for Ireland. John O'Sullivan was more successful in receiving financial assistance from the Irish state. He first applied in 1933, telling the Pensions Board that his son had been promised that if anything happened to him, his family would be looked after. 'I didn't want it up to now, but through a long period of idleness and my old age of seventy-five, I am afraid that my working time is nearly finished. It is therefore with great reluctance that I am asking you to use your offices to put forward my claim in front of those that are dealing with the matter.' The Dunnes had been provided for, he added. 'I understand there was a house purchased for them at Bray, but not a word of sympathy from your predecessors in my case.'[13]

Bill Ahern was indignant on his behalf: 'Aged and feeble, he has been through a lot and now in his old age I think it is a shame that such a man should have to depend on charity. Repeated requests have been made through various channels asking for help but so far nothing has been done.'

Seán MacCraith, the former intelligence officer for the IRA in London who was arrested after the Wilson assassination, pressed the case. He supported John O'Sullivan's application on the basis that:

> They carried out the legal orders from headquarters of the executive to execute a man sentenced to death. Many such executions were carried out in Ireland. I know for a fact that the orders for this execution as well as two others were given by the late General Michael Collins prior to the Treaty split. Practically all orders for action in London came from him. Both Dunne and O'Sullivan were deeply religious men and had they any doubts of the legality of the order, they would not have executed it.[14]

Art O'Brien added: 'I can bear witness to the fact that it has been a matter of keen disappointment both to their comrades in the IRA as well as to their many friends in and out of Ireland that the service and sacrifice of Commandant Dunne and Volunteer O'Sullivan have never been publicly and adequately recognised.'[15]

Pat O'Sullivan pleaded his father's case. John O'Sullivan had bronchial pneumonia and needed the assistance of two nurses. The medical bills were mounting up and his children did not have the means to support him. In 1939 O'Sullivan was eventually awarded a gratuity of £112.10.0 (£7,500 today) as a one-off payment, the maximum amount allowed to a dependant.

Pat O'Sullivan's application for a military pension failed despite his documented service in both London and Cork during the War of Independence and on the anti-Treaty side in the Civil War. O'Sullivan did not need the money, or so he said; it was the principle that mattered. Those who had served under him had received pensions. He had done more than his bit for Ireland. The sum was immaterial. 'There is not the slightest doubt that there has been a serious mistake made or a serious miscarriage of justice has been committed in my case,' he told Kevin Boland, the Minister for Defence, in 1959:

> I feel confident that the referee's decision will be squashed
> by the court. I realise it will be a costly affair to me at my
> advanced years, but to me and for the honour of my family it
> will be worth it, after all my brother gave his life for Ireland
> and it would be a discredit to his good name for me to allow
> the slur to remain that I had made a false claim for my service
> to Ireland.[16]

O'Sullivan was turned down for a pension as he was not considered to have been on 'active service' – an absurdity, as he pointed out, given the risks that he ran in using his tailoring business as a front for gunrunning, coupled with his duplicity at Ballincollig Barracks in stealing weapons from the British.

Despite multiple references from those he served with, his pension application came to nothing. This was typical of the mean-spirited approach to pension applications that so many endured from the new Irish state, especially so for English-born IRA veterans such as Dunne and the O'Sullivan brothers, who had nothing to gain materially from fighting for a country in which they did not live.

What of the third man, Denis Kelleher? Kelleher was later arrested in March 1923 at his digs in Clapham, south London, and deported to Ireland. His nemesis this time was not Britain, but the Free State government. He too had been arrested, along with Art O'Brien and others, in March 1922 and imprisoned in Ireland. His release after eleven weeks coincided with the end of the Civil War. Like many of the Irish revolutionary generation, he left behind his youthful revolutionary endeavours and returned to his native county, Cork. He joined the Refuge Assurance Company (later Irish Life) in 1924, and in 1939 became manager of the Cork branch, a position he held until his retirement in 1960. His anti-Treaty tendencies manifested themselves later in life when he served as a Fianna Fáil councillor on Cork Corporation.

Kelleher's afterlife was a cliché of middle-class respectability: insurance manager, golf club captain, local representative and a friend to the poor through his role as a committee member of the local charitable infirmary. He died in November 1972 at the age of seventy-one, leaving a widow and six children. Two of his sons, Humphrey and Olann, went on to become judges. Olann remains one. Another son, Michael, became a doctor, and a daughter, Gretchen, married Ted Crosbie, the publisher of the *Cork* (now *Irish*) *Examiner*, Cork's premier newspaper. Kelleher never revealed his connection with the Wilson shooting. It was only disclosed when his military service pensions file was released in 2020.[17]

Humphrey Kelleher recounted many stories about his father to his son Johnny. Johnny says he never heard of his grandfather's connection with the assassination of Wilson. 'It's entirely news to me. I have never heard anything like that.'

> It's perfectly possible that my father could have chosen not to tell me about this aspect of his father's activities – particularly as by the time I was old enough to hear his stories in the 1970s and beyond he, Humphrey Kelleher, had come to detest everything connected with not only the then Provos but what he called 'Fenianism' in general – but it is still surprising to hear that he didn't tell me anything about it (if we were to accept that it is true and that he knew). What I do know is

that my father always said that my grandfather was recruited into the IRB in London by Sam Maguire, via the Gaelic League, and subsequently into the IRA. That he told Ernie O'Malley that Collins and Maguire had met him subsequently to ask him to keep quiet about what he knew about Wilson's assassination. That he wrote to the press in 1953 to protest the claim that Dunne and O'Sullivan were not acting under orders, that he temporarily became acting director of the IRA in London in the aftermath of the assassination and stopped all activities.[18]

Sam Maguire returned to Ireland in March 1923 and was given the equivalent job he had in Britain with the new state's Department of Post and Telegraphs. A year later he was implicated in the Army Mutiny, a protest by officers who had been loyal to Michael Collins and resented the demobilisation of the National Army after the Civil War. He was dismissed by letter on 30 December 1924, but challenged this by insisting he had not been given a chance to answer the charges. His dismissal was justified by the Minister for Justice Kevin O'Higgins, with Maguire accused of being one of those who were 'talking and thinking in terms of a coup d'etat, in terms of suborning the forces of the State, civil and military'.[19] Penniless and disillusioned in the new state he had played his part in creating, Maguire died of tuberculosis at his family home near Dunmanway, County Cork, on 6 February 1927, at the age of just forty-nine. A year later his friends presented a cup in his name to the Gaelic Athletic Association. Sam Maguire is a household name in Ireland as the winning team in the All-Ireland senior football championship receives 'the Sam Maguire', or 'Sam' as it is more commonly known. His revolutionary activities have been mostly forgotten about.[20]

While he was pursuing a pension from the Irish state for himself and his family, Pat O'Sullivan was also pursuing vindication for the reputation of his brother and the man Joe called his best friend, Reggie Dunne. On 6 September 1953 the *Sunday Press* published extracts from Major Florrie O'Donoghue's book *No Other Law*, about the anti-Treaty leader Liam Lynch. In passing, O'Donoghue mentioned that when Dunne and O'Sullivan shot Wilson, 'they were not acting on the instructions of the army executive'.[21] What O'Donoghue wrote was correct but imprecise. There were two IRAs at the time of Wilson's shooting, and he did not specify that this only applied to the anti-Treaty side led by Lynch.

The extract provoked indignant correspondence with the newspaper and with O'Donoghue directly. Joe Dolan, one of Collins's Squad attached to the intelligence department of the pro-Treaty IRA GHQ and also his aide-de-camp, wrote to the paper in response to O'Donoghue's letter:

> This execution was ordered by Michael Collins because Sir Henry Wilson was the originator of the pogroms in the North in 1922. Michael Collins instructed Sam Maguire, who was O/C Britain all through the Anglo-Irish War, to carry out same. Sam Maguire conveyed the order to Reggie Dunne, an ex-Irish Guard in the 1914–1918 war and later O/C London IRA. Reggie Dunne and Joe O'Sullivan, ex-Leinster Regiment [*sic*], Dunne's right-hand man in the IRA, carried out the operations.[22]

Dolan was not correct that Maguire was O/C London, but that aside, it was the first time the specifics of Collins's involvement in the shooting had been made public in such a forthright manner, as previously they had been the subject of mere speculation.

This was followed a week later by a letter in the *Sunday Press* from Frank Lee, the chairman of the Association of Old IRA in London:

> The old IRA and Cumann na mBan put on record an emphatic protest and denial against the statement . . . that Commandant Reg Dunne and Volunteer Joseph O'Sullivan were not acting under the orders of the army executive when they shot and killed General [*sic*] Sir Henry Wilson in London.[23]

Dolan then wrote a second letter to the *Sunday Press*, this one much more emphatic than the last about Collins's involvement:

> All orders for major executions were issued by the director of intelligence, who was Michael Collins. Therefore, no amount of side-tracking or quibbling can alter the fact that the execution of Sir Henry Wilson was an official one. It is appalling that any Irishman, by suggesting otherwise, should seek to disparage those two patriots Dunne and O'Sullivan.[24]

Pat O'Sullivan wrote directly to O'Donoghue on 12 December. 'This passage has caused extreme hurt and pain to my family and myself and very considerable annoyance,' he stated. He did not hold back:

> You must agree that any of the younger generations in Ireland today could only infer from your book that the Wilson shooting was carried out by two ex-servicemen without orders from the IRA HQ – call it if you like the Army Executive. The fact remains that you stated that they acted without orders and that is what most readers remember. For years now we, the brothers and sisters of one of these men, have had to ensure

this vile and wicked slander by various authors and it would seem we have no redress, publish what you like – false or true – and be damned to the feelings of these boys' relatives. I was born in England as they were, I was forced into the British army, it did not weaken my love for Ireland even in the same No. 1 Cork Brigade as yourself and finished up wounded a few miles outside your own Cork City (Carrigrohane) so WHY must you attack these men just because, as you term them, they were ex-British servicemen 'acting without orders'. Acting without orders, perhaps as a stretch, could be understood in a very wide way in some point which you wished to make, but again where or what are you aiming at by adding the prefix 'ex-servicemen'?[25]

O'Donoghue was clearly taken back by the tone of the criticism. He protested that when he was referring to the men having acted without orders, he meant from the anti-Treaty side. O'Donoghue pointed out that Rory O'Connor had made the same point shortly after the shooting, as did Dorothy Macardle in her book *The Irish Republic*, and Pat O'Sullivan had not made a similar protest. He then added:

The reasons for its inclusion in a story of Liam Lynch are that Lynch was chief of staff of the IRA after the split in the Army, that the shooting of Wilson took place while he held that post and that it was necessary to indicate that the order did not come from him from the Executive under which he acted. These are matters of historical truth which had to be recorded.[26]

O'Donoghue drew attention to discrepancies between the account given by Pat O'Sullivan, in which he stated that the order to shoot Wilson was given before the Truce and confirmed during the Treaty negotiations, and that of Denis Kelleher. Kelleher stated that the instructions to shoot Wilson were 'contingent on the breakdown of the peace negotiations'.[27]

If the latter was clear, why was Wilson shot when the peace negotiations clearly had not broken down? O'Donoghue set out the areas that they had in common. Both agreed that O'Connor had not given the order for the shooting, 'so that the difference between us amounts to this – that you go further than I do and say Collins gave the order'.[28] He then challenged Lee and O'Sullivan to produce the evidence linking the shooting with Collins:

> I am not quite so unfamiliar with Dunne's character as to require any convincing that he was one of the very best, and that his action was dictated solely by patriotic motives. I have no doubt at all that your brother was an equally worthy patriot. So, there is no need to write this offensive nonsense about being fair to the dead. It would be much more to the point if you had given us any facts you may have which would enable me to put the truth on the record. May I therefore have the 'very important evidence' which is in your hands? I assure you if I get the evidence, I will include it in the book.[29]

Pat O'Sullivan disputed any notion that Rory O'Connor as O/C Britain could have ordered the shooting of Wilson. As Dunne's deputy, he was aware that all 'major orders, executions, shootings of named people etc were only to be carried out on instructions from GHQ, Dublin. In view of this order I fail to see how any O/C Britain could take it on himself to issue any such order.' He also disputed Kelleher's suggestion that the shooting of Wilson was predicated on a breakdown of the peace negotiations. On the contrary, it had been planned much earlier than that and there are 'men here to this day who were on the abortive job months earlier':

> I was the last and only IRA man who visited Reggie and my brother in Wandsworth prison and as a consequence can state from that visit that the order was given by Mick Collins, but I can state much more which would be very hurtful to men who are alive in Ireland today. I see no point in so doing. I have no wish to revive the bitter memories of the Civil War, enough is to say that one other officer of the London IRA should be able to tell us quite a lot more if they choose to do so.[30]

Who is he referring to here? Could it be Kelleher, the man who was supposed to have accompanied Dunne and O'Sullivan during the shooting? The end result was a rewritten paragraph in the printed edition of O'Donoghue's book, which includes the claim that Collins had ordered the shooting, but attributes the claim to the evidence of Pat O'Sullivan:

> In a booklet entitled *Remembrance*, published by the Association of Old IRA and Cumann na mBan London, it is stated that 'the order for his [Wilson's] execution had been given before the Treaty negotiations and was actually confirmed while the negotiations were in progress.' A brother of one of the executed men, Patrick O'Sullivan, who was vice-commandant of the London IRA, in a letter to the author states that the order was given by Michael Collins to Reggie Dunne and never subsequently cancelled. In any event it is clear that Dunne and O'Sullivan were acting upon orders which they accepted as official and therefore legitimate.[31]

The accumulated evidence was published in the *Sunday Press* on 10 August 1958, the thirty-sixth anniversary of the execution of Dunne and O'Sullivan. The article had a joint byline of Pat O'Sullivan and Frank Lee. 'The order was issued by Michael Collins, chief of the staff, and the direct order was conveyed to Commandant Dunne as battalion commander of the London IRA,' they stated.[32]

Pat O'Sullivan revealed that his brother had come to visit him while he was serving in Cork with H Company, First Battalion, Cork No. 1 Brigade. This confirms the earlier testimony of Seamus Lynch that Joe O'Sullivan had visited Ireland during the War of Independence. Pat O'Sullivan said it was while his brother was in Cork that he told him of the order to shoot Wilson and that the order had come directly from Michael Collins.

O'Sullivan and Lee claimed the documents they had were of 'historic importance', containing testimony from Art O'Brien, who said in 1939, 'It is my firm conviction and that of their immediate colleagues that in the execution of Sir Henry Wilson, Commandant Dunne and O'Sullivan were acting on orders they had received from Supreme Command Dublin.' O'Brien, as O'Sullivan and Lee explained, had sworn Reggie Dunne and Joe O'Sullivan into the IRA in 1919. Joe Dolan revealed that Wilson was shot on the orders of Collins, that he was a serving officer in the National Army at the time and 'I am willing to swear an affidavit as to the truth of my statement concerning the execution.'[33]

* * *

The London memorial committee that erected the Celtic cross memorial in Deansgrange hoped against hope that the remains of Dunne and O'Sullivan could one day rest there, though it looked legally impossible.

Under the Capital Punishment Amendment Act 1868, executed prisoners were to be buried in prison grounds and it was illegal to remove them. This put the mark of Cain on prisoners, and was intended to convey public and posthumous disgust at the deeds perpetrated by the executed individuals.

In August 1916, six years before Dunne and O'Sullivan faced the scaffold, Sir Roger Casement was hanged for treason. He was a Dublin-born Protestant who joined the British civil service as a teenager. He gained an international reputation for his work in exposing abuses in the rubber industry in the Congo Free State, a kleptocracy set up by King Leopold II of Belgium. He followed this up with another report, into the exploitation of the Putumayo Indians by the Peruvian Amazon Company, published in 1910.[34]

Casement was knighted for his services in 1911. While accepting this honour from the British Empire, Casement had already begun the process of becoming an Irish nationalist, seeing in British rule of Ireland echoes of the colonial exploitation he had encountered in other parts of the world. Once convinced of the cause of Irish nationalism, Casement threw himself into it with the same sense of single-minded devotion that he had given to the peoples of the Congo and the Amazon.

In the early stages of the First World War the Germans concentrated some 2,400 Irish-born prisoners together in a huge prisoner-of-war camp in Limburg an der Lahn, a town in Hesse to the north-west of Frankfurt. Casement, who travelled to Germany in late 1914, agreed to try to recruit an Irish Brigade from among the POWs to fight for Germany and against Britain.

Casement is now regarded as a great Irishman, but the prisoners regarded him as a charlatan and a nuisance, listening to him with mounting incredulity and no little irritation. 'As soon as the men realised who he was and what was his aim, they set upon him, and he was only saved by the German sentries from serious injury,' one prisoner remembered. Just fifty-six Irishmen joined Casement's Irish Brigade.[35]

Two years later Germany provided weapons for the Irish rebellion, albeit only a token amount, given that the Irish Republican Brotherhood had requested 200,000 guns. Some 20,000 confiscated Russian rifles, ten machine guns and a million rounds of ammunition sailed on the SS *Libau*, disguised for the purposes of the long voyage to Ireland as the Norwegian vessel, the *Aud*.

Casement travelled behind in a U-boat, U-19. German support had been half-hearted at best, he concluded, and the Rising was doomed. He wanted to convey that fact to the leaders before they embarked upon what he regarded as a suicidal mission. The *Aud* was intercepted by a Royal Navy squadron outside Queenstown (now Cobh), whereupon the crew changed into their German naval uniforms, ran up the ensign of the German Empire, scuttled the ship and then surrendered.

Casement arrived off the coast of Kerry on Good Friday 1916. He was arrested and immediately sent to London. His trial took place during the opening phase of the Battle of the Somme but eclipsed it in public interest. 'Casement's trial was so dramatic that the war news seemed secondary,' the novelist Mary Colum recalled.[36]

Casement was charged with high treason, defined under a 1351 statute as 'levying war against the King or being adherent to the King's enemies in his realm, giving them aid and comfort in the realm or elsewhere'.

Many well-known people called for a reprieve, but the anti-German atmosphere at the time and the private circulation of the so-called 'Black Diaries', which highlighted Casement's homosexuality, were designed to blacken his name in polite society. Casement's celebrated speech from the dock denied the right of an English court to sit in judgement on him:

> With all respect, I assert this court is to me, an Irishman, charged with this offence, a foreign court – this jury is for me, an Irishman, not a jury of my peers to try me on this vital issue, for it is patent to every man of conscience that I have a right, an indefeasible right, if tried at all, under this statute of high treason, to be tried in Ireland, before an Irish court and by an Irish jury.[37]

The circulation of the Black Diaries did not prevent Casement becoming a republican martyr. While awaiting execution in Pentonville Prison, he sent a letter to his cousin Gertrude Bannister, in which he wrote, 'Take my body back with you and let it lie in the old churchyard in Murlough Bay.'[38] Murlough Bay, a beauty spot on the north Antrim coast, was where he had spent much time with his extended family after he was left an orphan at the age of thirteen.

Casement's last wish was circulated in the Irish press and the repatriation of his remains was a goal of successive Irish governments, but the time never seemed to be right. In 1936 Éamon de Valera, the Free State leader, wrote to the British prime minister Stanley Baldwin. Baldwin was in favour, but the Home Office advised against it as it would set a precedent for the removal of the remains of other executed prisoners buried in prison grounds. Baldwin also feared the possibility of a 'recrudescence of controversy' and he politely turned down the invitation.[39]

Undeterred, de Valera tried again in 1953, when Churchill was prime minister. Once again, the British authorities demurred at releasing the body, the Home Secretary Sir David Maxwell Fyfe declaring, 'the matter is essentially one for a uniform rule. Either no bodies should be handed over, or the relatives should be given the option in every case of removing the corpse of an executed criminal for private burial.'[40]

The Irish government claimed an exception should be made for Casement as he was hanged for treason, not murder, and his motivations were political, not criminal, but the British feared that public demonstrations of support for Casement in Ireland would give offence to the families of British servicemen who had been killed by the Germans in the First World War. In addition, the Northern government would be sure to object to any attempt to repatriate his remains to Antrim.

In 1959 de Valera was replaced as Taoiseach by Seán Lemass. Although an Easter Rising veteran like de Valera, Lemass was forward-thinking and did not want the past to damage good relations between Britain and Ireland. Nevertheless, he wrote to Harold Macmillan, but he received the same response as de Valera, this time with a further caveat: the whereabouts of Casement's remains could not be established with any certainty.[41]

Things changed when Labour's Harold Wilson became British prime minister in October 1964. He had a large number of Irish constituents in his Huyton constituency outside Liverpool and was rumoured to be in favour of Irish unification. 'As soon as we talked to Wilson all these objections disappeared overnight,' Lemass revealed. 'The remains were found; they had not been buried in quicklime.' Lemass continued:

All the arguments of the Conservative government were completely phoney. Wilson brushed all this aside and said: 'That grave is number such and such . . . the body is there.' There was no pretence of lying or that sort. I liked Wilson.

There was no personal animosity between us at all. On the whole I think, from the Irish point of view, I found him to be by far the best prime minister in my time. To Wilson these were not problems and he was, of course, very much aware of the fact that he was not losing political support by conceding these things to us. The Conservatives would have been worried about the possibility of losing political support from their right wing, but Wilson was if anything gaining support from the Irish population in Britain and in particular his own constituency by these concessions of no great importance.[42]

Wilson's government made only one demand: Casement was not to be buried in Northern Ireland as it was bound to create disturbances. The British and Irish sides feared there might be ghoulish interest in the exhumations and possible objections, so a public announcement was not made until Casement's remains arrived in Dublin.

Casement was given a full state funeral on 1 March 1965. Tens of thousands of people lined the streets of Dublin from the Pro-Cathedral to Glasnevin Cemetery, where his body was buried in a plot purchased for him by his sister in 1925. The Taoiseach and most members of his government were there, along with the ambassadors of many countries. The now elderly President de Valera, aged eighty-one, gave the oration:

> We are glad to claim him, we are glad to have him back amongst us; and like the young I have mentioned, we too for the years that remain to us, will draw from here inspiration, resolution and hope. Every one of us must believe – and I do not think it presumption on our part to believe – that a man who was so unselfish, who worked so hard for the downtrodden and the oppressed and who so died, that their

man is in Heaven, with, I hope, all the other Irishmen who have given their lives for our country.[43]

* * *

Casement's repatriation set a precedent, and Pat O'Sullivan was quick to capitalise on it. He wrote to the Home Office in June 1966, praising the British government for their 'generous and courageous action' in repatriating Casement's remains to Ireland. O'Sullivan noted that the law too had changed in Britain. The Capital Punishment Amendment Act 1868 was repealed with the Murder (Abolition of Death Penalty) Act 1965, which not only abolished the death penalty but allowed for private reburials outside prison grounds.

The change in the law was driven by the case of Timothy Evans, who had been hanged in 1950 for the murder of his thirteen-month-old daughter Geraldine. Her murder and that of Evans's wife had been carried out by his neighbour John Christie, a serial killer. This blatant miscarriage of justice embarrassed the British government, as did several other high-profile cases. Evans's remains, along with those of others dubiously executed for murder, including James Hanratty and Derek Bentley, were exhumed and reburied elsewhere. The liberal-minded Home Secretary Roy Jenkins announced that he would look sympathetically on any application for an exhumation from prison grounds.[44]

The way was clear for the exhumation of Dunne and O'Sullivan. An application was made by the Labour MP Hugh Delargy, who had Irish parents and was a member of the Irish Anti-Partition League. There were no legal obstacles preventing their removal and reburial, but the attitude of the Irish government was in marked contrast to the enthusiasm with which it embraced the return of Casement's remains.

'[Hugh James] McCann, the permanent secretary of the Department of External Affairs [Department of Foreign Affairs], discussed the question informally with the British ambassador again today,' C. A. Lovitt, an official at the British Embassy in Dublin, wrote to the Home Office in November 1966:

> He was in a state of considerable embarrassment about it. He had evidently spoken to ministers and was giving his assessment of their views. He stressed that a decision on this case was one for us and that the Irish government for their part was neither asking for the remains to be returned nor requesting us not to send them back. The Irish government had, however, understood that the Casement repatriation was *sui generis* and would not be used as a precedent.[45]

McCann cited the impact that the repatriation would have on relations with Northern Ireland, and Lovitt dryly observed that the same arguments had been made regularly by the British government about the repatriation of Casement's remains:

> It was quite obvious to the ambassador that we had been right in guessing that, paradoxical as it may be, we should be causing embarrassment to the Irish government and to that extent doing harm to Anglo-Irish relations if we were to repatriate these two men. The Irish Government's attitude is strictly illogical, but then this is Ireland.[46]

The British sought assurances from their Irish counterparts that the repatriation of Dunne and O'Sullivan would not be an event with a paramilitary tinge as this would be regarded as offensive to unionists in the North, where Wilson was regarded as somebody who had died for Ulster. The reluctance of the Irish government to embrace the memory of Dunne and O'Sullivan was laid bare in a conversation between Sir Geoffrey de Deney of the Home Office and Sean Ronan of the Irish Ministry of Foreign Affairs in November 1966. In the course of a 'full and frank discussion', Ronan told his British counterpart:

> Most historians were agreed that the murder of Field Marshal
> Sir Henry Wilson was a totally unjust act, carried out at
> the behest of Michael Collins at a time when his mind was
> virtually unhinged. The Government would therefore not feel
> under any obligation to mark the occasion as a State affair
> and, although an application for a State funeral would almost
> certainly be received, it would be refused.[47]

Ronan expressed surprise that the British government would be prepared to facilitate the repatriation of the remains. 'Ministers in the Republic did not want to stir up trouble for the Northern Ireland government and create opportunities for extremists on both sides of the Border to exploit a situation to further their own ends,' Lovitt stated.

Within his own department McCann detailed in a secret memo why the Irish government felt the Wilson shooting was something best forgotten about:

> Needless to say, we would not suggest that the British should
> refuse the present application. Nevertheless, we recognised
> that the possibility did exist that the repatriation might
> reawaken interest and, possibly, controversy within one or
> other parts of Ireland in a matter which might better be
> regarded as an event of history not to be highlighted at the
> present time.[48]

McCann was writing at a time when the civil rights movement was gaining traction in Northern Ireland, and the prime
minister Terence O'Neill was trying to bring in reforms and was
being opposed by hardliners, most notably the Rev. Ian Paisley,
who had been jailed in June 1966 after inciting a riot in Belfast in
which dozens were injured. McCann had discussed the issue with
officials from the Northern Ireland Home Office. He noted the
details of their concerns:

> They did not object to these proposals in principle,
> particularly having regard to the Casement precedent. They
> have, however, pointed out that Sir Henry Wilson was a figure
> much more closely identified with the Ulster question than
> Casement and there is, therefore, a risk that these exhumations
> may inflame opinion in Ulster, particularly in view of the
> present imprisonment of the Rev. Paisley. They hope therefore
> that the authorities in the Republic will not lay too much
> stress on the re-interment, since the present delicate state
> of affairs in Northern Ireland might produce unwelcome
> reactions to undue celebrations. From our end this means in
> practical terms that we shall hope to avoid the exhumation and
> re-interment coinciding with the release of Paisley.[49]

McCann's minister, Frank Aiken, was equally unenthusiastic
and regarded 'the repatriation of Casement's body not as a precedent for a series to follow, but rather as a symbolic act representing the return of the bodies of all who died abroad in the cause of
Irish freedom and the identification and repatriation of which it
would be impossible to complete'.[50]

Nevertheless, the Irish government raised no objection publicly to the repatriation, but it did nothing to facilitate the event.
On 6 July 1967 the remains of Dunne and O'Sullivan arrived in

29 The repatriation of the remains of Dunne and O'Sullivan was widely covered
    in the *Irish Press* of 7 July 1967

Dublin, accompanied by Pat O'Sullivan and his wife. They were
received at the airport by the National Graves Association chairman Seamus McKiernan. Both coffins were draped in the Irish
tricolour, the one on Dunne's having once been placed on Terence
MacSwiney's coffin. Pat O'Sullivan declared at Dublin Airport

that he was doing this for the deceased parents of Reggie Dunne as much as to remember his own brother.

The remains were removed to the Pro-Cathedral, where a requiem Mass was celebrated. The procession moved through the streets of Dublin. Conspicuous by their presence were many of the republican organisations that desired an end to partition – Sinn Féin, Fianna Éireann and members of the old IRA. Conspicuous by their absence were any mainstream Irish politicians, although Taoiseach Jack Lynch sent his aide-de-camp.

As an official concession the flag on the GPO flew at half-mast as the funeral cortège made its way to Deansgrange Cemetery, seven miles from Dublin city centre. The inscription on the two men's headstone, given in both Irish and English, reads:[51]

In
Loving Remembrance of
Comdt. Reginald Dunne
And
Vol. Joseph O'Sullivan
I.R.A.
Who died for Ireland on the
10th August 1922
In Wandsworth Prison England
Also in memory of
Michael McInerney
Who died for Ireland
May they rest in peace.[52]

Orations were delivered at the graveside by Pat O'Sullivan and John Stephenson (Seán Mac Stíofáin), another London-born republican, who would become one of the founders of the Provisional IRA a few years later. Three men with revolvers fired shots over the grave. For Pat O'Sullivan, this was the fulfilment of years of striving for vindication for the two men. He wrote to Charlie Woods, the secretary of the National Graves Association, three days after the funeral:

Charlie,

A hurried note just before I leave dear Ireland. I would be so glad if you could do one more favour for me to add to all the many you have already done. Could you get someone to collect all the cards and wreaths at Deansgrange? Just because I shall always treasure them till I die, but also I want to write to the wonderful people who sent them and I have not their names etc. This is only a note. I shall be writing to you in full to thank you all for your great kindness and work which I will never be able to repay.

God bless, Pat[53]

* * *

Field Marshal Sir Henry Wilson's violent death ensured he had an elevated status in public opinion in Britain just as many started to question the actions of his peers and the unconscionable slaughter of the First World War. This changed with the publication of Major General Sir Charles Callwell's two-volume *Field Marshal Sir Henry Wilson, Bt, GCB, DSO: His Life & Diaries, etc.* in 1927.

Callwell was an Anglo-Irish officer like Wilson (his father was from Antrim, his mother from Galway) and was also a friend of the field marshal. He served as a staff officer in the First World War, after which he retired and published a number of books on the conflict in quick succession. He would in theory have been ideally suited to the sensitive task of putting Wilson's diaries and papers into book format. Callwell was commissioned by Lady Wilson to write the book, some felt so she could wreak vengeance on the politicians whom she blamed for his death, but hers was the wrong motive and Callwell the wrong biographer. He lacked the judgement to put some of Wilson's most provocative musings into their proper context, even while he stressed in the preface:

> Outspoken in conversation and outspoken by nature, Sir Henry was no less outspoken on paper – so much so that it has been found expedient to omit some passages, even though of undoubted interest, and that it has been thought desirable to exclude some of the forcible expressions concerning individuals which find a place in these records of his. He had contemplated compiling his memoirs himself so soon as he should find the requisite leisure for embarking on such a task and he had looked forward to making a commencement in the autumn of the very year in which he was struck down by the assassin's hand.[54]

One wonders what Callwell left out, because what he put in was shocking in its frankness and caused Wilson's posthumous reputation infinite harm. Callwell's biography was based on Wilson's diaries, which he had kept assiduously since 1893. Wilson used his diary to order his thoughts and let off steam. His nocturnal jottings were often made after long, trying days and amid the stress of war. Sometimes it appeared he did not have a good word to say about anybody. Lord Kitchener was 'ignorant', Kitchener's army the 'laughing stock of every soldier in Europe', Asquith 'frightened', his namesake President Woodrow Wilson 'that ass'.[55] The book confirmed people's worst suspicions about Wilson, his intriguing in the Curragh Incident, his undermining of the Liberal government, his contempt for the 'Frocks' and his obduracy with regard to Ireland.

In the 'battle of the memoirs', as it was called in the 1920s and 1930s, Wilson was bound to lose, with such a poor champion for his cause. In his *War Memoirs*, published in 1933, Lloyd George did not demur:

It is characteristic of Wilson's selfishness and ingratitude that the only comment he makes in his diary on the night of his appointment by me to the chief position in the Army was that it had been delayed for 11 days owing to my indecision. Eleven days spent in anxious conferences, in fighting through his policy and his promotion among ministers and on the floor of the House of Commons. Invariably to me personally he was effusive. Behind my back he was abusive. One can understand the imputation of treachery which was associated with his name, and which, by the entries of his diary, he has done his best to justify . . . There was a streak of mischief – not to say malice – in his nature which often made trouble and sought to make trouble. On the other hand, he was very anxious at this date to ingratiate himself with the commander-in-chief, who distrusted him through and through. You never can track down the motive in so labyrinthine a character as that of Sir Henry Wilson. But like all men of brilliant gifts and marked personality he had not only fervent admirers but implacable opponents in the Army. Professional officers were sharply divided into these two schools. The men at the top were strongly anti-Wilson. Some actively disliked him; most of them distrusted him. Both schools were right. He possessed intellectual gifts which justified admiration. But he also had attributes which explained and, to a large extent, gave warrant for the suspicion and lack of confidence so widely felt in him. He was whimsical almost to the point of buffoonery. He answered a serious question or expounded a grave problem in a vein of facetious and droll frivolity which was undignified in a man of his grave responsibilities. Habitually he jested over questions of life and death. This habit detracted from the weight and authority which his position and capacity ought to have given to his counsel.[56]

It took until the publication of the late Professor Keith Jeffery's book *Field Marshal Sir Henry Wilson: A Political Soldier*, published in 2006, to rescue Wilson's reputation from the shadow of his own nocturnal musings and to differentiate between his private thoughts and his public deeds. In the preface to his well-received book, Jeffery recounted that Wilson was best known nowadays for the circumstances behind his shooting rather than his military career. His reputation in life had been 'ruined' by the publication of Callwell's book:

> The impression given by the all-too-quotable passages is that of an over-ambitious, self-serving monster, with such violent passions and prejudices as to appear at times actually unbalanced. Yet Wilson was admired and respected by many of his colleagues; and he served with distinction in a series of very senior and important positions in the British military hierarchy before, during, and after the First World War.[57]

Wilson was never remembered as many of his fellow Anglo-Irish stock, like the Duke of Wellington, Lord Roberts and Field Marshal Sir Bernard Montgomery, had been, but neither was he reviled like many of his First World War contemporaries, particularly the 'Butcher' Haig (Field Marshal Sir Douglas Haig), who was blamed for his callous approach to a war that cost so many British lives. Wilson was simply forgotten about. The bronze memorial bearing his likeness, with its chilling inscription that he died 'within two hours of his unveiling the adjoining memorial', was erected less than a year after his death. It is in a corner under the larger memorial he unveiled and beside the one to Captain Charles Fryatt. Tens of thousands of commuters pass by it every day without a backward glance. There is no blue plaque outside 36 Eaton Place nor any memorial there recounting the terrible events of 22 June 1922.

His assassination, so shocking at the time, was superseded by more ruthless assassinations in more modern times. The Provisional IRA had none of the qualms its predecessor in the War of Independence had about the taking of life in Britain. During the modern-day Troubles, the IRA killed the Ulster Unionist MP Rev. Robert Bradford in 1981, Sir Anthony Berry, during the Brighton bombing that targeted Margaret Thatcher in 1984, and Ian Gow in 1990, the last MP killed by the Provisional IRA. The Brighton bomb was followed by a chilling statement from the Provos directed at Thatcher: 'Today we were unlucky, but remember we only have to be lucky once. You will have to be lucky always.'[58]

Thatcher's Northern Ireland spokesman Airey Neave was blown up by an Irish National Liberation Army (INLA) bomb in 1979 in the car park of the House of Commons. The attack on Neave was the one that bore the most resemblance to the Wilson assassination, as the INLA believed that he would wage war against republicans if he became Secretary of State for Northern Ireland. There are shields in the House of Commons to all those MPs who died at the hands of the IRA, and one to Jo Cox, but none to Wilson.[59]

Wilson did surface in public culture in the 1969 film *Oh! What a Lovely War*, when he was played by Michael Redgrave, the narrator of the BBC series *The Great War*, which was broadcast in 1964. The

BBC series *Peaky Blinders* referenced Wilson's assassination in the second series, when Tommy Shelby (played by Cillian Murphy), the head of the Birmingham crime gang the Peaky Blinders, assassinates Field Marshal Henry Russell on Derby Day 1922 at the Epsom racecourse. The final episode of the second series begins with Shelby writing a letter to be opened in the event of his death:

> Agents of the Crown have joined forces with pro-Treaty Fenians to arrange his murder. I believe the government intends to falsely blame the anti-Treaty IRA. The bullets I fire this afternoon will be the starting gun for the Civil War in Ireland.[60]

There the plot departs from the historic reality, as Shelby is put up to it by a crooked police inspector over from Belfast at the behest of Winston Churchill. It is an interesting take but not borne out by the facts.

13

Conclusion: Ireland's Sarajevo

The shooting of Field Marshal Sir Henry Wilson was Ireland's Sarajevo. When the Bosnian Serb teenager Gavrilo Princip shot dead Archduke Franz Ferdinand on 28 June 1914 he inadvertently started the largest war in history to that date. All the millions who died, the empires that ruptured, the states that broke up and the new ones that formed, the Bolshevik revolution – all occurred as a result of that one event.

The First World War would not have happened without the shooting of Franz Ferdinand. He was the strongest advocate for peace with Serbia and would have done everything possible to stop the Austro-Hungarian Empire going to war with Russia. Without his assassination, there would have been no ultimatum to Serbia, no mobilisation by Russia and no war. The interlocking series of alliances among the European powers might have brought the world to war under another pretext; then again, maybe not. The world had survived other moments of peril, such as the Agadir Crisis, without going to war. The German historian Fritz Stern described the First World War as the 'first calamity of the twentieth century, the calamity from which all other calamities sprang'.[1] The Second World War followed on directly as a consequence of the First.

Would the Irish Civil War have taken place if Wilson had not been shot? The counterfactual in history is by definition impossible to prove. There were many within the Provisional Government, Griffith and O'Higgins among them, who wanted an end to the stand-off in the Four Courts, by force if necessary. There was much bellicose rhetoric on the part of the anti-Treaty side too, but also a marked reluctance on both sides to engage in civil war. The anti-Treaty rebels had not taken the precaution of digging a tunnel under the Four Courts. Even while they were being surrounded by National Army troops, they were reluctant to make the first move.

'The [Free] Staters were taking advantage of the fact that we did not want to open fire on them. We were like rats in a trap,' Ernie O'Malley recalled in his posthumously published memoir *The Singing Flame*. In the Rotunda, under the vast dome of the Four Courts, the leadership of the anti-Treaty side debated which IRA sections might support them and which ones might not. They had made no preparation for war, despite all the rhetoric.[2]

The kidnapping of General J. J. 'Ginger' O'Connell by anti-Treaty forces was the immediate pretext, but the British ultimatum that followed the Wilson shooting would have forced a confrontation in any case. The use of British artillery – the National Army had none of its own – was a direct consequence of the Wilson assassination and emboldened many to resist the Provisional Government. The Irish Civil War would not have happened the way it did without the Wilson shooting, and Irish history would have been significantly different.

There is nothing inevitable in history. History is replete with moments of danger where the protagonists are compelled by random events into actions that lead to catastrophic and unintended consequences. Every powder keg needs a lit fuse. Without the spark there is no conflagration. Without the Irish Civil War the state would have had a less traumatic birth, but would always have struggled for legitimacy against those who insisted that nothing other than a thirty-two-county Irish republic was acceptable.

* * *

The facts of the Wilson shooting are not in dispute – Dunne and O'Sullivan killed him, were caught and executed. But on whose orders were they acting?

This question has been pertinent to the assassination for the last century. Attempts to answer it definitively have been stymied by two critical factors. The perpetrators, Dunne and O'Sullivan, died and left no written evidence behind them as to who gave them the order. They apparently told Pat O'Sullivan that Michael Collins had ordered the shooting, but we only have his word for that. There is also a lack of documentary evidence – a 'smoking gun' proving once and for all who ordered the shooting.

There are four primary theories:

1. Dunne and O'Sullivan acted of their own accord without instructions from anyone else.
2. The shooting was ordered by the anti-Treaty side.
3. The shooting was ordered by Michael Collins before the Truce and was never rescinded.
4. The shooting was ordered after the Truce by Michael Collins.

1. Dunne and O'Sullivan acted of their own accord without instructions from anyone else

Dunne and O'Sullivan were British soldiers before they joined the IRA. They understood the importance of the chain of command and of military discipline. In his extant correspondence, Dunne makes reference to discipline in his last letter to his father. 'You and I must not grouse when it comes to enduring discipline because we are good soldiers and Catholic Irishmen.'[3] He does so again in his letter to Rory O'Connor, when he praises the virtues of 'strict discipline, secrecy, cheerful obedience to orders and punctuality'.[4]

There is no evidence of either Dunne or O'Sullivan having been involved in maverick operations as IRA operatives. Everything they did followed instructions from GHQ. This was particularly the case in relation to the assassination plans. Both men were privy to the moves to assassinate high-ranking British personages and knew that these orders were issued from GHQ. They were intelligent men who knew the gravity of what they had been asked to do. This point was repeatedly made by their supporters. 'Both Dunne and O'Sullivan were deeply religious men and had they any doubts of the legality of the order, they would not have executed it,' Pat O'Sullivan stated. 'All major orders, executions, shootings of named people etc were only to be carried out on instructions from GHQ, Dublin.'[5] This, as far as we know, was the case when Pa Murray accosted Arthur Balfour in Oxford but demurred at shooting him because Collins had told him not to.

As O/C London, Dunne went about collecting intelligence on possible assassination targets in the knowledge that the order would come from Michael Collins. O'Sullivan scouted Lloyd George's car for a possible assassination. Far from being a maverick operation, the killing of Wilson was entirely consistent with earlier republican policy on the assassination of senior British military figures.

That Dunne and O'Sullivan acted of their own accord was Rex Taylor's conclusion in his book *Assassination*. He based this on a letter allegedly sent to Denis Kelleher by Dunne from jail. Dunne told Kelleher that they had gone to Eaton Place just to barrack and insult Wilson, not to kill him. For all they knew he might not turn up. As Wilson got out of the car, O'Sullivan, inexplicably to Dunne and without orders from his more senior officer, shot Wilson, and so the disaster for the pair began. The absence of an able-bodied accomplice or a getaway driver demonstrated that murder had not been on the mind of the pair when they killed Wilson. Taylor's theory begs a number of questions. Why did Dunne and O'Sullivan turn up with loaded guns if they had not intended to kill Wilson? Taylor's claim, which suggested that Dunne had sought to blame O'Sullivan for the shooting, enraged O'Sullivan's family. More seriously still, Taylor did not produce the letter that Dunne had allegedly sent to Kelleher. In a letter to the *Irish Press* in 1968 Frank Lee commented:

> The individual concerned [Rex Taylor] has been challenged several times by Joe O'Sullivan's brother, Pat, to produce this remarkable document, but has failed to do so. It is indeed a most fantastic suggestion that Reg and Joe went to Liverpool Street to barrack Wilson but were unable to do so and then proceeded to Eaton Place to shout abuse at Wilson and to help them do this carried two fully loaded Webley revolvers. There is, of course, not an atom of truth in this statement.[6]

Neither does Taylor appear to have had a copy of Dunne's own account of what happened, which was published in the *Irish Press* in 1948 and which mentions nothing about visiting Liverpool Street Station on the day of the killing.[7]

The best account to date of the shooting was given by the late historian Peter Hart in the November 1992 issue of the journal *Irish Historical Studies*. Hart stated that there was a plot to kill Wilson in 1921, but none in 1922, and therefore no 'solid evidence' to support a conspiracy theory linking Michael Collins or anyone else to the assassination. Hart concluded:

> In the absence of such evidence, we must accept the assertions of the murderers that they acted alone, in the (grossly mistaken) belief that Wilson was responsible for Catholic

murders in Belfast. My own hypothesis as to Dunne and O'Sullivan's motives cannot be definitely proved, but it fits not only with what we know of them and the London IRA and IRB but also with the general anarchy and proliferation of revenge killings in Ireland at the time. For two young Irish idealists to take matters into their own hands and shoot a hated foe was not a particularly unusual act in the summer of 1922.[8]

Yet Dunne in his statement, which was published in the *Irish Independent* two days after his death, never stated that he and O'Sullivan had acted of their own accord in killing Wilson. Hart was implying from Dunne's statement that they acted on their own, but Dunne remained silent on the issue. Dunne wrote the letter to whomever was going to be his successor in the London IRA, and it was smuggled out by Pat O'Sullivan. He was not going to commit to paper who had ordered him to carry out such a high-profile assassination.

The strongest evidence suggesting it was a maverick operation came from William 'Bill' Ahern, officer commanding in Great Britain at the time, who was quoted in a biography of Michael Collins written by Ulick O'Connor and published in 1996:

I am certain [said Ahern] that it was not authorised by Collins because in Dublin a short time before Wilson was killed, I met Reggie Dunne, who was second-in-command of the London Brigade, coming down the Dublin Quays to get the boat to London. He was looking very angry and I asked him what was the matter. He told me he'd come over to get permission from Collins to reactivate a pre-Treaty order to assassinate Wilson which had not been implemented. Collins told him on no account was he to undertake such a mission and had expressly forbidden him to proceed with it.[9]

Ahern's account is interesting, but not factually correct. There was no London Brigade and Dunne was O/C in London, not second-in-command. Moreover, Ahern gave a lengthy account of his activities to Ernie O'Malley in the 1940s and neglected to mention the significant detail of Collins having stymied Dunne. Instead, Ahern told O'Malley: 'They had instructions to shoot Wilson before the Truce, but the order was never countermanded.'[10] In 1953 Ahern told Maurice 'Moss' Twomey a similar story – the order to shoot Wilson had been taken before the Truce and was never countermanded. Therefore it still stood. Quite why he decided to change his story at such a late stage is difficult to understand and strains credulity.

2. The shooting was ordered by the anti-Treaty side

The British government rushed to blame the anti-Treaty side, but there is no evidence they were involved at all. Lloyd George sent the ultimatum to Michael Collins on the basis that incriminating documents were found on Reggie Dunne linking him with the anti-Treaty side. But the only document found on Dunne was a copy of the official IRA paper *An t-Óglách*, which was available in newsstands. The only other evidence advanced linking the anti-Treaty side with the shooting was a statement given by Frank Martin to Professor Liam Ó'Briain, Professor of Romance Languages at University College Galway (UCG), in 1949. Ó'Briain said Martin was an engineer in Galway and a member of the London company (*sic*) of the IRA in 1921 and 1922:

> The Four Courts people, he said, had decided to shoot Sir
> Henry Wilson. This would precipitate an attack on the Four
> Courts by the British military forces still in Dublin. The
> 'Portobello people' (that is, the Army under Mulcahy and Dáil

Éireann) could not stand by and see old comrades attacked by the British and would have to come to their assistance, and so the split would be healed up and we would be 'all one again fighting the British, and there would be no further question of the Treaty. After long consideration, I declined and Reggie Dunne got O'Sullivan to assist him in the job.' I [Ó'Briain] wanted at the time for Frank Martin to write down and sign before witnesses this statement, but the usual procrastination occurred.[11]

Nobody in London had ever heard of a Frank Martin, and Ernie O'Malley, a member of the Four Courts executive, said no such order to shoot Wilson was ever given. The statement issued by the Four Courts executive in the immediate aftermath of Wilson's killing that it had nothing to do with the shooting and would have admitted it if it had can be taken at face value.

3. The shooting was ordered by Michael Collins before the Truce and was never rescinded

This canard has been repeated many times in various guises over the years. It is correct, as we have seen, that IRA GHQ – and therefore Collins – ordered the assassination of Wilson, among many other senior figures in the British government and security apparatus, but those assassination plans against all persons were nullified by the Truce in July 1921. The terms of the Truce stated that the IRA was to cease 'attacks on Crown Forces and civilians . . . [and] *British government* [author's italics] and private property'. As has already been shown, Bill Ahern believed that the instructions to kill Wilson were issued pre-Truce and never cancelled. Seán MacCraith said, 'I know for a fact that the order for this execution was given by Collins prior to the Treaty split.'[12] This was correct but it did not mean that the order was still valid after the Treaty split. Another version of this claim was Denis Kelleher's assertion that Collins ordered the shooting in the event of negotiations breaking down. The talks did not break down and the Anglo-Irish Treaty was supposed to end all hostilities between Britain and Ireland. There is no mystery as to why Dunne and O'Sullivan shot Wilson. It is all in the statement they wished to address to the jury:

> He [Wilson] was at the time of his death the military advisor to what is colloquially called the Ulster Government, and as military advisor he raised and organised a body of men known as the Ulster Special Constabulary, who are the principal agents in his campaign of terrorism.[13]

Wilson did not become a military advisor to the Northern government until March 1922. Therefore the idea that an assassination order was still extant from *before* the Truce can be discounted. In short, Wilson was killed for what he did *after* he retired as CIGS in February 1922 and not beforehand.

4. The shooting was ordered after the Truce by Michael Collins

Why would Michael Collins, whose personal endorsement was critical to the passage of the Treaty through the Dáil, seek to undermine it so completely by ordering the assassination of the former head of the British army? This question is at the heart of the debate about the 'why' of the Wilson shooting.

The shooting of Wilson was entirely consistent with what Collins's biographer Tim Pat Coogan called Collins's 'Janus-faced' attitude to the Treaty:

> He stood in Dáil Éireann, arguing fiercely for the Treaty and the establishment of law and order in a democratic,

independent Irish State, while at the same time he acted with the vigour, intent and methodology of any chief of staff of the Provisional IRA to wreck the other state enshrined in that Treaty.[14]

Implicit in the Treaty was an acceptance of the Government of Ireland Act 1920, which established the Northern Ireland state. (It was superseded in the South by the Treaty.) Collins recognised that the Treaty was the best deal he could have got in the circumstances for the twenty-six counties of the Free State (the 'stepping-stone' theory), but he detested partition and did all he could to undermine it by both violent and non-violent means. His actions were a 'personal crusade against partition', the historian Robert Lynch concluded.[15]

Unlike many of his colleagues in the Provisional Government, Collins did not wholly trust that the Boundary Commission would provide the solution to partition by ceding Derry city, Tyrone and Fermanagh to the Free State. He witnessed first-hand Craig's opposition to the commission that Craig himself had proposed in 1919 to deal with border disputes. The destabilisation of the North to force a better settlement with the South was, therefore, the only way forward, Collins reasoned.

He sanctioned the cross-border kidnappings of dozens of loyalists that followed the arrests of the Monaghan footballers in January 1922, and then tried to pretend to his cabinet colleagues and to the British that he had nothing to do with it. He was involved in smuggling guns into the North and in planning for the failed Northern offensive of May and June 1922. He lied to his own cabinet colleagues and to Churchill about what was going on.

He detested Wilson and, as importantly, said so on several occasions. In a speech in Wexford in April 1922 he said:

We all know only too well the hopes and aims of the Orange North-East Ulster. They are well expressed to the world with a lightly veiled brutality in the language of Sir Henry Wilson. They want their ascendancy restored. They want the British back. British diehards and the mischief makers of the Sir Henry Wilson breed are leaving no stone unturned to restore British domination in Ireland.[16]

At the time little attention was paid to this speech. It was part of the inflammatory rhetoric on all sides occasioned by the disturbances in Ulster but, as we have seen, Collins made other comments about Wilson in public, describing him as a 'violent Orange partisan' while blaming him publicly for the actions of the British army in Belleek and Pettigo. Wilson, he concluded, had a *Morning Post* attitude to Ireland, named after a newspaper notorious for its reactionary imperialism. Collins was present in the visitors' gallery of the House of Commons when he heard Wilson say that British forces should not hesitate to cross the border if necessary.

Those searching for Collins's motivation for ordering the shooting need look no further than these statements. Seen from Collins's perspective, Wilson provided the impetus for the Craig government's ferocious crackdown on the IRA. If Wilson's words were not in themselves enough to damn him as a formidable enemy, those of Sir James Craig were. At his speech in the Northern parliament announcing Wilson's role as a military advisor, Craig said he had put aside £2 million to justify their pledge to Wilson to do everything he asked in his advice to them as to how to respond to the security threat. 'There was no better man to deal with the IRA. I would say if any man can devise means to meet these hordes of IRA and promoters of rebellion, that man is Sir Henry Wilson.'[17]

In the negotiations about the Irish constitution Lloyd George and Churchill noted that Collins was more animated in 1922 about the situation in the North than he was about the constitutional imbroglio in the South. Collins believed the Pettigo incident was intended to 'deflect world attention from the worse than Armenian atrocities that are a daily occurrence in Belfast . . . in this design they were largely assisted by certain powerful British influencers and unconsciously by some of our own people.'[18]

In a private unpublished note Collins sought to link the 'Orange North-East Ulster' with the personality of Wilson. 'They are well expressed to the world with a lightly veiled brutality in the language of Sir Henry Wilson.' Collins also believed that the British occupation of Pettigo in June 1922 presaged what might have happened if Wilson ended up in a position of influence within the British government. This is not as implausible as it sounds, given that the Tories could form a government on their own in Britain and did so in October 1922 under Wilson's friend Bonar Law. Yet it was not Wilson but Winston Churchill who was responsible for the overwhelming force used at Pettigo to teach the Free State a lesson that any incursions would be ruthlessly dealt with.

Collins may have cooled on assassination as a tactic, as suggested by his exchange with Seán Mac Eoin in March 1921. However, that took place at a stage when there was a real prospect of peace talks. Paradoxically, Collins may have felt it safer to pursue this tactic in relation to Wilson after the peace treaty had been signed.

Collins had ample reason to want Wilson dead, but you will search in vain for any paper trail of the assassinations that he ordered. Given the frequent raids on IRA premises, leaving any such evidence would have been foolhardy. Instructions to the men who shot fourteen British agents on Bloody Sunday 1920 were given orally to members of the Squad. Such a modus operandi would be understandable in the context of a guerrilla campaign with a better resourced enemy, but Collins was the chair of the Provisional Government set up under the Anglo-Irish Treaty.

Collins delegated the details to people he trusted to carry out assassinations in an efficient manner. In the case of the Wilson shooting, he trusted too much. Had he been aware of the details of what was planned for the shooting, he would certainly have objected to one of the assassins being a man with one leg and the pair being without a getaway car. There has been much speculation as to why O'Sullivan was involved in the shooting. The answer was given in a PS to Dunne's statement smuggled out of prison:

> To this report I wish to be noted particularly that the conduct of Joe O'Sullivan throughout this has been magnificent.
> He was one of the finest soldiers I have met. I have had momentary regrets about taking him on this job with me on account of his disability, but myself justified it on the following grounds.
> The notice was very short and he was at hand.
> His heart was set on it.
> He had the necessary courage (and he has not lost it either).[19]

The critical statement here is that the 'notice was very short and he was at hand'. This was why O'Sullivan was involved. Previous attempted assassinations by the IRA in London demonstrated that targets such as Wilson were elusive and chances had to be taken when they arose. Even so, there was no guarantee that he would turn up as he did at 36 Eaton Square. It was bad luck for all concerned that he did.

Collins might have calculated that a well-planned 'job', the favourite euphemism of the IRA, would have seen the assassins escape. The Provisional Government could issue a plausible and honest denial, along with a resounding denunciation of this wicked crime. After all, most of the cabinet would have had nothing to do with it.

Publicly, the British government would share the indignation of the public about the shooting of so distinguished a soldier. Privately, Collins might have believed they would not have been displeased that so vocal a critic was gone, along with his increasingly outdated views on Ireland and the Empire. British Cabinet Secretary Tom Jones regarded Wilson as a dangerous nuisance who was trying to restart the war in Ireland 'in order to embroil us on their side against the South and get us back into the pre-Treaty position'.[20]

On 28 April 1922 he noted 'another mischievous speech from Henry Wilson in today's *Morning Post* . . . a couple of weeks ago his right-hand man General [Arthur] Solly-Flood had the effrontery to try and get from the Disposals Board a supply of aeroplanes, bombs etc for use by the Ulster Specials to be paid for by the British Exchequer'. In the weeks before the shooting Jones revealed Lloyd George was worried that the actions of de Valera and Wilson would drag the British back into a civil war situation in Ireland.[21] It is a quirk of history that, at the time of his death, the British and Irish governments, once sworn enemies, regarded Wilson as their mutual foe.

Indeed, the British government did not blame its Irish equivalent for the shooting, but Collins miscalculated the depth of British unhappiness about the pact that preceded the general election, the continued tolerance of anti-Treaty rebels in the Four Courts and the increasing evidence that it was pro-Treaty and not anti-Treaty forces who were stirring up trouble in the North. The British attitude of 'extend and pretend' could not survive the effrontery of one of its best-known generals being shot dead on his own doorstep. The shooting of Wilson gave the British the opportunity to put an end to any ambivalence in Ireland about the terms of the Treaty.

In order to understand Collins's culpability in the shooting of Wilson, one has to understand that he was not just the chairman of the Provisional Government and therefore a public figure. He was also the president of the secretive Supreme Council of the Irish Republican Brotherhood (IRB). As Tim Pat Coogan said:

> There is a tendency on the part of some contemporary
> historians to ascribe Collins's Northern policy merely to his
> desire to keep the South's Republicans in line. But it went
> deeper than that. Collins was not only the head of the newly
> formed twenty-six-county Irish State. He was the head of the
> IRB, committed by conviction and by the oath administered to
> him by Sam Maguire to continue what was begun in 1916.[22]

There were many in the Provisional Government who thought a secret society like the IRB had no place in a democratic state, but the statesman Collins found it hard to shake off the secret-society leader Collins.

It is important to understand that at that fateful meeting in Mooney's pub on the night before the Wilson shooting, Sam Maguire was present and aware of what Dunne and O'Sullivan were about to do. Maguire and Dunne were members of the IRB (O'Sullivan too, probably), and they answered to Collins. The oath all three took was:

> In the presence of God, I, [name given], do solemnly swear
> that I will do my utmost to establish the independence of
> Ireland, and that I will bear true allegiance to the Supreme

Council of the Irish Republican Brotherhood and the Government of the Irish Republic and implicitly obey the constitution of the Irish Republican Brotherhood and *all my superior officers* and that I will preserve inviolable the secrets of the organisation [author's italics].[23]

Reflecting on the shooting almost thirty years later, Patrick Sarsfield (P. S.) O'Hegarty, a former member of the IRB Supreme Council, said the Wilson shooting had been an IRB job:

I have seen it stated that Sam was O/C [IRA] Britain. I don't believe that at all. He was almost certainly the head of the London IRB and would have been instructed to keep out of publicity and stick to his own job, which was vital. I believe that Dunne and O'Sullivan acted under his instruction as members of the organisation and not as members of the Irish Volunteers [IRA].[24]

O'Hegarty believed that Sam Maguire had been 'mad [keen] to shoot Wilson' and kept asking Collins for permission. O'Hegarty suggested that Collins gave the order in a fit of exasperation, telling Maguire: 'Get away to hell out of that and don't bother me and do whatever you like.' Although we only have a second-hand account from O'Hegarty, it chimes with what people observed of Collins after the Treaty was signed. He was overworked and overwrought, with many competing demands on his time. Nevertheless, O'Hegarty concluded, Collins was still morally responsible for the shooting.

In their biography *Michael Collins: The Man and the Revolution*, Anne Dolan and William Murphy maintained that Collins's involvement in the shooting remained a 'moot point', but stated that he was often impulsive and less than collegiate:

It raises very serious questions not just of his attitude to the Treaty, but of his capacity to lead and to strategise at all. If it was his command, then Collins [. . .] may well have started the Civil War he had done so much not to fight.[25]

If Collins was responsible for giving the order, how was that order conveyed to Dunne and O'Sullivan? In *Michael Collins: A Biography*, Tim Pat Coogan claimed that a woman named Peig Ní Bhraonáin, who worked as a courier for Collins, was sent to London with a dispatch. On 9 June 1922 she met a 'tall man called Tobin' in Euston Station. This presumably was Liam Tobin, one of Collins's closest colleagues. She believed the instructions were from Collins to Dunne to kill Wilson. 'Years later as she came near death, her conscience assailed her, not for Wilson, but for Dunne and O'Sullivan. On her deathbed she told her son the story for the first time,' Coogan wrote.[26]

This is third-hand information, but Tobin's grandson Brian Hand says he saw a document which proved his grandfather's involvement in the planning for the shooting:

In early August 1999 I was researching in the [Irish] Military Archives. There would be a daily readers' log to confirm this. I remember the reading room to be very quiet on these days and had struck up a good relationship with Commandant Peter Young, as I had been in and out of the archives since the spring researching Liam Tobin. Peter Young had let me see classified G files [Irish military intelligence files] on Tobin, Joe McGrath and Pat McCartan from the 1940s. Then he decided to take me to another room below the reading room which was full of files and he directed me to a wall of shelves on the left. He pointed out files of photographs and said some were of roadside shootings during the Civil War

that he thinks will never be released. He then retrieved a
two- or three-page document transcript and showed it to
me. It was an affidavit by Frank Thornton on the killing of
Henry Wilson and he showed me the final page, which was
the witness signature of Liam Tobin. I remember reading the
opening paragraph before Peter said, 'Sorry I can't show it to
you until it is declassified,' which he expected it would [be].
The conversation continued and I said something like, 'So it
confirms their involvement in the Wilson assassination?' And
he said, 'Yes' (again to the best of my memory). I thought it
was significant but not groundbreaking news, as I have always
believed that Liam was involved in it.[27]

Brian Hand said the document recounted a meeting with a courier at Euston Station in relation to the Wilson shooting. Could
this document conclusively prove Collins's involvement in the
shooting? When Hand went to retrieve the document from the
Irish Military Archives, it could not be located. Attempts by this
author to locate it were also unsuccessful. Denis Kelleher placed
Tobin in London around the time of the shooting. Tobin had also
come over the previous year with a view to assassinating Lloyd
George.

Collins's involvement in the shooting explains why he was prepared to send his best men to London, including Tobin, to rescue
Dunne and O'Sullivan, even while the Civil War was imminent. It
explains why Dunne included 'Micky Collins' in his list of people
to be remembered to in his last letter. It explains why Tobin and
Cullen went to Dunne's parents a year after the shooting and
handed them the deeds of the house in Florence Road, Bray,
where they were staying. It explains why Joe O'Sullivan's father
received the maximum gratuity possible from the Irish state.

Historians now know from Wilson's diaries and private correspondence that he despaired of military indiscipline from each and every side, but he kept his reservations private. He was reckless in his public speeches and careless about how his speeches were regarded by those who did not share his views. When the letter he wrote to Craig apologising about being unable to attend the opening of parliament was intercepted and made public, the *Irish Bulletin*, the propaganda sheet of the underground Irish government prosecuting the War of Independence, responded:

> This letter will live in history as the authentic proof of the military and political motives which dictated the partition of Ireland and the establishment of a parliament, so-called, in North-East Ulster. In the person of the Ulsterman, Sir Henry Wilson, the military and political policy of England are jointly embodied. He writes that his 'opinions on the Irish question are fairly well known'. His action in relation to the Irish question is also well known since the year 1913 when he took an important part in organising Sir Edward Carson's rebel army, down to the present day when as 'senior officer of the British army' he is organising and has from the beginning been organising the military terror in Ireland.[28]

These comments, made in June 1921 when Wilson was still a serving soldier, elicited no response from him or from any of his supporters. Time and again the Irish press and the liberal British press drew attention to Wilson's motivations and cast them in the worst possible light. He shrugged off the criticism. His good friend General Sir Nevil Macready noted:

> It is important to remember in view of events that occurred in the future that beyond putting forward proposals Henry

Wilson had no hand or part whatsoever in the carrying-out of the scheme or in directing the activities of the Ulster forces. I have always recorded that apart from putting before Sir James Craig certain suggestions of a most simple and common sense nature, all tending towards the maintenance of a discipline which would curb the over-zealous activities of men influenced to some extent by religious fervour, Henry Wilson had nothing whatsoever to do with the operations of the Specials since he left the War Office. He had become more and more in the eyes of the Southern Irish a leader of Ulster activities. This was not due to anything he had done or not done, but to the misdirected zeal of his political friends and the Diehard press who were never tired of quoting him, often inaccurately, and dwelling upon the value of his support to Ulster and her claims.[29]

Macready blamed the Irish press for perceptions of Wilson as the personification of all evil in Ulster and believed they had motivated Dunne and O'Sullivan to pull the trigger on him:

The two miscreants who murdered him were apparently not resident in Ireland, but I have never had a doubt that they were saturated with the lies they read in the Irish press and in similar publications in England and came eventually to believe that Henry Wilson was in truth the directing spirit of every activity which resulted in the death of a Catholic. The distorted outpourings of a certain section of the Irish press had in the past been the prelude of more than one assassination in Ireland and without doubt on this occasion it exercised its baleful influence on the imaginations of the misguided fanatics, who by their brutal deed robbed the Empire of a kindly and brilliant Irishman whose greatest ideal was the good of the land of his birth.[30]

Macready revealed that Wilson himself understood how he was perceived in nationalist Ireland:

> On more than one occasion he told me that he wished
> people would get out of their head the idea that he had
> any connection with the force [the Specials]. But when, in
> reported speeches and in press articles, the Southern Irish saw
> his name constantly quoted as a champion of Ulster's rights,
> they were not slow to attribute every incident that occurred in
> Belfast or elsewhere in Ulster, resulting in collisions between
> Orangemen and Catholics, to his personal initiative. Time and
> again I read in the Southern Irish press accounts of so-called
> outrages by Orangemen, for which it was claimed that Henry
> Wilson was responsible.[31]

Yet nobody was more to blame for the perception of Wilson in nationalist Ireland than Wilson himself. He was not at all chastened by the commentary that followed his letter to Craig in March 1922, when he wrote about Ireland being in a 'welter of chaos and murder'. The comments of his fellow Southern unionists ought to have given him pause for thought, but he carried on with the same inflammatory rhetoric until the end of his life, repeating that the British government had made a mess of Ireland, that a strong man needed to go into the South to crush resistance and that such measures would have the support of the British public. He continued to repeat his belief that the Irish were not capable of ruling themselves and, worst of all, stating in his letter of 11 June, published posthumously, that 'there is no Irish nation'.[32]

He never tried to counter the derogatory things said about him, and his private misgivings about the behaviour of the Specials in the North were just that – private misgivings. His comments that the British should reinvade the South, if taken at face value, made him an enemy of the new Irish state as well. These comments went beyond anything said by the most recalcitrant unionist, who, though they detested Irish nationalism, had resigned themselves to the reality of an Irish state. Nowhere in his private musings or his public utterances will you find any acknowledgement by Wilson that his fellow Irish people had the right to rule themselves, nor did he ever condemn the sectarian outrages perpetrated against the Catholic minority in the North. It is one of the great paradoxes of Wilson's life that a soldier so nimble and original in his thinking could be so wooden-headed on the critical issue of the fate of his own country, but then again he never understood Ireland as a country in the way his fellow Irish people did. After the Anglo-Irish Treaty of 6 December 1921 he wrote in his diary:

> I could not help recalling my advice to the Cabinet given repeatedly ever since Nov. 11th 1918. 'Come out of those places that don't belong to us & hang on like hell to those places that do' and contrasting that with L.G.'s [Lloyd George's] performances which have been, & are, the exact opposite – for he is coming out of those places that *do* belong to us viz. Ireland, Egypt & India, & he is hanging on to those places that do *not* belong to us viz. Silesia, Constantinople, Palestine and Mesopotamia. Wonderful.[33]

This passage is significant in its use of the word 'belong'. How do countries as disparate as Ireland, Egypt and India 'belong' to Britain? The supposition was typical of Wilson's unquestioning arch-imperialist worldview. The peoples of Ireland, Egypt and India would demonstrate in turn that they did not 'belong' to Britain. Wilson was right to warn that granting independence to Ireland would lead to a clamour for more self-determination across the Empire. He was wrong to think that this was a bad thing.

In *No Other Law*, Florrie O'Donoghue described Wilson as the 'most fanatically anti-Irish Irishman'.[34] Wilson, had he lived, might have seen that epithet as unfair. There is no evidence that either he or his family detested their fellow Irishmen and women on a personal level, but the charge is not unfair on a political level. Erskine Childers, shortly after Wilson's death, said Wilson through his honesty and frankness had showed what 'Orange imperialism' was really about – 'predatory militarism tipped with the deadly venom of sectarian bigotry. Eastern Ulster is its last breeding ground and the last stronghold of Orange imperialism just as England is the only country in the world which dares to permit it to flourish.'[35]

Wilson's blinkered imperialism is shown too in his support for General Reginald Dyer, the perpetrator of the Amritsar massacre of 13 April 1919, when British and Indian troops under his command opened fire on a peaceful crowd and killed at least 379 people, including forty-two children. Dyer's actions embarrassed Britain, but Wilson was one of his biggest champions, seeing the controversy solely through its impact on the reputation of the British army rather than on the victims of the massacre. 'We should have many Dyer cases both in India and in Ireland, and if we did not stand by our own soldiers we should lose their confidence.'[36]

In 1940, eighteen years after the death of Wilson, Amritsar would claim the life of a fellow Irish imperialist. Sir Michael O'Dwyer, an Irish Catholic from Soloheadbeg, where the Irish War of Independence began in 1919, was shot dead by a Sikh nationalist, Udham Singh, in London. O'Dwyer was the governor of the Punjab when the Amritsar massacre occurred and gave retrospective justification to it. Singh's two-decade-long attempt to track him down and assassinate him was the subject of Anita Anand's book *The Patient Assassin*, published in 2019.

Wilson showed no interest in fairness or even-handedness in public. For a man who held such a senior position in the British army and whose judgement was trusted by politicians during the First World War, his subsequent utterances were unworthy. In his brief spell as a politician he exhibited neither tact nor judgement.

He made a bad situation much worse, but so did his assassination. Wilson, despite his manifest faults, detested military indiscipline from wherever it came. He may have hated the IRA, but he also detested the Black and Tans and the Specials. He was consistent at least in that regard.

He was not responsible for the pogroms in the North. If anything, his proposals, partisan as they were, were designed to stop this kind of arbitrary killing on the part of state forces. Wilson did not expel Catholic workers from the shipyards or burn them from their homes, throw bombs at children in Weaver Street or shoot down the McMahon family. Communal strife in Ulster was centuries old and continued long after his death. His irresponsible rhetoric emboldened some of those responsible for these outrages, but it was not sufficient to justify his death.

Dunne and O'Sullivan were intelligent men, uncommonly well educated for their time and deeply religious. Yet despite their Catholic faith, they performed an un-Christian act and broke the Fifth Commandment, 'Thou shalt not kill.' In 1993 Terence Sheehy wrote to the National Library of Ireland. His friend Fr Richard Magan, SJ, taught Dunne and had sent him a picture taken of Dunne in his cricket gear at St Ignatius College. Dunne, Magan revealed, had been inspired by the teachings of the Jesuits' founder St Ignatius Loyola on the morality of assassination. In the Jesuit catechism, Ignatius writes:

> To kill a king who tyrannizeth is so far from treason that
> it should rather be esteemed as an act of justice and zeal,
> being agreeable to nature, law, scripture and the practice and
> precepts of holy men.[37]

Philosophers and theologians have pondered the morality of assassination for millennia. In his 2015 book *Not in God's Name: Confronting Religious Violence*, Britain's chief rabbi Jonathan Sacks coined the phrase 'altruistic evil' to explain why good people do bad things in the name of religion or nationality. Only in fiction are great evils committed by 'caricatures of malevolence', he observed. Real people are more complicated. 'Evil committed in a sacred cause in the name of high ideals . . . turns ordinary people into cold-blooded murderers of schoolchildren.'[38] Assassination has been a policy tool of governments, guerrillas and individuals with grudges. Collins had no doubt it was morally appropriate in certain circumstances. The comments he made after the assassination of fourteen British officers during the War of Independence might equally be applied, in his worldview, to the Wilson shooting.

> My one intention was the destruction of the undesirables
> who continued to make miserable the lives of ordinary decent
> citizens. I have proof enough to assure myself of the atrocities
> which this gang of spies and informers have committed.
> Perjury and torture are words too easily known to them. If
> I had a second motive it was no more than a feeling such as
> I would have for a dangerous reptile. By their destruction
> the very air is made sweeter. That should be the future's
> judgement on this particular event. For myself, my conscience
> is clear. There is no crime in detecting and destroying, in war-
> time, the spy and the informer. I have paid them back in their
> own coin.[39]

In another era Dunne would have become a teacher, a Jesuit priest or maybe a poet or author; O'Sullivan, perhaps a master tailor like his father or a diligent civil servant. But they were part of one of the unluckiest generations in history, pitched into a war beyond their comprehension, physically and mentally damaged by what they witnessed.

They returned from the First World War looking for a purpose, like millions of others. They found it in Irish nationalism. Two days after Wilson was assassinated, the German foreign minister Walther Rathenau was shot dead by ex-servicemen from the far right. Germany's defeat in the First World War produced a generation of embittered and radicalised veterans, which in turn would lead to the disaster of Hitler coming to power.

The First World War and its aftermath was a time when a lot of good people did very bad things, when high-minded individuals like Dunne and O'Sullivan indulged their basest instincts. As they said in their statement justifying the killing, they had joined the British army 'voluntarily, for the purpose of taking human life'.[40] What was legal, state-sponsored killing in Flanders and France was illegal on the streets of London.

They went to the scaffold believing they had done the right thing.

Identity is complex, Irish identity especially so. That two British-born Irish nationalists killed an Irish-born British imperialist is the greatest irony of this tragic affair. All three men died for countries they were neither born nor raised in. Having endured so much, Dunne and O'Sullivan made sense of the post-war world by embracing their parents' country, which they claimed as their own. They would never have passed Norman Tebbit's 'cricket test'. In 1990 Tebbit, formerly a prominent minister in Margaret Thatcher's Conservative government, questioned the loyalty of the children of South Asian and Caribbean immigrants to Britain. Which cricketing Test team did they support, England or that of their parents' country? 'Are you still harking back to where you came from or where you are?' Tebbit said in an interview in the *Los Angeles Times*.[41] It is a question that children of immigrants everywhere often ask themselves.

Tebbit's comments came from an ignorance of the dual identities that the children of immigrants often have to wrestle with, between their home country and that of their parents. This duality is part of what makes multicultural societies so dynamic and interesting, creating, among other things, great literature, music and cuisine. The band the Pogues, for instance, possessed a uniquely London-Irish identity. In the case of some, though, the duality is impossible to reconcile and they become alienated from the country of their birth, as Dunne and O'Sullivan did. Dunne and O'Sullivan find their contemporary echo in the story of Dermot (Diarmaid) O'Neill, the last Provisional IRA operative to be shot dead by the security forces in the Troubles and the only IRA man to be killed in Great Britain. O'Neill was born and raised in Hammersmith, west London. He attended the prestigious London Oratory School and became interested in both Irish and Basque nationalism. He was shot dead on 23 September 1996 by the Metropolitan Police during a raid on a guesthouse in Hammersmith, having been under surveillance for six weeks before he was killed. Police discovered evidence that he and others were planning a bombing campaign in London.

Frank Lee, another British-born IRA volunteer, said Dunne and O'Sullivan's actions had saved Ireland:

Any Irishman . . . must come to the conclusion that the liquidation of Wilson was justified and in shooting Wilson,

Reg and Joe saved Ireland from a terrible holocaust as there is no doubt that it was Wilson's intention to wage a ruthless and bloody war against the people of Ireland.[42]

There were many who supported his view that the assassination of Wilson was justified and who felt vindicated by events afterwards. In their booklet published in 1953, the London Memorial Committee set up to honour Dunne and O'Sullivan stated: 'The violent pogroms in the North of Ireland immediately lessened in their vicious intensity and murder soon ceased to stalk the streets of the nationalist areas of its towns and cities.'[43]

Art O'Brien was of the same view: 'It was understood at the time that the execution of Sir Henry Wilson was decided upon in order to put an end to the wholesale massacres of Irish nationalists in Belfast for which Sir Henry Wilson was held to be responsible. After the death of Sir Henry Wilson these massacres did in fact terminate immediately.'[44]

The killings did not terminate immediately, but they did peter out as a result of the Wilson shooting, though not for the reasons that Dunne and O'Sullivan's supporters claimed. They were already waning following the assassination of William Twaddell in May 1922, which led to the mass arrest and detention of republicans in Northern Ireland. Craig's administration refitted an American cargo ship, the SS *Argenta*, and turned it into a prison ship. It was anchored in Belfast Lough and three hundred prisoners were held in cages on board, before being transferred to prisons in the area. It is estimated that 1,700 republicans left Belfast between April and June, with many of the prime instigators of the violence fleeing south to participate in the Civil War. With the outbreak of hostilities in the South on 28 June 1922, the North slipped off the agenda.

*

As Alan F. Parkinson pointed out in his book *A Difficult Birth: The Early Years of Northern Ireland 1920–25*, 'The main consequence of the Civil War on IRA activity in Northern Ireland was the redeployment of personnel for action in the south and west of the island, thereby significantly curbing the number of operations in Belfast and its surrounding areas, to the great good fortune of James Craig's government.'[45]

The number of IRA attacks declined, as did the number of revenge attacks on Catholics by loyalists and the Specials, although tit-for-tat killings took place in July during the marching season and sporadic violence occurred in September, when five people died in sectarian attacks. The last victim of the pogroms was Mary Sherlock, a Catholic woman, who was shot dead on 5 October. By the end of October Northern Ireland entered a state of perpetual sullenness and unresolved conflict lasting until the abortive border campaign of 1956 to 1962, followed by the next explosion of extended communal violence in 1969, which then continued for twenty-five years.

In 1968 Bernard Ash's *The Lost Dictator* was published, portraying Wilson as a dangerous right-wing extremist. The 1960s were not a good decade for the reputation of First World War generals, following the publication of Alan Clark's *The Donkeys* in 1961, which popularised the phrase 'lions led by donkeys'. Ash portrayed Wilson as a ruthless man whose contempt for Irish nationalists also extended to the English working classes, the trade unions and socialists in general. He posited that had Wilson lived he would have led a Diehard takeover of the Tory party and headed an authoritarian government that would have made common cause with Hitler and Mussolini in the 1930s. Dunne and O'Sullivan, Ash concluded, had done not just Ireland but Britain a favour by taking out Wilson when they did:

> Under his vivid and reckless leadership the extremists would
> quickly have gained control of the Conservative party and
> the Conservative leadership – on which without doubt his
> sights were already set – would in due course have fallen to
> him as well. Who else was there? There was not a leader on
> the horizon, nor anyone who could compete with Wilson
> for fire, the capacity to rouse men, inspire their loyalty,
> consolidate their ranks. What these years would have brought
> beggars the imagination. One has only to begin to think of
> the consequences of an attempted re-conquest of Ireland,
> subjugation of India, Egypt and other lands where there
> was already more than mere stirring of the will to achieve
> independence. One has only to think of the consequences
> of governing England, of military confrontation with the
> forces of organised labour in a decade soured by depression
> and riddled with industrial revolution. Had his life not been
> cut short at that particular time things would have been very
> different; the history of his country and of the world in the
> 1920s and beyond might have been incalculably changed.[46]

As a piece of counterfactual history, Ash's book is enormously
engaging, though most observers reckoned that Wilson lacked the
tact to be a successful politician. It is a reminder, though, that contempt for Wilson was not just confined to Ireland.

In reality nobody benefited from Wilson's shooting. It left a wife
without her husband. Cecil Wilson died suddenly in London from
a heart attack in April 1930, aged sixty-eight. 'She never recovered
from the shock of the Field Marshal's death,' her niece Leonora
Trench said at the time of her death.[47]

It left Reggie Dunne's grieving parents without their only child and the O'Sullivans without a beloved son and brother. In a short time all those centrally involved in the British assassination campaigns – Dunne, O'Sullivan, Collins, Brugha and Rory O'Connor – were dead. A day after the Wilson shooting RUC and A-Specials shot dead three Catholics – Seamus McAllister (eighteen), John Gore (twenty-two) and John Hill (thirty) – in Cushendall, County Antrim. One of the Specials who shot John Gore was heard to say, 'You are one of the bastards who shot Wilson.'[48]

30 Reggie and Joe's final resting place in the republican plot of Deansgrange Cemetery, Dublin

All three men were found dead behind an alleyway in the town, and so it continued until the end of May 1923. The Civil War curdled Irish politics for generations and destroyed the lives of so many who could have benefited the new Irish state – Collins, Griffith and Childers among them.

The assassination of Wilson occurred a year to the day after the speech by King George V at the opening of the Northern Ireland parliament. There he asked Irishmen to 'pause, to stretch out the hand of forbearance and conciliation, to forgive and to forget, and to join in making for the land which they love a new era of peace, contentment, and goodwill'.[49]

It was not contentment or goodwill but great hatred that motivated Henry Wilson. Great hatred of Wilson motivated Dunne and O'Sullivan, great hatred motivated the sectarian strife in the North and the Civil War, and those hatreds lingered for generations afterwards. It was the worst of times and almost destroyed the new Irish state wished for by Irish nationalists for centuries. The fact that it survived at all is its greatest achievement.

Glossary of Terms

Act of Union 1800: The Act of Union abolished the Irish parliament and integrated Ireland into the United Kingdom.

Anglo-Irish Treaty: On 6 December 1921 the Anglo-Irish Treaty was signed between representatives of Dáil Éireann and the British government. Under its terms, the twenty-six counties were given Dominion status on a par with Canada – self-government within the British Empire, with the king as head of state. The Treaty created the Irish Free State, which was set up on a provisional basis and came into being a year later on 6 December 1922.

Chief of the Imperial General Staff (CIGS): The role held by Wilson was the professional head of the British army, with responsibility for overall strategic direction. The symbolic head of the British army is the monarch. Wilson was also the chief military advisor to the British government from February 1918 to February 1922. The title is now Chief of the General Staff.

Cumann na mBan (the Women's Council): The women's auxiliary of the Irish Volunteers (*see below*) was founded in April 1914 to 'advance the cause of Irish liberty and to organise Irishwomen in the furtherance of this object'. It was involved in the Easter Rising and the War of Independence. Cumann na mBan became heavily anti-Treaty and was banned by the Free State government in January 1923.

Cumann na nGaedheal: The pro-Treaty party was founded in 1923 and ruled the Irish Free State until 1932. In 1933 it merged with smaller parties to form Fine Gael, historically the second-largest party in Irish politics.

Dáil Éireann (Assembly of Ireland): Dáil Éireann was set up in January 1919 as the first independent Irish parliament by the seventy-three Sinn Féin MPs elected in the British general election of 1918. It was banned by the British government in August 1919. The First Dáil was replaced by the Second Dáil in May 1921. It sent emissaries to negotiate the Anglo-Irish Treaty and narrowly approved the treaty in January 1922 by sixty-four votes to fifty-seven.

Fenians: Founded in 1858 in Paris by James Stephens and John O'Mahoney, the Fenians was a republican organisation that wanted an independent Irish republic and was prepared to use violence to achieve its aims. The Fenians staged a short-lived rebellion in 1867.

Fianna Fáil (Soldiers of Destiny): Party founded in 1926 by Éamon de Valera from those who opposed the Treaty. The dominant force in Southern Irish politics from 1932 to 2011 and the largest party (by seats) at the 2020 Irish general election.

Four Courts: The Four Courts building on Dublin's north quays was and remains the heart of the Irish judiciary. It was built in 1776 from a design by the architect James Gandon. It was almost destroyed in 1922 but has since been rebuilt.

Home rule: Home rule was devolution for the island of Ireland. It was envisaged that the Irish would have complete control over entirely local matters, while the UK continued to run foreign affairs and the armed forces.

Home Rule Act: The Third Home Rule Act was passed by the House of Commons in 1912 and given royal assent in September 1914, but was suspended for the duration of the First World War. It was never implemented and was replaced by the Government of Ireland Act 1920 and the Anglo-Irish Treaty 1921.

Irish Free State (*Saorstát Éireann*): The Irish Free State succeeded Southern Ireland as the name of the twenty-six-county entity. It came into being on 6 December 1922, one year after the Anglo-Irish Treaty was signed. Northern Ireland opted out of the Free State a day later.

Irish Parliamentary Party (IPP): Also known as the Irish Party, the IPP was the dominant force in Irish nationalist politics from the 1870s until the British general election of December 1918. The party supported home rule, and its leader John Redmond backed the British army war effort in the First World War.

Irish Republican Army (IRA): The name adopted by the Irish Volunteers in August 1919. IRA volunteers had to swear an oath to Dáil Éireann. In April 1921 Dáil Éireann took responsibility for the actions of the IRA. After the Treaty, anti-Treaty forces retained the name IRA, while pro-Treaty forces became known as the National Army.

Irish Republican Brotherhood (IRB): A secret, oath-bound organisation dedicated to the overthrow of British rule in Ireland and the establishment of an Irish republic. Michael Collins, Sam Maguire, Dunne and O'Sullivan were all members of the IRB, while Collins was president at the time of the Wilson shooting.

Irish Unionist Alliance (IUA): Set up in 1891 as an all-Ireland party opposed to home rule for Ireland. It was supported by a third of voters in the general election of 1900 but was superseded by the Ulster Unionist Party (UUP), which was founded in 1905 and operated only in Ulster.

Irish Volunteers (IV): Founded in November 1913 as a nationalist counterpoint to the Ulster Volunteer Force (UVF) to 'secure and maintain the rights and liberties common to the whole people of

Ireland'. The IV split over Irish Party support for the British war effort in September 1914 and staged the Easter Rising in 1916.

Irish War of Independence: Lasting from 21 January 1921 to the Truce of 11 July 1921, the war was fought between the IRA and Crown forces represented by the Royal Irish Constabulary (RIC), the Black and Tans, Auxiliaries and the British army. Approximately 2,200 people were killed. It ended in a military stalemate.

National Army: Created in January 1922 as the army of the Irish Free State (set up in provisional form for the first year). At its height during the Civil War it had a strength of 55,000 men, many of them ex-British army veterans of the First World War.

Nationalists: Irish nationalists wanted more freedom from Britain. They were predominantly though not exclusively (Sam Maguire being a case in point) Catholics. The term 'nationalist' is often used in this period of the Irish revolution (1916–23) to distinguish those who followed the constitutional path to home rule, i.e. Irish Parliamentary Party supporters, from republicans, who were separatists and prepared to use violence to achieve their goals.

Northern Ireland: Created following the Government of Ireland Act 1920, Northern Ireland legally came into being on 3 May 1921 as a self-governing entity within the United Kingdom.

Partition: The Government of Ireland Act 1920 made partition official. In November 1919 a parliamentary committee chaired by Walter Long agreed to a proposal for two parliaments, with a council of Ireland to discuss issues of mutual interest and a view to unity at some point in the future. It was accepted by Ulster Unionists, and the Northern Ireland parliament began in June 1921. The act was superseded in the South by the Anglo-Irish Treaty.

Phoenix Park murders: Chief Secretary for Ireland Lord Frederick Cavendish and the Under-Secretary for Ireland Thomas Burke in 1882 were the first significant public figures to be assassinated by Irish republicans since the Act of Union of 1800. Five members of the Invincibles, a splinter group of the Fenian movement, were hanged for the killings. Comparisons have been made between the murders and the assassination of Wilson.

Provisional Government: The first Irish government was set up in January 1922 and operated on a provisional basis until the Irish Free State came into being in December of that year.

Republicans: Those who want complete separation from Britain, including the demand that the British monarch would not be the head of state.

Sinn Féin (Ourselves Alone): Founded in 1906 by Arthur Griffith, Sinn Féin was a fringe movement until 1916, when it was erroneously blamed for the Easter Rising. It became the dominant force in Irish politics after the British general election of 1918. The three main parties in the Republic, Fianna Fáil, Fine Gael and Sinn Féin, all claim lineage from the original Sinn Féin.

Southern Ireland: The name given to the twenty-six counties of what is now the Republic of Ireland by the British government through the Government of Ireland Act 1920.

Teachta Dala (TD; member of the house): The Irish equivalent of MP.

Truce: The Truce of 11 July 1921 ended the War of Independence. It was signed between representatives of Sinn Féin and the British government. British forces were to cease 'pursuit of Irish officers and men, or war materials or military stores'. The IRA was to cease 'attacks on Crown Forces and civilians . . . [and] British government and private property'.

Ulster Special Constabulary (USC): Also known as the 'Specials', the USC was set up as an auxiliary to the Royal Irish Constabulary in the six counties in 1920. It was organised into three groups: A-Specials, a full-time auxiliary; B-Specials, who were armed part-time officers; and the C-Specials, who were older, unarmed volunteers who guarded infrastructure. Wilson did not create or command the Specials, but his name was frequently evoked when they were mentioned.

Ulster Volunteer Force (UVF): Set up in January 1913 as an armed militia to stop the introduction of home rule into Ulster.

Unionists: Those who want to keep Ireland in the United Kingdom per the Act of Union 1800. One hundred years ago, most unionists were clustered in the north-east of Ireland, where they were a majority, but there were also 300,000 who could be identified as Southern unionists, including the Wilson family.

Acknowledgements

This book arose out of my previous one, *Wherever the Firing Line Extends: Ireland and the Western Front*, on the stories behind First World War memorials with an Irish connection. The last chapter in the book is about Robert Armstrong, who is memorialised in Valenciennes (St Roch) Communal Cemetery in France. He served with the Irish Guards in the war and got a job afterwards as a gardener with the Imperial (now Commonwealth) War Graves Commission. During the Second World War he joined the French Resistance, was captured by the Nazis and died in Waldheim prison camp in 1944. Armstrong grew up on the Currygrane estate, where his father James was the steward and estate manager. In researching Armstrong's life, I realised that the assassination of Wilson, a major event in its time, had been under-researched and was now largely forgotten.

I would like to thank my agent Faith O'Grady at Lisa Richards and the team at Faber & Faber of Laura Hassan, Anne Owen, Laura Hassan, Mo Hafeez and Hannah Turner for their support. It was a privilege to work with my editor Eleo Carson, copyeditor Mark Bolland and proofreader Ian Bahrami.

My good friends Martin Doyle, Tommy Conlon and the historian Gerard Shannon provided invaluable input. Bill King supplied information about the Great Eastern Railway Society and Dr Eileen Reilly-Prunty sent me her BA (Hons) thesis on the Wilson family. Michael Boulton and Paul Raffield were unfailingly polite and helpful in all my inquiries about the O'Sullivan family, as was Brian Hand in relation to his grandfather Liam

Tobin. Commandant Daniel Ayiotis of the Military Archives and Sandra Heise of the National Museum of Ireland supplied me with documents. I wish to acknowledge the wonderful work of Cécile Chemin-Gordon and the team at the Irish Military Archives, who since 2014 have been involved in digitising, cataloguing and making publicly available the Military Service Pensions Collection (MSPC), which has been the source of much of the new material used in this book. John Dorney's website 'The Irish Story' (https://www.theirishstory.com) was an important source of information, especially in relation to the Irish Civil War.

Rex Taylor's book *Assassination: The Death of Sir Henry Wilson and the Tragedy of Ireland* (1961) and Keith Jeffrey's *Sir Henry Wilson: A Political Soldier* (2007) were valuable references throughout. Professor Jeffrey's death in 2016 was a major loss to Irish historical research. Gerard Noonan's *The IRA in Britain, 1919–1923* and Dr Mary MacDiarmada's *Art O'Brien and Irish Nationalism in London, 1900–25* are two valuable additions to the neglected study of Irish republicanism in Great Britain.

The Brady brothers, Aidan and Noel, and Noel's wife Patricia showed me around the old Currygrane estate and Currygrane Lake. It is a beautiful part of the world and people should visit.

London and Longford are two places I know well, having lived in both. The London-Irish, many of whom are family and friends, are a redoubtable people and have taught me a lot about the complexity of identity.

I would like to thank my brothers John and Conor for their help with the book, and finally my wife Rebecca and my children Rosamund and Leo for their love and support.

Notes

Abbreviations for archives referenced:

BMH – Bureau of Military History
HO – Home Office
IMA – Irish Military Archives
INA – Irish National Archives
MSPC – Military Service Pensions Collection
NGI – National Gallery of Ireland
NLI – National Library of Ireland
NMIA – National Museum of Ireland Archive
TNA – The National Archive
UCDA– University College Dublin Archives

TIMELINE
1 Tim Pat Coogan, *Michael Collins: The Man Who Made Ireland* (Dublin 2002), p. 373

1 ASSASSINATION: 'HERE, IN THE MIDDLE OF OUR OWN METROPOLIS, HE HAS BEEN MURDERED'
1 'History and Projections', https://www.youtube.com/watch?v=_7jCioztj_c. London was the largest city in the world for almost a century until overtaken by New York in 1925
2 *Great Eastern Journal*, October 2014
3 'Charles Fryatt: The man Executed for Ramming a U-Boat', *BBC News*, 15 July 2016, https://www.bbc.com/news/uk-england-essex-36745439, retrieved October 2021
4 'The Funeral of Edith Cavell', https://www.westminster-abbey.org/abbey-commemorations/commemorations/edith-cavell, retrieved October 2021
5 The UK National Archives list 886,000 dead from the UK. See https://www.nationalarchives.gov.uk/help-with-your-research/research-guides/deaths-first-and-second-world-wars/. The Robert Schuman Centre lists 1,114,914 British Empire dead
6 *Great Eastern Journal*, October 2014
7 Keith Jeffery, 'Wilson, Sir Henry Hughes', *Dictionary of Irish Biography* (online), https://www.dib.ie/biography/wilson-sir-henry-hughes-a9074, retrieved October 2021

8 Bernard Ash, *The Lost Dictator: Field Marshal Sir Henry Wilson* (London, 1968), p. 34

9 Winston Churchill, *The World Crisis 1911–1918* (New York, 1923), p. 760

10 Keith Jeffery, *Field Marshal Sir Henry Wilson: A Political Soldier* (Oxford, 2006), p. 81

11 *Scotsman*, 23 June 1922

12 Rudyard Kipling, 'Recessional', 1897

13 *Scotsman*, 23 June 1922

14 Jeffery, *Field Marshal Sir Henry Wilson*, p. 88. The Wilsons agreed to take a thirteen-and-a-half-year lease on 36 Eaton Place in 1910

15 The Metropolitan Police's descriptions of Dunne and O'Sullivan were widely circulated in the British press

16 John Keegan, *The First World War* (London, 1999), p. 365

17 IMA/BMH, WS945, Sorcha Nic Diarmada, 1954

18 *Dundee Courier*, 3 July 1922

19 UKNA, HO282/50, the murder trial of Reginald Dunne and Joseph O'Sullivan. All the witness statements are collated here

20 *New York Times*, 23 June 1922

21 Ibid.

22 Ibid.

23 (IMA/BMH) Document No. 247. This contains a copy of Reggie Dunne's statement

24 *New York Times*, 23 June 1922

25 Ibid.

26 Ibid.

27 IMA/BMH, Document No. 247

28 The island of Great Britain consists of England, Scotland and Wales. The United Kingdom included Ireland until December 1921, and now includes Northern Ireland. The official name of the British state is the United Kingdom of Great Britain and Northern Ireland. The UK is not Great Britain

29 William Manchester, *The Last Lion: Winston Spencer Churchill, Visions of Glory 1874–1932* (London, 2015), p. 111

30 Ruth Winston, *Events, Dear Boy* (London, 2012), p. 8

31 John Spencer, 'Soldier-Diplomat: A Reassessment of Sir Henry Wilson's Influence on British Strategy in the Last 18 Months of the Great War', unpublished PhD thesis, University of Wolverhampton, January 2018, https://ethos.bl.uk/OrderDetails.do?uin=uk.bl.ethos.737822, retrieved October 2021

32 *Hansard*, House of Commons debates, 22 June 1922, vol. 155, cc1514–16

33 Ibid.

34 *New York Times*, 23 June 1922

35 *Hansard*, House of Lords debates, 22 June 1922, vol. 50, cc1093–6

36 'Archduke Franz Ferdinand Pt. 1: Igniting the Powder Keg', Assassination podcast, Spotify, https://open.spotify.com/episode/7jjgre7LMBuXzRxqElNbmr, retrieved October 2021. See also 'After WWI, Hundreds of Politicians Were Murdered in Germany', history.com, https://www.history.com/news/political-assassinations-germany-weimar-republic, retrieved October 2021

37 *Hansard*, House of Lords debates, 22 June 1922, vol. 50, cc1096

38 Ibid.

39 Ernest Hemingway, *The Sun Also Rises* (New York, 1926), p. 108

40 *Illustrated London News*, 10 September 1921

41 *Hull Daily News*, 17 October, 1921

42 Dáil Éireann debates, 19 December 1921. Vol. T, no. 6

43 Paul McMahon, *British Spies and Irish Rebels: British Intelligence and Ireland 1916–1945* (Woodbridge, 2008), p. 46

44 *Hansard*, House of Commons debates, 15 December 1921, vol. 149, cc133–258

45 Terence de Vere White, *Kevin O'Higgins* (Kerry, 1966), pp. 83–4

46 *Irish Times*, 13 February 1922

47 Coogan, *Michael Collins: The Man Who Made Ireland* (Dublin 2002), p. 373

48 General Sir Nevil Macready, *Annals of an Active Life*, vol. 2 (London, 1924), p. 340

49 Ibid.

50 Coogan, *Michael Collins*, p. 374

51 *Hansard*, House of Commons debates, 26 June 1922, vol. 155, cc1693–811

52 Michael Hopkinson, *Green Against Green: The Irish Civil War* (Dublin, 2004), p. 44

53 *Irish Examiner*, 3 July 2012

54 *Irish Times*, 28 June 1922

55 Michael Fewer, *The Battle of the Four Courts* (Croydon, 2018), p. 141

2 HENRY WILSON – THE EARLY YEARS: 'I AM AN IRISHMAN'
1 'Currygrane House, Currygrane, Longford', National Inventory of Architectural Heritage, https://www.buildingsofireland.ie/buildings-search/building/13400910/currygrane-house-currygrane-county-longford, retrieved October 2021

2 Eileen Reilly-Prunty, 'The Wilson Family of Currygrane, Co. Longford 1650–1930', BA research project for BA (Hons) degree, Maynooth University, 1990

3 *The Times*, 12 April 1897

4 *Longford Leader*, 3 May 1924

5 J. Mackay Wilson, 'Bird Life at Currygrane, Co. Longford', *The Irish Naturalist*, vol. 27, no. 7 (July 1918), p. 111

6 *Northern Whig*, 10 May 1922

7 Maire Coleman, 'Mac Eoin, Seán', *Dictionary of Irish Biography* (online), https://www.dib.ie/biography/mac-eoin-sean-a5033, retrieved October 2021

8 IMA/BMH, WS716, General Seán MacEoin, 1957

9 Keith Jeffery, 'Field Marshal Sir Henry Wilson: Myths and the Man', *Journal of the Society for Army Historical Research*, vol. 86, no. 345 (Spring 2008), pp. 57–82

10 Ash, p. 3

11 *Melbourne Argus*, 24 June 1922

12 *Irish Independent*, 27 December 1901

13 *Kilkenny People*, 3 October 1908

14 *Irish Times*, 8 June 1914

15 *The Times*, 14 March 1914

16 Reilly-Prunty, 'The Wilson Family of Currygrane, Co. Longford 1650–1930'

17 Ibid.

18 Joe Lee, *The Modernisation of Irish Society 1848–1918* (Dublin, 1973), p. 56

19 Paul Bew, *Ireland: The Politics of Enmity 1789–2006* (Oxford, 2007), p. 568

20 Alvin Jackson, *Home Rule: An Irish History 1800–2000* (London, 2003), pp. 30–1

21 James Lydon, *The Making of Ireland: From Ancient Times to the Present* (Oxford, 1998), p. 310

22 Jeffery, *Field Marshal Sir Henry Wilson: A Political Soldier*, p. 70

23 Sir Charles Callwell, *Field Marshal Sir Henry Wilson: His Life and Diaries*, 2 vols (London, 1927), vol. 1, p. 9

24 Ibid., p. 52

25 Ibid., p. 42

26 Ibid., p. 88

27 Ibid., p. 100

28 Ibid., p. 96

29 Ibid., p. 143

30 Ibid., p. 122

31 Keith Jeffery, 'Wilson, Sir Henry Hughes', *Dictionary of Irish Biography* (online), https://www.dib.ie/biography/wilson-sir-henry-hughes-a9074, retrieved October 2021

32 Callwell, vol. 1, p. 162

33 Ibid., p. 139

34 Ibid., p. 141

35 Ash, p. 62

36 Viscount Esher, *The Tragedy of Lord Kitchener* (London, 1921), p. 85

37 Callwell, vol. 1, p. 183

38 Sir John French, *1914* (London, 1919), p. 109

39 Callwell, vol. 1, p. 301

40 Jeffery, *Field Marshal Sir Henry Wilson: A Political Soldier*, pp. 156–8

41 Callwell, vol. 1, p. 279

42 Jeffery, *Field Marshal Sir Henry Wilson: A Political Soldier*, p. 195

43 Callwell, vol. 2, p. 20

44 Ibid.
45 Churchill, p. 760
46 Callwell, vol. 2, p. 193
47 Ibid., p. 48
48 Ibid., p. 159

3 WILSON – THE POST-WAR YEARS: 'NEVER DAUNTED, NEVER DISMAYED'
1 Callwell, vol. 2, p. 164
2 *Irish Times*, 21 January 2019
3 Callwell, vol. 2, p. 241
4 Ibid., p. 201
5 Ibid., p. 203
6 Jeffery, *Field Marshal Sir Henry Wilson: A Political Soldier*, p. 258
7 *Irish Times*, 26 July 1919
8 Callwell, vol. 2, p. 206
9 Ibid., p. 207
10 Ibid., p. 216
11 Diarmaid Ferriter, *The Transformation of Ireland 1900–2000* (London, 2004), p. 222
12 Callwell, vol. 2, p. 219
13 Jeffery, p. 206
14 Callwell, vol. 2, p. 236
15 Ibid., p. 237
16 'Mixed Messages from America on Irish Independence', RTÉ/Century Ireland, https://www.rte.ie/centuryireland/index.php/articles/mixed-messages-from-america-on-irish-independence, retrieved October 2021
17 Callwell, vol. 2, p. 265
18 Ibid., p. 238
19 Ibid., p. 255
20 Ibid., p. 251
21 Ibid.
22 Jeffery, *Field Marshal Sir Henry Wilson: A Political Soldier*, p. 270
23 Callwell, vol. 2, p. 267
24 Rex Taylor, *Assassination: The Death of Sir Henry Wilson and the Tragedy of Ireland* (Michigan, 1961), p. 56
25 *Irish Independent*, 5 November 1920
26 IMA/BMH, WS767, Patrick Moylett, 1952
27 Cain Ulster Text of the Anglo-Irish Treaty, https://cain.ulster.ac.uk/issues/politics/docs/ait1921.htm, retrieved November 2021
28 Callwell, vol. 1, p. 301
29 Jeffery, *Field Marshal Sir Henry Wilson: A Political Soldier*, p. 274
30 Callwell, vol. 2, p. 519

NOTES

4 HENRY WILSON AND ULSTER: 'THE ORANGE TERROR'

1 Keith Jeffery, *The Military Correspondence of Field Marshal Sir Henry Wilson* (London, 1985), p. 274
2 Ibid, p. 285
3 Ibid.
4 *Irish Times*, 19 November 1921
5 *Northern Whig*, 8 March 1922
6 *Hansard*, House of Commons debates, 3 August 1914, vol. 65, cc1809–32
7 *Irish Times*, 23 June 1920
8 Alan F. Parkinson, *A Difficult Birth: The Early Years of Northern Ireland, 1920–25* (Dublin, 2020), p. 23
9 'Northern Cabinet Calls in More Troops to Deal with Ongoing Violence in Belfast', RTÉ/Century Ireland, https://www.rte.ie/centuryireland/index.php/articles/northern-cabinet-calls-in-more-troops-to-deal-with-ongoing-violence-in-belf, retrieved October 2021
10 Michael Hopkinson, 'The Craig–Collins Pacts of 1922: Two Attempted Reforms of the Northern Ireland Government', *Irish Historical Studies*, vol. 27, no. 106 (Nov. 1990), pp. 145–58
11 *Hansard*, House of Commons debates, 28 March 1922, vol. 152, cc1281–96
12 *Hansard*, House of Commons debates, 14 February 1922, vol. 150, cc808–9
13 *Freeman's Journal*, 22 March 1922
14 Robert John Lynch, *The Northern IRA and the Early Years of Partition 1920–1922* (Dublin, 2006), p. 122
15 Bridget Hourican, 'Nixon, John William', *Dictionary of Irish Biography* (online), https://www.dib.ie/biography/nixon-john-william-a6216, retrieved October 2021
16 Statement of Robert Dunne, House of Lords, Lloyd George papers, F97/1/230
17 *Irish Times*, 31 March 1997
18 Patrick Concannon, 'Michael Collins, Northern Ireland and the Northern Offensive, May 1922', *The Irish Story* (online), https://www.theirishstory.com/2019/08/12/michael-collins-northern-ireland-and-the-northern-offensive-may-1922/#.YYlrSFXP3IU, retrieved November 2021
19 Matthew Lewis, 'The Fourth Northern Division and the Joint IRA Offensive, April–July 1922', *War in History*, vol. 21, no. 3 (July 2014), pp. 302–21
20 Ibid.
21 Kieran Glennon, *From Pogrom to Civil War* (Cork, 2015), p. 187
22 *Belfast Newsletter*, 20 March 1922
23 Ibid.
24 *Irish Independent*, 22 March 1922
25 Ibid.
26 *Irish Independent*, 20 March 1922; *Freeman's Journal*, 23 March 1922
27 Callwell, vol. 2, p. 337

28 Ibid., p. 341
29 *Freeman's Journal*, 1 May 1922
30 *Belfast Telegraph*, 25 May 1922
31 *Freeman's Journal*, 9 June 1922
32 *New York Herald*, 11 June 1922
33 *Irish Independent*, 7 June 1922
34 *Belfast Newsletter*, 19 June 1922
35 *Belfast Telegraph*, 23 June 1922

5 REGINALD DUNNE: 'THE BLOOD THAT'S IN THEM'

1 NLI, MS2653, Reginald Dunne's final letters
2 Ibid.
3 Statement of Robert Dunne, House of Lords, Lloyd George papers, F97/1/230
4 IMA/BMH, WS902, Mary MacGeehin, 1953
5 David Fitzpatrick, 'Irish Emigration in the Later 19th Century', *Irish Historical Studies*, vol. 22, no. 86 (September 1980), pp. 126–43
6 Ireland population 1841, 8,199,853; Ireland population 1911, 4,390,219 (All-island Census)
7 C. R. L. Fletcher and Rudyard Kipling, *A School History of England* (Oxford, 1911), p. 22
8 Dáil Éireann debates, 10 January 1922, vol. T, no. 17
9 *Sunday Bee* (Omaha), 10 September 1922
10 IMA/BMH, WS902, MacGeehin
11 NLI, MS2653, Dunne
12 Douglas Hyde, 'The Necessity for De-Anglicising Ireland', speech delivered at the Irish National Literary Society, 25 November 1892, https://www.thefuture.ie/wp-content/uploads/1892/11/1892-11-25-The-Necessity-for-De-Anglicising-Ireland.pdf, retrieved October 2021
13 *An Claidheamh Soluis*, 19 September 1908
14 *An tÉireannach*, August 1911
15 Fitzpatrick, 'Irish Emigration in the Later 19th Century'
16 Peter Hart, 'Operations Abroad: The IRA in Britain 1919–1923', *The English Historical Review*, vol. 115, no. 460 (February 2000), pp. 71–102
17 Martin Harkin, 'Mary Dunne, A Mother's Struggle for Recognition', *The Irish Story* (online), https://www.theirishstory.com/2020/09/17/mary-dunne-a-mothers-struggle-for-recognition, retrieved October 2021
18 NLI, MS2653, Dunne
19 'About the Parish', Roman Catholic parish of Stamford Hill, https://parish.rcdow.org.uk/stamfordhill/about-the-parish/, retrieved October 2021
20 NLI, MS2653, Dunne
21 Patrick McGilligan, *Alfred Hitchcock: A Life in Darkness and Light* (London, 2004), p. 125

22 Ibid., p. 22
23 IMA/BMH, Document No. 247, Robert Dunne statement
24 TNA, service records for the First World War, WO363, Reginald Dunne
25 Rudyard Kipling, *The Irish Guards in the Great War: The First Battalion* (New York, 1923), p. 259
26 IMA/BMH, Document No. 247, Robert Dunne statement
27 Ibid.
28 Hart, 'Operations Abroad', p. 71
29 IMA/MSPC, MSP34REF57116, Pat O'Sullivan
30 Hart, 'Operations Abroad', p. 72
31 IMA/BMH, WS902, MacGeehin
32 William Murphy, *Political Imprisonment and the Irish, 1912–1921* (Oxford, 2014), p. 171
33 IMA/MSPC, MSP34REF8677, Frank Lee
34 UCDA, P17b/99, Ernie O'Malley papers, Bill Ahern
35 Ibid.
36 Roger Swift and Sheridan Gilley (eds), *The Irish in Britain, 1815–1939* (Maryland, 1989), p. 18
37 IMA/MSPC, MSP34REF27243, Denis Carr
38 Ibid.
39 IMA/MSPC, MSP34REF52661, Martin Walsh
40 Gerard Noonan, *The IRA in Britain, 1919–1923: 'In the Heart of Enemy Lines'* (Liverpool, 2014), p. 153
41 Michael Barry, *Fake News and the War of Independence* (Dublin, 2021), pp. 112–16
42 UCDA, P17b/99, Ahern
43 UCDA, P17b/107, Ernie O'Malley papers, Denis Kelleher
44 Noonan, p. 174
45 Dave Hannigan, 'When the IRA Tried to Burn Down Old Trafford in 1921', *Irish Times*, 3 February 2021, https://www.irishtimes.com/sport/soccer/dave-hannigan-when-the-ira-tried-to-burn-down-old-trafford-in-1921-1.4474954, retrieved October 2021
46 IMA/MSPC, MSP34REF19573, Thomas Morgan
47 IMA/BMH, WS1678, William O'Keeffe
48 *Hansard*, House of Commons debates, 21 February 1921, vol. 138, cc624–723
49 Hart, 'Operations Abroad'
50 Ibid.
51 UCDA, P7/A/29, Richard Mulcahy papers, 'Report on a Visit to Britain', September 1921
52 Ibid.
53 IMA/BMH, WS965, Sorcha McDermott, 1954
54 NLI, MS8430, O'Brien papers

6 JOSEPH O'SULLIVAN: AN OLD FENIAN FAMILY

1 *Freeman's Journal*, 5 March 1847
2 Central Statistics Office (Ireland), 'Distribution and Changes in the Population', 1926, p. 13, https://www.cso.ie/en/media/csoie/census/census1926results/volume10/C_1926_V10_Chapter_II.pdf, retrieved November 2021
3 Jim Barry (O'Sullivan family relative), email correspondence with author
4 Paul Raffield, email correspondence with author
5 *Hansard*, House of Commons debates, 26 June 1922, vol. 155, cc1693–811
6 Information on the O'Sullivan boys' war service was provided by Michael Boulton
7 IMA/MSPC, MSP34REF57116, O'Sullivan
8 Ibid.
9 Ronan McGreevy, 'The Man Who Fought for Three Armies', *Irish Times*, 1 February 2020, https://www.irishtimes.com/news/ireland/irish-news/the-man-who-fought-for-three-armies-british-ira-and-free-state-1.4159106, retrieved October 2021
10 *The Revolution Papers*, 16 August 2016, p. 33
11 Tom Barry, *Guerilla Days in Ireland* (Dublin, 1949), p. 2, with the permission of Mercier Press
12 Stephen Gwynn, *John Redmond's Last Years* (New York, 1919), p. 190
13 Ronan McGreevy, *Wherever the Firing Line Extends: Ireland and the Western Front* (Dublin, 2016), pp. 187–95
14 IMA/BMH, WS1511, Gerald Doyle, 1956
15 National Museum of Ireland archive (NMIA) – MacDonnell collection
16 Ibid.
17 IMA/MSPC, MSP34REF19466, Denis Kelleher
18 Frances Stevenson, *Lloyd George: A Diary* (London, 1971), p. 218
19 Thomas Jones, *Whitehall Diary, Vol. I* (London, 1969), p. 40
20 IMA/MSPC, MSP34REF32335, William Smyth
21 IMA/MSPC, MSP34REF57116, O'Sullivan
22 Ibid.
23 Ibid.
24 Ibid.
25 IMA/MSPC, DP6925. John O'Sullivan's application for a dependant's allowance because of his son's service to Ireland contains testimonials from many people, including Art O'Brien and Bill Ahern
26 Ibid.
27 IMA/MSPC, MSP34REF57116, O'Sullivan
28 *Southern Star*, 26 August 1922. Joe O'Sullivan's final letter was widely circulated in the Irish press
29 IMA/MSPC, MSP34REF57116, O'Sullivan
30 UCDA, P17b/107, Kelleher
31 IMA/MSPC, DP6925

7 PLANNING: 'THE WILSON JOB IS ON'

1 Senan Molony, *The Phoenix Park Murders: Conspiracy, Betrayal and Retribution* (Cork, 2006), p. 51

2 IMA/BMH, WS402, Richard Walsh, undated.

3 James Quinn, 'Brugha, Cathal', *Dictionary of Irish Biography* (online), https://www.dib.ie/biography/brugha-cathal-a1077, retrieved October 2021

4 IMA/BMH, WS1447, John Gaynor, 1956

5 Ibid.

6 Ibid.

7 *Irish News*, 1 November 2018

8 IMA/BMH, WS369, William Whelan, 1950

9 IMA/BMH, WS386, Joseph Good, 1956

10 Ibid.

11 Ibid.

12 Ibid.

13 Ibid.

14 Ibid.

15 *Irish Times*, 21 January 2019. My account of the intended assassination of John French is based on evidence from the Bureau of Military History and Dan Breen's account of the incident

16 Ibid.

17 Ibid.

18 Ibid.

19 Charles Townshend, *The Republic: The Fight for Irish Independence, 1918–1923* (London, 2013), p. 299

20 IMA/BMH, WS615, Frank Thornton, 1950

21 IMA/BMH, WS158, Patrick Murray, 1957

22 Ibid.

23 Ibid.

24 IMA/BMH, WS684, George Fitzgerald, 1952

25 IMA/BMH, Patrick Murray

26 Mark Duncan, 'Ireland's Lord Lieutenant: "A Fount of All That Is Slimy in Our National Life"', RTÉ/Century Ireland, https://www.rte.ie/centuryireland/index.php/articles/irelands-lord-lieutenant-a-fount-of-all-that-slimy-in-our-national-life, retrieved October 2021

27 IMA/BMH, WS1716, General Seán MacEoin

28 Ibid.

29 IMA/MSPC, MSP34REF20497, Shaun Cody

30 UCDA, P17b/99, Ahern

31 IMA/MSPC, MSP34REF55889, Mary Egan

32 UCDA, P17b/100, Ernie O'Malley papers, Seán McGrath

33 UCDA, P17b/107, Ernie O'Malley papers, Denis Brennan

34 IMA/MSPC, MSP34REF38812, Denis Brennan

35 IMA/BMH, WS903, Michael Cremen, 1953

36 *Pall Mall Gazette*, 21 June 1922

37 IMA/BMH, WS814, Patrick Daly, 1953

38 Uinseann Mac Eoin (ed.), *Survivors* (Dublin, 1980), pp. 243–4

39 IMA/MSPC, MSP34REF19466, Kelleher

40 IMA/MSPC, WS900, Joe Dolan, 1953

8 AFTERMATH: 'THE ASSASSINATION HAS HORRIFIED THE WHOLE CIVILISED WORLD'

1 Robert C. Self (ed.), *The Austen Chamberlain Diary Letters* (Cambridge, 1995), p. 426

2 'Of the dead nothing but good is to be said' (from the Latin)

3 Jeffery, *Field Marshal Sir Henry Wilson: A Political Soldier*, p. 287

4 *Hansard*, House of Commons debates, 26 June 1922, vol. 155, cc1693–811

5 Ibid., cc1705

6 *Weekly Dispatch*, 25 June 1922

7 *Belfast Newsletter*, 23 June 1922

8 *Belfast Telegraph*, 28 June 1922

9 *Cork Examiner*, 27 June 1922

10 *Evening Echo*, 27 June 1922

11 *The Times*, 23 June 1922

12 *Irish Independent*, 23 June 1922

13 *Belfast Telegraph*, 23 June 1922

14 *New Statesman*, 24 June 1922

15 *Evening Herald*, 23 June 1922

16 *Morning Post*, 24 June 1922

17 *Hansard*, House of Lords debates, 26 June 1922, vol. 50, cc.1150–63

18 Ibid.

19 Ibid.

20 *Irish Independent*, 1 July 1922

21 Ibid., 6 July 1922

22 *Irish Times*, 18 July 1922

23 *Irish Independent*, 23 June 1922

24 *Irish Times*, 23 June 1922

25 *Freeman's Journal*, 23 June 1922

26 *Belfast Newsletter*, 23 June 1922

27 *Belfast Telegraph*, 24 June 1922

28 Ibid.

29 Ibid.

30 'Confidential Report from Count Gerald O'Kelly de Gallagh to Joseph P. Walshe (Dublin) (178/30)', https://www.difp.ie/volume-3/1930/progress-report-on-paris-legation/1102/#section-documentpage, retrieved October 2021

31 *Belfast Telegraph*, 24 June 1922
32 Ibid.
33 *Irish Independent*, 23 June 1922
34 *New York Times*, 23 June 1922
35 *Evening Star*, 23 June 1922
36 *Irish Times*, 23 June 1922
37 UCDA, UCD P150/1588, De Valera papers
38 *Cork Examiner*, 27 June 1922
39 *Evening Echo*, 23 June 1922
40 Ibid.
41 *Freeman's Journal*, 25 July 1922
42 O'Brien memo, 24 June 1922 (NLI, MS 8421/31)
43 *Belfast Newsletter*, 27 June 1922
44 Ibid.
45 *Hansard*, House of Commons debates, 26 June 1922, vol. 50, cc1695–705
46 *Belfast Newsletter*, 27 June 1922
47 *Belfast Telegraph*, 27 June 1922
48 *Belfast Newsletter*, 27 June 1922
49 Marie Coleman, 'O'Connell, Jeremiah Ginger', *Dictionary of Irish Biography* (online), https://www.dib.ie/biography/oconnell-jeremiah-joseph-j-j-ginger-a6561, retrieved October 2021
50 *Hansard*, House of Commons debates, 30 June 1922, vol. 155, cc2551–8. A copy of the proclamation of the Provisional Government was read into the record of the House by Winston Churchill
51 *Belfast Newsletter*, 3 July 1922

9 RESCUE: KIDNAPPING THE PRINCE OF WALES

1 *Cork Evening Echo*, 22 June 1922
2 'Michael Collins', Elections Ireland, https://electionsireland.org/candidate.cfm?ID=6695, retrieved October 2021
3 IMA/BMH, WS945, Diarmada
4 UCDA, P17b/097/098, Ernie O'Malley papers, Joe Sweeney
5 'The Man Who Found a Caravaggio in Dublin', *Irish Times*, 17 February 2018, https://www.irishtimes.com/life-and-style/people/the-man-who-found-a-caravaggio-in-dublin-1.3393582, retrieved October 2021
6 Florence O'Donoghue (ed.), *IRA Jailbreaks 1918–1921* (Dublin, 1971), p. 18
7 Ibid., p. 49
8 Ibid., p. 74
9 *Pall Mall Gazette*, 27 October 1919
10 O'Donoghue, 1971, p. 285
11 Ibid., pp. 181–92
12 UCDA, P17b/99, Ahern
13 IMA/BMH, WS903, Cremen

14 Ibid.
15 Ibid.
16 UCDA, P17b/99, Ahern
17 IMA/MSPC, MSP34REF36970, Ambrose Bettridge
18 TNA, HO144/3689
19 Ibid.
20 *The Times*, 19 July 1922. There are many comprehensive accounts of the trial. *The Times*' account is the most detailed
21 Ibid.
22 Ibid.
23 Ibid.
24 Ibid.
25 Ibid.
26 Ibid.
27 Ibid.
28 Ibid.
29 *Portsmouth Evening News*, 27 July 1933
30 Jeffery, *Field Marshal Sir Henry Wilson: A Political Soldier*, p. 276
31 IMA/MSPC, MSP34REF19466, Kelleher
32 IMA/MSPC, MSP34REF9241, John Joseph Carr
33 Ibid.
34 IMA/MSPC, MSP34REF19466, Kelleher
35 IMA/MSPC, MSP34REF9241, Carr
36 *Evening Echo*, 4 August 1922
37 Ibid.
38 Ibid.
39 *Derry Journal*, 9 August 1922
40 *Irish Independent*, 9 August 1922
41 Ibid.
42 *Daily News*, 10 May 1916
43 *Manchester Guardian*, 8 August 1922
44 UCDA, Document 194, Hugh Kennedy papers
45 *Freeman's Journal*, 10 August 1922

10 EXECUTION: 'THE FELON'S CAP IS THE NOBLEST CROWN AN IRISH HEAD CAN WEAR'
1 National Museum of Ireland Archive (NMIA). The last wills and testaments of Dunne and O'Sullivan are in a tranche of papers sold at auction in 2014 by Whyte's auctioneers in Dublin, comprising the archive of their solicitor James Hyndman MacDonnell. This also contains a copy of Dunne's and O'Sullivan's last letters to their fathers and the petition that was circulated after their trial and sentencing, calling for a reprieve. The archive was purchased at auction by the National Museum of Ireland in Collins Barracks

and remains uncatalogued. The original archive can be seen at https://www.
whytes.ie/art/1922-22-june-assassination-of-sir-henry-wilson-
by-reginald-dunn-and-joseph-osullivan-london-ira/146279/?SearchString=&
LotNumSearch=&GuidePrice=&OrderBy=&ArtistID=&ArrangeBy=list&Nu
mPerPage=15&offset=359, retrieved October 2021

2 Ibid.

3 NLI, MS2653, Dunne

4 Statement of Robert Dunne, House of Lords, Lloyd George papers,
F97/1/230

5 *Daily Express*, 28 June 1922

6 Ibid.

7 NLI, MS2653, Dunne

8 Ibid.

9 Ibid.

10 TNA, HO144/3689

11 Wilfred Owen, 'Dulce et Decorum Est', 1920 (published posthumously)

12 Rupert Brooke, 'The Soldier', 1914

13 Patrick Pearse, *Peace and the Gael* (Dublin, 1915), p. 216

14 *Workers' Republic*, 25 December 1915

15 *Irish Times*, 9 March 2016

16 Ibid.

17 Joe Lee and Brian O'Conchubhair, *Kerry's Fighting Story 1916–1921* (Cork,
2009), p. 163

18 NLI, MS2653, Dunne

19 NMIA holdings, last wills and testaments of Dunne and O'Sullivan

20 Ibid.

21 Ibid.

22 NLI, MS2653, Dunne

23 NMIA holdings, last wills and testaments of Dunne and O'Sullivan

24 NLI, MS2653, Dunne

25 Ibid.

26 *Irish Independent*, 9 August 1922

27 NLI, MS2653, Dunne

28 *Leeds Mercury*, 11 August 1922

29 'Wandsworth Prison, London', Capital Punishment UK, http://www.
capitalpunishmentuk.org/wands.html, retrieved October 2021

30 *Irish Independent*, 12 August 1922

31 Ibid.

32 'President Wilson's Address to Congress, Analyzing German and Austrian
Peace Utterances' (delivered to Congress in Joint Session on 11 February
1918), https://wwi.lib.byu.edu/index.php/President_Wilson%27s_Address_
to_Congress,_Analyzing_German_and_Austrian_Peace_Utterances, retrieved
November 2021

33 Macready, vol. 2, p. 661 (see Chapter 13 for more details)

34 Ibid.

35 Irish Capuchin Archives, *Irish Bulletin*, 5 June 1922

36 *Irish Bulletin*, 5 June 1921

37 *Irish Independent*, 12 August 1922

38 Ibid.

11 THE IRISH CIVIL WAR: 'THE MADNESS FROM WITHIN'

1 Hopkinson, *Green Against Green*, p. 182

2 Tim Pat Coogan, *De Valera: Long Fellow, Long Shadow* (London, 2015), p. 284

3 Ibid., p. 287

4 *Cork Examiner*, 27 March 1922

5 Ibid., 31 March 1922

6 *Cork Examiner*, 10 April 1922

7 Ibid.

8 Hopkinson, *Green Against Green*, p. 72

9 *Irish Independent*, 27 March 1922

10 Ibid., 3 April 1922

11 Dorothy Macardle, *The Irish Republic* (Dublin, 1937), p. 714

12 The text of the Anglo-Irish Treaty is at https://cain.ulster.ac.uk/issues/politics/docs/ait1921.htm

13 *Hansard*, House of Commons debates, 31 May 1922, vol. 50, cc884–908

14 Ibid., c2197

15 *Irish Times*, 6 June 1922

16 T. Ryle Dwyer, *'I Signed My Death Warrant': Michael Collins & the Treaty* (Cork, 2006), p. 278

17 Hopkinson, *Green Against Green*, p. 115

18 Whyte's auctioneers, copy of the Proclamation, https://www.whytes.ie/art/1922-28-june-proclamation-at-the-four-courts-by-the-anti-treatyira-forces-the-start-of-the-civil-war/127339/?SearchString=&LotNum-Search=&GuidePrice=&OrderBy=&ArtistID=&ArrangeBy=list&NumPer-Page=15&offset=108, retrieved November 2021

19 Michael Gallagher, 'The Pact General Election of 1922', *Irish Historical Studies*, vol. 22, no. 84 (September 1979), pp. 404–21

20 Fewer, p. 152

21 Hopkinson, *Green Against Green*, p. 121

22 Michael Fewer, 'What Really Happened in the Four Courts at the Start of the Civil War', *Irish Times*, 3 December 2018, https://www.irishtimes.com/culture/books/what-really-happened-in-the-four-courts-at-the-start-of-the-civil-war-1.3718291, retrieved October 2021

23 Ernie O'Malley, *The Singing Flame* (Dublin, 1978), p. 114

24 Caitriona Crowe, 'Ruin of Public Record Office Marked Loss of Great archive', *Irish Times*, 30 June 2012, https://www.irishtimes.com/opinion/

ruin-of-public-record-office-marked-loss-of-great-archive-1.1069843,
retrieved October 2021.

25 Ibid.

26 Trinity College Dublin, 'A Calendar of Irish Chancery Letters, c.1944–1509',
https://chancery.tcd.ie/content/destruction-irish-chancery-rolls-1304-1922,
retrieved January 2022

27 Ibid.

28 O'Malley, p. 102

29 Quinn, 'Brugha, Cathal'

30 'When Ruairí Met Máire' (TG4 Leargás), YouTube, 2003, https://www.
youtube.com/watch?v=nTXa1lNRHj4, retrieved October 2021

31 Hopkinson, *Green Against Green*, p. 124

32 William Murphy, 'Lynch, William Fanaghan (Liam)', *Dictionary of Irish
Biography* (online), https://www.dib.ie/biography/lynch-william-fanaghan-
liam-a4949, retrieved October 2021

33 Hopkinson, *Green Against Green*, p. 128–9

34 Ibid., pp. 147–8

35 Ibid., pp. 154–5

36 Ibid., p. 152

37 Ibid., pp. 142–71

38 Ibid., pp. 198–9

39 IMA/MSPC, MSP34REF57116, O'Sullivan

40 Hopkinson, *Green Against Green*, p. 164

41 *Irish Independent*, 11 August 1922

42 Ibid.

43 Colum Kenny, *The Enigma of Arthur Griffith: 'Father of Us All'* (Newbridge,
2020), p. 1

44 Dáil Éireann debate, 7 January 1922, vol. T, no. 15

45 *Westmeath Independent*, 19 August 1922

46 *Irish Times*, 3 June 2020

47 INA, FIN/COMP/2/14/21, James Mackay Wilson compensation file

48 *Longford Leader*, 3 May 1924

49 Thomas Mohr, 'Religious Minorities Under the Constitution of the Irish
Free State, 1922–1937', *American Journal of Legal History*, vol. 61, issue 2, June
2021, pp. 235–72

50 Interview with Doug Armstrong, grandson of James Armstrong, by the
author

51 Ronan McGreevy, *Wherever the Firing Line Extends: Ireland and the Western
Front* (Dublin, 2016), pp. 324–37

52 Terence Dooley, 'The Tale of Ireland's "House Burning Mania" of 1919–
1923', *Country Life* online, https://www.countrylife.co.uk/architecture/
the-tale-of-irelands-house-burning-mania-of-1919-1923-221446, retrieved
October 2021

53 UCDA, P67/2, Twomey papers, Liam Lynch, IRA General Orders 9/12/22

54 Hopkinson, *Green Against Green*, p. 221

55 Collins to Joe O'Reilly, widely reported since then

56 T. Ryle Dwyer, 'Michael Collins and the Civil War', in John Crowley, John Borgonovo, Mike Murphy, Donal Ó Drisceoil and Nick Hogan (eds), *Atlas of the Irish Revolution* (Cork, 2017), pp. 725–9. There are many accounts of Collins's last journey. See also S. M. Sigerson, *The Assassination of Michael Collins: What Happened at Béal na mBláth?* (Loughborough, 2013)

57 Joe Connell, 'A Timeline of Michael Collins' Death in August 1922', Irish Central, https://www.irishcentral.com/roots/history/michael-collins-death-timeline, retrieved October 2021

58 Ibid.

59 'Emmet Dalton Remembers', 1978 RTÉ documentary, YouTube, https://www.youtube.com/watch?v=SLrGnImYCwU&t=586s, retrieved October 2021

60 Coogan, *Michael Collins*, p. 364

61 'Emmet Dalton Remembers', 1978 RTÉ documentary

62 'The Shadow of Béal na mBláth', 1991 RTÉ documentary, YouTube, https://www.youtube.com/watch?v=8k4kFtHKc4A&list=PLF7667FA2D605E4B1P, retrieved October 2021

63 IMA, Department of Defence file 2/21085 (1924)

64 *Irish Times*, 22 August 2021

65 See Paddy Cullivan's website, https://www.paddycullivan.com/event-details/the-murder-of-michael-collins

66 Tom Barry, p. 183

67 Coogan, *Michael Collins*, p. 382. De Valera is alleged to have made the comments to Joe McGrath, a former IRA volunteer and prominent businessman, in 1966, when de Valera was asked to be the patron of the Michael Collins Foundation. The quote is disputed

68 Patrick J. Twohig, *The Dark Secret of Béalnablath: The Michael Collins Story* (Cork, 1991), p. 64

69 Kevin O'Higgins, 'The Quenching of Our Shining Light', in Sean Ghall et al., *Arthur Griffith, Michael Collins* (Dublin, 1923), p. 42

70 Eunan O'Halpin, *Defending Ireland: The Irish State and Its Enemies Since 1922* (Oxford, 1999), p. 11

71 Dáil Éireann, 10 January 1922, vol. T, no. 17

72 *Irish Times*, 11 December 2015

73 Ibid.

74 Ibid.

75 Ibid.

76 *Irish Times*, 4 December 1922

77 Maryann Gialanella Valiulis, *Portrait of a Revolutionary: General Richard Mulcahy and the Founding of the Irish Free State* (Newbridge, 1998), p. 181

78 Dáil Éireann, 8 December 1922, vol. 2, no. 3

79 Stephen Collins, 'On the Run and in Disguise: Why WT Cosgrave Dressed Up as "Br Doyle" and Dyed His Hair Blazing Red', *Irish Times*, 18 October 2014, https://www.irishtimes.com/news/politics/on-the-run-and-in-disguise-why-wt-cosgrave-dressed-up-as-br-doyle-and-dyed-his-hair-blazing-red-1.1967433, retrieved October 2021

80 Ibid.

81 Hopkinson, *Green Against Green*, pp. 240–1

82 'No Other Law'; text of Éamon de Valera's proclamation can be found at http://www.nootherlaw.com/archive/legion-of-the-rearguard.html, retrieved October 2021

83 Hopkinson, *Green Against Green*, p. 273

84 IMA/MSPC, Patrick Murray

85 Dáil Éireann, 20 March 1923, vol. T, no. 41

86 Mary MacDiarmada, *Art O'Brien and Irish Nationalism in London, 1900–25* (Dublin, 2020), p. 173

87 Tim Pat Coogan, quoted in 'The Madness from Within', RTÉ TV documentary broadcast in 1998

12 REPATRIATION: 'THE IRISH GOVERNMENT'S ATTITUDE IS STRICTLY ILLOGICAL'

1 'A Brief History of the National Graves Association', http://www.nga.ie/history.php, retrieved October 2021

2 TNA, DO 182/137, 'Repatriation of the Remains of Joseph O'Sullivan and Reginald Dunne', formerly 2-WES 9/207/3. Copies of most of these documents are in the Irish National Archives at DFA/10/2/484.

3 Peter Hart, 'Michael Collins and the Assassination of Sir Henry Wilson', *Irish Historical Studies*, vol. 28, no. 110 (Nov. 1992), p. 158

4 NLI, MS8430, O'Brien papers. Copies of several letters from Mary Dunne are in this collection

5 IMA/BMH, WS902, MacGeehin

6 Ibid.

7 Diarmaid Ferriter, 'Revolutionary Ireland: Defiance, Youth and Pessimism', *Irish Times*, 15 October 2019, https://www.irishtimes.com/culture/heritage/revolutionary-ireland-defiance-youth-and-pessimism-1.4037518, retrieved October 2021

8 Diarmaid Ferriter, 'A Window into the Soul of Ireland', *Irish Times*, 17 January 2014, https://www.irishtimes.com/culture/heritage/a-window-into-the-soul-of-ireland-1.1657510, retrieved October 2021

9 IMA/MSPC, DP1462. The file relates to claims made by Mary Dunne for a dependant's allowance in respect of her son Reginald Dunne

10 Ibid.

11 Ibid.

12 Ibid.

13 Ibid.
14 John O'Sullivan's application for a dependant's allowance includes testimonials from Art O'Brien and Seán McGrath
15 Ibid.
16 IMA/MSPC, MSP34REF57116, O'Sullivan
17 IMA/MSPC, MSP34REF19466, Kelleher
18 Email correspondence with author
19 *Southern Star*, 15 September 2018
20 Marie Coleman, 'Maguire, Sam', *Dictionary of Irish Biography* (online), https://www.dib.ie/biography/maguire-sam-a5365, retrieved October 2021
21 *Sunday Press*, 6 September 1953
22 Rex Taylor, pp. 211–19
23 *Sunday Press*, 13 September 1953
24 Ibid.
25 NLI, MS31, 285 (1–4), Florence O'Donoghue papers
26 Ibid.
27 Ibid.
28 Ibid.
29 Ibid.
30 Ibid.
31 Rex Taylor, pp. 211–19
32 *Sunday Press*, 10 August 1958
33 Ibid.
34 McGreevy, pp. 70–6
35 *Irish Times*, 14 April 2014
36 Alison Garden, *The Literary Afterlives of Roger Casement, 1899–2016* (Oxford, 2020), p. 105
37 Roger Casement's speech from the dock: Speakola.com, https://speakola.com/political/roger-casement-speech-from-dock-2011, retrieved October 2021
38 Lucy McDiarmid, *The Irish Art of Controversy* (Cornell, 2005), p. 186
39 Chris Reeves, 'The Penultimate Irish Problem: Britain, Ireland and the Exhumation of Roger Casement', *Irish Studies in International Affairs*, vol. 12 (2001), pp. 151–78
40 Ibid.
41 *Irish Times*, 2 June 2018; see also UCDA, P311, Seán Lemass's interviews with Dermot A. Ryan
42 Ibid.
43 *Irish Independent*, 2 March 1965
44 Julian B. Knowles, 'The Abolition of the Death Penalty in the United Kingdom', Death Penalty Project, https://www.deathpenaltyproject.org/wp-content/uploads/2017/12/DPP-50-Years-on-pp1-68-1.pdf, retrieved October 2021
45 TNA, PCOM 8/367; INA, DFA/10/2/484
46 Ibid.

47 Ibid.
48 Ibid.
49 Ibid.
50 Ibid.
51 See photographic plate
52 The inscription in Irish on the gravestone reads: *I ndil-cúimne ar Ragnall ua Duinn, Ceann cata oglaigh na hÉireann agus ar Seosam Ua Súilleabain oglac, a tug a n-anamana ar son na h-éireann i Sasanaib (Wandsworth Prison) an 10 lá na Mí na Lugnasa 1922, Ar déir dé go raib a n-anmain.* National Graves Association Archive (shown to the author by NGA chairman Matt Doyle)
53 NGI archives
54 Callwell, vol. 1, p. viii
55 *New York Times*, 6 October 1927
56 David Lloyd George, *War Memoirs*, vol. 5 (London, 1933), p. 2,818
57 Jeffery, *Field Marshal Sir Henry Wilson: A Political Soldier*, p. viii
58 Peter Taylor, *Brits: The War Against the IRA* (London, 2001), p. 265
59 Henry Hill ('Portcullis'), 'A Shield for Sir Henry', *The Critic*, 16 July 2021, https://thecritic.co.uk/a-shield-for-sir-henry, retrieved October 2021. See also Alistair Lexden, 'Remembering Sir Henry Wilson, the MP the IRA Assassinated – and the Commons Forgot', Conservativehome.com, https://www.conservativehome.com/platform/2021/08/alistair-lexden-remembering-sir-henry-wilson-the-mp-the-ira-assassinated-and-the-commons-forgot.html, retrieved October 2021
60 BBC One, *Peaky Blinders* TV series, series 2, episode 6 (2014). Writer/creator: Steven Knight

13 CONCLUSION: IRELAND'S SARAJEVO
1 Fritz Stern, quoted in David Fromkin, *Europe's Last Summer: Who Started the Great War in 1914?* (New York, 2004), p. 6
2 O'Malley, p. 81
3 NLI, MS2653, Dunne
4 UCDA, P7/A/29, Richard Mulcahy papers, 'Report on a Visit to Britain, September 1921'
5 NLI, MS31, 285 (1–4), Florence O'Donoghue papers
6 *Irish Press*, 25 June 1968
7 *Irish Press*, 25 December 1948. This is the first time that Dunne's account of the shooting is made public
8 Hart, 'Michael Collins and the Assassination of Sir Henry Wilson', p. 170
9 Ulick O'Connor, *Michael Collins and the Troubles* (New York, 1996), pp. 195–6
10 UCDA, P17b/99, Ahern
11 IMA/BMH, WS No.3, Liam O'Briain
12 Seán MacCraith, UCDA, P17b/100, Ernie O'Malley papers
13 *Irish Independent*, 12 August 1922

14 Coogan, *Michael Collins*, p. 333

15 Anne Dolan and William Murphy, *Michael Collins: The Man and the Revolution* (Cork, 2018), p. 194

16 Coogan, *Michael Collins*, p. 334

17 *Cork Examiner*, 15 March 1922

18 Coogan, *Michael Collins*, p. 341

19 IMA/BMH, Document No. 247, Dunne statement

20 Tom Jones, *Whitehall Diaries*, vol. 3 (London, 1969), p. 202

21 Ibid., p. 198

22 Coogan, *Michael Collins*, p. 376

23 'The Irish Republican Brotherhood', That Irishman, http://thatirishman. com/the-irish-republican-brotherhood/, retrieved October 2021

24 IMA/BMH, WS897, Patrick Sarsfield (P. S.) O'Hegarty, 1953

25 Dolan and Murphy, p. 322

26 Coogan, *Michael Collins*, p. 376

27 Email correspondence with author

28 Rex Taylor, p. 114

29 Macready, vol. 2, p. 660

30 Ibid.

31 Ibid., p. 661

32 *Daily Mail*, 23 June 1922

33 Imperial War Museum Holdings, 'A Catalogue of the Papers of Field Marshal Sir Henry Wilson (1864–1922)', 1/1–1/41, personal diaries 1883–1922

34 Florence O'Donoghue, *No Other Law* (Dublin, 1954), p. 255

35 Rex Taylor, p. 116

36 Nigel Collett, *The Butcher of Amritsar: General Reginald Dyer* (London, 2006), p. 361

37 Ignatius of Loyola, *The Jesuit Catechism* (London, 1681), p. 14

38 Rabbi Jonathan Sacks, *Not in God's Name: Confronting Religious Violence* (London, 2015), p. 205

39 Coogan, *Michael Collins*, p. 164

40 *Irish Independent*, 12 August 1922

41 *Los Angeles Times*, 19 April 1990

42 Rex Taylor, p. 117

43 NLI, 'Remembrance: Reginald Dunne and Joe O'Sullivan', London Memorial Committee, Florence O'Donoghue papers (1954)

44 IMA/MSPC, DP6925, John O'Sullivan

45 Parkinson, p. 522

46 Ash, p. 278

47 *Evening Herald*, 15 April 1930

48 Christopher Magill, *Political Conflict in East Ulster, 1920–22: Revolution and Reprisal* (Woodbridge, Suffolk), 2020, p. 108

49 *Irish Independent*, 23 June 1922

Select Bibliography

Ash, Bernard, *The Lost Dictator: Field Marshal Sir Henry Wilson* (London, 1968)

Barry, Michael, *Fake News and the War of Independence* (Dublin, 2021)

Barry, Tom, *Guerilla Days in Ireland* (Dublin, 1949)

Bew, Paul, *Ireland: The Politics of Enmity 1789–2006* (Oxford, 2007)

Callwell, Sir Charles, *Field Marshal Sir Henry Wilson: His Life and Diaries*, 2 vols (London, 1927)

Churchill, Winston, *The World Crisis 1911–1918* (New York, 1923)

Collett, Nigel, *The Butcher of Amritsar: General Reginald Dyer* (London, 2006)

Coogan, Tim Pat, *De Valera: Long Fellow, Long Shadow* (London, 2015)

—— *Michael Collins: The Man Who Made Ireland* (Dublin, 2002)

Dháibhéid, Caoimhe Nic, *Seán MacBride: A Republican Life 1904–1946* (Liverpool, 2011)

Dolan, Anne, and William Murphy, *Michael Collins: The Man and the Revolution* (Cork, 2018)

Dwyer, T. Ryle, 'Michael Collins and the Civil War', in John Crowley, John Borgonovo, Mike Murphy, Donal Ó Drisceoil and Nick Hogan (eds), *Atlas of the Irish Revolution* (Cork, 2017), pp. 725–9

Esher, Viscount Reginald, *The Tragedy of Lord Kitchener* (London, 1921)

Ferriter, Diarmaid, *The Transformation of Ireland 1900–2000* (London, 2004)

Fewer, Michael, *The Battle of the Four Courts* (Croydon, 2018)

Fitzpatrick, David, 'Irish Emigration in the Later 19th Century', *Irish Historical Studies*, vol. 22, no. 86 (September 1980), pp. 126–43

Fletcher, C. R. L., and Rudyard Kipling, *A School History of England* (Oxford, 1911)

French, Sir John, *1914* (London, 1919)

Fromkin, David, *Europe's Last Summer: Who Started the Great War in 1914?* (New York, 2004)

Garden, Alison, *The Literary Afterlives of Roger Casement, 1899–2016* (Oxford, 2020)

Glennon, Kieran, *From Pogrom to Civil War: Tom Glennon and the Belfast IRA* (Cork, 2013)

Gwynn, Stephen, *John Redmond's Last Years* (New York, 1919)

Hart, Peter, 'Michael Collins and the Assassination of Sir Henry Wilson', *Irish Historical Studies*, vol. 28, no. 110 (November 1992), pp. 150–70

—— 'Operations Abroad: The IRA in Britain 1919–1923', *The English Historical Review*, vol. 115, no. 460 (February 2000), pp. 71–102

Hemingway, Ernest, *The Sun Also Rises* (New York, 1926)

Hopkinson, Michael, 'The Craig–Collins Pacts of 1922: Two Attempted Reforms of the Northern Ireland Government', *Irish Historical Studies*, vol. 27, no. 106 (November 1990), pp. 145–58

—— *Green Against Green: The Irish Civil War* (Dublin, 2004)

Ignatius of Loyola, *The Jesuit Catechism* (London, 1681)

Jackson, Alvin, *Home Rule: An Irish History 1800–2000* (London, 2003)

Jeffery, Keith, 'Field Marshal Sir Henry Wilson: Myths and the

Man', *Journal of the Society for Army Historical Research*, vol. 86, no. 345 (Spring 2008), pp. 57–82

—— *Field Marshal Sir Henry Wilson: A Political Soldier* (Oxford, 2006)

—— *The Military Correspondence of Field Marshal Sir Henry Wilson* (London, 1985)

Jones, Tom, *Whitehall Diaries*, vol. 3 (London, 1969)

Keegan, John, *The First World War* (London, 1999)

Kenny, Colum, *The Enigma of Arthur Griffith: 'Father of Us All'* (Newbridge, 2020)

Kipling, Rudyard, *The Irish Guards in the Great War: The First Battalion* (New York, 1923)

Lee, Joe, *The Modernisation of Irish Society 1848–1918* (Dublin, 1973)

—— and Brian O'Conchubhair, *Kerry's Fighting Story 1916–1921* (Cork, 2009)

Lewis, Matthew, 'The Fourth Northern Division and the Joint IRA Offensive, April–July 1922', *War in History*, vol. 21, no. 3 (July 2014)

Lloyd George, David, *War Memoirs*, vol. 5 (London, 1933)

Lydon, James, *The Making of Ireland: From Ancient Times to the Present* (Oxford, 1998)

Lynch, Robert John, *The Northern IRA and the Early Years of Partition 1920–1922* (Dublin, 2006)

Mac Eoin, Uinseann (ed.), *Survivors* (Dublin, 1980)

Macardle, Dorothy, *The Irish Republic* (Dublin, 1937)

MacDiarmada, Mary, *Art O'Brien and Irish Nationalism in London, 1900–25* (Dublin, 2020)

McDiarmid, Lucy, *The Irish Art of Controversy* (Cornell, 2005)

McGilligan, Patrick, *Alfred Hitchcock: A Life in Darkness and Light* (London, 2004)

McGreevy, Ronan, *Wherever the Firing Line Extends: Ireland and the Western Front* (Dublin, 2016)

McMahon, Paul, *British Spies and Irish Rebels: British Intelligence and Ireland 1916–1945* (Woodbridge, 2008)

Macready, General Sir Nevil, *Annals of an Active Life*, 2 vols (London, 1924)

Magill, Christopher, *Political Conflict in East Ulster, 1920–22: Revolution and Reprisal* (Woodbridge, 2020)

Manchester, William, *The Last Lion: Winston Spencer Churchill, Visions of Glory 1874–1932* (London, 2015)

Molony, Senan, *The Phoenix Park Murders: Conspiracy, Betrayal and Retribution* (Cork, 2006)

Murphy, William, *Political Imprisonment and the Irish, 1912–1921* (Oxford, 2008)

Noonan, Gerard, The *IRA in Britain, 1919–1921: 'In the Heart of Enemy Lines'* (Liverpool, 2014)

O'Connor, Ulick, *Michael Collins and the Troubles* (New York, 1996)

O'Donoghue, Florence, *No Other Law* (Dublin, 1954)

—— (ed.), *IRA Jailbreaks 1918–1921* (Dublin, 1971)

O'Halpin, Eunan, *Defending Ireland: The Irish State and Its Enemies since 1922* (Oxford, 1999)

O'Higgins, Kevin, 'The Quenching of Our Shining Light', in Sean Ghall et al., *Arthur Griffith, Michael Collins* (Dublin, 1923)

O'Malley, Ernie, *The Singing Flame* (Dublin, 1978)

Parkinson, Alan F., *A Difficult Birth: The Early Years of Northern Ireland, 1920–25* (Dublin, 2020)

Pearse, Patrick, *Peace and the Gael* (Dublin, 1915)

Self, Robert C. (ed.), *The Austen Chamberlain Diary Letters* (Cambridge, 1995)

Sigerson, S. M., *The Assassination of Michael Collins: What Happened at Béal na mBláth?* (Loughborough, 2013)

Swift, Roger, and Sheridan Gilley (eds), *The Irish in Britain, 1815–1939* (Maryland, 1989)

Taylor, Peter, *Brits: The War Against the IRA* (London, 2001)

Taylor, Rex, *Assassination: The Death of Sir Henry Wilson and the Tragedy of Ireland* (Michigan, 1961)

Townshend, Charles, *The Republic: The Fight for Irish Independence, 1918–1923* (London, 2013)

Twohig, Patrick J., *The Dark Secret of Béalnablath: The Michael Collins Story* (Cork, 1991)

Valiulis, Maryann Gialanella, *Portrait of a Revolutionary: General Richard Mulcahy and the Founding of the Irish Free State* (Newbridge, 1998)

White, Terence de Vere, *Kevin O'Higgins* (Kerry, 1966)

Wilson, J. Mackay, 'Bird Life at Currygrane, Co. Longford', *The Irish Naturalist*, vol. 27, no. 7 (July 1918), p. 11

Winston, Ruth, *Events, Dear Boy* (London, 2012)

Index

Page numbers for illustrations are shown in *italics*. HW = Henry Wilson

Act of Union (1800), 49, 53
Agadir Crisis (1911), 61
Ahern, William 'Billy,' 152, 154, 157, 186, 207, 252, 255, 338, 371–2
Aiken, Frank, 119, 329, 337–8, 357
Altnaveigh massacre (1922), 120
Amritsar massacre (1919), 388
Anderson, Sir John, 255–6
Anglo-Irish Treaty (1921): boundary provisions, 112–13, 375; Collins negotiates, 21, 26–7, 98, 377; Collins fails to respect, 211–12, 374–6; creation of Irish Free State, 26, 29, 98; Dáil passes, 241; depicted in Mac Eoin memorial, 44; Griffith's role, 315–16; HW's opinions, 8, 98–9, 387–8; IRA's divided opinions, 160–2, 188, 211, 212–13, 295, 297; oath of allegiance, 26–7, 29, 98, 298, 300, 301, 331; *see also* Craig–Collins pacts; Irish Free State; Provisional Government
anti-Treaty IRA: formation and constitution, 296–7; seize *Upnor*, 296; in Britain, illegal deportation, 330–1; size and weaponry, 296, 302, 310; *see also* Four Courts occupation (1922); Irish Civil War (1922–3)
arms supply to IRA, 152–5, 172, 181, 185–6, 187, 209–10, 330
Armstrong, James, 316, 317, 319
Armstrong, Robert, 318–19
Army Emergency Powers Resolution (1922), 325, 328
Army Mutiny (1924), 342
Arran, Earl of (Viscount Sudley), 266
arson: in Britain, War of Independence, 158, 159, 182; Currygrane House, 45, 316; during Irish Civil War, 313, 319, 330
Ash, Bernard, 47, 67, 394–5
Ashe, Thomas, 279
Asquith, Herbert, 19, 20, 65, 66, 67, 69, 76–7
assassination, morality of, 389–90

assassination of Archduke Franz Ferdinand, 22, 366
assassination of HW: planning, 208–10, 211, 212–17; Collins's involvement (disputed), 343–8, 356, 368, 373–83; other theories about, 368–73; third man (Kelleher), 215–16, 341–2, 346–7; assassination, 10–13, 17, 236, 245, 259; pursuit and arrest of assassins, 14–17, 236; news travels to Westminster, 17–21, *17*, 22–3; political response, 20, 21, 219–20, 225–6, 232–3; press response, 222–32, 232, 242; Four Courts garrison response, 233; royal response, 23, 24, 221; other arrests, 234–5; inquest, 235–6; IRA denies involvement, 334; influence on Irish Civil War, 367; impact on Belfast pogroms, 393, 394; *see also* Dunne, Reginald 'Reggie'; O'Sullivan, Joseph 'Joe'
assassinations, political (other), 22, 190–1, 364
Aston, Ernest Albert (E. A.), 93–5
Auxiliaries, 85, 184–5

Balfour, Arthur, Lord, 205, 240, 369
Bantry Bay, role in Irish history, *42*, 164–7
Barrow, Sir George, 6
Barry, Kevin, 92–5
Barry, Tom, 167–8, 174–5, 301, 323
Barton, Robert, 250
Bathurst, Lord and Lady, 226
Battle of Dublin (1922), 307–8
Battle of Passchendaele (1917), 10, 177–8
Battle of the Boyne (1690), 50–1
Battle of the Marne (1914), 69
Battle of the Somme (1916), 37, 103, 176; Ulster Tower memorial, 103–4
Beardsley, Aubrey, 275
Belfast Boycott, 35, 36, 112, 297
Belfast pogroms (1920–2), 106–7, 108–12, 113–14, 115–20, *116*, 291–2; HW's role and opinions, 114–15, 120–3, 125–6, 389; impact of HW's assassination on, 393, 394; statistics, 34–5, 106, 111, 113, 114; *see also* War of Independence (1919–21)

Belfast Protestants' Association, 109–10
Birkenhead, Earl of, 226
Birrell, Augustine, 43–4
Black and Tans, 85
Boer War (1899–1902), 58–9
Boland, Harry, 325, 331
Bonar Law, Andrew, 198–9, 221–2, 242
border tensions and warfare (1922), 126–8
Breen, Dan, 201, 202
Brennan, Denis, 212–13
Brooke, Rupert, 278
Browne, Agnes and Martin, 153–4
Brugha, Cathal, 193, 194, 195, 196, 197–9,
    206, 207–8, 209, 307–8
Burke, Henry, 190, 191, 224
Butt, Isaac, 53–4
Byrne, Vincent 'Vinny', 200

Callwell, Major General Sir Charles, 56, 57,
    59, 82, 83, 125–6, 360–1, 363
Carr, Denis, 149, 153, 154–5
Carr, John Joseph (J. J.), 149, 153, 154–5,
    210, 264–5, 266
Carson, Edward, Lord, 20, 64, 67, 104, 108,
    240
Carter, Colonel J. F. C., 256
Carty, Frank, 251–2
Casement, Sir Roger, 279, 287, 349–54
Catholicism: in British schools, 141, 143;
    of Dunne, 131, 141, 272, 273, 276–7,
    285–6, 369, 389; Ne Temere decree, 318;
    of O'Sullivan, 276–7, 282–4, 285–6, 369,
    389
Cavendish, Frederick, Lord, 190, 191, 224
Chamberlain, Austen, 20, 218–19
Childers, Erskine, 325–7
Churchill, Winston: supports home
    rule, 64; on War of Independence, 28,
    113–14, 117; on electoral pact, 299;
    on Public Records Office destruction,
    306; intervenes in border warfare, 127;
    defends police protection removal,
    220; demands action over Four Courts
    occupation, 31, 34, 241–3; describes HW
    in The World Crisis, 62, 74
Clones Affray, 113
Collins, Michael, 25, 325; birthplace,
    42, 167; time in London, 133–5; head
    of IRB, 380; IRA Squad, 200, 377–8;
    organises jailbreaks, 250; seeks IRA
    publicity, 157, 158; and attacks on
    British government, 202–6, 208; and
    Fovargue's shooting, 183–4; meets
    Dunne and O'Sullivan, 188; negotiates
    Anglo-Irish Treaty, 21, 26–7, 98, 377;

fails to respect Treaty, 211–12, 374–6;
    Craig–Collins pacts, 34–5, 112–13,
    117–18; organises Northern Offensive,
    118–19, 375; criticises HW, 124, 128,
    129, 375–6, 377; and 1922 election,
    247–8, 298, 300–1; involvement in HW's
    assassination (disputed), 343–8, 356, 368,
    373–83; response to HW's assassination,
    248–9; response to Griffith's death, 315;
    ambush and killing, 320–3; funeral, 325;
    reaction to death, 323–4; biographers, see
    Coogan, Tim Pat; Dolan, Anne; Murphy,
    William; O'Connor, Ulick; The Path to
    Freedom, 324; public opinions of, 24–5,
    323–4; quoted, 124–5, 128, 135, 248,
    315, 390
communism, HW's views on, 77, 80, 126
Connolly, James, 278, 279
conscription: HW supports, 60, 73, 74; in
    Ireland, plans for (1918), 73, 147, 192–3,
    199; in rest of UK (1916), 73, 144, 191–2
Coogan, Tim Pat, 374–5, 380, 382
Cork, Civil War violence, 309, 312–13
Cosgrave, William T., 315, 319, 328–9, 336
Cowes Week, regatta, 262–3, 263
Craig–Collins pacts, 34–5, 112–13, 117–18
Craig, Sir James: establishes USC, 110–11;
    response to Weaver St bombing, 114;
    HW advises, 120–2, 123, 376; response
    to HW's assassination, 47; other
    mentions, 104, 375
Cremen, Michael, 213, 253–4
Cullen, Tom, 249, 253, 254, 334–5, 383
Cullivan, Paddy, 323
Cumann na mBan (female IRA auxiliary),
    151–2, 210, 213–14, 295
Curragh Incident (1914), 64–7
Currygrane House and estate, 39–46, 40,
    42, 51, 81, 316–17, 317, 318, 319
Curtain, Tomás Mac, 110

Dáil Éireann (Assembly of Ireland):
    establishment, 28, 78–9; Belfast Boycott,
    112; see also de Valera, Éamon; Griffith,
    Arthur
Dalton, Major General Emmet, 36–7,
    308–9, 311, 313, 320, 321, 322, 324
Daly, Patrick, 214
de Gallagh, Count Gerald O'Kelly, 230
de Valera, Éamon, 325; prison escape,
    250; Churchill on, 241; on HW's
    assassination, 212, 233; Fianna Fáil party
    enters Dáil, 298; appeals for Casement's
    repatriation, 351–2; speaks at Casement's
    funeral, 353–4; on Collins, 324;

rhetorical style, 294; other mentions, 192, 297, 300, 337, 338
Diehards, 105–6, 123
Dillon, Seán 'John', 182–3, 209
Dolan, Anne, 381–2
Dolan, Joe, 215–16, 343–4
Donoughmore, Earl of, 225
Doyle, Martin, 173–4
Dublin, 295; Battle of Dublin, 307–8; Celtic cross memorial to Dunne and O'Sullivan, 333; graves of Dunne and O'Sullivan, 359, 396; IRA conventions, 295–7; Public Records Office destruction, 303–6, 304; see also Four Courts occupation (1922)
Dunne, Mary (Reggie's mother), 132, 135, 272–3, 282, 284, 285, 334–5, 336–8, 383
Dunne, Reginald 'Reggie', 12, 147; early life and family, 42, 132, 135–6, 140–1, 143, 389; response to Easter Rising, 143–4; serves with Irish Guards, 11, 140, 141, 144–6, 277, 368; attends college, 146–7, 147; IRA/IRB activities, 148, 149, 150–1, 155, 184, 185, 188, 206–7, 210, 211, 369; response to MacSwiney's hunger strike, 279; views on Anglo-Irish Treaty, 160–1, 162–3; response to Belfast pogroms, 117, 291–2; Cumann na mBan accuse of cowardice, 213–14; plots to assassinate HW, 210, 212–17, 380–1; theories about assassination order, 368–83; assassinates HW, 11–13, 245, 259; pursuit and arrest, 14–17, 15, 236; appears in Police Court, 234, 245, 246; awaits trial, 131, 136–7, 272–3, 275–6; IRA rescue plans, 249, 252–6; trial and appeal, 227–8, 246, 258–62, 266–7; public petition and support, 267–71, 281–2; awaits execution, 141, 145, 272, 276–7, 280, 281, 282, 284, 285; execution, 285–7, 286, 313; will, 272, 279; early requests for reburial, 333–4; memorial, 333; posthumous reputation, 343–8, 355–6, 393; exhumation and reburial, 354–60, 358, 396; adopted Irish identity, 391–2; appearance, 11, 158; Catholicism, 131, 141, 272, 273, 276–7, 285–6, 369, 389; influence on Hitchcock, 141–3; love of music, 135–7, 140, 274; mental health, 146–7; personality, 11, 131, 150, 160; quoted (court addresses), 260–1; quoted (disallowed court statement), 288–92, 374, 378, 391; quoted (letters home), 131, 136–7, 141, 272–3, 275–6, 282, 284, 368; quoted (other letters), 160–1

Dunne, Robert (Reggie's father), 132, 135, 140–1, 273–5, 334–5, 383
Dyer, General Reginald, 388

Eadie, Katie, 235
Easter Rising (1916): background, 68, 278; German support, 350; rebellion and fighters, 70–1, 134, 140, 143–4, 193–4, 197, 352; aftermath, 71, 144, 147, 278–9
Egan, Mary, 210
electoral pact (1922), 30, 298–301
Ellis, John, 212, 287
Ennis, Tom, 37–8
Eoin, Seán Mac ('Blacksmith of Ballinalee'), 44–5
Esher, Lord: The Tragedy of Lord Kitchener, 62, 68
exhumation from prison grounds and repatriation: legality, 349, 354; Casement, 351–4; Dunne and O'Sullivan, 354–60, 358, 396

farmers, land ownership, 53
farms, IRA attacks on, 158, 159, 182
Fenian movement, 52–3, 150, 167, 186, 190–1
Fenian rebellion (1867), 52–3
Ferdinand, Franz, assassination, 22, 366
First World War: prelude to and HW's preparations, 60–2, 68, 366; German POW camp, 349–50; Battle of the Marne (1914), 69; German bombing campaigns, 2–3; Battle of the Somme, see Battle of the Somme (1916); Battle of Passchendaele (1917), 10, 177–8; German Spring Offensive (1918), 72–4, 145, 192; end of, 6, 74; army demobilisation, 74, 77; HW's role in, 3, 6–7, 21, 60, 68–70, 71–4, 81, 230–1; Irish Guards and battalions, 144–6, 147, 175–6; Irish recruits to British army, 174–6; patriotism and War Poets, 277–8
FitzAlan, Lord, 97, 99, 207, 240
Fitzgerald, George, 202, 205–6
Foch, Marshal Ferdinand, 6, 7, 60, 61, 73, 230–1, 239
Four Courts occupation (1922), 295; initial impasse, 30, 31, 366–7; and HW's assassination, 224, 233, 372–3; Churchill and Lloyd George demand action, 31–4, 241–3; siege, 35–8, 243–4, 302–6, 303, 366–7; arrests, 306
Fovargue, Vincent, 183–4
French, Sir (later Lord) John: and Home Rule Bill (1912), 65, 66; on

INDEX

Irish parliament, 79; IRA attempts to assassinate, 81, 84, 199–202; poorly received in Dublin, 80–1; autobiography, 69; other mentions, 68, 70, 137
Fryatt, Captain Charles, 2, 364

Gaelic Athletic Association (GAA), 134, 342
Gaelic League, 136, 137–40, 148, 193
Gaelic Revival, 137
Gaynor, John, 194–6
general amnesty (1917), 178
general elections: Dec. 1918, 28, 75, 76–7, 107; June 1922, 29–30, 298–301, 302
George V, King, 23, 24, 67, 221, 397
German Plot arrests (1918), 81, 249
German Spring Offensive (1918), 72–4, 145, 192
Good, Joe, 197–9
Gough, Hubert and Johnnie, 65–6, 68
Government of Ireland Act (1920), 82–3, 96, 98
Great Famine (1845–51), 166
Great War: see First World War
Greenwood, Sir Hamar, 92, 156, 205–6
Griffith, Arthur, 98, 232–3, 314–16
Gwynn, Stephen, 175

Hart, Peter, 370–1
hayricks and farms, IRA attacks on, 158, 159, 182
Hitchcock, Alfred, 141–3
Home Rule Act (1914), 67–8
Home Rule Bill (1886) (defeated), 54
Home Rule Bill (1912) (passed), 63, 66–7, 107
home rule movement, 53–4, 140; see also nationalists and republicans
Humphreys, Travers, 234
hunger strike protests: Ashe, 279; MacSwiney, 90–2, 91, 158, 182, 202, 204, 205, 208–9, 279
Hyde, Douglas, 137–8

India: Prince of Wales's tour of, 23–4; Amritsar massacre (1919), 388; HW's posting to, 57
Invincibles, 190–1
IRA (Irish Republican Army): anti-Treaty IRA, see anti-Treaty IRA; attacks on Britain, 155–60, 182, 184–5, see also specific targets; Barry's execution, 92–5; and Belfast pogroms, 106–7, 108–9, 110–12, 113–14, 117–20; and border warfare, 126–8; companies in Britain, 148–63, 186, 194–5, 210, 212, 213–14,

253, 255; conventions in defiance of Provisional Government, 28, 295–7, 301, 308; Currygrane House arson, 45; divided opinion on Anglo-Irish Treaty, 160–2, 188, 211, 212–13, 295, 297; Ellis's attempted assassination, 211–12; ex-servicemen joining, 173–5; failed kidnap attempts, 265–6; female auxiliary (Cumann na mBan), 151–2, 210, 213–14, 295; Fovargue's assassination, 183–4; HW's assassination, see assassination of HW; HW's opinions, 8, 87–8, 97, 98–9, 101, 102, 129; jailbreaks during War of Independence, 249–52; Northern Offensive, 118–20; pensions, see pensions for veterans; plans to rescue Dunne and O'Sullivan, 249, 252–6; plots and attempts to assassinate British government members, 182–3, 192–208; size and organisation, 27–8, 70, 148, 150; Troubles (1969–95), 106, 364, 392; typhoid plot, 156; War of Independence activities, 27–8, 79, 83–5, 92–6, 147, 148, 155–60, 167–8, 182, 184–5, 187, 200, 308; weapons supply to, 152–5, 172, 181, 185–6, 187, 209–10, 330; see also Irish Volunteers (later IRA); Provisional IRA; Sinn Féin
IRB (Irish Republican Brotherhood), 134, 148–9, 211, 214, 380–1; see also assassination of HW
Ireland, map, 42
Irish Civil War (1922–3): build-up, 38, 294–302, 367; Four Courts occupation, see Four Courts occupation (1922); Battle of Dublin, 307–8; in 'Munster Republic', 309–13, 309; 'big house' attacks, 45, 316, 319, 330; short truce, 310; ambush and killing of Collins, 320–3; Army Emergency Powers Resolution and prisoner executions, 325–7, 328–9; other killings by republicans, 328, 329; atrocities by government troops, 329; ceasefire, 329; statistics, 308, 330; long view, 331–2, 397
Irish Constitution (1937), 331
Irish diaspora, 132–3
Irish Free State: see Anglo-Irish Treaty (1921); Provisional Government
Irish Guards regiment, 144–6, 147
Irish parliament (1782–1800), 53
Irish Parliamentary Party (IPP), 63, 75, 191
Irish Potato Famine (1845–51), 166
Irish Self-Determination League (ISDL), 151, 234–5

Irish stereotyping and prejudices against, 134–5, 223, 224–5
Irish Unionist Alliance (IUA), 48
Irish Volunteers (later IRA): formation, 67, 107, 137, 140; and the Easter Rising, 140; reorganised into IRA, 148; see also IRA (Irish Republican Army)
Irish War of Independence: see War of Independence (1919–21)

Jeffery, Keith, 363
Jones, Tom, 379

Kelleher, Denis: early life, 159; IRA activities, 159, 182, 253, 264, 265; as 'third man', 215–16, 341–2, 346–7; arrest and release, 340; later life, 341; death, 216; quoted, 159, 182, 215, 264, 265, 346
Kerry, Civil War violence, 309, 311–12
'Khaki election' (Dec. 1918), 28, 75, 76–7, 107
Kipling, Rudyard, 9, 134, 145

Labour Party National Executive, 222
land acts, 53
Lea-Wilson, Captain Percival and family, 248–9
Lee, Frank, 151, 344, 348, 370, 392–3
Lemass, Seán, 352
Limerick, Civil War violence, 309, 310–11
Liverpool, IRA attack on, 157
Liverpool Street Station, 1–3, 4, 8–9
Lloyd George, David: leads coalition government after 'Khaki election' (1918), 75, 76–7; response to War of Independence, 83, 85–9, 92–5, 96–7, 113; response to Lord French's assassination attempt, 202; threatened by IRA, 182–3; close call with IRA Squad, 202–3; and Free State constitution negotiations, 300; worried about HW, 379; response to HW's assassination, 18–19, 20, 221; demands action over Four Courts occupation, 30–4; portrayal of HW in War Memoirs, 362–3; relationship with HW, 71, 72, 82, 84; other mentions, 6, 7, 59
Local Government Act 1898, 52
London: Gaelic League, 136, 138–40, 148; IRA attacks and planned attacks on, 156, 157–8, 159, 160; IRA companies, 148, 149–52, 153–5, 156, 160–2, 186, 194–5, 210, 212, 213–14, 253; Irish community in, 135–6, 138–40, 141, 195
Long, Walter, 82–3

Lovitt, C. A., 355, 356
Lynch, Liam, 301, 308–10, 319, 329, 343, 345

Mac Diarmada, Seán, 278–9
Mac Eoin, Seán, 207–8, 264; memorial, 44
Macardle, Dorothy, 298–9
McCann, Hugh James, 355, 356–7
MacCraith, Seán (Seán McGrath), 188, 211, 234–5, 339, 373
MacDonnell, James Hyndman, 227, 254, 266, 267–9, 281, 285, 333
MacGeehin, Mary, 136, 285, 335, 337
McGilligan, Patrick, 141–3
McGrath, Seán (Seán MacCraith), 188, 211, 234–5, 339, 373
McKelvey, Joe, 301, 328
McMahon family massacre, 115–17, 116
Macready, General Sir Nevil, 31–3, 85, 86, 89–90, 96–7, 238, 384–6
MacSwiney, Terence (hunger strike), 90–2, 91, 158, 182, 202, 204, 205, 208–9, 279
Maguire, Sam, 134, 155, 167, 182, 212, 254, 342, 380–1; and HW's assassination, 214, 215; Sam Maguire Cup, 134, 342
Manchester, IRA attacks and planned attacks on, 155–6, 158
map of Ireland, 42
Mauser (weapon), 152, 196, 197
Maxwell, General John 'Conky', 71
Mayo, Earl of, 123–4
Mellows, Liam, 301, 328
Midleton, Earl of, 225–7
migration from Ireland, 132–3
Moncheur, Ludovic, Baron, 231
Morning Post, altercation with Earl of Midleton, 224–7
Mountbatten, Louis, Lord, 256–8, 257
Moylett, Patrick, 97
Mulcahy, General Richard, 84, 161–2, 192–3, 194–6, 197–8, 334
'Munster Republic' in Irish Civil War, 309–13, 309
Murphy, Mick, 209–10
Murphy, William, 381–2
Murray, Pat 'Pa', 203–5, 206, 212, 330, 369

Napoleon, attempted Bantry Bay landings, 165–6
National Army, 35–8, 126–8, 243–4, 302–6, 303, 342, 366–7; see also Irish Civil War (1922–3)
National Graves Association (NGA), 333, 358, 360
nationalists and republicans: see anti-Treaty

IRA; Easter Rising (1916); Fenian movement; home rule movement; IRA (Irish Republican Army); Irish Volunteers (later IRA); Sinn Féin
Neenan, Con, 214–15
Nicholson, John, 104
Nine Years' War (1593–1602), 164
Northern Ireland: creation in Government of Ireland Act (1920), 82–3, 96, 98; Belfast pogroms, *see* Belfast pogroms (1922–3); map, *42*; *see also Ulster entries*
Northern Ireland parliament, state opening, 101, *102*, 397
Northern Offensive (May 1922), 118–20

Ó'Briain, Liam, 372–3
O'Brien, Arthur 'Art': family background, 148; offices, 148–9, 235; anti-Treaty sentiments, 212, 330; arrest and deportation, 330–1; on Dunne and O'Sullivan, 162, 339; on HW's assassination, 339, 393; other mentions, 254, 334
O'Connell, Lieutenant General J. J. 'Ginger', 35, 36, 243, 367
O'Connor, Rory, 155, 157, 160–1, 296–7, 301, 306, 328, 331, 346
O'Connor, Ulick, 371
O'Donoghue, Florence 'Florrie', 249, 294, 320, 343–7, 388
O'Duffy, Eoin, 111–12
O'Dwyer, Sir Michael, 388–9
O'Hegarty, Diarmuid, 33–4
O'Hegarty, Patrick Sarsfield, 381
O'Higgins, Kevin, 29, 126, 324, 330–1, 342
O'Keeffe, William, 158
O'Malley, Ernie, 304, 306, 367, 372
O'Neill, Denis 'Sonny', 322–3
O'Neill, Dermot (Diarmaid), 392
Orangemen, 108, 119–20; *see also* Ulster unionists
O'Sullivan, Aloysius (Joe's brother), *169*, 170
O'Sullivan, Dennis (Joe's brother), *169*, 171
O'Sullivan, Donal 'Cam' (O'Sullivan Beara), 164–5
O'Sullivan, Eugene Jr (Joe's brother), *169*, 171
O'Sullivan, Eugene Sr (Joe's uncle), 168
O'Sullivan, John Jr (Joe's brother), *169*, 171, 187–8
O'Sullivan, John Sr (Joe's father), 167, 168–70, *169*, 188, 189, 284, 338–9, 383
O'Sullivan, Joseph 'Joe', *12*, *169*, *172*; early life and family history, *42*, 166,

168, 169–70, *169*, 171; military service, 10, 170, *172*, 173, 176–9; injury and rehabilitation, 178–9, 180; girlfriend, 179–81; employment, 179, 188; IRA activities, 180–6, 188, 369; sees HW in workplace, 188–9; plots to assassinate HW, 214–17, 380–1; theories about assassination order, 368–83; assassinates HW, 11–13, 245, 259; pursuit and arrest, 14–16, *15*, 236; appears in Police Court, 234, 245–6; IRA rescue plans, 249, 252–6; trial and appeal, 227–8, 246, 258–62, 266–7; public petition and support, 267–71, 281–2; awaits execution, 181, 187–8, 272, 276–7, 280–5; will, 272; execution, 285–7, *286*, 313; early requests for reburial, 333–4; memorial, 333; posthumous reputation, 343–8, 355–6, 393; exhumation and reburial, 354–60, *358*, *396*; adopted Irish identity, 391–2; appearance, 10, *169*, *172*; Catholicism, 276–7, 282–4, 285–6, 369; personality, 10, 179–80, 181; quoted (court addresses), 261, 262; quoted (letters home), 280–4, *283*
O'Sullivan, Mary Ann (Joe's mother), 168, *169*, 187
O'Sullivan, Pat (Joe's brother), *169*; military service, 171–2; IRA activities, 168, 182, 185, 187, 280, 312; pension applications, 186, 339–40; protects posthumous reputations of Joe and Dunne, 343–8, 369; and repatriation of Joe and Dunne, 354, 358–60
Owen, Wilfred, 277–8

Paisley, Rev. Ian, 357
Parkinson, Alan F., 394
parliaments in Ireland: *see* Dáil Éireann; Irish parliament (1782–1800); Northern Ireland parliament, state opening
partition of Ireland: *see* Government of Ireland Act (1920)
Pearse, Patrick, 137, 139, 167, 278, 279
pensions for veterans: application process, 336, 340; John O'Sullivan (for Joe), 188, 189, 338–9, 383; Mary Dunne (for Reggie), 336–8; Pat O'Sullivan, 186, 339–40
Pershing, General John, 231
'Peter the Painter', 196–7
Pettigo–Belleek triangle, British–Irish troop warfare, 126–8, 377
Phoenix Park murders (1882), 190–1, 224
police in Ireland: *see* Auxiliaries; Black and

Tans; Royal Irish Constabulary (RIC);
    Ulster Special Constabulary (USC)
police protection for ministers and HW,
    219, 220
Prescott-Decie, Brigadier General Cyril,
    227
press response to HW's assassination,
    222–32, 232, 242
Prince of Wales (future King Edward VIII),
    23–4, 262–3, 265
Protestantism: ascendancy, 50, 51–2, 53;
    decrease, 317–18
Provisional Government: establishment
    and mandate to rule, 24, 28–30, 99, 112,
    241; IRA conventions in defiance of, 28,
    295–7, 301, 308; Churchill's ultimatum
    to, 240–3; Four Courts impasse, 30, 31,
    366–7; Four Courts siege, 35–8, 243–4,
    302–6, 303, 366–7; and Irish Civil War,
    310, 325, 326; handling of Collins's
    killing, 323; other mentions, 232, 235; see
    also Anglo-Irish Treaty (1921); National
    Army
Provisional IRA, 359, 364, 392
Public Records Office destruction, 303–6,
    304

Raffield, Paul, 170
Redmond, John, 67
Republic of Ireland, map, 42
Republic of Ireland Act (1948), 331
republicans and nationalists: see anti-Treaty
    IRA; Easter Rising (1916); Fenian
    movement; home rule movement; IRA
    (Irish Republican Army); Irish Volunteers
    (later IRA); Sinn Féin
'Revenge for Skibbereen', 166
Roberts, Frederick 'Bobs', Lord, 58, 59
Ronan, Sean, 356
Royal Irish Constabulary (RIC) (later Royal
    Ulster Constabulary): IRA attacks on, 79;
    and Belfast pogroms, 84–5, 88, 108–9,
    111, 117, 119; other mentions, 227
Russia, 72, 78, 366

Sacks, Jonathan, 389–90
St Ignatius College, Stamford Hill, 141,
    143, 389
Salisbury, Marquess of, 22–3
sectarian violence: see Belfast pogroms
    (1920–2); Easter Rising (1916); Irish
    Civil War (1922–3); Troubles (1969–95);
    War of Independence (1919–21)
Seely, John, 66
Shanahan, Joe, 184

Sharkey, Paddy, 200
Shaw, George Bernard, 269–71
Shortt, Edward, 219–20, 271
signal boxes, IRA attacks on, 159
Singh, Udham, 388–9
Sinn Féin: German Plot arrests, 81,
    249; 'Khaki election' success (1918),
    28, 75, 77, 107; establishes parallel
    administration, 28, 85; negotiates Anglo-
    Irish Treaty, 97; 1922 election, 30,
    298–301, 302; HW's opinions, 8, 87–8,
    97, 98–9, 101, 102, 129; see also IRA (Irish
    Republican Army)
Smith, Frederick Edwin (F. E.), 20–1
Smyth, Lieutenant Colonel Gerald Bryce,
    108–9
Special Powers Act (1922), 114–15, 120,
    125, 292
Swanzy, Oswald, 110

Taylor, Rex, 369–70
Tebbit, Norman, 391–2
telegraph poles, IRA attacks on, 159
Thornton, Frank, 202–3, 215, 383
Tobin, Liam, 249, 334–5, 382–3
Treaty of Versailles (1919), 78, 79, 80
Troubles (1969–95), 106, 364, 392
Twaddell, William, 119–20, 393
typhoid plot, IRA, 156

Ulster, general election results, 107–8
Ulster Council (IRA) and Northern
    Offensive, 118–20
Ulster Special Constabulary (USC), 32,
    110–11, 113, 117, 119–20, 125, 127;
    HW's opinions, 121, 122–3
Ulster Tower memorial (The Somme),
    103–4
Ulster unionists: oppose Home Rule
    Bills (1886 and 1912), 54, 63; Curragh
    Incident (1914), 64–7; accept parliament
    for Ulster (1919), 83; accept Government
    of Ireland Act (1920), 96; see also Carson,
    Edward, Lord; Orangemen
Ulster Volunteer Force (UVF), 63–4, 65,
    67, 107, 108, 115
unionists: geographic clusters (19th
    century), 54; response to Government
    of Ireland Act (1920), 96; views on home
    rule (1919), 83; see also Ulster unionists

Walsh, Martin, 155
Walsh, Richard, 192–3
War of Independence (1919–21): start of,
    79; Irish public in, 88; IRA in, 27–8, 79,

83–5, 92–6, 147, 148, 155–60, 167–8, 182, 184–5, 187, 200, 308; Terence MacSwiney's hunger strike, 90–2, *91*, 158, 182, 202, 204, 205, 208–9, 279; Truce, 26, 97, 111, 210, 212, 251; HW's opinions, 84, 85–90, 97; jailbreaks during, 249–52; Mac Eoin memorial, 44; US's opinions, 87; *see also* Anglo-Irish Treaty (1921); Belfast pogroms (1920–2)

weapons, supply to IRA, 152–5, 172, 181, 185–6, 187, 209–10, 330

Whelan, William 'Bill', 196, 198

Wilson, Arthur (HW's brother), 45

Wilson, Field Marshal Sir Henry, *4, 5, 61*; ancestry, 50–1; early life and family, 39, 41–3, 45–6, 47–9, 52, 54–5; education, 54–5; military career, 3, 6–7, 21, 55–62, 68–70, 71–4, 77–8, 79–82, 99–100; prepares for war, 60–2, 68, 81; role in Curragh incident, 64–7; role in First World War, 3, 6–7, 21, 60, 68–70, 71–4, 81, 230–1; decides not to stand as MP, 71–2; as CIGS (senior military advisor), 3, 7, 79–81, 99–100, 104–105; role in Treaty of Versailles, 79–80; receives honorary degree, 80–1; made field marshal, 81–2; opinions on government response to War of Independence, 84, 85–90, 97; intervenes over transporting MacSwiney's remains, 91–2; opposes Barry's execution, 93; nearly drowns at Cowes, 263; opinions on Anglo-Irish Treaty, 8, 98–9, 387–8; visits O'Sullivan's workplace, 188–9; declines to attend state opening of Northern Ireland parliament, 101–2, 384; opinions on state of Ireland and need for British intervention, 101–3, 129–30, 386–7; unveils war memorials, 103–4; opinions on electoral pact, 299–300; as MP for North Down, 3, 47, 101, 105–6, 389; loses police protection, 219, 220; role in and opinions on Belfast pogroms, 114–15, 120–3, 125–6, 389; unveils monument at Liverpool Street Station, 3–4, *4*, 8–9; assassination, *see* assassination of HW; political tributes, 221–2; press tributes, 229; international tributes, 230–1; funeral, 221, 236–40, *237, 239*; memorial to, 363–4; appearance, 4–5, *5*, 57, *61*, 79–80; Currygrane House and estate, 39–46, *40, 42*, 51, 81, 316–17, *317, 318, 319*; depiction in *The Tragedy of Lord Kitchener*, 62, 68; Eaton Place, 10, 11–12, *12*, 17; as imperialist, 8, 63–4, 89, 105–6, 376, 387–8; Irish identity, 7–8, 43–4, 46–7; marriage, 57; personality, 5–6, 55, 56, 57, 59, 68, 69, 79–80, 82, 361–3; posthumous reputation, 360–4, 388, 394–5; public opinion of during life, 93–5, 123–4, 126, 127–9, 384–6; quoted (address to cabinet), 99; quoted (address to House of Commons), 299–300; quoted (diaries), 58–9, 62, 65, 66, 69, 70–1, 72, 74, 75, 79–80, 81, 82, 84, 85, 86, 87, 88, 89, 92, 97, 98–9, 361, 387; quoted (letters), 46–7, 89, 101, 102–3, 120–2, 129–30, 386; quoted (speeches), 8–9, 43–4, 55, 126; referenced in popular culture, 364–5; rhetorical style, 6, 8–9, 55, 60, 62, 74, 386, 389; as unionist, 3, 7–8, 47, 49–50, 54, 63–4, 65, 83, 95, 101–3, 105, 229; views on communism, 77, 80, 126

Wilson, Harold, 352–3

Wilson, James Mackay 'Jemmy' (HW's brother), 43, 44, 45, 46, 48–50, 81, 152, 316–17

Wilson, James Sr (HW's father), 41–3, 47–8, 51, 52

Wilson, John, 50

Wilson, Lady Cecil Mary (HW's wife), 13, 57, 219, 221, 238, *239*, 240, 395

Wilson, William (HW's grandfather), 51

Wilson, Woodrow (US president), 87, 361

Wimborne, Lord, 265

Wormwood Scrubs demonstrations, 150–2

Ypres, Battle of Passchendaele (1917), 10, 177–8